The First World War

1914–1918

Gerd Hardach

University of California Press
Berkeley and Los Angeles

University of California Press
Berkeley and Los Angeles

Library of Congress Catalog Card Number: 75-17142

Copyright © 1977 by Gerd Hardach

First Paperback Printing 1981

ISBN 0-520-04397-9

Printed in the United States of America

1 2 3 4 5 6 7 8 9

History of the World Economy in the Twentieth Century
General Editor: Wolfram Fischer

To young I.

Contents

List of Tables

The translators are most grateful to Mr Michael Miller of the School of Social Studies of the University of East Anglia for his help in reading over parts of this book.

Introduction

Du fond de son sac à malice
Mars va sans doute à l'occasion
En sortir un vrai délice
Qui me fera grosse impression.
En attendant je persévère
A dire que ma guerre favorite
Celle mon colon que je voudrai faire
C'est la guerre de quatorze dix-huit.

– Georges Brassens, *La Guerre de 14–18*

The First World War unquestionably represents an important climacteric in economic history. However, the significance of that climacteric is variously interpreted. Essentially there are four themes, whose order of priority depends on the observer's viewpoint: the decay of the 'classical' capitalist world economy based on Great Britain and the gold standard; the progress of industrialization overseas brought about by the temporary economic paralysis of Europe; the long-term effect of structural changes in the economies of the warring industrial countries, more especially the merging of the economy and the apparatus of state; and finally, the development of the international labour movement from its nadir in August 1914 to its triumphant culmination in the Russian October revolution.

I have endeavoured to the best of my ability to do justice to these various aspects and to place them in a common context which might be described as the 'crisis of the capitalist world economy'; whether I have succeeded is another matter. Nor would I, of course, claim to have produced anything approaching a comprehensive bibliography for the individual themes. I have deliberately placed the main emphasis of this study on Europe at the expense of overseas developments; the Great War was a European event, and the structural changes that took place in the world economy as a result of that war originated in Europe. Though in itself of great interest, the question of the import of the Great War to industrialization outside Europe can only be answered within the context of the long-term development of the countries concerned. All in all, I hope that the reader will find this book, whatever its shortcomings, a useful guide to the hitherto relatively neglected field of the international economy from 1914 to 1918.

In the course of a work of any length a writer necessarily accumulates a considerable debt of gratitude. For their help with the bibliography, and in reading over certain sections of this work, I have to thank a number of colleagues, notably Professor Stefano Fenoaltea of Philadelphia, Dr Heiko Haumann of Freiburg, Professor Herbert Matis of Vienna, Dr Henner Papendieck of Berlin, Professor Sidney Ratner of New Brunswick and Professor Arnt Spandau of Johannesburg. The manuscript as a whole was subjected to a thorough and most helpful critical scrutiny by Professor Wolfram Fischer. Among the librarians to whose hospitality I am indebted are those of the Bibliothèque de Documentation Internationale Contemporaine in Paris–Nanterre, the London School of Economics, the Imperial War Museum, and the Institut für Weltwirtschaft in Kiel.

G.H.

1

The International Economy, Imperialism, War

Economic historians often bypass the period from 1914 to 1918[1] and, indeed, so far as the economic historian is concerned, the First World War is a thankless episode; for one of the central themes of this period is the destruction of an international economy often nostalgically referred to as 'the good old days': 'What an extraordinary episode in the progress of man that age was which came to an end in August 1914.'[2] The liberal observer could point with satisfaction to substantial economic growth, to the unhampered movement between nations of goods and capital, to unrestricted travel. He was at most marginally concerned with poverty and oppression; militarism and imperialism, racial and cultural rivalries, monopolies and restrictions were to him 'little more than the amusements of his daily newspaper'.[3] Numerous examples might be adduced to fill out this description of the multilateral international economy. Apart from a brief interlude during

1. W. Ashworth, *A Short History of the International Economy since 1850*, 2nd ed., Longman, 1962; P. T. Ellsworth, *The International Economy. Its Structure and Operation*, Macmillan, New York, 1950; D. Landes, *The Unbound Prometheus. Technological Change and Industrial Development in Western Europe from 1750 to the Present*, Cambridge University Press, 1970.

2. J. M. Keynes, *The Economic Consequences of the Peace, Collected Writings*, vol. II, Macmillan, London, 1971, p. 6.

3. ibid., p. 7.

the eighties and nineties, world trade steadily expanded from 1870 to 1914, a process which suffered no more than a temporary setback as a result of protectionist aspirations. The trade in industrial goods, though subject to greater fluctuations, increased on the whole more rapidly than the trade in raw materials and food. In other words, economic growth and industrial specialization were, as a basis of international trade, more important than the division of the world into industrial countries and non-industrialized primary producers. And since the gold standard merged the major national currencies into a kind of world currency, a multilateral adjustment of the balance of payments of individual countries met with no technical difficulties. The international economy possessed an efficient financial nerve centre in the City of London, whose position in turn rested on Great Britain's vast international creditor position, which had accrued to her in the course of history.

As and when necessary, the Bank of England could, by slight changes in bank rate, repatriate British and attract foreign funds; the Bank's own gold reserve was relatively small. The peculiar structure of Britain's balance of payments was of particular significance to the stability of the world economy. The export of capital and the adverse balance of trade on the one hand, and invisible income from shipping, insurance and interest on the other, more or less matched each other, so that residual gold flows were unimportant.[4] The Bank of England did not constantly increase its reserves to the detriment of other countries, nor did it continuously lose gold. This system was dependent on complex multilateral interconnections. Vis-à-vis India and a few other overseas countries Great Britain had an export surplus which partially offset what were, incidentally, very large import surpluses, while those countries in their turn had substantial export surpluses vis-à-vis the rest of the world. Unilateral changes in a country's export performance or the trend of its imports might easily disrupt this system and, indeed, a disruptive factor of this kind was not only potentially but actually present in the deteriorating export performance of British industry.

Towards the end of the nineteenth century, and for reasons that

4. On British foreign trade see A. H. Imlah, *Economic Elements in the Pax Britannica. Studies in British Foreign Trade in the Nineteenth Century*, Harvard University Press, Cambridge, Mass., 1958; S. B. Saul, *Studies in British Overseas Trade, 1870-1914*, Liverpool University Press, 1960.

still cannot be explained, the British economy underwent an appreciable loss of dynamism as compared with its closest competitors, the U.S.A. and Germany and, by the beginning of the twentieth, was very far from being the undisputed 'workshop of the world'. In the iron and steel industries as well as in the more technologically advanced sectors (the chemical, electrical and, most recent of all, the automobile industries), Britain had been outstripped by the U.S.A. and Germany. During the decades that preceded the war, her share of world trade declined from 20 per cent (1876–80) to 14 per cent (1911–13), a tendency which may be explained partly by the spread of industrialization and economic development overseas, but may also perhaps point to a relative drop in economic efficiency.[5] The fact that Britain nevertheless maintained a favourable balance of payments which enabled her to retain and expand her international creditor position may be attributed to the high yields from her foreign investments and to income from shipping. In the years between 1911 and 1913 Great Britain was able to finance on average 84 per cent of her net capital exports out of the return on previous foreign investments, while the British mercantile marine represented about one-third of the world's tonnage.[6]

Because at this time the economic progress of individual nations was subjected to close observation and comparison, a kind of national rivalry entered into the international economy. Britain's leading role as the hub of the world economy was no longer uncontested, although in the pre-war years it was not as yet possible to identify a successor. Contemporaries were no less fascinated by Anglo–German rivalry than were historians at a later date. But Germany had neither the world-wide, comprehensive trading connections nor the strong creditor position that would have enabled her to lay serious claim to the status of an economic world power. True, Germany's external trade was not significantly less than that of Great Britain, but it was very largely confined to the Continent and for that reason did not present any serious competition to British exports outside Europe. The legend of the German commercial traveller who always, in every market in the world, got in

5. W. Ashworth, *An Economic History of England, 1870-1939*, Methuen, 1960, reprint 1969, p. 147.

6. ibid., p. 154; United Nations, *International Capital Movements during the Inter-war period*, Lake Success, 1949, p. 15.

just ahead of his British counterpart is not statistically verifiable. Germany's foreign investments in 1913/14 are estimated at some 5·8 billion dollars, and hence amounted to barely one-third of Britain's foreign investments. In terms of the extent and regional distribution of foreign trade, America seemed the likeliest candidate for economic world power. Her net debtor position in 1913 was still considerable, but for the previous twenty years she had achieved export surpluses, so that her emergence as a net creditor could be expected within the foreseeable future. In as much as export demand was crucial to prosperity, there was a rational basis for the rivalry between the great powers in the field of external trade. During the pre-war years there had been an increase in the proportion of exports and, since these were regarded by both Britain and France as pacemakers for economic development, they were of the utmost importance to incomes and employment.[7] The material results of a more or less successful foreign trade policy could thus be considerable. Because of the operation of the gold standard, a policy of economic stabilization based on internal demand was not feasible, even had it been compatible with the prevailing liberal climate of opinion; hence governments were to some extent compelled to pursue an aggressive policy in the field of foreign trade, this being at the same time the only possible kind of counter-cyclical policy.[8]

This rivalry between the leading industrial powers is an indication of the considerable strain that was imposed on the outwardly stable and – from a liberal viewpoint – harmonious international economic system. An area of conflict hardly less significant was the mounting rivalry between the great powers over the economic exploitation of the world, a rivalry which, epitomized in the term 'imperialism', has given a name to a whole epoch.[9] The non-industrialized 'primary producing countries' were integrated into the international capitalist economy as sources of raw

7. See e.g., P. Deane and W. A. Cole, *British Economic Growth 1688-1959*, 2nd ed., Cambridge University Press, 1967, pp. 311ff; C. P. Kindleberger, *Economic Growth in France and Britain, 1851-1950*, Harvard University Press, Cambridge, Mass., 1964, pp. 264-87.

8. See J. M. Keynes, *The General Theory of Employment, Interest and Money*, Macmillan, London, 1951, pp. 381ff.

9. For 'classic' contemporary analyses see J. A. Hobson, *Imperialism: A Study*, George Allen & Unwin, London, 1902.

material, as outlets for manufactured goods and as spheres of influence for capital exports. The economic penetration of these countries generally began with politico-military action. The fact of their being restricted to the primary sector perpetuated their

TABLE 1

THE FOREIGN TRADE OF THE GREAT POWERS, 1913

| | Exports | | Imports | | Total foreign trade | |
	Billion[10] dollars	Share (per cent)	Billion dollars	Share (per cent)	Billion dollars	Share (per cent)
Great Britain	2·6	14	3·2	16	5·8	15
U.S.A.	2·4	13	1·8	9	4·2	11
Germany	2·4	13	2·6	13	5·0	13
France	1·3	7	1·6	8	3·0	8

SOURCE: League of Nations, *Memorandum on Balances of Payments and Foreign Trade Balances, 1910–1924*, 2 vols, Geneva, 1925, vol. I, p. 90.

The shares relate to reported world trade of 37·8 billion dollars, or some 93 per cent of total world trade.

economic and hence also their political dependence. We need only consider the foreign trade of the industrial powers to see how specialized the international economy had become. Taking the

TABLE 2

REGIONAL DISTRIBUTION OF THE GREAT POWERS' FOREIGN TRADE 1913 (PER CENT)

| | Exports to | | | Imports to | | |
	Europe	North America	Other continents	Europe	North America	Other continents
Great Britain	35	10	55	44	24	32
U.S.A.	60	17	23	48	8	44
Germany	75	8	17	54	17	29
France	70	7	23	53	11	36

SOURCE: League of Nations, *Memorandum on Balances of Payments and Foreign Trade Balances, 1910–1924*, 2 vols, Geneva 1925, vol. 1, pp. 112ff.

average for the years 1911 to 1913, more than 80 per cent of the imports of the leading industrial countries (Great Britain, U.S.A., Germany, France) consisted of raw materials and foodstuffs,

10. A billion equals one thousand million.

whereas 60 per cent of their exports was made up of manufactures.[11]

The investment policy of the industrial countries in non-industrialized regions further promoted the latter's enforced restriction to the primary sector. Capital exports were concentrated on the infrastructure (railways, harbour installations, public

TABLE 3

FOREIGN INVESTMENTS ON THE EVE OF THE FIRST WORLD WAR (1913–14)

Creditor	Billion dollars	Debtor	Billion dollars
Great Britain	18·0	Europe	12·0
France	9·0	U.S.A. and Canada	10·5
Germany	5·8	Latin America	8·5
U.S.A.	3·5	Asia	6·0
Belgium, Netherland,		Africa	4·7
Switzerland	5·5	Australia	2·3
Other countries	2·2		
	44·0		44·0

SOURCE: United Nations, *International Capital Movements in the Inter-War Period*, Lake Success, 1949, p. 2. The figures are in each case gross; e.g. the U.S.A. was creditor to the extent of 3·5 billion dollars, and debtor to the extent of 6·8 billion dollars.

utilities), and on the mineral resources and agriculture of the recipient countries. In the fifty years between 1865 and 1914, nearly 70 per cent of British investment abroad was devoted to the infrastructure, 12 per cent to mining and agriculture and a mere 4 per cent to the industrial sector.[12] The aim was a rapid improvement in export performance which would guarantee real interest payments on, and the amortization of, foreign credits, an aim best served by investment in the infrastructure and in the primary sectors. In retrospect investment of this nature is therefore also held to have been particularly successful.[13] Nevertheless it is, of

11. Calculations based on League of Nations, *Industrialization and Foreign Trade*, 1945, pp. 158, 166.

12. M. Simon, 'The Pattern of New British Portfolio Foreign Investment, 1865-1914', A. R. Hall, ed,. *The Export of Capital from Britain 1870-1914*, Methuen, London, 1968, pp. 23ff.

13. See D. North, 'International Capital Movements in Historical Perspec-

course, true that the capital exports of the industrial countries were, at best, no more than moderately beneficial to the development of indigenous industries overseas.

There seems little doubt that restriction to the primary sector was disadvantageous to the non-industrialized nations, since the greater opportunities for growth afforded by the secondary and tertiary sectors thus eluded them. Moreover, in the long run, the terms of trade moved against countries exporting foodstuffs and raw materials: taking the relative price of raw materials and foodstuffs to manufactured goods in the period 1876–80 as 100, the corresponding index for 1911–13 is 93.[14] It is by no means certain, however, that the industrial nations' economic and political oppression of the non-industrialized countries was as expedient as they then believed, at least so far as their own interests were concerned. True, the non-industrialized countries' political and economic dependence created the precondition for the remarkably unfair exchange which resulted in the poor primary producing countries subsidizing the rich industrial nations. But this exchange meant that the economic efficiency of the primary producers, and hence their importance to the industrial countries, was restricted, whereas industrialization and economic growth would, on the contrary, have served to raise the exchange to a more intensive level. And this must also have benefited the industrial countries.[15]

There might conceivably have been an international trade structure whereby many would have gained and only a few lost, and which would therefore certainly have been preferable. But such an alternative was foreign to the contemporary consciousness and, indeed, militated immediately against those concrete economic

tive', R. F. Mikesell, ed., *US Private and Government Investment Abroad*, University of Oregon Books, Eugene, Or., 1962, p. 32.

14. United Nations, *Relative Prices of Exports and Imports of Underdeveloped Countries*, Lake Success, 1949, p. 22. Also, League of Nations, *Industrialization and Foreign Trade*, 1945. A country's terms of trade denote the ratio of export to import prices. Falling terms of trade in the primary producing countries mean that, in return for an equal volume of imports (e.g. machinery), more materials and foodstuffs have to be exported. A formal model of the terms of trade is elaborated by M. K. Atallah in his book *The Long-Term Movement of the Terms of Trade between Agricultural and Industrial Products*, Netherlands Economic Institute, Delft, 1958.

15. For details, see League of Nations, *Industrialization and Foreign Trade*, 1945.

interests which, directly or indirectly, profited by the exploitation of the dependent territories.

There is a well-known theory of Lenin's to the effect that 'on both sides the 1914 war was an imperialist war (i.e. a war of rapine and plunder), a war for the division of the world, for the division and redivision of colonies, for financial capital's "spheres of influence", etc.'[16] Lenin demonstrated that economic history prior to the Great War was potentially productive of conflict. Germany was a comparative late-comer in the race to carve up the world and hence, in relation to her productivity, was under-represented. Of this discrepancy the ruling classes were very well aware and efforts were made to alter the position. In 1913, for instance, Walter Rathenau wrote: 'We need land on this earth . . . We must continue to receive what is necessary from future apportionments until such time as we are satiated to approximately the same degree as our neighbours.'[17] The problem posed by Lenin thus remains as pertinent as ever to historical research. 'It is questionable,' he writes, 'whether, given capitalism, there is any way other than war of getting rid of the disproportion between the development of the productive forces and the accumulation of capital on the one hand and, on the other, the distribution of colonies and financial capital's "spheres of influence".'[18] Lenin's hypothesis has since been substantiated in as much as students of diplomatic history prior to the Great War now almost unanimously hold that Germany was the real aggressor in the summer of 1914.[19] This marks historiography's departure from the earlier, reassuring assumption that responsibility for 'stumbling' into the war was shared equally between all the powers. Fritz Fischer and a number of Marxist writers, by stressing Germany's peculiar responsibility for the war

16. V. I. Lenin. *Der Imperialismus als höchstes Stadium des Kapitalismus* (*Vorwort zur französischen und deutschen Ausgabe*), *Ausgewählte Werke in zwei Bänden*, vol. I, Dietz, Berlin, 1960, pp. 711f.

17. W. Rathenau, 'Deutsche Gefahren und neue Ziele', *Neue Freie Presse*, 25 December 1913, reprinted in *Gesammelte Schriften*, vol. I, Berlin, 1918, p. 270. Cit., from W. Gutsche, 'Erst Europa – und dann die Welt. Probleme der Kriegszielpolitik des deutschen Imperialismus im Ersten Weltkrieg', *Zeitschrift für Geschichtswissenschaft*, 12, 1964.

18. V. I. Lenin, *Der Imperialismus als höchste Stadium der Kapitalismus*, *Ausgewählte Werke in zwei Bänden*, vol I. Dietz, Berlin, 1960, p. 790.

19. For detailed account, see I. Geiss's documentation, *Julikrise und Kriegsausbruch 1914. Eine Dokumentensammlung*, 2 vols, Verlag für Literatur und Zeitgeschehen, Hanover, 1963–4.

have, by the same token, begun to shed light on the economic motives underlying German imperialist policy.[20]

August 1914 was not merely a time of crisis for the international capitalist economy, it was also a time of crisis for the international labour movement. In the pre-war period, the workers' parties and the trade unions, as the organizations of a class largely excluded from the benefits conferred by industrial progress,[21] had made impressive headway. As seen by the Second International, the labour movement was not a community of interests intrinsic to the system, but an anti-capitalist power, a position which manifested itself primarily in resistance to imperialism and war – and this not least at the Extraordinary Congress of Basle of 1912.[22] But during the crucial weeks of July and August the forces of socialism proved too weak to organize any effective resistance to the war. This was not fortuitous. The discrepancy between the reality and the programme of the Second International, a discrepancy which became manifest when nearly all the workers' parties and trade unions endorsed the warlike policy of their respective countries, was not simply the product of 1914.

The political course of the 1914 'July crisis' has been amply documented[23] so that only the more important dates need be referred to here. On 28 June 1914 the Austrian heir-apparent and his wife were assassinated in Sarajevo. In Austria both govern-

20. See F. Fischer, 'Der Griff nach der Weltmacht', *Die Kriegspolitik des kaiserlichen Deutschland 1914-18*, 3rd ed., Droste, Düsseldorf, 1964; F. Fischer *Weltmacht oder Niedergang. Deutschland im Ersten Weltkrieg*, Europäische Verlags-Anstalt, Frankfurt, 1965; F. Fischer, *Krieg der Illusionen. Die deutsche Politik von 1911 bis 1914*, Droste, Düsseldorf, 1969; W. Gutsche, 'Erst Europa – und dann die Welt'; J. Kuczynski, *Darstellung der Lage der Arbeiter in Deutschland von 1900 bis 1917/18 (Die Geschichte der Lage der Arbeiter unter dem Kapitalismus*, vol. IV). Akademie-Verlag, Berlin, 1967.

21. Cotton goods, for instance, were the mainstay of the British export trade but, with an average weekly wage of 20s. the workers in the cotton industry were living below the 'poverty line' which, according to Bowley, was 23s. See A. Bowley, *Prices and Wages in the United Kingdom 1914-1920*, Clarendon Press, Oxford, 1921; A. Bowley, *Some Economic Consequences of the Great War*, Thornton Butterworth, London, 1930, p. 162.

22. See G. Haupt, *Der Kongress fand nicht statt. Die sozialistische Internationale 1914*, Europa-Verlag, Vienna/Frankfurt/Zurich, 1967. For further literature see Chapter 7.

23. For detailed documentation, see *inter alia*, Geiss, *Julikrise und Kriegsausbruch 1914*.

ment and military saw in the assassination an opportunity for a show of force against Serbia and in this they had the support of their German counterparts who, in the circumstances, risked a bid for imperial power by way of and beyond the Austro–Serbian conflict. Austria's declaration of war on Serbia on 28 July was the signal for general mobilizations and declarations of war and, on 4 August, German troops marched into Belgium. The war arrayed against each other first the industrial nations of Europe, then those of the rest of the world, with far-reaching consequences that were also to affect neutrals both on the European continent and overseas.

2

The Allied Blockade of the Central Powers

Pre-war planning and international law

The outbreak of war in 1914 demolished at one stroke the complex web of international relations, for the legislation of the belligerents prohibited trading with the enemy. In addition, each side endeavoured to cut the other off from the world's markets by means of an offensive economic war. The Allies encircled the Central Powers in an ever tighter blockade. For its part the German government sought, by means of a commercial war fought with U-boats, to isolate Britain economically. The longer the war went on the more both parties pinned their hopes on economic warfare. The Great War, is has been said,

> was as much a war of competing blockades, the surface and the submarine, as of competing armies. Behind these two blockades the economic systems of the two opposing groups of countries were engaged in a deadly struggle for existence, and at several periods of the war the pressure of starvation seemed likely to achieve an issue beyond the settlement of either the entrenched armies or the immobilized navies.[1]

When hostilities began, economic warfare was subject to certain internationally agreed rules based on the experiences of the nine-

1. J. A. Salter, *Allied Shipping Control. An Experiment in International Administration*, Clarendon Press, Oxford, 1921, p. 1.

teenth century, rules which represented a compromise between the strategic interests of the warring parties and the commercial interests of the neutrals.[2] These rules were first codified and internationally agreed in the Declaration of Paris of 1856, in connection with the peace negotiations after the Crimean War. The declaration provided for two 'legitimate' economic measures in time of war: the blockade of an enemy's coasts or ports and the confiscation of his goods or vessels on the high seas.

At the Second Peace Conference at the Hague in 1907 the question of economic warfare was again tabled. One concrete result was the setting up in the same year of an international prize court, a body to which appeals could be made from national prize courts. In this way the final decision in cases of dispute was taken out of the hands of the belligerents whose position as at once judge and interested party had been unsatisfactory. But so long as there continued to be divergencies over the rules of economic warfare the international court lacked an objective legal basis. This shortcoming was to be made good at a conference of the interested powers (Great Britain, France, Germany, the U.S.A., Austria–Hungary, Italy, Japan, Russia, Spain and the Netherlands) which met in 1908 and, the following year, agreed the Declaration of London.

This document very largely endorsed the rules laid down in the Declaration of Paris and sought, by clarifying definitions, to clear up contentious questions. The right to blockade was reinforced. In future it would be a question of the effectiveness of the block-

2. Basic material on the Allied blockade policy may be found in the official histories: A. C. Bell, *A History of the Blockade of Germany, Austria-Hungary, Bulgaria, and Turkey, 1914–1918*, H.M.S.O., 1937. This history of the blockade, written from the British standpoint, was first published for official use only; it was not until 1961 that it became available to the general public. The French standpoint is given in L. Guichard, *Le Blocus Naval Economique* (*Travaux du Service Historique de l'Etat-Major Général de la Marine*), undated, duplicated manuscript (available at the Bibliothèque d'Histoire Contemporaine, Paris-Nanterre and elsewhere). The substance of this account may be found in L. Guichard, *Histoire du Blocus Naval (1914-1918)*, Payot, Paris, 1929. A study of the blockade up till the time of America's entry into the war has been made by M. C. Siney, *The Allied Blockade of Germany 1914-1916*, University of Michigan Press, Ann Arbor, 1957. Also recommended: M. W. W. P. Consett, *The Triumph of Unarmed Forces (1914-1918)*, Williams & Norgate, London, 1923; M. Parmelee, *Blockade and Sea Power. The Blockade, 1914–1919, and its Significance for a World State*, Hutchinson, London, 1924.

ade, i.e. of the ability of the blockading power to maintain an effective patrol line off an enemy's ports and coasts. The blockading of neutral ports and littorals was not permitted. As a basis for prize regulations on the high seas, goods were divided into three groups: absolute contraband, conditional contraband and free list goods.

Absolute contraband comprised warlike material such as arms, munitions, and military equipment. In case of war a belligerent power could extend this list by making a unilateral declaration. Absolute contraband *en route* to neutral recipients was confiscable in accordance with the doctrine of 'continuous voyage' if there was good reason to believe that the ultimate destination was enemy territory.

Conditional contraband comprised non-warlike goods which might also be used for military purposes, notably foodstuffs, forage, fuel, lubricants and clothing. Enemy conditional contraband was confiscable if there was good reason to believe that it would be put to warlike use (e.g. if consigned to a government agency) and, of course, in accordance with the right of blockade, if intercepted off a blockaded enemy port. But neutral conditional contraband was excepted, nor was it subject to the doctrine of 'continuous voyage'.

Finally, there was a 'free list' of goods which might in no circumstances be declared contraband. This comprised in particular raw materials for industry and agriculture such as ores, cotton and fertilizers. Thus, in accordance with the law of blockade, such goods were liable to seizure only when off an enemy port.

After the signing of the Declaration of London, it was thought that Britain, as the nation most closely concerned, would ratify it; but this was never done. Hence the declaration was a legal instrument of doubtful value, quite aside from the obvious difficulty of enforcing the observance of international agreements at a time of conflict. Neither in the Italo–Turkish War (1911/12), nor in the Balkan Wars (1912/13) did the belligerents abide by the Declaration of London.

Restricted blockade

In its first phase the blockade might be described as restricted because it was largely still conducted in accordance with the international agreements of the pre-war period. This phase lasted from August 1914 to March 1915. The military prerequisites for the Allied blockade had already been created soon after the outbreak of war. German cruisers and armed merchantmen in foreign waters were intercepted and destroyed by superior Allied forces. The two battle fleets now confronted one another in a state of deadlock. They remained in port and thus successfully defended their home waters but neither side wanted to risk a decisive battle off the other's base. The sea battles imposed by circumstances – the Battles of the Dogger Bank (January 1915) and the Skagerrak (May 1916) – only served to strengthen the naval strategists of both sides in this determination. This stalemate enabled the Allies to retain the upper hand in the economic war since, without impairing the combat potential of the battle fleet, the Admiralty was able to detach sufficient cruisers and lighter units for the high seas blockade. Moreover the world's merchant fleets were so distributed as to provide a useful springboard for the Allies' blockade policy. In 1914 the steamer tonnage throughout the world amounted to some 26 million gross tons. Of this, the Allies possessed 59 per cent (the British Empire alone accounting for 48 per cent), the Central Powers 15 per cent (Germany 12 per cent), and the neutrals 27 per cent.[3] In the first few days of the war the merchant vessels belonging to the Central Powers disappeared from the oceans of the world; hence those countries could only conduct their overseas trade by way of neutral shipping which, however, was also in Allied employ.

The high seas blockade whereby Allied naval forces controlled the approaches to the North Sea and the Mediterranean was not a blockade within the meaning of the Declaration of London, and the term 'blockade' was studiously avoided in official circles. The aim was to deny the Central Powers imports of contraband; imports on the 'free list' however, and goods exported by the Central Powers in neutral vessels, were not molested. Thus the Allies adhered fundamentally to the terms of the Declaration; it was a blockade that conformed to 'prize law'. Nevertheless, it was imposed more stringently than envisaged by the Declaration, partly because of an elastic interpretation of the latter's terms and partly as a result of various formal amendments. Here the Allies placed the emphasis on two factors: firstly, a tightening up of the

3. See Siney, *The Allied Blockade of Germany*, p. 259.

prize regulations combined with an extension of the contraband list and, secondly, more rigorous controls on the trade of the neutrals, not only on the high seas but also, and above all, within the neutral countries themselves.

Of Germany's neutral neighbours, the Netherlands were the most important from the point of view of indirect foreign trade.[4] After the outbreak of war that country had, like other neutrals, experienced difficulty in securing its normal imports because of the general disruption of international economic relations. The Dutch economy was dependent on the import of industrial raw materials, fertilizers and forage and, as early as 1 August 1914, a virtual embargo was placed on the export of essential goods. Before long the British government was pressing for an intensification of the embargo, more especially after foodstuffs and forage had been added to the absolute contraband list and become subject to the doctrine of continuous voyage. Though the Dutch government pleaded its neutrality, it could not wholly disregard the wishes of Britain, since the latter controlled the approach routes along which essential imports reached the Netherlands. It was also in the interests of the Dutch economy to conclude mutual agreements which would obviate the risk of arbitrary confiscation by the Allies. The first negotiations to this end took place between the British government on the one hand and, on the other, the Dutch government, the Holland–America Line and the Commissie voor den Nederlandschen Handel, a central information and negotiating agency set up on a voluntary basis in September 1914. The upshot was an undertaking by the Holland–America Line and several other shipping companies to refuse to handle contraband destined for the Central Powers, in return for which the British government agreed to relax its controls. These agreements were superseded when the Nederlansche Oversee Trustmaatschappij (N.O.T.) was founded in November 1914. The N.O.T. was a private organization and, while helping to promote it, the Netherlands government carefully avoided entering into any legal ties that might jeopardize its own neutrality. The N.O.T. guaranteed that any commodities shipped to it, or any finished goods manufactured from those commodities, would not be re-exported to the

4. See C. van Manen, *De Nederlandsche Overzee Trustmaatschappij. Middelpunt het Verkeer van Onzijdig Nederland met het Buitenland tijens den Wereldoorlog, 1914 to 1918*, Nijhoff, The Hague, 1935.

Central Powers, and accordingly kept a check on its associated shipping companies, merchants and producers. The British government for its part accepted the N.O.T.'s guarantee as sufficient assurance that all shipments to the N.O.T. would remain in neutral hands. This compromise gave the Allies greater control over Dutch imports, while the Netherlands on their side were assured of essential imports from overseas for their own domestic use. In quantitative terms the agreement was at first of small significance. Generally speaking it applied only to contraband: primarily food-stuffs, forage and such raw materials as the Allies had by degrees added to the contraband list. Dutch merchants might take advantage of the agreement, though not compelled to do so – nor, clearly, could they be expected to relinquish out of hand their profitable transit trade with the Central Powers. At the beginning of 1915 the N.O.T.'s imports amounted to no more than some 2.5 per cent of total imports into Holland. But the creation of this body was the first indication that, under economic pressure from the Allies, neutral traders were prepared in some measure to co-operate. As the war went on the N.O.T. became what was virtually a government agency controlling the entire foreign trade of the Netherlands.

In August 1914 the Danish government imposed an embargo on the export of various goods in order to safeguard the country's food supplies.[5] Three months later the list was extended to correspond approximately to the Allied contraband list; complete conformity was rejected by the Danes on the grounds of their neutrality. British complaints about an increase in the transit trade, followed by threats to seize Danish imports of contraband goods generally, led in January 1915 to the first Anglo–Danish agreement in which the Danish government undertook rigidly to enforce its own export prohibitions while for its part the British government accepted that undertaking as sufficient guarantee that the goods imported would remain on Danish soil. Meanwhile negotiations had been proceeding between the British government and private Danish agencies regarding the establishment of a trust along the lines of the N.O.T. Already by the end of 1914 the British had concluded an agreement with Denmark's largest ship-

5. See E. Cohn, *Danmark under den Store Krig*, Gad, Copenhagen, 1928. Revised English trans. in H. Westergaard, ed., *Sweden, Norway, Denmark and Iceland in the World War*, Yale University Press, Newhaven, 1930.

ping line, the United Steamship Company, whereby the latter undertook to ensure that contraband carried in its own vessels would not find its way to the Central Powers; in return, the British government promised to relax its controls. At the beginning of 1915 the British embarked on similar negotiations with the associations representing trade (Grosserer Societat) and industry (Industriraad). The first agreement, which provided for voluntary export prohibitions on contraband goods not included in the Danish list, was concluded in February 1915.

The Netherlands and Denmark were the first countries to introduce the trust system. At the end of 1914 an agreement was reached with Sweden whereby that country's government undertook to prohibit the re-export of contraband goods, albeit with certain reservations such as the right to re-export them freely to the other Scandinavian countries. Italy, Norway and Switzerland also undertook not to re-export imported contraband goods but did not enter into any formal agreement nor, in the case of the first two countries, was any lasting pressure brought to bear by the British government for fear of alienating pro-Allies sentiment. As for Switzerland, there was for the time being little danger of any appreciable transit trade with the Central Powers, since the Allied blockade precluded imports via the North Sea ports and those arriving via the French and Italian Mediterranean ports barely sufficed to meet her own needs, so congested was the transport system in that area. Negotiations and Allied investigations were still proceeding when, in March 1915, the blockade policy entered a new phase.

By February the system of restricted blockade had to some extent seen its day. The neutral neighbours of the Central Powers had all more or less pledged themselves to refrain from re-exporting contraband goods. All, however, insisted that they were free to export their own products to the Central Powers which would consequently continue to receive Dutch and Danish foodstuffs, Norwegian and Swedish ores, and Swiss manufactures.

The efficacy of the restricted blockade policy is difficult to gauge; a certain time elapsed before the diverse measures began to take effect and this meant that they coincided with the general disruption of international economic relations resulting from the war, a disruption which would have come about even in the absence of economic sanctions. Worse still, there is a lack of statistics on the foreign trade of the Central Powers. The control of shipping approaching the North Sea and the Mediterranean was virtually complete. Out of a total of 2,466 vessels entering the North Sea in the first six months of 1915, 2,132 were inspected.[6] In the northern approaches an average of two, and in the Channel an average of twelve, vessels were brought in each day during 1915.[7] On the other hand it is apparent from the foreign trade figures of the Central Power's neutral neighbours that, despite almost total control of neutral shipping, the restricted blockade was being circumvented in no mean fashion. Exports by the northern neutrals, consisting partly of domestic products and partly of re-exports, were appreciably larger in real terms during the first months of the war and in 1915 than they had been in peacetime. What particularly disturbed those concerned with implementing the blockade was the fact that Britain was clearly becoming an entrepôt for overseas products which were reaching the Central Powers *via* the Netherlands and Scandinavia; indeed, it seemed probable that British manufactures were also finding their way to the enemy along the same route. By comparison with peace-time figures, the northern neutrals'[8] share of British exports had doubled during the first months of the war, while their share of British re-exports had actually trebled. Particularly striking was the vast absolute increase in British re-exports to the northern neutrals. That the neutrals would increasingly route their imports via Britain after the outbreak of war was only to be expected, since British exports to neutral ports did not run the risk of confiscation and were generally subject to fewer delays than direct shipments between neutral countries. And precisely because a less careful watch was kept on British exports, the Central Powers might equally be expected to use this route to obtain those imports which, by the terms of the blockade, were deemed 'unlawful'. This could safely be assumed when total neutral imports of the categories in question rose. According to the official British account of the blockade, Great Britain was 'not so much a pipe or a channel as an open sluice gate' for the import by the Central Powers of oil and

6. R. Lank, *Der Wirtschaftskrieg und die Neutralen 1914-1918*, Junker & Dünnhaupt, Berlin 1940, pp. 11ff.

7. Siney, *The Allied Blockade of Germany*, pp. 124f.

8. Holland, Denmark, Norway and Sweden.

linseed, flax, tea and cocoa, British tin, Egyptian and Indian cotton, and Australian wool, meat and corn.[9]

TABLE 4

UNITED KINGDOM: EXPORTS AND RE-EXPORTS, 1913–15

Quarter	Re-exports millions of pounds	Share of northern neutrals		Domestic exports millions of pounds	Share of northern neutrals	
		millions of pounds	Per cent		millions of pounds	Per cent
1913 III	20·1	1·7	8·5	84·2	8·6	10·2
IV	24·0	1·6	6·7	84·2	9·1	10·8
1914 I	26·1	1·7	6·5	83·3	9·2	11·0
II	26·5	1·8	6·8	77·9	9·2	11·8
III	14·5	1·7	11·7	53·0	6·8	12·8
IV	16·1	5·3	32·9	44·5	8·1	18·2
1915 I	19·1	6·6	34·6	50·7	9·9	19·5
II	26·7	7·1	26·6	62·2	10·5	16·9
III	21·0	4·6	21·9	58·9	9·4	16·0
IV	19·9	4·2	21·1	64·5	9·7	15·0

SOURCE: M. Siney, *The Allied Blockade of Germany, 1914–1916*, University of Michigan Press, Ann Arbor, 1957, pp. 261ff.

Within the British government, opinion was divided over the increasing flow of exports and or re-exports which might well be finding their way to the enemy via the neutrals. Strict enforcement of the blockade was opposed primarily by the Board of Trade which had constituted itself the mouthpiece of those business interests whose first concern was to build up Britain's position in the world market and, wherever possible, to penetrate markets previously dominated by Germany. On the other hand, both during and after the war, bitter accusations were levelled against the British businessman for having, as it were, made a profit on either side of the battle line. After the intensification of the economic offensive in the summer of 1915 there was a fall-off in Britain's re-export trade, due primarily to the rationing of neutral imports.

9. Bell, *A History of the Blockade*, p. 246.

The unrestricted blockade, March 1915 to March 1917

In March 1915 the economic offensive entered upon a new phase with the initiation of a policy of unrestricted blockade. It was now that the Allies announced their intention of stopping all shipping movements to and from the ports of the Central Powers and all goods entering and leaving those countries via neutral ports. The intensification of the blockade was officially described as a reprisal for the German government's introduction of unrestricted U-boat warfare; however, it may be supposed that this was no more than a convenient pretext, for attempts to increase the scope of the economic war had already been made by the Allies.

In their view, unrestricted blockade could be effective only if, as previously in the case of restricted blockade, more or less massive pressure was brought to bear on the neutrals so as to secure their cooperation. The moment for the intensification of the blockade was well chosen since the neutrals regarded the unrestricted U-boat offensive launched in February 1915 as by far the greater menace to their trade and shipping; consequently, despite formal protests, the reactions of the U.S.A. and the Central Power's neutral neighbours to the Allied measures were relatively mild.

The first negotiations over the implementation of an unrestricted blockade were conducted with the Netherlands where the prerequisites for a comprehensive system of control already existed in the shape of the N.O.T. Holland was particularly hard-hit by the extension to German exports of the economic offensive, since she re-exported to her own colonies appreciable quantities of German manufactures. From March 1915 onwards these re-exports became subject to the Allied blockade, in accordance with the doctrine of 'continuous voyage'. The Allies held to be 'of German origin' goods in which materials previously supplied by Germany constituted more than 25 per cent by value. Under the terms of an Anglo–Dutch agreement of April 1915, certain exceptions were made in the case of German goods for re-export to the Dutch colonies. Control of re-exports was vested in the N.O.T. which thereafter arranged for the onward shipment of a substantial portion of German exports. In July 1915 the N.O.T. undertook to restrict the import of all articles, irrespective of origin, to the quantity required for internal consumption. This was the first step towards rationing; until the end of the year quarterly import quotas were laid down for essential raw materials, foodstuffs and forages. The quotas were negotiated solely with the N.O.T. but the British regarded these as applicable to all imports and accordingly confiscated any quota goods not consigned to that body. From that time until the end of 1915 the N.O.T.'s share of the Dutch import trade rose to nearly 40 per cent.

In the case of Switzerland, negotiations were necessarily rather more protracted, for the previous round of talks on the restricted blockade had failed to produce any concrete result.[10] The Swiss government had done no more than give a guarantee in December 1914 to the effect that imported contraband would remain on Swiss soil, but no official agreement had been concluded. The principal difficulty lay in the close economic ties between Switzerland and Germany; unlike the latter's other neutral neighbours, Switzerland exported considerable quantities of her own finished goods to Germany. Hence the Swiss authorities felt small inclination to add to the contraband list finished goods that contained raw materials such as copper. That, however, was precisely what the Allies wanted. Despite initial difficulties, the substance of an agreement was reached as early as April 1915. A list was drawn up of goods which, regardless of their raw material base, qualified as 'domestic' products and might be freely exported: e.g. chocolate, condensed milk, silk, clothing and timepieces. Import quotas were based on normal pre-war imports. So far as the exchange of industrial goods between Germany and Switzerland was concerned, licences were granted for the export of a small quantity of products containing contraband metals, the permitted weight of non-ferrous metals (copper, zinc, tin, lead, nickel) for this purpose being limited to 850 tons a year. A trust on the Dutch pattern, the Société de Surveillance Suisse, was formed to handle all restricted imports of contraband goods. The talks took longer than expected because of the political objections raised on both sides, independently of the negotiating parties. October 1915, however, saw the conclusion of a treaty that was substantially the same as the draft treaty of April.

10. For recent publications on the blockade policy vis-à-vis Switzerland, cf. see D. D. Driscoll, *Anglo-Swiss Relations 1914-1918. With special Reference to the Allied Blockade of the Central Powers*, diss., University of London, 1968; H. Ochsenbein, *Die Verlorene Wirtschaftsfreiheit 1914-1918. Methoden ausländischer Wirtschaftskontrollen über die Schweiz*, Stämpfli, Berne, 1971.

In August 1915 negotiations began with the Danish trade associations, the Industriraad and the Grosserer Societat, and culminated in an agreement in November of that year. By its terms, the British government guaranteed the Danes imports at the pre-war level, both for their own domestic consumption and for re-export to Norway and Sweden. The export of finished goods to the Central Powers was permitted providing that imported constituents did not amount to more than 20 per cent of the export value. To a lesser degree, exceptions were allowed to the embargo in the shape of goods that might be exported to Germany for the purpose of exchange, thus enabling Denmark to import such commodities as the Germans would only deliver in return for contraband, and which the Allies were unable to supply. It was, from the Danish viewpoint, an extremely favourable agreement, considering the more rigorous principles Britain had meanwhile decided to adopt in regard to her blockade policy. For while the British government still proceeded on the assumption that an effective blockade could be conducted only with the cooperation of the neutrals, there was a strong body of public opinion which repudiated the agreement and clamoured for the adoption of a more stringent policy. The agreement of November 1915 made no provision for import quotas, but the principle of rationing was discussed during the talks and was accepted by the Danes; by February 1916 import quotas had been laid down for seventy-five articles in all. Of importance to the Danes was the fact that forages were not included in the lists until the beginning of 1917, for the import of this commodity was a necessary prerequisite for Denmark's substantial export trade in meat and animal fats.

No general agreement on rationing was reached with Norway and Sweden although in the summer of 1915 individual treaties were concluded between the British government and various Norwegian trade associations.[11] At the end of the year a general trade agreement proposed by the Norwegian government was rejected by the British government which, in the light of its experiences over the Danish agreement, deemed it too difficult to reach a settlement

11. See W. Keilhau, *Norge og Verdenskrigen*, Aschehoug, Oslo, 1927. Revised English trans. in Westergaard, ed, *Sweden, Norway, Denmark and Iceland in the World War*, and O. Riste, *The Neutral Ally: Norway's Relations with Belligerent Powers in the First World War*, Universitetsforlaget, Oslo, and Allen & Unwin, London, 1965.

that would be acceptable both to Norway and to public opinion at home. Hence where Norway was concerned the blockade policy was based on a series of individual agreements. Import quotas for a number of commodities were laid down in the so-called 'branch agreements' or settlements with the firms concerned and/or their associations. The first agreements related to cotton rationing (effective from November 1915), petroleum products and lubricants (effective from December 1915) and raw materials for the manufacture of margarine (effective from March 1916). For the control of imports regarding which no quotas had as yet been settled, 'trust agreements' after the Dutch and Danish model were concluded with the leading shipping companies between May and November 1915. From time to time, when imports seemed too high, the British government intervened with unilateral rationing measures.

Negotiations with Sweden, which began in July 1915, proved exceptionally difficult.[12] This was partly due to the attitude of the Swedish government: because the traditional ruling circles were in sympathy with the Central Powers, the government made a major political issue of the protection of neutral trading interests. Unlike the governments of Holland, Denmark and Norway, therefore, that of Sweden was determined to conduct the negotiations itself and not to permit any separate talks with individual firms or associations. This was disadvantageous to the British delegation which would have preferred to bypass the government and conclude agreements direct with the import and shipping interests; from past experience in the Netherlands, Denmark and Norway, they had found that individual businessmen were more inclined than their governments to ignore political considerations and come to terms with the Allied blockade policy. In the face of Allied economic pressures, the Swedish government could bank on the fact that an appreciable proportion of Allied shipments to Russia passed through Swedish territory. Hence the Russians repeatedly urged caution upon their allies, fearing that trans-shipments might be held up and perhaps even that Sweden might ultimately

12. See E. Heckscher, ed., *Bidrag till Sveriges ekonomiska och sociala historia under och efter väldskriget*, Norstadt, Stockholm, 1926. Revised English trans. in Westergaard, ed., *Sweden, Norway, Denmark and Iceland in the World War*.

enter the war on the side of the Central Powers. In view of Germany's successful offensive against Russia in the spring and summer of 1915, such fears were understandable. In the circumstances the two delegations agreed in August of that year on a draft treaty which contained important concessions to the Swedes. The draft envisaged a 'normalization' of imports and an embargo upon the re-export of all essential imported goods; however, the fixing of quotas and the administration of the embargo were left to the Swedish government which, if past experience was anything to go by, would almost certainly place a generous interpretation upon its mandate. But hardly had the delegations agreed the draft treaty than the political situation changed. In October Germany's offensive in the east ground to a standstill so that Russia no longer felt herself to be so greatly imperilled. At the same time the possibility of Sweden's accession to the Central Powers began to recede and this, paradoxically enough, precisely because of the defeats suffered by Russia in the summer of 1915, for now the pro-war faction could no longer argue that Sweden must anticipate a threat from that quarter. In these relatively favourable circumstances, the British government refused to ratify the draft treaty and instead submitted a counter-proposal in line with its customary rationing policy. But this proved unacceptable to the Swedes and negotiations were broken off. However, it had meanwhile been found that a compromise solution based on a system of exchanges was perfectly practicable even in the absence of any formal agreement. In return for Allied permission to import essential commodities (e.g. coal) into Sweden, the government granted licences for through-shipments to Russia, for which purpose the Aktiebolag Transito was formed; officially a private concern, this organization was in effect controlled by the Allies.

By the end of 1915 the latter had established with the neutral states contiguous to the Central Powers a system of treaties and informal compromises which enabled them effectively to ration neutral imports. The Allied rationing system not only restricted the transit trade, but also the export of domestic products from the neutrals to the Central Powers, in so far as such products contained imported raw materials and semi-manufactures – almost inevitable in the case of industrial finished goods. There were certain products which were not covered by the rationing system but which nevertheless were of some importance to the enemy;

these included fish, agricultural produce (more especially from Denmark and Holland) and ores from Scandinavia. In this case 'purchasing agreements' were intended as far as possible to absorb the neutrals' export surpluses and thus divert them from the Central Powers, at the same time ensuring that the Allies should receive from the neutral countries specific shipments which might otherwise, given a free market, find their way to the enemy. Open market purchasing would have driven the Allies into expensive competition with the Central Powers and to obviate this they brought economic pressure to bear on neutral governments with the aim of securing for themselves contractually agreed quotas of neutral exports at fixed prices.

The blockade system was strengthened by postal controls, by the regulation of British deliveries of bunker coal to neutral vessels and also by 'black lists' and navicerts, measures which must, if only briefly, be touched on here although the particular efficacy of each is difficult to assess.

Firms held to be agents for the Central Powers were placed on a black list first published in February 1916 and appearing regularly thereafter; anyone dealing with these firms risked being black-listed himself. The primary aim of this procedure was the intensification of the blockade; for instance, German firms overseas, which had previously been supplying the Central Powers with wheat from Argentina or coffee and rubber from Brazil via the contiguous European neutrals found their business connections disrupted by the introduction of the black lists. The system had the secondary aim of causing lasting damage to German business interests overseas.

Under the navicert system, the exporter could have his shipment to one of the neutral states adjoining the Central Powers inspected by the British consulate prior to dispatch.[13] If, in the British view, both the shipment and the consignee were unexceptionable, a certificate, or 'navicert', was issued which ensured that the goods would not be detained by a blockading vessel. This procedure assisted the Allies in the task of control and relieved the exporter of the risk of confiscation. It was introduced in 1916, primarily for the benefit of North American exporters; similar agreements

13. See monograph, H. Ritchie, *The 'Navicert' System during the World War*, Carnegie Endowment for International Peace, Washington, 1938.

had been concluded with the steamship companies of Denmark in November 1914 and with those of Norway in 1915.

At much the same time as the unrestricted blockade came into force in northern waters, the Allies closed the last loophole in the south. British naval units controlled the approaches to the Mediterranean at Gibraltar and Suez, while French, and later Italian, warships blockaded the Austrian ports, this being a close blockade within the meaning of the Declaration of London.

After Bulgaria's entry into the war on the side of the Central Powers, the Allies extended the official blockade to the Bulgarian littoral. The blockade in the Mediterranean was conducted more or less independently of the operation in the North Sea and in accordance with its own rules: namely, those laid down by the Declaration of London. In the overall context of Allied blockade policy the Mediterranean, however, counted as no more than a secondary theatre of war.

At the end of 1916 the Allies took stock of their policy. The system of import rationing, combined with the measures mentioned above, such as black lists, navicerts and controls on bunker fuel, appeared to have largely halted the flow of imports from overseas to the Central Powers; in January 1917 the British War Cabinet approved a memorandum submitted to them by Lord Cecil, which opened with the words: 'All the available evidence tends to show that, with some minor exceptions, no goods from overseas are getting through to Germany.'[14] The domestic production of neutral countries adjoining the Central Powers still continued to provide the latter with supplies of varying importance. Despite the blockade, Sweden was delivering appreciable quantities of iron ore, wood pulp and foodstuffs. Swedish exports of food to Germany were under-estimated by the Allies, while wood pulp was important in that it had become a substitute for cotton in the German powder and explosives industry. Norway provided fish, copper pyrites and nickel, but shipments had been much reduced as a result of the agreements of the summer of 1916. Denmark and Holland were primarily a source of farm produce – meat, bacon, ham, cheese and eggs – which, given the deplorable state of the German livestock industry, were also important. There was some doubt as to the quantities involved; according to the French they were sufficient to support the German armies on the

14. Bell, *A History of the Blockade*, p. 605

Western Front. In the view of the British Blockade Ministry, these residual imports could hardly be stopped, even if economic pressure were stepped up. Hence the guiding principle of the blockade policy was to be the enforcement of agreements already in existence, with the supplementary aim, as from the beginning of 1917, of pressing for a formal agreement with Sweden. For the exchange system, which had at first appeared eminently practicable, even in the absence of a formal agreement, no longer seemed effective enough in the light of the experience of 1916.

Generally speaking, the end of that year found the Allies rather more sceptical about the efficacy of the commercial war than they had been when, full of high hopes, they had first initiated the unrestricted blockade. Germany's combat efficiency had not been appreciably impaired by the economic offensive. Moreover, expert opinion was unanimous in declaring that the blockade system had been seriously breached by the defeat of Romania whose oil and grain were now readily accessible to the enemy.[15] In a memorandum submitted to the inter-Allied conference in Paris in November 1916, Lloyd George expressed the pessimistic view that the success of the blockade had been set at naught by the Romanian defeat.[16] In fact, the Central Powers' economic position was far more unfavourable than the Allies supposed. Hindenburg's ambitious programme of August/September 1916, and the setbacks resulting from the transport and coal crisis and the food crisis in the winter of 1916/17, were indications that the country's economic resources were all but exhausted, though not necessarily in consequence of the blockade.

The blockade after America's entry into the war

The launching of the unrestricted U-boat offensive by the German government in February 1917, and America's entry into the war in April, ushered in the third phase of the blockade policy. Unrestricted U-boat warfare brought about an immediate and sensible

15. On the economic exploitation of Romania by the Central Powers, see G. Antipa, *L'occupation ennemie de la Roumane et ses conséquences économiques et sociales.* Presses Universitaires de France, Paris, 1929. Also summed up in D. Mitrany, *The Effect of the War in South-Eastern Europe,* Yale University Press, New Haven, 1936.

16. See D. Lloyd George, *War Memoirs,* 6 vols, Nicholson & Watson, London, 1933-6, vol. II, pp. 914ff.

reduction in neutral shipping. In February, March and April a total of 313 vessels entered the ports of Germany's neutral neighbours (Denmark, Holland, Norway, Sweden); in 1915, over the same period, the number had been 1,070. Thus, if only because of the transport situation, imports into neutral countries fell well below the level of the import quotas negotiated with the Allies. It may be assumed that there was likewise a drop in exports from the neutrals to the Central Powers, but this assumption is difficult to substantiate because, shortly afterwards in April 1917, the U.S.A. entered the war and hence also the economic war. The effect of this was to render more impenetrable the blockade round the Central Powers. It was not only that neutral business interests were thenceforward deprived of their foremost, if not always successful advocate, the U.S.A.; with no less rigour than the other Allies, that country immediately subordinated its foreign trade and its shipping to the prosecution of the economic war. In May 1917 America introduced the system of black lists, bunker control and navicerts, albeit with certain reservations with regard to her economic interests in South America. U.S. naval units cooperated, not only in combating the U-boat offensive, but also in the control of neutral shipping, and America also played a part in the rationing of neutral imports. This last was of crucial importance to Germany's neutral neighbours since their imports of grain, meat, animal feeds, oil and metals largely derived from the U.S.A.

America's first export embargo was ratified by Congress in June 1917 and put into force the following month. The main purpose of the embargo and of the accompanying declaration of intent was to initiate a new round of talks with Germany's neutral neighbours and to induce them to cut down their exports to the Central Powers. The means of coercion used to bring these neutrals to the conference table was strict adherence to the export restrictions. In August, textiles were included in the export embargo and the British government followed the American lead in placing a ban on virtually all exports to Scandinavia, Holland and Switzerland.

At first the neutral countries showed little inclination to negotiate. To the surprise of the British blockade authorities they had, despite import rationing, succeeded in accumulating sufficient stocks to enable them to defy the embargo, at least for a time. Moreover, the exchange of goods between the Scandinavian countries was on the increase. Despite political affinities, such transactions had fallen off slightly after the outbreak of war as a result of an increase in exchanges with the belligerents. Not until the spring of 1917, with the introduction of unrestricted U-boat warfare and the drastic curtailment of imports from overseas, did private initiative lead to an intensification of the exchange of goods between the Scandinavian countries; indeed, a further extension of these activities seemed called for if business was not to lose its resilience in the face of the Allied embargo. In the course of these transactions Denmark supplied agricultural products and animal feeds; Norway, fish, fertilizers and ores; and Sweden iron and steel, timber and assorted manufactured goods.[17] As regards certain staples, however – more especially grain, coal and oil – all the Scandinavian countries were dependent on the world market; in the long run, therefore, they were bound to become sensitive to Allied pressure.

In October 1917 the neutrals entered into negotiations whose duration and outcome varied in accordance with the situation of each of the countries concerned. American representatives had by now joined the Allied delegations. For the better coordination of blockade policy, a permanent Allied Blockade Committee had been set up; it met for the first time in March 1918 in London, four months after a joint agreement had been concluded with the Swiss, a treaty which largely endorsed all previous agreements and import quotas. On the advice of her European Allies, and France in particular, America withdrew her demand for a more rigid control over Swiss exports. For the French government deemed it expedient to take account, not only of the tide of political opinion which was now gradually turning against the Central Powers, but also of Switzerland's economic importance to the Allies.

The negotiations that preceded this agreement were expedited both by the extent of Switzerland's economic dependence and by the relatively favourable terms proposed. Discussions with the northern neutrals were more protracted, firstly because of the Allies' more exacting demands which called for a drastic reduction in exports, and secondly because, for a variety of reasons, these neutrals were less prepared to make concessions. In December 1917 the U.S.A. released several shipments, or 'Christmas

17. See E. Heckscher, 'Sweden', in H. Westergaard, ed., *Sweden, Norway Denmark and Iceland in the World War*.

TABLE 5

THE U.S. EMBARGO. AMERICAN EXPORTS TO THE CENTRAL POWERS'
NEUTRAL NEIGHBOURS (MILLIONS OF DOLLARS)

	June 1915 to June 1916	June 1917 to June 1918
Denmark	55·9	5·0
Netherlands	97·5	6·4
Norway	53·6	25·2
Sweden	52·0	4·1
Switzerland	8·0	21·2

SOURCE: A. C. Bell, *A History of the Blockade of Germany, Austria-Hungary, Bulgaria, and Turkey 1914–1918*, H.M.S.O., 1937, p. 668.

presents', to Holland and Scandinavia. This was not simply a gesture of good will, but was aimed at dissuading the neutrals from looking to the Central Powers for economic support. However, no trade agreements were ratified before the spring of 1918 – Norway signed in April, Sweden in May, while Denmark did not sign until September of that year. As for the Netherlands, negotiations were not formally concluded until after the end of the war. Although America relaxed the embargo and, from time to time, authorized essential shipments to Holland, the quantities were far smaller than the import quotas under the rationing system. It was only after the Armistice, on 25 November 1918, that a general trade agreement was concluded with the Nederlandsche Overzee Trustmaatschappij. Hence the American embargo was an all-important factor in the economic offensive and contributed materially to the efficacy of the unrestricted blockade, as is evident from the decline in the foreign trade of the northern neutrals. The trade agreements concluded with those countries in connection with the embargo reduced to a trickle their exports to the Central Powers, but by that time the failure of the 1918 spring offensive had already sealed Germany's fate.

The significance of the blockade

After the war many Germans held that the blockade had 'starved' their country and had forced it to sue for peace. The imputation was that the enemy had been able to win only by resorting to the 'unfair' method of the 'hunger blockade'. In this way attention was distracted from the military defeat – 'unbeaten in the field' was a phrase often heard after 1918. Indeed, some people actually believed that a study of the high wartime mortality rate among the civilian population could produce an accurate estimate of the number of deaths caused by the blockade. Non-German authors have subscribed not only to these calculations, but also to the view that the blockade was a war-winning weapon.[18] However, a broadly-based economic system such as that of the Central Powers bears little more than a superficial resemblance to a beleaguered fortress, compelled to surrender for lack of supplies.

The blockade was effective only in so far as it excluded the Central Powers from the international division of labour. There was a considerable range of raw materials, held to be of strategic importance, which, if they existed at all within the Central Powers' sphere of influence, were only to be had in inadequate quantities. Among these were saltpetre, cotton and various non-ferrous metals. The Central Powers, and in particular Germany as the economic leader in that system of alliances, sought to adapt themselves to their isolation by radical changes in their economies – i.e. the development of ersatz industries, the intensive exploitation of such raw materials as were available, the introduction of economy measures and, finally, the recovery of raw materials from waste and from plant not required for the war effort.[19] The production of artificial nitrogen in Germany, already a technical possibility before the war and promoted on a large scale after her economic isolation, was a genuine breakthrough so far as the further development of the productive forces was concerned. Other efforts proved less successful, so that the term 'ersatz' has retained somewhat pejorative connotations. At best considerable

18. See Bell, *A History of the Blockade;* M. Olson, *The Economics of Wartime Shortage. A History of British Food Supply in the Napoleonic War and in World Wars I and II*, Duke University Press, Durham, 1963.

19. On Germany's raw materials supply, see O. Goebel, *Deutschlands Rohstoffwirtschaft im Weltkrieg*, Deutsche Verlags-Anstalt, Stuttgart/Berlin/Leipzig, 1930, and A. Müller, *Die Kriegsrohstoffbewirtschaftung 1914-1918 im Dienste des deutschen Monopolkapitals*, Akademie-Verlag, Berlin, 1955. On Austria: R. Riedl, *Die Industrie Österreichs während des Krieges*, Hölder-Pichler-Tempsky, Vienna, 1932. Since the lesser Allies had no domestic munitions industry, the supply of raw materials was for them no more than a peripheral problem; see G. T. Danaillow, *Les effets de la Guerre en Bulgarie*, Presses Universitaires de France, Paris, 1932, and A. Emin, *Turkey in the World War*, Yale University Press, New Haven, 1930.

production facilities were called for; at worst the only result, despite enormous expenditure, was an inferior ersatz product or else complete failure which in turn involved recourse to existing stocks.

Again, the beleaguered fortress is a false analogy because, in the case of a well-developed economy, restrictions on foreign trade affect only a small area of economic activity. In the pre-war years, German imports amounted on average to 20 per cent of the net national product, and exports to 18 per cent.[20] During the war imports fell to 40 per cent of the pre-war figure; on the other hand, the even greater drop in exports released capacity for the manufacture of armaments,[21] an aspect often overlooked when assessing the blockade. On balance, the Central Powers drew more heavily on the resources of other countries during the war than at any previous time. Between August 1914 and December 1918, Germany's import surplus amounted to some 12 billion gold marks as compared with the Allied figure of 4–5 billion for the same period.[22] This trend is borne out by the foreign trade statistics of the neutrals. In 1913, for instance, Norway's trade with Germany showed an import surplus of 110 million kroners, whereas from 1915 to 1918 her export surpluses averaged 23 million kroners a year.[23] In addition to the Central Powers' commerce with other countries, account must be taken of the supplies they obtained by their more or less barefaced depredations in the occupied territories.[24]

20. W. Hoffmann, F. Grumbach and H. Hesse, *Das Wachstum der deutschen Wirtschaft seit der Mitte des 19. Jahrhunderts*, Springer, Berlin/Heidelberg/New York, 1965, p. 151.

21. The deciine relates to the value of foreign trade expressed in gold marks; see Kleine-Natrop, *Devisenpolitik in Deutschland vor dem Kriege und in der Kriegs- und Nachkriegszeit*, Preiss, Berlin, 1922, p. 11. No trade figures were published in respect of the war years and no source is given by Kleine-Natrop. As a Reichsbank official he may have had access to the bank's confidential files.

22. ibid., p. 11. According to information provided by the Reichskreditgesellschaft, Austro-Hungarian import surpluses rose at current prices from 0·8 billion kronen in 1914 to 3·2 billion kronen in 1917. From 1914 to 1917 they amounted in all to 11 billion kronen. See W. A. Brown, *The International Gold Standard Reinterpreted, 1914-1934*, 2 vols, Ams Press, New York, 1940, vol. I, p. 53.

23. See Riste, *The Neutral Ally*, p. 236.

24. For information as to the quantities of foodstuffs imported via contiguous neutrals and from occupied territories, See H. Loewenfeld-Russ, *Die Regelung der Volksernährung im Kriege*, Hölder-Pichler-Tempsky, Vienna, 1926, pp. 361-403.

Since the real economic contribution made by other countries to a nation's war economy consists not so much in imports as in the import surplus, these data would seem to show that the blockade was only moderately successful. Indeed the Central Powers' import surpluses were limited as much by Allied economic sanctions as by the extent to which the neutrals were prepared to grant credit. It would appear that, in financing her import surpluses, Germany had largely exhausted her credit facilities abroad. The prerequisites for any marked increase in the import balance – gold reserves of corresponding magnitude or easily realizable investments abroad – were not to hand, nor would it seem probable that

TABLE 6

GERMAN FOREIGN TRADE, 1913–18 (BILLIONS OF GOLD MARKS)

	Foreign trade at current prices			Foreign trade in gold marks			Gold mark index (1913 = 100)	
	Im-ports	Ex-ports	Balance	Im-ports	Ex-ports	Balance	Im-ports	Ex-ports
1913	10·8	10·1	0·7	10·8	10·1	0·7	100	100
1914								
Jan–July	6·4	6·0	0·4	6·4	6·0	0·4	79	74
Aug–Dec.	2·1	1·4	0·7	2·1	1·5	0·6	—	—
1915	7·1	3·1	4·1	5·9	2·5	3·4	55	25
1916	8·4	3·8	4·5	6·4	2·9	3·5	59	29
1917	7·1	3·5	3·6	4·2	2·0	2·2	39	20
1918	7·1	4·7	2·4	4·2	2·8	1·4	39	28
Aug 1914 to Dec 1918	31·8	16·5	15·3	22·8	11·7	11·1	—	—

SOURCE: Foreign trade 1913 (merchandize trade) from W. Hoffman, F. Grumbach, H. Hesse, *Das Wachstum der deutschen Wirtschaft seit der Mitte des 19. Jahrhunderts*, Springer, Berlin/Heidelberg/New York, 1965, p. 817. Foreign trade 1914–18 from Kleine-Natrop, *Devisenpolitik in Deutschland vor dem Kriege und in der Kriegs- und Nachkriegszeit*, Preiss, Berlin, 1922, p. 11.

neutral governments or business interests would have been agreeable to any substantial increase in credit.[25] The blockade posed a number of problems for those directing the wartime economic policy of the Central Powers, and the necessary process of adjust-

25. For the German view, Kleine-Natrop, *Devisenpolitik*. The money and capital markets of the neutrals were visibly somewhat over-burdened with

ment placed a considerable burden on the economies of those countries – that of Germany in particular. But the tremendous economic decline of the Central Powers between 1914 and 1918 was caused less by the blockade than by the excessive demands made on their economies by the war. The blockade also seriously affected the economies of the European neutrals; despite the initial wartime boom and the high profits deriving more especially from shipping and commerce, there can be no doubt that the economic consequences of the war were negative so far as the neutrals were concerned.

---

claims denominated in marks and other currencies against Germany. For example, in Sweden various methods were discussed and tried out for dealing with the accumulation of such claims. On Scandinavia, see Westergaard, ed., *Sweden, Norway, Denmark and Iceland in the World War*. On Holland see G. Vissering and J. Westerman Holstijn, 'The Effect of the War upon Banking and Currency', in H. B. Greven, ed., *The Netherlands and the World War; Studies in the War History of a Neutral*, vol. IV, Yale University Press, New Haven, 1928.

3

Commercial Warfare
and the U-Boat

Prior to 1914, commercial warfare played no more than a subordinate role in German naval planning.[1] In 1907 Admiral Tirpitz wrote a memorandum in which he mentioned commercial warfare as a possible form of retaliation against a British high seas blockade, but no plan was drawn up for this contingency. During the winter of 1913/14, a commercial war employing cruisers and armed

1. On pre-war planning and the U-boat campaign generally, from the German viewpoint, see A. Spindler, *Der Handelskrieg mit U-Booten. Der Krieg zur See 1914-1918*, 5 vols, Mittler, Berlin/Frankfurt, 1932-66; also B. Stegemann, *Die deutsche Marinepolitik 1916-1918*, Duncker & Humblot, Berlin, 1970. From the British viewpoint, see comprehensive official accounts in: *The History of the Great War*, by direction of the Historical Section of the Committee of Imperial Defence; C. E. Fayle, *Seaborne Trade*, 3 vols, Murray, London, 1920-24; A. Hurd, *The Merchant Navy*, 3 vols, Murray, London, 1921-29; H. Newbolt, *Naval Operations*, vols. IV and V, Longmans, London, 1928-31; the economic and social history of the Great War published by the Carnegie Foundation; C. E. Fayle, *The War and the Shipping Industry*, Oxford University Press, 1927; J. A. Salter, *Allied Shipping Control. An Experiment in International Administration*, Clarendon Press, Oxford, 1921. For the official French version, see A. Laurens, *La guerre sous-marine*, (Travaux du service historique de l'Etat-Major de la Marine), duplicated ms, undated (available at the Bibliothèque d'Histoire Contemporaine, Paris-Nanterre and elsewhere); A. Laurens, *Le blocus et la guerre sous-marine, 1914-1918*, Colin, Paris, 1924; *Histoire de la guerre sous-marine allemande (1914-1918)*, Société d'Editions Géographiques, Maritimes et Coloniales, Paris, 1930.

merchantmen was the subject of a naval staff exercise. According to this study, the prospects of causing Britain grievous damage by means of a commercial war were very favourable; however, the study was based on dubious statistical evidence and, worse still, disregarded the problems of supplying the units engaged. From the beginning of 1914, U-boat officers were of the opinion that commercial warfare was the task to which the new submarine arm was best suited. The technical prerequisites had existed since 1910, when the first ocean-going submarines were commissioned, the older boats being suitable only for operations in coastal waters. Though a proposal for a commercial war employing U-boats was submitted to Tirpitz in June 1914, no further action was taken.

After the outbreak of war it soon became apparent that, in view of Allied naval superiority and the absence of an adequate logistical base, the Central Powers could not in fact conduct an effective commercial war with surface vessels. The operations carried out by the few German cruisers and armed merchantmen in foreign waters were of no economic relevance. On the other hand, the notion of a commercial war employing submarines was given general impetus when, in September 1914, several British warships were sunk by two German U-boats in surprise attacks. These unexpected successes gave rise to undue optimism over the submarine, both in official quarters and among the public. Generally speaking, once the element of surprise was lost, these relatively slow vessels were of little use against enemy warships. Hence, in October 1914, individual U-boat commanders, acting partly on their own initiative, began to attack merchant vessels. So far as possible they sought to abide by the rules of the Declaration of London. This *ad hoc* beginning coincided with the start of a controversy, conducted at the highest level, on the principles of commercial warfare waged with U-boats.

The U-boat offensive against merchant shipping represented an entirely new form of sea warfare and hence was difficult to subsume under existing international law. Strict adherence to the terms of the Declaration of London was virtually impossible. A submarine could neither load confiscated contraband, nor could it escort into harbour the vessels it had stopped. The sinking of merchantmen, permissible only in exceptional cases under the terms both of the Declaration and of the German prize regulations, inevitably became the rule in the U-boat offensive. Moreover

U-boats were not capable of accommodating the crews of the vessels they sank. Hence U-boat warfare 'in accordance with the prize regulations' involved a distinctly 'abridged' procedure: the submarine commander would simply dispatch a boarding party to establish the nationality of the intercepted vessel and the destination of her cargo and then, should he decide to sink her, allow the crew sufficient time to take to the boats. In such a situation the surfaced U-boat was in danger of being rammed or exposed to superior fire power. However, as experience was to show, this 'abridged' procedure based on the prize regulations was still regarded by the Allies and neutrals as admissible under international law.

But in November 1914 the naval authorities began to advocate a different view, namely the doctrine of unrestricted U-boat warfare, of 'sinking without warning'. This postulated an extensive 'barred zone' off the British and French coasts within which all shipping, regardless of flag, would be attacked and sunk without warning. Such procedure was clearly contrary to established international law but so, too, was the unrestricted blockade of the Central Powers by the Allies from March 1915 onwards. Hence, during and after the war, Germans tended to regard the one as offsetting the other under international law. But to all save the Germans there was a marked distinction between the confiscation of goods and the sinking without warning of ships, together with their helpless crews and passengers.

The controversy that took place inside Germany was essentially a debate between naval and political leaders, and was not concerned with the niceties of international law. For the civil no less than the naval authorities had always interpreted unrestricted submarine warfare as an admissible retaliatory measure against prior Allied infringements of the rules of naval warfare, an interpretation that was subsequently endorsed by the Parliamentary Investigating Committee of the Weimar National Assembly.[2] The government, however, feared that unrestricted submarine warfare would cause the neutrals, and in particular the United States, to react in a manner unfavourable to the Central Powers, and for a

2. See Spindler, *Der Handelskrieg*, vol. 1, pp. 42ff also, A. Spindler, *Völkerrecht im Weltkrieg 1914-1918. Dritte Reihe im Werk des Parlamentarischen Untersuchungsausschusses*, 4 vols, Deutsche Verlagsgesellschaft für Politik und Geschichte, Berlin, 1927.

time this disadvantage was held to outweigh any potential advantages. Hence the discussion was always, as it were, 'technocratic', concerning on the one hand, the prospects of success held out by the U-boat campaign and, on the other, the possible disadvantages and risks involved, which might even extend to America's entry into the war. But in addition the controversy over unrestricted submarine warfare may be seen as perfectly illustrating the political balance of power in Germany.[3] Politically speaking, there were three distinct 'U-boat crises', – the first in the winter of 1914/15 the second in the winter of 1915/16 and the third in the winter of 1916/17. From an economic viewpoint, the U-boat campaign is of interest only from February 1917 onwards, after the third 'U-boat crisis'. However, a short account of preceding events will afford a better understanding of the period in which the U-boat campaign first assumed the dimensions of a blockade.

From November 1914 Admiral Pohl, Chief of Naval Staff, was the main advocate of unrestricted submarine warfare. Among the naval leaders, opinion was at first divided. The staff, unlike their chief, were inclined to temporize; they advised the government not to introduce unrestricted submarine warfare before some telling blows had been inflicted on land, when Germany would be in a stronger position vis-à-vis the neutrals. Tirpitz also warned against the introduction of unrestricted submarine warfare on the grounds that the forces available were not powerful enough to deal a decisive blow, and went on to describe as 'rodomontade' the claim that an effective U-boat blockade could, at that point of time, be imposed upon Britain. In January 1915 there was a shift of emphasis, for the naval staff now supported Pohl while Tirpitz, if he still had any reservations kept them to himself. Thenceforward the government found itself confronted by a resolute naval leadership who backed up their case with exaggerated claims for the efficacy of U-boat warfare. The naval chiefs themselves were clearly under the impression that there was no time to lose, February being the month in which Argentina began shipping wheat to

3. See G. Ritter, *Staatskunst und Kriegshandwerk. Das Problem des Militarismus in Deutschland*, 4 vols, Oldenburg, Munich, 1960-68, vol. III, p. 145; B. Kaulisch, 'Die Auseinandersetzung über den uneingeschränkten U-Bootkrieg innerhalb der herrschenden Klassen im zweiten Halbjahr 1916 und seine Eröffnung im Februar 1917', F. Klein, ed., *Politik im Krieg 1914-1918*, Akademie-Verlag, Berlin, 1964

Britain. The Supreme Army Command, hitherto somewhat sceptical, now also declared themselves in favour of unrestricted
submarine warfare, more especially since Admiral Pohl had
assured them that his submarines could effectively disrupt the
movement of Allied troops across the Channel. Moreover, under
the influence of intensive propaganda, the public also began to
press for a U-boat offensive. During a crucial discussion on 1
February 1915, therefore, the Chancellor finally gave his assent
to unrestricted U-boat warfare.

On 4 February 1915, the German government declared the
waters surrounding Great Britain and Ireland, including the
Channel, to be a military area, announced that after 18 February
enemy merchantmen found in this area would be sunk without
warning, and also drew attention to the dangers to which neutral
shipping might be exposed as a result of mistaken identity or other
accident. The proclamation was justified on the flimsy pretext that
it had been issued in retaliation against the Allies' infringement of
international law in November 1914, when they had declared the
North Sea a military area. A compromise proposal by the U.S.A.
on 20 February 1915, whereby Germany would abstain from
unrestricted submarine warfare, in return for which Great Britain
would permit the import under American control of foodstuffs
for the German civilian population, was turned down by both
belligerents.[4] The German government demanded the unrestricted
import not only of foodstuffs, but of all industrial raw materials,
in other words a complete suspension of the Allied blockade. The
Allies, for their part, were just beginning to discover and develop
the blockade as a decisive weapon, and clearly regarded it as more
effective than submarine warfare – not, as it happened, without
justification.

The first U-boat campaign, quite aside from any moral considerations, is generally regarded as a resounding failure. In a
tactical sense it was not necessarily so. Losses of Allied and neutral
shipping through enemy action, which had averaged 61,000 gross
tons per month in the first six months of the war, almost doubled
in the six months from March to August 1915 when the monthly

4. See Ritter, *Staatskunst*, vol. III. pp. 157ff; and M. C. Siney, *The Allied
Blockade of Germany, 1914-1916*, University of Michigan Press, Ann Arbor,
1957, p. 65.

average was 116,000 gross tons.[5] But the expectation that Britain's economy would be grievously damaged thereby proved illusory. Her civilian supplies remained unaffected, as did her armaments industry, which did not really get under way until the summer of 1915.

In effect, the resources available when the U-boat campaign was launched were too modest to justify the high hopes of the German leaders. On 10 February 1915 the navy had at its disposal a total of twenty-seven U-boats. Most of these were of the older type, suitable only for coastal work. In the case of the ocean-going boats account had to be taken of the periods devoted to repair and of the long time spent on passage – approximately two-thirds of a normal seventeen-day mission. On average, no more than three 'blockade stations' with one U-boat apiece could be maintained off the west coast of England. The naval staff would not appear to have envisaged an effective blockade of the coast or even of individual ports, although they clearly over-estimated the striking power of the U-boats themselves and were, furthermore, responsible for the grave misconceptions harboured by the government and the general public. It was hoped, however, that a few spectacular sinkings would achieve a shock effect and thereby deter the neutrals from trading with England – a false speculation, as it turned out.

At international level the first U-boat campaign had unexpectedly grave repercussions. The Allies' immediate response was to intensify the blockade. No doubt they had intended to do this in any case, but the U-boat campaign provided them with a welcome pretext for describing these measures as a reprisal. Above all the Germans had under-estimated neutral opposition, America's reaction being particularly sharp. The dispute reached its climax when, on 7 May 1915, the British passenger liner *Lusitania* was sunk without warning with the loss of more than a thousand lives, including a large number of Americans. There was nothing accidental about the attack, quite the contrary. The naval staff cherished the belief that the sinking of passenger vessels would act as a powerful deterrent, and the torpedoing of the *Lusitania* was hailed as a 'victory' in the German Press. Only when a wave of indignation swept the United States did the German government,

5. Figures for sinkings, as also below, from Salter, *Allied Shipping Control*, pp. 355ff.

fearful of an open breach, urge the naval staff to moderate the U-boat campaign. After the sinking of the *Arabic* on 19 August 1915, again with the loss of American lives, attacks without warning on passenger steamers were expressly prohibited. The following month the U-boat campaign was brought within the limits of commercial warfare 'in accordance with the prize regulations', and all operations off the west coast of Britain were called off.

Though this brought a temporary lull in the conflict with the United States, the controversy in Germany continued unabated. The naval staff had of necessity deferred to the politicians but continued to regard unrestricted submarine warfare as the proper course. Hence the next political 'U-boat crisis' in the winter of 1915/16 followed almost inevitably from the Supreme Army Command's call for unrestricted U-boat warfare in support of its forthcoming Verdun offensive. Having by-passed the Chancellor and gained the Emperor's assent, the navy embarked on an 'intensified' U-boat campaign on 12 February 1916. Officially this campaign was directed exclusively against armed merchant vessels, but in practice was hardly to be distinguished from 'unrestricted' warfare. In April 1916 sinkings rose to 183,000 gross tons as against an average of 120,000 gross tons between September 1915 and January 1916 – the period of the restricted campaign; but this increase is attributable to the general stepping up of the U-boat campaign rather than to sinkings without warning. Nevertheless such sinkings continued as before to produce 'incidents', among them the torpedoing of the French passenger vessel, *Sussex*, which revived the conflict with the U.S.A. Once again the Emperor, under pressure from the political leaders, shrank from the possibility of an open breach. In May 1916, the practice of sinking without warning was abandoned, and at the same time the German navy reduced the scope of its restricted U-boat campaign.

With the institution of the Third Supreme Army Command under Hindenburg and Ludendorff in August 1916, decisions affecting U-boat warfare finally became the province of the service chiefs. In October of the same year the naval staff intensified its campaign within the limits of the 'prize regulations'. This was held to be a purely military measure which did not have to be referred to the government and hence was extraneous to the dispute over sinking without warning. The stepping-up of the restricted campaign was sufficient to raise the monthly sinkings to more than

300,000 gross tons, a figure never previously attained. For the first time the U-boat menace began to arouse serious concern in Britain. The tactical successes scored by the U-boats, combined with Germany's relatively favourable position after the defeat of Romania, prompted the service chiefs to renew their demands for a resumption of sinking without warning. In January 1917 it was decided at Imperial Headquarters to initiate unrestricted U-boat warfare on 1 February. Responsibility for this step cannot be laid wholly at the door of the military and naval leaders, for it was finally endorsed by the Chancellor. In business circles, too, it gained considerable support.

The decision was based on a memorandum produced by the naval staff in December 1916, in which it was assumed that monthly sinkings of 600,000 tons were an attainable target, an estimate similar to that already made during the 'second U-boat crisis' in January. In the view of the naval staff, a view based on expert business opinion, losses of this order would render Britain's economic position untenable within a matter of months and compel her government to sue for peace. As Admiral Holtzendorff put it in his memorandum: 'I can say without hesitation that, as circumstances are now, we can force Britain to her knees within five months by means of unrestricted U-boat warfare.'[6] In the opinion of the naval staff there was no effective means of defence against the U-boat. In particular the convoy system, in which merchantmen were escorted by destroyers or other warships, was regarded as impracticable on technical and economic grounds; as will be seen, there was a remarkable consensus of opinion on this point between the German admirals and their British counterparts. The memorandum went on to consider, while attempting to minimize, the possible military and economic consequences of America's entry into the war. It was suggested that shortage of shipping space would preclude any increase in American shipments of war material and also prevent the dispatch of an American expeditionary force.

At the beginning of February the unrestricted U-boat campaign was launched with a fleet of 110 submarines. The target, in terms of tonnage sunk, had soon been reached and, indeed, exceeded: in April 1917 the Allies and neutrals lost 866,000 gross tons, no less than 526,000 of which belonged to Britain and the Empire.

6. Cit. from B. Kaulisch, *Die Auseinandersetzung*, p. 111.

One out of every four vessels that left the United Kingdom during this month for a foreign port, failed to return. There were many in England who voiced the opinion that the war would be lost within a matter of months failing the early discovery of an effective counter-measure. Indeed experts believed that if sinkings continued at the current level, the unrestricted U-boat offensive would, by the end of the year, have reduced the British merchant fleet from some 8·4 million gross tons to 4·8 million gross tons. The carrying capacity of these remaining vessels was estimated at between 1·6 and 2 million tons a month, of which 1·4 million tons alone would have to be earmarked for food supplies.[7] The situation was made even gloomier by the fact that naval experts were obviously at a loss. Admiral Jellicoe who, at the end of 1916, had been appointed First Sea Lord with the explicit task of combating the U-boat menace, was unable to find an answer. Nevertheless, five months later, on 1 July 1917, the Allies were still in the war, and eighteen months after that they had emerged victorious.

The U-boat menace was overcome in various ways. Immediate counter-measures included the convoy system to reduce losses and an increase in shipbuilding to fill the gaps. In addition there were economic counter-measures whose effect was more far-reaching: for instance, centralized control of available Allied and neutral merchant shipping, control of imports and a complete restructuring of domestic production and consumption. These measures against unrestricted U-boat warfare were given added force by the accession of a new ally: in February 1917 the United States broke off diplomatic relations with Germany and, in April, they entered the war.

The convoy system

The story of the introduction of the convoy system makes strange reading. For although in principle a time-honoured feature of naval practice and, in the event, the only effective defence against U-boat attack, this method was for long opposed by the Admiralty.[8] It was objected that there were insufficient warships to provide escorts, that the masters of merchant vessels were

7. Newbolt, *Naval Operations*, vol. IV, p. 385.

8. Cf. ibid, vols IV and V; D. Lloyd George, *War Memoirs*, 6 vols, Nicholson & Watson, London, 1933-6, vol. III.

incapable of manoeuvring within a compact group and, finally, that the system was uneconomical because the speed of the whole convoy was governed by that of the slowest ship; arguments which, though not wholly illogical, were to be proved wrong in practice. Since the end of 1916 the system had been canvassed by the younger generation of naval officers, who were later joined by the 'technocrats' in the newly established Ministry of Shipping, and also by a number of politicians, more especially Lloyd George, who threw his entire weight behind it. From February 1917 onwards, colliers bound for France were escorted in what were known as 'controlled sailings', an experiment that proved completely successful. Out of the 4,000 ships or so that were escorted across the Channel in March, April and May 1917, only nine were lost. In April, at the height of the U-boat campaign, the Admiralty was virtually compelled to experiment with the convoy system for longer voyages. The first inward convoys arrived in May, one of sixteen vessels from Gibraltar and another of twelve vessels from Hampton Roads (U.S.A.). The number of convoys increased rapidly and, from August onwards, the system was regularly extended to outward bound vessels. At the beginning of the U-boat campaign one out of every ten vessels sailing to or from Britain was sunk. By April 1917 the proportion had risen to one in four, but after the introduction of the convoy system, losses dropped to less than 1 per cent. Absolute losses of Allied and neutral merchant shipping fell from a monthly average of 630,000 gross tons in the first six months of unrestricted U-boat warfare to a monthly average of 296,000 gross tons in the fifteen months from August 1917 to October 1918. Thus, while the seas were still by no means safe, losses had been reduced to an economically acceptable level.

Increase in shipbuilding

Side by side with the reduction in losses, there was an appreciable increase in Allied and neutral shipbuilding. In 1914 the monthly average tonnage entering service worldwide, but excepting the Central Powers, was 201,000 gross tons, rather more than two-thirds of it in Great Britain and the Dominions. During the first two war years, British production fell to less than two-fifths of the 1914 figure, a drop that was clearly due to a contraction of capacity imposed by the war since, in terms of profitability, the outlook for shipping was exceedingly bright. In 1917, in response to the U-boat campaign, shipbuilding was greatly stepped up by means of priority allocations of steel, the release of shipyard workers from military service and the rigorous rationalization of production; towards the end of the war 76 per cent of all new vessels were 'standard ships' constructed from uniform plans. Ultimately the total new tonnage entering service was almost as great as in 1914

TABLE 7

NEW CONSTRUCTION OF MERCHANT VESSELS (THOUSAND GROSS TONS AND ABOVE) DURING THE WAR

	Monthly average (thousand gross tons)	Share			
		Great Britain and Dominions		U.S.A.	
		thousand gross tons	Per cent	thousand gross tons	Per cent
1914	201	142	71	17	8
1915	99	55	56	15	15
1916	140	53	38	42	30
1917	243	102	42	83	34
1918	450	132	29	253	56

SOURCE: J. A. Salter, *Allied Shipping Control. An Experiment in International Administration*, Clarendon Press, Oxford, 1921, p. 361.

TABLE 8

UNITED KINGDOM: MERCHANT FLEET AND FOREIGN TRADE, 1913–18

	Merchant fleet (million gross tons)	Imports (million tons)	U.K. share of inward sailings (Per cent)
1913	18·6	54·5	66
1914	19·1	46·4	67
1915	19·2	46·6	68
1916	18·2	44·3	67
1917	15·9	37·3	81
1918	15·7	35·2	85

SOURCE: C. E. Fayle, *The War and the Shipping Industry*, Oxford University Press, 1927, pp. 415, 425; C. E. Fayle, *Seaborne Trade*, 3 vols, Murray, London, 1920–24, vol. III, p. 477.

Only steamships and motor vessels are here subsumed under the heading merchant fleet. The percentage of vessels entering British ports is based on tonnage, not numbers.

and, in the last few months before the Armistice, monthly losses in the British merchant marine were more than offset by new construction. The largest contribution to the expansion of the Allied merchant fleet, however, was made by the U.S.A. which emerged from the war as the chief shipbuilding nation. In 1914 American production amounted to 17,000 gross tons a month, little more than a tenth of British production. By 1916, in consequence of the heavy demand for shipping, this figure had risen to an average of 42,000 gross tons a month. The same year saw the setting up of the Shipping Board, an official body whose task was further to expand the merchant fleet. After America's entry into the war, her shipbuilding programme became vastly more ambitious; as a new industry it could exploit to the full all the advantages of rationalization. Ships were no longer 'built' but 'produced' from standard finished components which simply had to be assembled in the yards. By 1918 the U.S.A. was turning out 253,000 gross tons a month, more than half of all Allied and neutral production. In 1917 Allied and neutral losses of shipping through enemy action amounted to 6·1 million gross tons, while new construction totalled 2·9 million gross tons.

In 1918 losses through enemy action amounted to 2·5 million gross tons, and new construction to 5·4 million gross tons, i.e. a net loss of 3·2 million gross tons had been converted into a net gain of 2·9 million gross tons.

Centralized control of shipping

After the outbreak of war, the Admiralty began to requisition merchant vessels for essential war purposes. In so far as the Admiralty did not operate the vessels itself, the owners were paid at fixed rates, under what was known as 'blue-book rates' which, though they were well below the rapidly rising freight rates on the open market, still allowed the owners a fairly handsome profit. After the end of 1915 ships were requisitioned at 'blue-book rates' for the import of grain for civilian consumption. Initially the object of the intervention was not the control of all shipping space in accordance with wartime economic priorities, but merely the control of freight rates whose rapid rise had increased the price of imports, especially food, and aroused general indignation at the profits being made by the ship-owners. The simple statistical facts, according to Stamp, were that vessels to the value of 200 million pounds earned a profit of 20 million pounds in 1913 and 250 million pounds in 1916; what the man in the street wanted to know was who was footing the bill.[9] Towards the end of 1916 the question was no longer simply one of controlling freight rates for essential imports, since the economic situation as a whole had now taken a turn for the worse, because of, among other things, the poor harvest in 1916 and the increasing losses caused by the 'restricted' U-boat campaign. Plans for centralized control had already been prepared under Asquith and were introduced immediately after the change of government. In December 1916 Lloyd George set up a new Ministry of Shipping consisting largely of the former Transport Department of the Admiralty. He also informed Parliament that shipping was to be nationalized 'in the true sense of the word'.[10] What this actually meant did not at first become clear if only because the man appointed Minister of Shipping, Sir Joseph Maclay, was a prominent ship-owner who laid stress on the positive virtues of free enterprise. Ultimately nationalization amounted to no more than the extension of requisitioning at 'blue-book rates' to all shipping in the early months of 1917. From then on the main problem was that the essential requirements of the various government departments (War Office, Ministry of Munitions, Board of Trade and Ministry of Food) were in excess of the shipping space available, and this quite apart from private demand. Consequently the various departmental requisitions were initially submitted to a joint committee of the ministries concerned (the Tonnage Priority Committee) which cut them down in accordance with the capacity available. The Ministry of Shipping then decided upon the allocation of individual vessels. In the event of there being any spare capacity, the space was offered on the free market by the shipping companies acting on behalf of the Ministry. In 1917 the British merchant fleet was apportioned roughly as follows:[11] 100 vessels as auxiliaries and a further 300 as naval transports (16 per cent); seventy as troopships and a further 335 for the supply of the land forces (17 per cent); 350 for raw material imports for the munitions industry (15 per cent);

9. J. Stamp, *Taxation during the War*, Oxford University Press, 1932, p. 120.
10. Lloyd George, *War Memoirs*, vol. III, p. 1230. For detailed information on shipping control, cf. Fayle, *The War and the Shipping Industry*, pp. 191–221.
11 Salter, *Allied Shipping Control*, p. 77.

750 for essential civilian imports (31 per cent); and 500 on loan to Allies (21 per cent). Despite the pass to which she had been brought by the U-boat campaign, Britain was bound, in the interests of the common war effort, to make shipping available to her Allies. In the early years of the war this was little more than an informal expedient, predominantly commercial in character. It was not until the end of 1917 that effective inter-Allied control of shipping and imports was introduced, by which time the U-boat war had already been decided. In fact the prime concern of the inter-Allied administrators was no longer to combat the submarine menace but rather to coordinate the transport of the American Army and the shipment of supplies for the Allies.

Control of imports

The control of shipping also meant the control of imports in accordance with criteria imposed by the war economy. In 1917 British imports amounted to 37 million tons, as against 55 million tons in 1913, i.e. no more than two-thirds of the pre-war level.[12] A breakdown of these figures shows that imports of foodstuffs fell by 5·6 million tons or 28 per cent, industrial raw materials and finished products (including arms and munitions) by 12·8 million tons or 39 per cent. True, the U-boat menace had receded by 1918, but now the transport of American troops and supplies was making considerable demands on shipping space. Hence British imports in 1918 were on average no higher than in the previous year. A reduction of this order was bound to have a far-reaching effect, both on the country's food supplies and on its industrial production. A crisis could only be avoided by confining imports strictly to such goods as were immediately essential to these two sectors. The rationing of imports was effected by means of the allocation of shipping space and the determination of priorities by the aforementioned Tonnage Priority Committee, on which the various ministries were represented. Each ministry drew up a programme of imports affecting its own province, and subsequently took care of their distribution. This official machinery handled approximately 90 per cent of all imports. Here particular impor-

12. Salter, *Allied Shipping Control*, p. 352; C. E. Fayle, *Seaborne Trade*, 3 vols, Murray, London, 1920-24, vol. III, p. 477.

tance was attached to the Ministry of Food which was set up at the end of 1916 and incorporated two existing, autonomous controls, the Wheat and Sugar Commissions. The final months of the war, from March 1918 onwards, saw the formation of an inter-Allied organization whose task was to coordinate individual import programmes. The only commodity to be affected was wheat, for the Armistice intervened before planning could take effect in other spheres.

Attention was not confined solely to individual import quotas; external trade as a whole was reorganized having regard to the shortest possible shipping routes. This resulted in concentration on the North Atlantic and the emergence of America as the chief supplier. Her share of British imports rose from 25 per cent in 1914 to 43 per cent in 1917 and 49 per cent in 1918; at the same time Britain's traditional trade relations with Australia, the Far East and South America dwindled in importance.[13] This tendency was probably inevitable in any case for the enormous rise in freight rates was bound to bring changes in the fields of production and transport, and hence in the structure of world trade, as compared with before the war; but the process was accelerated by government intervention.

A third consequence of import control was the drop in exports, not because they competed with imports for shipping space, but because a brake was placed on raw materials for exporters. This development may be clearly seen in the cotton industry which, in the early years of the war, ranked as an essential war industry since it was an important earner of foreign exchange. But with the contraction of shipping space, raw materials and foodstuffs assumed greater importance than raw cotton; at the same time the foreign exchange problem retreated into the background in 1917 when the American government granted the necessary dollar credits. Consumption of raw cotton which, in 1916, still amounted to 90 per cent of the pre-war figure, had dwindled to 68 per cent by 1918. True, rising prices meant that exports had increased in value, but quantitatively the figures for 1918 show a 51 per cent reduction in cotton yarn and a 48 per cent reduction in cotton piece goods as

13. ibid, vol. III, Appendix. Also M. Olson, *The Economics of the Wartime Shortage. A History of British Food Supply in the Napoleonic War and in World Wars I and II*, Duke University Press, Durham, 1963, pp. 87ff.

compared with pre-war.[14] This deliberate brake on exports was to have far-reaching economic consequences: the British government financed its increasing import surplus with foreign credits whose repayment proved a heavy burden during the post-war years. Moreover, British industry lost export markets which proved difficult to win back after the war.

Re-structuring of the economy

Finally, one of the answers to the U-boat campaign was the extensive restructuring of the country's economy. A number of controls had already been introduced under Asquith, but after the change of government in December 1916, Lloyd George's administration immediately set about creating a comprehensive system of state intervention, a process accelerated by the U-boat campaign. The most important immediate problem, and one which it was neither possible nor desirable to leave to the market, was the distribution of imported goods in short supply. First and foremost we should cite food control which, within a few months, came to embrace everything that was eaten and drunk by 40 million people.[15] But other fields were also affected. To return to the cotton industry, for instance: the availability of raw cotton determined the degree of activity of the mills and hence also the situation of the workers and the profits of the employers. Here again the decision was not left to the market but, in June 1917, became the responsibility of the Cotton Control Board, a new body consisting of representatives of the employers, trade unions and the Board of Trade.[16] Another far-reaching problem was the reorganization of home production with a view to economizing on imports. Most impressive of all was the reorganization of agriculture: within the two years 1916–18 nearly 7·5 million acres of pasture were ploughed up, an area that represented roughly three-quarters of the arable land that had been turned over to grass in the fifty years preceding the war.[17] Production of wheat and potatoes rose by 40 per cent

14. H. D. Henderson, *The Cotton Control Board*, Clarendon Press, Oxford, 1922, p. 75.

15. W. Beveridge, *British Food Control*, Oxford University Press, 1928, p. 2.

16. See Henderson, *The Cotton Control Board*.

17. See T. H. Middleton, *Food Production in War*, Clarendon Press, Oxford 1923 pp. 207-57; and Olson, *The Economics of the Wartime Shortage*, pp. 98ff.

as compared with pre-war. Even allowing for the loss of production in stock farming, food production still showed an overall increase of 24 per cent in terms of calorie content. In industry, reorganization meant above all restrictions on investment activity.

In conclusion, let us again compare the planning of the U-boat blockade with its results. According to the German naval staff's memorandum of December 1916, an unrestricted U-boat campaign would force the British government to sue for peace within five months. This was based on the assumption that German submarines would sink 600,000 gross tons of shipping a month. Eventually the convoy system made such a figure unattainable, but within the period laid down by the German naval staff the tonnage sunk not only reached but actually exceeded the expected level; in the five months from February to June 1917, sinkings averaged 647,000 gross tons a month. When, in July 1917, regular convoys were introduced, the battle should, according to the German forecast, already have been decided. The naval staff was disappointed in its hopes that fear of sinking without warning would deter neutral and perhaps even Allied ship-owners and crews from entering the dangerous zones. Indeed, Allied and available neutral shipping was concentrated more than ever before on the dangerous supply routes to Britain, France and Italy. Hence the naval staff's mistake consisted less in faulty technical planning than in over-estimating the economic consequences of the U-boat campaign. The expectation that it would be possible to 'starve out' an industrial nation in a matter of months was false; here there is a close parallel with the blockade of the Central Powers which was likewise consistently over-rated by the Allies. Whether the unrestricted U-boat campaign was a decisive factor in the war, whether, that is, in Gerhard Ritter's words, it 'set Germany finally and decisively on the road to destruction'[18] is a political rather than an economic question. The assertion rests on the hypothesis that Germany's defeat was due to America's entry which in turn was occasioned by the unrestricted U-boat campaign. However there are others who hold the view that the United States would in any case have entered the war and that, quite aside from American military intervention, the defeat of the Central Powers had been a

18. G. Ritter, *Staatskunst*, vol. III, p. 145.

foregone conclusion, economically speaking, as early as August 1914.

A fundamental misconception underlying the Allied blockade no less than the German U-boat campaign was the over-estimation by both sides of the degree of dependence of industrial countries on foreign trade. The growth of economic interdependence on a worldwide scale, which had been observable prior to 1914, was interpreted as a vital concomitant of industrialization. But in reality the decisive factor was not industrialization *per se*, but the liberal-capitalist framework in which it took place. One of the lessons learnt from the war and the post-war period is that industrial countries can achieve a measure of self-sufficiency, irrespective of whether their economic systems are based on socialism or state monopoly.

4

Armaments Policy

The aim of wartime economic policy is, as Bertrand Russell very pertinently observed to J. M. Keynes on the latter's appointment to a Treasury post during the First World War: 'maximum slaughter at minimum expense'.[1] Technically, wartime economic policy presented itself as a question of optimalization, in other words the allocation of a country's available resources as ingeniously as possible among the armed forces, the armament industry, the producers of capital goods and the suppliers of the civilian population with the ultimate aim of inflicting the greatest possible damage on the enemy. In the European wars of the nineteenth century the economies of the belligerent nations were seldom fully mobilized – hence the tendency to identify wartime economic policy with financial policy. Only during the course of the Great War did it (again) become apparent that economic warfare was principally a matter of real resources, of labour, raw materials and productive capacity.

Arming for war signified the disruption of the world economy in two respects. According to Kenneth Boulding, the armaments industry is, first and foremost, a component in an international system of threat and conflict, as distinct from all other industries

1. Cit. from W. K. Hancock, *Four Studies of War and Peace in this Century*, Cambridge University Press, 1961, p. 18.

whose relation is one of international exchange.[2] Hence each gambit in the power struggle marked another step away from mutual dependence. The European war eroded to a quite unprecedented degree the resources of the European industrial powers and thus simultaneously undermined the world economy, at least two-thirds of which was at that time identifiable with the economy of Europe. Moreover, the war also disrupted the capitalist world economy in an abstract sense, namely by challenging, in unmistakable terms, its very *raison d'être*. The historical justification for the capitalist system lay in the tremendous development of the productive forces as described by Marx and Engels in the Communist Manifesto.[3] Keynes and other liberals also saw in this the social justification for the capitalist system with all its inequalities and injustices; the concentration of wealth, they held, was the prerequisite for rapid capital accumulation which ultimately would benefit the many because a new and higher level of the productive forces would make possible a better life for all. The Great War, which destroyed the fruits of years of accumulation, set these arguments at naught. It showed that the relations of production, i.e. the social conditions of production, were becoming incompatible with the productive forces. This particular effect of the Great War was apparent not only to the socialist critics of the system, but also and equally to those thoughtful liberals whose concern was the long-term stability of the capitalist system. Keynes has put this very clearly:

> It was not natural for a population, of whom so few enjoyed the comforts of life, to accumulate so hugely. The war has disclosed the possibility of consumption to all and the vanity of abstinence to many. Thus the bluff is discovered; the labouring classes may be no longer willing to forgo so largely, and the capitalist classes, no longer confident of the future, may seek to enjoy more fully their liberties of consumption so long as they last, and thus precipitate the hour of their confiscation.[4]

2. See K. Boulding, 'The Role of the War Industry in International Conflict', *The Journal of Social Issues*, 23, 1967.

3. See K. Marx and F. Engels, 'Manifesto of the Communist Party', *Selected Works*, Lawrence & Wishart 1968.

4. J. M. Keynes, 'The Economic Consequences of the Peace', *Collected Writings*, Macmillan, London, 1971, vol. II. p. 13

The Central Powers

Germany

It is evident that the German government had long been planning and preparing for war.[5] Nevertheless, when war came, its economic preparedness, aside from a few currency laws, proved inadequate in the extreme.[6] The problems of waging economic warfare in a conflict having an 'industrial' character, had not even been remotely anticipated. For this conservative approach, a number of reasons may be adduced, the most important being, perhaps, that everyone – and not just the Germans – continued to adhere to the concept of a short war. In the view of Schlieffen, the Chief of Staff, protracted hostilities between industrial countries were altogether inconceivable – a view he did not revise even after the Russo–Japanese campaign which in many respects anticipated the war of attrition that was soon to be conducted in the trenches on the Western Front. He wrote:

> Out there in Manchuria they may face each other for months on end in impregnable positions. In Western Europe we cannot allow ourselves the luxury of waging a war in this manner. The machine with its thousand wheels, upon which millions depend for their livelihood, cannot stand still for long . . . We must try to overthrow the enemy quickly and then destroy him.[7]

After his retirement, he again stressed this point:

> Such wars [of long duration] are, however, impossible at a time when a nation's existence is founded on the uninterrupted continuance of its trade and industry; indeed a rapid decision is essential if the machinery that has been brought to a standstill is to be set in motion again. A strategy based on attrition is unworkable when the livelihood of millions demands the expenditure of thousands of millions . . .[8]

5. See F. Fischer, *Krieg der Illusionen. Die deutsche Politik von 1911 bis 1914*, Droste, Düsseldorf, 1969.

6. On Germany's industrial preparations for war, see L. Burchardt, *Friedenswirtschaft und Kriegsvorsorge. Deutschlands wirtschaftliche Rüstungsbestrebungen vor 1914*, Boldt, Boppard, 1968.

7. Cit. from Reichsarchiv pub., *Kriegsrüstung und Kriegswirtschaft, vol. I: Die militärische, wirtschaftliche und finanzielle Rüstung Deutschlands von der Reichsgründung bis zum Ausbruch des Weltkrieges*. Mittler, Berlin, 1930, pp. 327ff.

8. Cit. from Reichsarchiv pub. *Kriegsrüstung*, p. 328.

Schlieffen's notion of the 'rapid decision' was to exert a crucial influence upon the views of both General Staff and civil service regarding the probable duration of the war. Moltke, who succeeded him, is known to have thought otherwise. On the whole he would seem to have been less optimistic than his predecessor over the prospect of a rapid victory; at any rate he did not entirely exclude the possibility of a 'protracted' war of at most two years' duration. In 1914 the General Staff, presumably influenced by their chief, also assumed that the war would not last more than two years; but in their eyes this was always the maximum, not the probable, duration. The economic deliberations of both the civil service and the Prussian War Ministry postulated a nine months' war.

Given these premises, there was no need for a plan that would provide for the mobilization of large sections of the economy. Moreover the military experts grossly under-estimated the probable consumption of material. A sufficient reserve of weapons, munitions, clothing and equipment was built up in peacetime to meet the requirements of mobilization. Economic planning also provided for the replacement, in case of war, of material destroyed, but the possibility of a constant increase in the consumption of such material and the need for a correspondingly high output to offset it were entirely overlooked. Consequently no provision was made for factories, outside the actual armaments industry, to go over to the production of weapons, ammunition and other warlike equipment; rather it was believed that the peacetime capacity of the munitions plants would suffice.

The armaments industry was partly in private, partly in public ownership. The public sector comprised the 'army workshops' of the larger Federal States – Prussia, Bavaria and Saxony – which were responsible not only for the development and proving, but also for the mass production of war material (rifles, grenades, small arms ammunition, powder and explosives, swords, etc.). Before the war the Prussian army workshops employed some 16,000 workers; in terms of value, the public factories supplied approximately 40 per cent of requirements. Hence the lion's share of the contracts went to the private sector. None of the private firms confined themselves exclusively to the production of war material but some, through their close contacts with the military, acquired the character of specialist 'armourers'. The industry was a considerable exporter and, in the case of some firms, the share capital was internationally owned. A well-known example of this was the Anglo–German Nobel Trust which had subsidiaries in various countries; not until August 1915, and then under pressure from public opinion, was this combine wound up.[9]

After war had broken out, it soon became apparent that planning in the field of armaments during the last years of peace had been inadequate, quite apart from the fact that only part of the last major programme, introduced in 1912, had been completed. The military authorities were taken unawares by an expenditure of war material with which they were not organized to cope. The various procurement agencies flooded the armaments industry with contracts, bidding against each other for supplies and thereby forcing up prices. In the expectation of a short campaign the armed forces were extravagant in their use of *matériel* and, at the height of the Battle of the Marne in early September, the artillery is alleged to have expended more ammunition than during the whole of the 1870/71 war. By October 1914 reserves of weapons and ammunition were exhausted, the armed forces depended for their supplies on current production, and there was even talk of a 'munitions crisis'.[10]

9. See W. J. Reader, *Imperial Chemical Industries: A History*, vol. I, *The Forerunners, 1870-1926*, Oxford University Press, 1970.

10. The most thoroughgoing study of German armaments policy so far undertaken is that by G. Feldman, *Army, Industry and Labour in Germany 1914-1918*, Princeton University Press, 1966. The emergence of state monopoly capitalism is the central theme of a number of Marxist studies, among them: K. Grossweiler, *Grossbanken, Industriemonopole, Staat. Ökonomie und Politik des staatsmonopolistischen Kapitalismus in Deutschland 1914-1932*, Deutscher Verlag der Wissenschaften, Berlin, 1971 ; J. Kuczynski, *Zur Frühgeschichte des deutschen Monopolkapitals und des staatsmonopolistischen Kapitalismus (Die Geschichte der Lage der Arbeiter unter dem Kapitalismus*, vol. XIV), Akademie-Verlag, Berlin, 1962; A. Schröter, *Krieg-Staat-Monopol 1914-1918. Die Zusammenhänge von imperialisticher Kriegswirtschaft, Militarisierung der Volkswirtschaft und staatsmonopolistischen Kapitalismus in Deutschland während des ersten Weltkrieges*, Berlin, 1965, recently recapitulated in F. Klein, ed., *Deutschland im Ersten Weltkreig*, 3 vols,. Akademie-Verlag, Berlin, 1970. Also of interest, with special reference to the Hindenburg Programme is R. B. Armeson, *Total Warfare and Compulsory Labor*, Nijhoff, The Hague,1964. Statistical information in R. Wagenführ, *Die Industriewirtschaft*. Hobbing, Berlin, 1933, pp. 21ff. Interest-group policies are analysed in F. Zunkel, *Industrie und Staatssozialismus. Der Kampf um die Wirtschaftsordnung in Deutschland 1914-1918*, Droste, Dusseldorf, 1974.

Government controls were first introduced in the sphere of raw materials.[11] Before 1914, the structure of Germany's foreign trade was typical of an industrial country, in that it involved an exchange of industrial products for raw materials and foodstuffs. In the four pre-war years (1910–13) 43 per cent of imports consisted of raw materials.[12] Prior to 1914, Germany's supply of raw materials in the event of war had been discussed from time to time by various authorities but no preparations had been made, chiefly because a brief campaign was envisaged.

The proposal for the control of raw materials originated in the private sector, and this during the very early days of the war. There has been much wrangling as to who actually deserves the credit, a question which has now been decided. A number of industrialists, amongst whom was Rathenau, made representations to the government with a view to effecting the central distribution of various raw materials: in particular the pickings that might be expected from Belgium. On the other hand, the idea of long-term planning of raw material supplies – an idea which, unlike the rosy view prevalent in official circles, envisaged the possibility of a protracted war – clearly derived from Wichard von Moellendorf, a senior executive in A.E.G. Rathenau adopted this plan which, thanks to his political contacts, he was able to put over far more effectively than any private individual, and soon he was claiming it for his own. The very fact that Moellendorf was thrust into the background is symptomatic, since his idea was part of a more comprehensive scheme, namely a modified economic system in which the aim would be 'the common weal' rather than profit. Rathenau, however, and the other industrialists who later took part in raw materials control, never left any room for doubt as to 'industry's right to make money'.[13]

On 13 August 1914 the Kriegsrohstoffabteilung (War Raw Materials Department) or K.R.A. was set up within the Prussian

11. See A. Müller, *Die Rohstoffbewirtschaftung 1914-1918 im Dienste des deutschen Monopolkapitals*, Akademie-Verlag, Berlin, 1955. For a purely descriptive account, see O. Goebel, *Deutschlands Rohstoffwirtschaft im Weltkrieg*, Deutsche Verlags-Anstalt, Stuttgart/Berlin/Leipzig, 1930.

12. W. Hoffmann, F. Grumbach and H. Hesse, *Das Wachstum der deutschen Wirtschaft seit der Mitte des 19. Jahrhunderts*, Springer, Berlin/Heidelberg/New York, 1965, p. 160.

13. See L. Burchardt, 'Walter Rathenau und die Anfänge der deutschen Rohstoffbewirtschaftung im Ersten Weltkrieg', *Tradition*, 15, 1970.

War Ministry which, with the assent of the war ministries in the other Federal States, was given responsibility for the control of raw materials throughout Germany. As an authority, the K.R.A.'s main tasks were administrative and supervisory: for instance, the vetting and licensing of requisitions submitted by the procurement agencies, the commandeering and allocation of raw materials, the expansion of the ersatz industries, and other more general economic matters relating to raw materials control. Within the department there were numerous sections, some twenty-five in all, each of which was responsible for a particular commodity. The idea underlying the control of raw materials was that those in short supply should be purchased, stored and resold by centralized authorities in accordance with economic wartime priorities. 'War Raw Materials Corporations' were set up to handle the technical-commercial side of control. By September 1914 the Kriegschemikalien A.G., the Kriegsmetall A.G. and the Kriegswollbedarf A.G. (wool) were already in existence, to be followed by the Kammwoll A.G. (tops) in October, and the Kriegsleder A.G. (leather) in November. Most of the others came into being during the first months of 1915. At the beginning of 1918 the K.R.A. administered twenty-five of these corporations. They were private undertakings (most of them incorporated with limited or unlimited liability) owned or controlled by the raw material consumers themselves. At the same time they also ranked as trust organizations for the K.R.A. and, as such, acted in an official capacity.

Initially, centralized control was envisaged only in respect of raw chemicals, textile fibres (cotton) and non-ferrous metals (copper), i.e. essential raw materials almost all of which had to be imported. The synthetic fixation of nitrogen is usually regarded as the most noteworthy example of cooperation between government and industry. The industrial preparation of synthetic ammonia from the nitrogen in the air had not begun until 1913 and then only in a very modest way because of high production costs.[14] When the import of Chilean nitrate ceased with the outbreak of war, nitrogen supplies became a crucial problem in the production of food and munitions. At this point the state stepped in and,

14. The plant in question is that of the *Badische Anilin- & Sodafabrik* at Oppau near Ludwigshafen which had been in operation since September 1913 see H. Mauersberg, *Deutsche Industrien im Zeitgeschehen eines Jahrhunderts*, Fischer, Stuttgart, 1966, p. 322.

within a short period, synthetic production had been expanded to an extent which, from the summer of 1915 onwards, permitted a steady increase in the output of powder and explosives. Moreover, nitrogenous fertilizers continued to be available to agriculture, if in somewhat reduced quantities. Had the synthetic fixation of nitrogen not been developed on a large scale, a shortage of munitions might well have brought the German war machine to a halt at the beginning of 1915. Non-ferrous metals and raw materials for the textile industry came under centralized control at approximately the same time as nitrogen, to be followed in due course by all materials relevant to the war effort. The initial incentive for raw materials control came from the interruption of imports due to the Allied blockade but, as the war went on, the emphasis shifted to the general scarcity which, in the final analysis, was attributable to a ubiquitous shortage of factors of production. From 1916 onwards steel and coal, the basis of German industrial production, were commandeered and distributed by a central authority.

In retrospect, the German raw materials administration is of interest primarily as a 'model' instance of cooperation between government and industry. Despite much talk of a fundamental change of system, there was no departure whatever from normal capitalist relations of production; rather it was a matter of certain interested parties gaining a privileged position vis-à-vis the rest of industry as a result of their close involvement in the machinery of government. The War Raw Materials Corporations had, it is true, been set up for the public good. Nevertheless, they were able to procure substantial advantages for industrialists and other interested parties, either by allocations of raw materials, or by the adjustment of buying and selling prices, or by the negotiation of government subsidies. The idea was that government control combined with 'a responsible attitude' on the part of private mandatories would curb individual interests. But this proved illusory – not by chance, but inevitably. To Rathenau and the other initiators of raw materials control it was 'self-evident that trade and industry had a well-established right to make money and to enjoy the greatest possible freedom of movement'.[15] The principle of unrestricted maximization of profits, even in the exceptional circumstances of war, was upheld by the War Corporations and within the K.R.A. As one of its officials (Troeger) wrote in a memoran-

15. Goebel, *Deutschlands Rohstoffwirtschaft*, p. 23.

dum for internal consumption: 'The exploitation of the national emergency to promote private interests does not mean that capitalism is decadent; rather it is the logical outcome of capitalism's basic views and a fruitful field for the employment of capitalist expertise.'[16] The K.R.A.'s control of the private Raw Materials Corporations did nothing to restore the balance since the central organization's staff (some of whom had the formal status of reserve officers) had been largely recruited from industry or were at any rate closely connected with it. Rathenau was an industrialist and of his successor, Major Koeth, it has been reliably stated that not only did he have a personal bias in favour of heavy industry, but he chose his colleagues accordingly.[17] The government commissars appointed by the Prussian War Ministry and, later, the German Treasury to control the Raw Materials Corporations were generally industrial advisers to the K.R.A. and hence not altogether disinterested. Thus, for instance, Rathenau (A.E.G.) and Porten (Metallgesellschaft) in their capacity as government commissars, were put in charge of the Kriegsmetall A.G. In fact private industry and the state did not confront each other from opposite poles; rather, the government machine, both as regards personnel and ideology, was dependent on industry and more especially upon individual groups inside industry.

The connection between interested parties and the raw materials controls was apparent from the very start, since only *consumers* of raw materials – and the larger firms at that – were invited to set up the War Corporations. The ownership and control of these corporations were the subject of stubborn dispute, especially since it soon transpired that the corporations were giving their own shareholders preferential treatment in the allocation of raw materials. A further cause for complaint was the fact that requisitioned materials were bought in at a figure considerably lower than the market price. Again the corporations gave their customers the benefit of advantageous 'average prices' which, because of the high cost of imports, had to be subsidized by the state. Finally, by means of direct subsidies and higher permitted prices, the state financed the construction by the larger undertakings in the

16. Cit. from ibid, p. 175.
17. The reference here is to the man who was later to be head of the War Bureau, Groener. See W. Groener, *Lebenserinnerungen. Jugend, Generalstab, Weltkrieg*, Vandenhoeck & Ruprecht, Göttingen, 1957, p. 352

chemical and metal industries of new plant for the recovery and processing of raw materials. The main beneficiary of these controls was quite patently big industry, at the expense of the public purse and the small and medium-sized firms.

The control of raw materials, though important in its own sphere, can in no way be equated with the machinery controlling armaments as a whole. Neither the state-run K.R.A. nor the private War Raw Materials Corporations were concerned with the broader aspects of munitions policy. The long-term armaments programme and the concomitant contracts were determined during discussions between government and industry. On the official side the person primarily responsible was the Prussian War Minister, though he was not without competitors in the shape of the Supreme Army Command and the regional army commanders who maintained their own contacts with the armaments industry. The private side was represented primarily by the War Committee for German Industry, an amalgamation of the two great industrial federations. Besides this, leading industrialists maintained direct contact with all the relevant military and civil authorities, up to and including the Emperor himself.

During the early months of the war Germany and her allies enjoyed overall superiority so far as war materials were concerned. Large industrial capacity, the full exploitation of technical innovations, and the ability to mobilize the country's economic resources for the prosecution of the war gave the German war machine a measure of superiority in the industrial field also. After the 'munitions crisis' of October 1914, there was a drive for the mass production of war materials. Armaments workers were released from military service and the nitrogen problem was gradually resolved by the production of synthetic ammonia. Yet despite a steady rise in the production of armaments, Germany began to fall behind when, in the summer of 1915, the British government stepped up industrial mobilization. At first this gradual shift in the relative strength of the German and Allied war industries went unnoticed in Berlin. In June 1916, the munitions supply position was regarded by the Prussian War Ministry as so satisfactory that quality standards were drastically raised. Large contracts for ammunition of inferior quality ('pig-iron grenades') previously awarded to the industry, were not renewed. However, the enormous expenditure of material in the Verdun offensive and in the defensive operations against the Allied attacks on the Somme soon necessitated a complete reversal of this policy. The 'Somme Programme' of August 1916 gave overriding priority to the maximum possible increase in production. But this new programme was quickly overtaken by internal events. The change in the military leadership at the end of the same month ushered in a new phase in which the initiative in regard to armaments policy no longer rested with the War Ministry but with the Supreme Command.

The Third Supreme Army Command under Hindenburg, with Ludendorff as his immediate adviser, was set up on 29 August 1916. The change had been preceded by lengthy intrigues in the course of which military, political and industrial interests had converged. The principal underlying motives appear to have been widespread dissatisfaction with the Second Supreme Army Command after the débacle at Verdun, the unexpected strength of the British offensive on the Somme and, finally and more generally, the efforts of conservative circles, and of industrialists in particular, to extend their power, an aim they hoped to achieve through some form of military dictatorship. Indeed, policy was determined by the Third Supreme Army Command to a quite unprecedented degree (even allowing for the not inconsiderable influence hitherto wielded by the military) and there is some justification for the assertion that this represented a swing towards overt military dictatorship. In the field of armaments policy the new warlords introduced a fresh phase by demanding that all resources be ruthlessly mobilized for war. Only two days after taking office, on 31 August 1916, the Third Supreme Army Command presented the Prussian War Minister with detailed proposals for the large-scale expansion of armaments production, proposals which were soon to become known as the Hindenburg Programme.[18]

This programme was based on the assumption that since, in terms of numbers, the armies of the Central Powers would grow progressively weaker than those of the Allies, industry must offset this imbalance by raising the armies' efficiency with the help of

18 This text, like other important documents concerning the armaments policy of the Third Supreme Army Command, is quoted in E. Ludendorff, ed., *Urkunden der Obersten Heeresleitung über ihre Tätigkeit 1916/18*, 4th ed., Mittler, Berlin, 1922. On the armaments policy of the Hindenburg-Ludendorff era, see also H. Weber, *Ludendorff und die Monopole. Deutsche Kriegspolitik 1916–1918*, Akademie-Verlag, Berlin, 1966.

'machines' (weapons and munitions). Cited as being of particular urgency were ammunition, artillery, machine guns, mortars, aircraft and materials for fortification. Production targets were set very high indeed. Explosives production was to be doubled within the shortest possible space of time (from 6,000 to 12,000 tons a month); the production of mortars was also to be doubled and that of machine guns to be trebled. The Supreme Command deluded both itself and others into thinking that its 'utopianly ambitious programme'[19] could still turn the scales if only the nation was prepared to devote itself exclusively to 'the service of the Fatherland'.

It would, of course, be wrong to ascribe the Hindenburg Programme solely to undue power-seeking on the part of the military; the programme corresponded in every way to the demands of the armaments industry. For various reasons the industrialists were dissatisfied with the Prussian War Ministry's armaments policy. In particular they accused the military bureaucracy of releasing insufficient labour and of pursuing a 'prices' rather than 'production' policy. More recently they had resented the attempts of the War Ministry to keep armaments profits within reasonable bounds, a case in point being the revelations made by the War Raw Materials Department in July 1916 regarding the huge excess profits of the steel producers. The War Ministry's patent failure correctly to assess the armaments situation in the summer of 1916 gave the industrialists a welcome pretext for advancing their own interests in the guise of 'patriotism'. Their criticism of current procurement policy, accompanied by the demand for a substantial increase in war production was set out in a memorandum of 23 August 1916 addressed to the Chancellor and a few other select persons, among them Hindenburg and Ludendorff. When, on 28 August – the day before the new Supreme Command was appointed – the Chancellor met Hindenburg and Ludendorff to discuss the memorandum, he found those gentlemen 'already in the picture and firmly determined to forge ahead'.[20]

The formulation of the Hindenburg Programme coincided with the reorganization of the government machinery controlling the

19. H. Herzfeld, *Der Erste Weltkrieg*, dtv, Munich, 1968, p. 262.
20. K. Helfferich, *Der Weltkrieg*, 3 vols, Ullstein, Berlin, 1919, vol. II, p. 255.

war economy – a reorganization whose explicit aim was to make that machinery more efficient and readily supervisable. Another, less publicized, aim was to strengthen the direct influence of the Supreme Army Command at the expense of the Prussian and the Imperial governments. In the industrialists' memorandum of 23 August 1916, it had been proposed to entrust all questions of policy affecting the war economy to a central body, the 'Supreme War Bureau' which was to be an independent military authority (independent more particularly of the political leadership). The Third Supreme Army Command adopted this proposal and, by the beginning of November, had brought the War Bureau into being. As a sop to the politicians who had no desire whatever to see a 'military-economic dictatorship', the new organization was nominally incorporated into the existing machinery as a department of the Prussian War Ministry; at the same time its head was made Deputy War Minister. But in fact the Bureau was much more an organ of the Supreme Army Command, especially since its first chief, General Groener, was still regarded as a trusted member of the Hindenburg-Ludendorff team. The War Bureau was put in charge of the War Raw Materials Department, the Labour and War Substitutes Department (responsible for the conscription and release of labour) and, lastly, the Arms and Munitions Procurement Bureau (W.U.M.B.A.)[21] which not long before had replaced the former Prussian Ordnance Department. On the face of it, then, the machinery for administering the war economy had become more compact, though personal differences impeded cooperation not only between the hitherto more or less independent departments now forming part of the new War Bureau, but also between the Bureau and the remaining, older departments of the War Ministry.

In a broader sense, the expression 'Hindenburg Programme' connotes not only the new production targets demanded of the armaments industry by the Third Supreme Army Command, but also a whole series of fundamental structural changes calculated to bring about the full-scale mobilization and militarization of the economy and society, changes which would ensure the fulfilment of the armaments programme. Central to this programme, in the view of the Supreme Army Command, was the total mobilization of labour. Indeed, the announcement of production targets on

21. Waffen- und Munitionsbeschaffungsamt

31 August 1916 was accompanied by a call for the 'total mobilization' of all persons: women, juveniles, disabled servicemen and prisoners of war were to be impressed to step up armaments production. The Supreme Army Command further demanded the general introduction of Sunday work and, 'where necessary', of compulsory measures. Universities and training colleges were to be closed down. The urgency of these demands was emphasized in a passionate exhortation to the effect that 'only by making full use of all our resources and our highly developed industry in the service of the war, can we hope to attain final victory'.[22] A few days later, the Supreme Army Command placed before the Chancellor detailed proposals in which they substantiated their demand for the total mobilization and militarization of labour.[23] In essence their representations called for a 'war production law' envisaging compulsory labour service for the entire population, including women (characteristic of their whole attitude was the allusion to 'untold thousands of childless service wives who are only a burden on the state'). Where men were concerned, compulsory service was to be part and parcel of general compulsory military service, and was to be extended to all males between the ages of fifteen and sixty, who would then be directed either into the forces or into the armaments industry. One of the more important aims was to restrict freedom of movement, as had already been requested on more than one occasion by industry.

The result of these demands was the promulgation in December 1916 of the Patriotic Auxiliary Service Law. During the drafting there had been considerable differences between the Supreme Army Command and industry on the one hand and the government on the other. The military anticipated that rigorous militarization would mobilize additional reserves of labour. In this they had the support of conservative industrialists, who regarded the militarization of labour as a favourable opportunity for reducing labour turnover and keeping down wages. To this the government objected that no reserves worth mentioning remained to be mobilized and went on to express the fear that a rigorous compulsory service law would meet with strong political resistance. In the final draft of the law, the demands of the Supreme Army Command and industry were considerably cut down. While

22. Ludendorff, ed., *Urkunden der Obersten Heeresleitung*, pp. 63ff.
23. ibid., pp. 65ff.

general compulsory service was introduced for men aged between seventeen and sixty, it was not part and parcel of compulsory military service; hence the workers retained their civilian status. However, their freedom of movement was generally restricted, although it was expressly stated that the prospect of a higher wage constituted sufficient grounds for a change of job. Compulsory service for women was entirely abandoned, being obviously quite unnecessary. Widespread poverty meant that women were in any case compelled to work and there were always several applicants for every vacancy.

What worried liberal critics almost as much as compulsory service was the proposed inclusion of the means of production in total mobilization. All suitable factories were to be turned over to the manufacture of weapons and munitions, while the remainder were to be ruthlessly stripped of their labour, raw materials and machinery. Earlier policy had been to permit as many factories as possible to operate, although at reduced capacity, so that their proprietors could keep them turning over without undue loss until the war was over; this consideration was no longer to apply. December saw the setting-up of the 'Standing Committee for the Integration of Factories'. Its task was to close down the smaller less efficient enterprises and those not essential to the war effort, so as to release extra labour, materials and machinery for the larger units in the armaments industry.

The deportation of workers from Belgium and Poland, which formed part of the policy of general mobilization and militarization, represented a particularly dark chapter in Germany's industrial history.[24] In its search for labour, the armaments industry had early shown an interest in the occupied territories and, with the

24. See at greater length, Armeson, *Total Warfare and Compulsory Labor*; W. Gutsche, 'Zu einigen Fragen der staatsmonopolistischen Verflechtung in den ersten Kriegsjahren am Beispiel der Ausplünderung der belgischen Industrie und der Zwangsdeportation von Belgiern', F. Klein, ed., *Politik im Krieg 1914–1918*, Akademie-Verlag, Berlin, 1964. Earlier accounts in: L. von Köhler, *Die Staatsverwaltung der besetzten Gebiete, vol. I: Belgien*, Deutsche Verlags-Anstalt, Stuttgart/Berlin/Leipzig, 1927; F Passelecq, *Déportation et travail forcé des ouvriers et de la population civile de la Belgique occupée*, Presses Universitaires de France, Paris, 1928; F. Zunkel, 'Die ausländischen Arbeiter in der deutschen Kriegswirtschaftspolitik des Ersten Weltkrieges', G. A. Ritter, ed., *Enstehung und Wandel der modernen Gesellschaft*, Gruyter, Berlin, 1970.

help of the military administrators, had set up recruiting offices in Belgium and Poland. By the summer of 1916 some 75,000 workers had been engaged in Poland and perhaps 12,000 in Belgium. Results in the latter country were disappointing, particularly in view of the large number of unemployed, estimated at 500,000 in March 1915 and 650,000 nine months later.[25] The large majority of Belgian workers were not prepared to work for an industry whose products were all too clearly destined for use against their own country. During a discussion of the Hindenburg Programme on 16 September 1916 between the Supreme Army Command and industry, the latter demanded amongst other things the conscription of Belgian workers. At first the government and the military administrators objected to compulsory measures on political grounds but in October 1916 they ceded to the pressure of the Supreme Army Command and the industrialists. On 26 October the deportations began. The workers were arbitrarily rounded up in Belgium and brought to Germany under the harshest conditions (in cattle wagons or open trucks, without heating or sufficient food). On arrival, they were housed in concentration camps,[26] pending allocation to the munitions factories. Ultimately this move proved mistaken from every point of view. In October 1916 the industry had reported a requirement of 'several hundred thousand' Belgian workers, whereupon the Supreme Army Command instructed the military administration in Belgium to deport 20,000 men a week. In fact the industry was in no way geared to an influx of this order, and the workers remained in their concentration camps for several weeks. In December, therefore, the number of deportations was reduced to 2,000 a week. Moreover, it became apparent that, though workers might be deported, they could not be forced to engage in skilled labour. Hence the economic value of the deportations was soon shown to be questionable. At the same time there were unexpectedly sharp repercussions abroad, notably in the Netherlands – repercussions which, having regard

25. See Köhler, *Die Staatsverwaltung*, p. 142; J. Pirenne and M. Vauthier' *La législation et l'administration allemandes en Belgique*, Presses Universitaires de France, Paris, 1925, p. 50.

26. It was considered expedient to hush up these matters. During a meeting held at the Ministry of the Interior on 17 October, 1916, the various officials concerned agreed to avoid the word 'camp' and to substitute the expression 'places of accommodation for industrial workers'. See E. Ludendorff, ed., *Urkunden der Obersten Heeresleitung*, p. 128.

to food imports, the German government could not afford to ignore. In February 1917 the deportations were discontinued and repatriation began; by the middle of the year the operation was officially declared to have been completed. Nevertheless, several thousand conscripted Belgian workers would appear to have been retained in Germany. In addition, there were the so-called 'voluntary' workers who, as often as not, had signed on under extreme duress.

Since the new targets set by the Hindenburg Programme called for continuous increases in the output of arms and munitions, large-scale investments were required – not just in the armaments industry proper, but also in associated fields, from materials right through to the infrastructure. After production targets had been agreed in September 1916 between the Supreme Army Command and leading industrialists, the industry set to work 'with burning zeal'.[27] The construction of new factory complexes, new blast furnaces and even new bridges over the Rhine was put in hand. There is no longer any way of discovering precisely how coordination was effected between individual sectors. This would seem to have been a somewhat rough-and-ready affair, capacity in many cases being expanded without any regard for planning. In making its demands, the Supreme Army Command had always assumed that general compulsory service and the suspension of activities not essential to the war effort would release sufficient resources to increase current armaments production, and at the same time expand the capacity of the industry itself. In Hindenburg's and Ludendorff's view, an unequivocal military order would take care of the rest; on a number of occasions they explicitly refused to concern themselves with the feasibility of the programme— while the industrialists for their part were content with the fact that maximum production targets had been set and contracts placed accordingly. Clearly the question of the attainability or otherwise of these goals, when viewed within the overall economic context, was of little concern to them either. Those most likely to harbour reservations on this score were the men in the government and in the Prussian state agencies responsible for economic questions, but it was only after the event that they learned of the

27. M. Bauer, *Der grosse Krieg in Feld und Heimat*, Osiander, Tübingen, p. 120.

agreements between the Supreme Army Command and the industrialists, and they did not take part in the planning.

It soon became apparent that the Hindenburg Programme was over-taxing the German war economy. First the transport system broke down. Even before the extra demands made on it by the programme the rail network had already been over-loaded by the extension of the fronts (Romania's entry into the war in August 1916) and the rising volume of industrial goods in transit. But at the same time it was short of plant because of the iron and steel industry's concentration on exports and on deliveries of armaments. From mid-October 1916 production was interrupted at a number of factories because lack of rolling stock had held up deliveries of coal. As a result of the exceptionally cold winter of 1916/17 the coal and transport crisis became more acute. By the beginning of 1917 it was already apparent that the shortfall in supplies of coal was due not only to the inadequate transport system, but to the fact that coal production generally was lagging behind requirements. Here the problem proved to be one of labour: no miners, no coal. In the field of metals, the scarcity of raw materials had become so acute by the summer of 1916 that recourse had to be had to the recovery of non-ferrous metals from production plant and finished goods. In the course of this 'mobilization of metal', a host of articles was melted down, including electrical wiring and the copper equipment used in breweries, distilleries, sugar refineries and hotels; also church bells, statues, town hall roofs and even window catches and door handles. In occupied Belgium, industrial plant and whole stretches of railway line were dismantled and taken to Germany, partly for reassembly and partly as scrap.[28]

Ultimately, the crucial bottleneck proved to be the excessive demands made on the labour force. The hope that the Auxiliary Service Law of December 1916 would secure additional operatives for the armaments industry was soon shown to be illusory. Even before the passing of the law, those workers who had not been called to the colours were already employed in essential industries (this being a condition of their deferment); moreover the high wages paid in the armaments industry had acted like a magnet. In areas where under-employment persisted, there were obstacles

28. See C. Kerchove de Denterghem, *L'Industrie Belge pendant l'occupation allemande, 1914–1918*, Presses Universitaires de France, Paris, 1927.

to mobility which no legislation could remove. For instance, Lusatian weavers could hardly fill the vacancies for skilled metal workers in the armament factories of the Ruhr. This being the case, the industry clamoured even more loudly than before for the release of skilled craftsmen from the armed forces. The Third Supreme Army Command showed itself more responsive than its predecessors to these demands; indeed it did not have much choice. In September 1916 1·2 million workers were released from military service and a further 1·9 million the following July.[29] Not only were there too few workers but, after two years of war, the labour force was becoming ever less inclined to make sacrifices in the interest of the war effort. These anti-war sentiments were further compounded by the breakdown of the food distribution system in the winter of 1916/17. Between January and March 1917 there were a number of strikes in the Ruhr, in Berlin and elsewhere, when demands were put forward for higher wages and better rations. The unrest reached its height on 16 April with mass strikes in Leipzig and Berlin. The immediate cause was an official announcement of a reduction in the bread ration. But what lent the strikes especial weight were the political demands put forward, partly as a result of general war weariness, partly under the impact of the Russian February revolution. In June and July 1917 there was another wave of strikes, centred principally on the Ruhr and Upper Silesia.

As a result of various bottlenecks, actual production was clearly lagging behind target figures. In February 1917 steel production amounted to 1,187,000 tons, i.e. 250,000 tons below the target figure and 225,000 tons less than in August 1916; powder production amounted to 6,400 tons as opposed to a target figure of 7,500. By now the War Bureau under Groener had already come to regard the excessive demands of the Hindenburg Programme as pernicious, too much labour and material having been invested in new plant which, owing to shortage of raw materials, could not then be put into production. The Supreme Army Command implicitly admitted its miscalculation when, in February 1917, it decided that investment programmes were to be drastically cut down in favour of current output. The construction of all plant due to come into production later than the spring of 1917 was

29. E. von Wrisberg, *Erinnerungen an die Kriegsjahre im Königlichen Preussichen Kriegsministerium*, 3 vols., Koehler, Leipzig, 1921–22, vol. II, p. 90.

halted. Priorities were introduced for the allocation of steel, a commodity which was to remain a bottleneck in armaments production. At the top of the list came locomotives, machine guns, aircraft, and barbed wire; also such plant (for the production of powder, explosives, fertilizers, and substitute feeds) as was capable of completion before the spring of 1917. After investment had been cut back and all efforts concentrated on speeding up output of the maximum possible quantity of weapons and munitions, production rose more rapidly. By the autumn of 1917 the production programme for machine guns and light artillery had been fulfilled; in April 1918, powder production reached 12,000 tons, though the target figure had meanwhile been increased to 14,000 tons. However, these target figures were attained at the expense of long-term productive capacity. Many of the new factories upon which work had been begun remained 'industrial ruins', only partially completed. Despite far-reaching restrictions on civilian consumption, coal and steel, the staples of industrial production, remained in exceedingly short supply and the transport system was still over-loaded. But from now on the main limiting factor in the field of armaments was the productivity of the labour force and the extent to which it was prepared to cooperate.

The difficulties besetting the implementation of the Hindenburg Programme were the undoing of Groener who, when he first became chief of the War Bureau, had enjoyed the confidence of the Supreme Army Command. Now, however, his realistic view of the military and economic situation had earned him Ludendorff's disapproval. This apart, he had also made himself unpopular in heavy industry because, in July 1917, he had submitted to the new Chancellor a memorandum prepared by his department, proposing government restrictions on industrial profits. Joint representations by the Supreme Army Command and leading industrialists led to Groener's dismissal in August 1917 and his replacement by General von Scheuch, a product of the traditional bureaucracy of the Prussian War Ministry.

In June 1918, after the failure of the spring offensive, the Supreme Army Command once again endeavoured to turn the tide by renewing its demand for the total mobilization and militarization of the economy. By and large the proposals were the same as in the autumn of 1916: compulsory military service for all men aged between fifteen and sixty; compulsory service for women; a military order binding workers to their place of work; and disciplinary measures to ensure higher output. If there was one concession to the tense social situation, it was the call for the control of industrial profits – a call now actually taken up by the Supreme Army Command. The civil and military agencies responsible for the war economy could do no more than again draw attention to the utopian nature of the new proposals and point out that, since all possible manpower had already been mobilized, nothing further was to be gained by attempts at reorganization. In this connection it is interesting to note the War Bureau's objection that, whereas the workers were agreeable to military control of industry, the factory owners were not, and 'refused to submit to the military authorities'.[30] The Supreme Army Command made what was tantamount to an admission of the hopeless pass to which the war economy had come when, in July 1918, the country's economic predicament was first officially made known to the commanders in the field who, according to Groener, had hitherto been largely kept in the dark as to how things stood in the sphere of armaments and substitute products.[31] Germany's armaments policy was to remain utopian right up to the end. Shortly before the collapse, in September 1918, heavy industry and the military leadership agreed an ambitious U-boat programme, the Scheer Programme – yet another scheme to force Britain to her knees.

The fact that, as the war went on, the Central Powers progressively improved their coordination of military operations and thereby came very close to achieving a common strategy, might lead us to look for a similar process in the sphere of their economies. However, there was little sign of a centrally coordinated Central European war economy which might have made up for the fact that the individual members of the alliance were no longer integrated into the world trading system. Germany, Austria–Hungary, Bulgaria and Turkey pursued largely independent economic policies and such limited exchanges as took place were based mainly on bilateral agreements.

30. Cit. from E. Ludendorff, ed., *Urkunden der Obersten Heeresleitung* p. 111.

31. See ibid., pp. 172ff. Also Groener, *Lebenserinnerungen*, p. 377.

Austria–Hungary

Austria–Hungary was the only one of Germany's allies with a domestic armaments industry.[32] From the beginning of the war Austria subjected her economy to rigorous militarization in the matter of direct supplies to the forces. Munitions factories and other undertakings essential to the war effort were placed under military control in accordance with the War Production Law of 1912. This enabled the War Ministry to commandeer the output of weapons, munitions, etc. (naturally against compensation) rather than operate indirectly through the price mechanism. This apart, it was the workers who were most affected by the practical effects of military control, since the employees of a militarized concern were bound to their place of work and were subject to military discipline and law. State intervention was not confined to armaments factories as such: the end of 1914 saw the establishment of a raw materials control on the German pattern. Finally, in 1917, the authorities reacted to the growing shortages in a manner not untypical of the German-speaking countries. They set up a comprehensive organization to administer the war economy under the joint control of the private sector (the newly formed self-governing associations) and the civil service (the Trade Ministry's General Commissariat for the War Economy in association with an inter-departmental coordinating body known as the War and Transitional Economy Commission). This development irresistibly calls to mind Robert Musil's *Man Without Qualities*, since clearly more attention was paid to perfecting the apparatus than to the results achieved: in August 1918, for instance, when the Allies were preparing for their Balkan offensive and when building in Austria had long been suspended for lack of labour and materials, a Building Trades Association was set up whose eight occupational groups embraced every kind of building worker, from architect to navvy.[33] In fact, central control consisted essentially in direct production orders placed by the military, and in the allocation of labour, raw materials and coal. Up to the end, war-

32. See R. Riedl, *Die Industrie Österreichs während des Krieges*, Hölder-Pichler-Tempsky, Vienna, 1932; G. Gratz and R. Schüller, *Der wirtschaftliche Zusammenbruch Österreich-Ungarns. Die Tragödie der Erschöpfung*, Hölder-Pichler-Tempsky, Vienna, 1930.
33. See Riedl, *Die Industrie Österreichs*, p. 80.

time economic policy was bedevilled by the failure to control overlapping between the military authorities and the agencies responsible for general economic policy in the civil sector. Nor was any solution found to the problem, peculiar to the Habsburg Monarchy, of the politico-economic particularism of Austria and Hungary, a problem which was not alleviated but rather exacerbated by the common emergency. The general shortages, which manifested themselves sooner and more palpably than in Germany, eventually thrust aside all other considerations. In 1918 the production of arms and munitions fell below the monthly average for 1914; the troops, who had already suffered untold hardships in the winter of 1917/18, were ill-fed, ill-clad and ill-shod, while supplies of industrial consumer goods to the civilian population had long since dried up.

Bulgaria and Turkey

Neither Bulgaria nor Turkey possessed a domestic armaments industry and hence both were entirely dependent on their allies.[34] The Central Powers promised considerable aid to Bulgaria in order to win over the government of that country. Under the terms of a German–Bulgarian military convention concluded in the autumn of 1915, Germany was to supply war material 'in so far as this is possible, having regard to our domestic requirements'.[35] According to estimates made by the Prussian War Ministry, Germany delivered war material to a total value of 616 million marks to Turkey and 1,074 million marks to Bulgaria.[36] In return, those countries supplied mainly raw materials and foodstuffs. Turkey's shipments consisted of ores, wool, cotton, leather, wheat and a few other foodstuffs; Bulgaria supplied ores, food of various kinds and, more especially, tobacco. But the great expectations Germany had nourished, particularly in view of the blockade, regarding the mineral deposits and farm produce of Turkey and, later, Bulgaria, were to be disappointed. This was due on the one hand to the difficult transport situation and, on the other, to the

34. See G. T. Danaillow, *Les effets de la guerre en Bulgarie*, Presses Universitaires de France, Paris, 1932; A. Emin, *Turkey in the World War*, Yale University Press, New Haven, 1930.
35. E. von Wrisberg, *Erinnerungen*, vol. II, p. 187.
36. ibid, pp. 288ff.

fact that, being underdeveloped, these countries had only a limited production capacity which, being already strained by the war, could not even cope with home demand. The Balkans and Turkey were among German imperialism's prime objectives, but the economic exploitation of these territories called for investment, especially in the infrastructure which, in wartime, was clearly out of the question.[37]

Economic cooperation between the Central Powers came to grief largely as a result of general pressure of circumstances. Towards the end of the war the Austro–Hungarian, Bulgarian and Turkish forces were noticeably less well-provided with food, clothing and arms and munitions than the Germans; on the other hand, supplies in Germany were such that they could not easily have been restricted in order to permit larger shipments to her allies. Right up to the end, Germany never regarded such aid as a contribution to the common war effort, but rather simply as a *quid pro quo*. If we are to believe Ernst von Wrisberg who, as director of the General War Department in the Prussian War Ministry, played an important part in armaments policy, German imperialism's thrust towards the Caucasus was a more or less altruistic 'gesture of support to the friendly state of Georgia'.[38] This frame of mind was not calculated to incline the departments responsible for Germany's armaments policy to make any substantial concessions to their allies, the less so since they mistrusted the wartime economic policy of these states. Beyond Germany's borders, it was generally thought, all was inefficiency, muddle and corruption. At the political level the failure of economic cooperation between the Central Powers was due primarily to Germanys' claim to supremacy vis-à-vis her weaker allies. Basically, the momentum of Germany's imperialism was directed, if somewhat more covertly, as much against her allies as against her enemies. Hence when Germans talked about greater economic coordination among the Central Powers, what they meant was the rigorous subjection of their allies to the wartime economic policy of the German Empire. Germany never showed any understanding for the particular

37. See F. G. Weber, *Eagles on the Crescent. Germany, Austria and the Diplomacy of the Turkish Alliance 1914-1918*, Cornell University Press, Ithaca, 1970; L. Rathmann, *Stossrichtung Nah-Ost 1914-1918*, Rütten & Loening, Berlin, 1963.

38. Von Wrisberg, *Erinnerungen*, vol. III, p. 235.

economic conditions or interests of her partners, an arrogance which, at a higher level, was equally apparent in the discussion of war aims. Conversely, in Austria–Hungary, Bulgaria and Turkey, Germany's claim to supremacy provoked mistrust and anti-German sentiment which in turn were hardly conducive to cooperation within the alliance. Behind the official façade of that alliance the Central Powers drew further and further apart as the war continued.

The Allies

Great Britain

In the Allied camp the principal economic power was Great Britain, although not to such a marked extent as Germany on the other side. Until the outbreak of war British armaments policy was based on strategic plans, elaborated in concert with the French government, which envisaged an expeditionary force of six divisions.[39] Thus Britain was not armed either for a major or a protracted war effort. Calculations were based on a conflict lasting three to eight months, an almost incredibly optimistic estimate in view of what was known of Germany's armament drive. Lord Kitchener, who became head of the War Office on 6 August 1914, was an exception in that he held Germany to be militarily far stronger than France and Russia; from this he deduced that in a war that might continue for years, Britain would have a much heavier burden to bear than was generally anticipated.

In fact the armed forces were very rapidly expanded, but neither Kitchener nor anyone else foresaw the economic consequences which the strategic plans were to bring in their wake. On the contrary, the popular expectation of a short war ('over by Christmas') was bound up with a general conviction that the conflict would in no way impinge on the normal economic life of the country ('business as usual')[40] This was in complete agreement

39. See P. Guinn, *British Strategy and Politics 1914 to 1918*, Oxford University Press, 1965. For a detailed account of British armaments policy, see the official *History of the Ministry of Munitions*, 12 vols., 1921–22, available at the Imperial War Museum, London, and elsewhere.

40. See Lloyd George, *War Memoirs*, 6 vols, Nicholson & Watson, London, 1933–6, vol. II, p. 710.

with prevailing liberal attitudes which were in any case mistrustful of the state where business interests were concerned; the most important task, in the view of those responsible for wartime economic policy in the Board of Trade, was to convince the commercial world that there would be no state intervention of any kind.[41] To safeguard the requirements of the armed forces, the government had statutory powers which on paper were very far-reaching. The much-amended Army Act, which dated back to Victorian times, provided the authority for the requisitioning of existing supplies. This legal authority may be compared with Germany's requisitioning legislation which originally was concerned in much the same way with the immediate requirements of the forces, but later became the formal authority for far-reaching intervention in the economy. A second legal authority was the Defence of the Realm Act, which was promulgated for the first time in August 1914 and several times amended. It gave the government the right to requisition, in whole or in part, the production of any concern manufacturing arms, munitions or other essentials of war.[42]

Later amendments to the Defence of the Realm Act further extended the government's rights of control, notably the amendment of March 1915 which empowered it to determine the production of essential undertakings, to issue instructions to the workers employed, and to adjudicate on the recruitment of labour.

Because of its basically liberal outlook and pragmatic approach, the government showed itself reluctant to make use of what were technically very far-reaching powers. On the whole, armaments policy during the early months of the war was consistent with a system of free enterprise; direct controls were a rare exception, an example being the requisitioning of transport. The War Office inundated the domestic munitions industry as well as a number of Canadian and American firms with orders for arms and munitions at attractive prices, the performance of the contracts being left entirely to the manufacturers. When they accepted these orders the suppliers counted on being able to build up capacity, but with the rapid increase in overall government requirements, skilled

41. S. J. Hurwitz, *State Intervention in Great Britain. A Study of Economic Control and Social Response, 1914–1919*, Columbia University Press, New York, 1949, p. 65

42 Cit. from E. V. Morgan, *Studies in British Financial Policy 1914–1925*, Macmillan, London, 1952, p. 45.

workers, machinery and raw materials were soon in such short supply that deliveries fell behind. By the end of 1914 the government had placed contracts at home and abroad for some 10 million shells, but in fact no more than half a million were produced; the position was the same with regard to other war material.

The worst bottleneck in the armaments industry proved to be the shortage of skilled labour. Since there was no conscription in Britain, there was no ready-made system of priorities and deferments. The recruiting offices accepted anyone who volunteered and was found fit. In the first three months of the war, 75,000 volunteers enlisted each week and by the end of the year enlistments were still running at 30,000 weekly. According to Board of Trade statistics the various branches of the munitions industry (metals, chemicals, shipbuilding) had, by the summer of 1915, lost between 16 and 24 per cent of their workpeople.[43]

At an early stage the industry attempted to offset the shortage of skilled labour by recruiting unskilled workers and at the same time standardizing production processes. This, however, affected the vital interests of the skilled workers. The craft unions, which set the tone in the armaments industry, succeeded, after some bitter disputes, in exacting from their employers a series of concessions affecting security of employment and the preservation of the skilled status of their members. For if large masses of unskilled workers were to pour into the factories and take over a substantial part of the production process, this would inevitably jeopardize the jobs and wage-scales of what had hitherto been the 'workers' aristocracy'. Hence there was at first vehement opposition to the 'dilution' programme, that is, the replenishment of a factory's labour force with unskilled workers, more especially women. Attempts by certain firms to introduce dilution against the wishes of the workers and their unions were met with strikes. At the same time, however, negotiations were proceeding between employers and unions in an endeavour to find a compromise that would be acceptable to both sides. In March 1915, after the government had stepped in, these talks resulted in the Shells and Fuses Agreement, in accordance with which the unions agreed to accept dilution for the duration of the war. In return the employers undertook to revert after the war to the old conditions and not to use dilution

43. See H. Wolfe, *Labour Supply and Regulation*, Clarendon Press, Oxford, 1923.

as a pretext either for dismissing skilled workers or for reducing wages.[44]

This agreement was also in keeping with the intentions of the government which, while backing the employers, was anxious in so far as possible to maintain social peace. In February 1915 a Committee on Production was set up to investigate conditions in the armaments industry. On the basis of its recommendations, the government and the unions concluded the Treasury Agreement at the end of March. In essence this agreement may be regarded as defining and giving concrete expression to a policy based on an industrial truce. The unions expressed their readiness to cooperate in the implementation of the armaments policy; they assented to dilution for the duration of the war, renounced strike action in the war industries and accepted the principle of compulsory arbitration in labour disputes, either by courts on which both sides were equally represented or by government committees. While the agreement was a distinct feather in the government's cap, its concrete benefits would, of course, become manifest only as and when it was invoked. Meanwhile the armaments policy based on 'business as usual' was heading for a crisis.

From G.H.Q. in France came a stream of increasingly urgent memoranda, complaining about the inadequacy of the equipment, both in quality and quantity.[45] As may be seen from the following minute written in January 1915 by Sir John French, the supply of material was in fact the decisive factor after the transition to trench warfare:

> Breaking through the enemy's lines is largely a question of expenditure of high explosive ammunition. If sufficient ammunition is forthcoming, a way out can be blasted through the line. If the attempt fails, it shows, provided that the work of the infantry and artillery has been properly coordinated, that insufficient ammunition has been expended, i.e. either more guns must be brought up, or the allowance of ammunition per gun increased.[46]

But the real show-down came when G.H.Q. attributed the failure

44. For a detailed account of dilution, see G. D. H. Cole, *Trade Unionism and Munitions*, Clarendon Press, Oxford, 1923.

45. See Lloyd George, *War Memoirs*, vol. I, pp. 124ff.

46. Cit. from P. Guinn, op. cit., p. 49. Sir John French was Chief of the Imperial General Staff and also, from August to December 1914, commanded the British Expeditionary Force in France.

of the British May offensive at Festubert to the inadequacy of the equipment[47] and made public their censure of the War Office. The 'shells scandal', together with the fiasco in the Dardanelles, led to the resignation of the first Asquith government.

Armaments policy necessarily ranked high on the Asquith coalition government's list of priorities. In this the prime mover was Lloyd George, the former Chancellor of the Exchequer, who in June 1915 became chief of the newly created Ministry of Munitions. The fact that responsibility for armaments had been withdrawn from Lord Kitchener, the Minister for War, and invested in a new ministry was more than a mere formality. Thereafter armaments policy was framed in close collaboration with industry. Lloyd George prided himself on the fact that his ministry, in striking contrast to a traditional department, possessed the distinct advantage of being an out and out 'businessman's organization', since its most important posts were occupied by 'captains of industry' turned civil servants for the duration.[48] Although the munitions programme laid down by the War Office had as yet by no means been fulfilled, the Ministry of Munitions again substantially raised the target figures which, in some cases, were doubled. To obtain information about likely requirements, Lloyd George had bypassed the War Office and gone directly to British and French officers in the field, thereby fomenting not a few inter-departmental squabbles. Weapons and munitions were ordered by his ministry in quantities which the War Office expressly declared to be excessive but which, in the event, proved correct. Subsequently the target figures were several times raised.

By now the era of 'business as usual' was over. An organization was in process of development which would permit the gradual incorporation of the country's industrial capacity into the armaments industry, and here the ministry no longer hesitated to intervene directly in production. 'Industrial control' might well be seen as the slogan of this new policy. Originally, 'control' had been interpreted quite literally. According to a memorandum of March 1915, full use was to be made of the powers conferred by the Defence of the Realm Act, and large armaments firms such as Vickers Armstrong, Birmingham Small Arms and Coventry

47. See C. R. M. F. Cruttwell, *A History of the Great War 1914–1918*, 2nd ed., Oxford University Press, 1940, p. 158.
48. Lloyd George, *War Memoirs*, vol. I, p. 245.

Ordnance were to be subject to government directives. As a result of stubborn resistance on the part of the firms concerned, this plan was dropped. Thenceforward the word 'control' meant in practice nothing more than governmental coordination of private business activities and the limitation of private profits, or at all events an attempt in that direction.[49]

A more effective measure of control over the armaments industry was brought about by the expansion of the public sector. In addition to the traditional military establishments at Woolwich, Waltham Abbey, Enfield and Farnborough some seventy 'national factories' were already in operation by the end of 1915 and over 200 by the end of the war. Some of these were newly built, others had been taken over from private owners who were compensated on the basis of their pre-war profits. The government munitions factories specialized in the mass production of relatively unsophisticated war material such as rifles, shells, small arms ammunition, powder and explosives. The factories had a substantial share of the market (50 per cent) in these products and were regarded as pioneers in the application of standardized manufacturing techniques. An incidental advantage of some import was that the cost accounts of the government factories enabled the authorities to maintain a better check on the pricing methods of private industry.

The private sector, too, was considerably expanded. When placing its contracts, the War Office had given preference to the military establishments and the few established armaments firms. By contrast, the new Ministry of Munitions was anxious to coopt as many undertakings as possible, not only in order to bring about a rapid rise in production, but also to create the necessary prerequisites for increased output in the long term, a purpose for which the traditional armaments industry was in any case too small. By the end of the war the greater part of industry was employed either directly or indirectly in the production of armaments. The entry of new firms into the sector also meant that in some cases the government was able substantially to force down prices of war material. In the first few months of the war, the established firms had asked for and been paid pre-war prices, and had sometimes even succeeded in negotiating an increase on the

49. See *History of the Ministry of Munitions*, 12 vols, 1921–22, vol. I, part 2, pp. 68ff.

grounds that they needed to expand, despite the fact that higher volume would result in a lower cost per unit. From the start the newcomers based their costings on bulk quantities and were, moreover, eager to enter the business; hence they accepted lower prices. The standard projectile in the field artillery, for example, was the eighteen-pounder high explosive shell which, at the beginning of 1915, cost the government up to 32s. apiece (or approximately a week's wage for one worker). By the middle of 1915 firms outside the traditional armaments industry were offering the shell at 20s., and by the end of the year the Ministry of Munitions was able to impose a price of 12s. 6d. which still, by the manufacturers' own admission, left them with a profit. An analysis of production processes by the Ministry produced an estimated cost of between 9s. and 10s.

The amalgamation of governmental bureaucracy and armaments industry into an organization having a state monopolistic tendency was effected comparatively quickly and without any major friction. A far more difficult problem, however, was the integration of the trade unions and the labour base into the system.[50] With the Munitions of War Act of July 1915 the government acquired wide statutory powers vis-à-vis the workers. Under the terms of this act the government could declare any undertaking essential to the war effort to be a 'controlled establishment'. In the case of such establishments, any rule that might limit productivity was prohibited; wages might only be altered with government consent; and profits were fixed at a flat 20 per cent above the average for the two years immediately preceding the war. So far as the controlled establishments were concerned, therefore, many of the principles became legally binding which had previously been agreed on a voluntary basis between employers, unions and the government in the Shells and Fuses Agreement and the Treasury Agreement. In addition there was government control of wages, a counterpart of the control of profits demanded by the unions. Organization of production in the non-controlled establishments continued to be subject to the voluntary agreements of March 1915. In one important respect, however, the law went far beyond all previous agreements in that it bound the workers to their place of employment.

50. G. D. H. Cole, *Trade Unionism and Munitions;* also, by the same author, *Workshop Organization*, Clarendon Press, Oxford, 1923.

It was a policy that met with considerable resistance. True, the unions were in principle prepared to cooperate and they accepted most of the terms of the Munitions of War Act. But they were flatly opposed to the restriction on freedom of movement, a measure which also led to protests in the factories as did, to an even greater extent, the practice of dilution, despite the fact that the union leaders had likewise agreed to this in principle. On Clydeside and in various other centres there was overt resistance, but the disturbances were neither statistically representative of labour as a whole, nor did they have any material effect on production. They did, however, point to the fact that the armaments policy was limited by the degree of strain the industrial truce could withstand. That limit was also discernible in what the government did *not* do. Originally Lloyd George had aimed at compulsory service for civilians whereby the authorities would have the right to direct an operative to any place of work they chose. But in view of the opposition it might arouse, this plan was dropped. Instead, a comparatively innocuous form of labour service, the War Munitions Volunteer Scheme, was introduced on a non-compulsory basis in June 1915.

Lloyd George remained at the Ministry of Munitions for no more than a year. In June 1916 he became War Minister in succession to Kitchener who had met his end while travelling to Russia.[51] In his memoirs Lloyd George claims, not without justification, to have brought about a turning point in the British war industry. Production of munitions had been enormously increased, and an organization built up which ensured that the momentum was maintained. The mobilization of industry on the lines of a state monopoly was the counterpart of the mobilization of the population by means of general military service.

In June 1916 the British launched their offensive on the Somme with enormous superiority in *matériel*. When in October Colonel Groener was sent by Hindenburg and Ludendorff to view the scene of operations, he was immensely impressed by the unremitting shellfire laid down by the Allies.[52] Not long afterwards, as

51. The cruiser 'Hampshire', aboard which Kitchener was travelling to Russia to discuss British Military aid and general questions of strategy, struck a mine on 5 June 1916 and sank with the loss of almost all her crew. Lloyd George wanted to reincorporate the Ministry of Munitions into the War Office but this would have made him too powerful for the liking of his political rivals. See Guinn, *British Strategy and Politics 1914 to 1918*.

52. See Groener, *Lebenserinnerungen*, pp. 326ff.

head of the War Bureau, Groener was responsible for implementing the Hindenburg Programme, the aim of which was to mobilize all available economic resources in a final attempt to turn the scales. Here we have a concrete example of the way in which an intensified armaments drive by one antagonist evokes a corresponding reaction on the part of the other.

During the period that followed the summer of 1916 historical interest shifts from armaments policy to the general economic measures with which the British government reacted to the U-boat campaign. For the decisive economic battle was fought out in 1917 in the course of that campaign, a point on which both friend and foe were agreed. At the same time armaments production continued, of course, to expand, while the new problem facing Lloyd George's successors at the Ministry of Munitions[53] was that of organizing the large-scale production of the new chemical and technical weapons (poison gas, aeroplanes, tanks).[54] Churchill, too, was in favour of a single Ministry of Munitions for both services, but here he met with opposition from the tradition-conscious Admiralty with the result that only in the case of aircraft was production administered by the Ministry of Munitions for army and navy alike.

Towards the end of 1916 it became clear that the country's economic resources, given the vast demands of the war, were by no means as inexhaustible as people had optimistically imagined in the summer of 1914. There were not enough skilled workers; coal and steel, those essential industrial staples, were no longer plentiful and there were bottlenecks in the supply of foodstuffs. Even dyed-in-the-wool liberals were induced by increasing scarcity to advocate government controls which, no longer confined to the armaments industry, eventually embraced the entire economy of the country. The first moves towards an extension of controls were made while the coalition government under Asquith was still in power. However, the chief credit for the full mobilization of the British industry economy – in response partly to the heavy

53. E. S. Montagu from July to December 1916, C. Addison from December 1916 to July 1917, Winston Churchill from July 1917 to January 1919 and, lastly, A. Weir (Lord Inverforth) until the ministry was abolished in March 1921.

54. On aircraft production, see more recently, P. Fearon, 'The Formative Years of the British Aircraft Industry, 1913–1924', *Business History Review*, 43, 1969.

demands of the war and partly to the intensification of the U-boat campaign – is generally accorded to the new government, the 'great coalition' consisting of Tories, Liberals and Labour under Lloyd George, which assumed office on 6 December 1916. A number of new ministries were formed, visible tokens of the expansion of executive authority. At first it was intended that industrial mobilization should also comprise general compulsory service, something that had already been mooted in the summer of 1915. But in the end this plan was again shelved out of consideration for the Labour Party.

In 1917, the ever-lengthening casualty lists meant that the armed forces had again to be given priority in the allocation of manpower. Despite the plight of industry, the factories were rigorously combed for potential heroes. Many workers who had been trained during the first phase of dilution were called up and replaced by women. Finally, the government even deemed it necessary to call up skilled workers, although this violation of a tabu was bound to provoke a virulent dispute with organized labour. For the jingoist phase was long since over, and the unions – although not openly admitting as much – adhered stubbornly to the opinion that in practice it was their duty to keep their members out of uniform. However, prompted by the German spring offensive, they gave way yet again in order that all available manpower might be thrown into the great defensive battle. Between March and September 1918 a further 900,000 men were called to the colours. To buttress the military presence on the Continent, substantial cuts were made in the economic programme for 1919, but armaments production remained unimpaired. As everyone knows, these measures paid off: the autumn of 1918 brought victory for the Allies.

France

In common with the other belligerents, *France* failed either to anticipate a protracted war or to make adequate economic preparations.[55] After the commencement of hostilities, large armies

55. For a brief survey, see Gerd Hardach, 'Französiche Rüstungspolitik 1914–1918', H. A. Winkler, ed., *Organisierter Kapitalismus*, Vandenhoeck & Ruprecht, Göttingen 1973. A projected study of the armaments industry by Albert Thomas has not been published. Some information on armaments

were rapidly mobilized, but the economic significance of the call-up was not at first apparent, for in its wake the war had brought a general crisis, including massive unemployment. Moreover the economy suffered a heavy blow in the early loss of the northern and north-eastern frontier areas. The industrial region round Briey in Lorraine fell into enemy hands as early as August 1914. Later, the French High Command was to be criticized for its

TABLE 9

UNITED KINGDOM; MUNITIONS PRODUCTION, 1914–18 (IN UNITS)

	1914	1915	1916	1917	1918
Guns	91·0	3390·0	4314·0	5137·0	8039·0
Tanks	—	—	150·0	1110·0	1359·0
Machine guns (thousand)	0·3	6·1	33·5	79·7	120·9
Aircraft (thousand)	0·2	1·9	6·1	14·7	32·0
Aero-engines (thousand)	0·1	1·7	5·4	11·8	22·1
Rifles (million)	0·1	0·6	1·0	1·2	1·1
Shells (million)	0·5	6·0	45·7	76·2	67·3
Powder and explosives (thousand tons)	5·0	24·0	76·0	186·0	118·0

SOURCE: *History of the Ministry of Munitions*, 12 vols, 1921–22, vol. X, part 1; vol. XII, parts 1, 3 and V.

failure to recognize the wartime importance of heavy industry and hence to make adequate dispositions for the protection of Longwy-Briey.[56] But having regard to the initial superiority of the Germans, it is a moot point whether a better-prepared defence of the region would have saved the day. When the front was stabilized in November 1914, after the Battle of the Marne and the race to the sea, the fighting line passed through the heart of the industrial region of northern France. Though the occupied territory represented only 6 per cent of the whole, those living and working there before the war constituted 10 per cent of the population and 14 per cent of all industrial workers. Hardest hit were the centres of heavy industry: in 1913 64 per cent of the country's pig iron,

policy is to be found in: C. Reboul, *Mobilisation Industrielle, vol. I: Les fabrications de guerre en France de 1914 à 1918*, Berger-Levrault, Nancy/Paris/Strasbourg, 1925. On the industry generally, A. Fontaine, *L'industrie française pendant la guerre*, Presses Universitaires de France, Paris.

56. See P. Bruneau, *Le rôle du Haut Commandement au point de vue économique de 1914 à 1921*, Berger-Levrault, Nancy/Paris/Strasbourg, 1924, p. 16.

58 per cent of its steel and 40 per cent of its coal had been produced in the occupied territory.[57]

Inadequate planning, the massive call-up, and the early loss of important industrial centres resulted in a general shortage of supplies for the front. Peacetime stocks of arms and munitions were quickly exhausted and production was slow in getting under way. Daily output of the 'seventy-five' shell, the field artillery's standard projectile, amounted to 14,000 units at a time when a single battery was expending as much as 1,000 rounds a day. In September the High Command was calling for supplies of 700,000 shells a week. The early advent of this 'ammunition crisis' led the government to revise its armaments policy in the same month. Whereas in peacetime, war material had largely been manufactured in government ordnance and munition factories (shells, for example, were supplied wholly by government factories), it was now proposed to shift the main responsibility for production on to private industry. At meetings between the War Minister and the leaders of the steel and chemical industries in September and October 1914, preparations were made to mobilize the private sector for armaments production. Industrial mobilization passed through three distinct phases. During the first, steps were taken to speed up supplies as much as possible by turning over to munitions work all firms that seemed in any way suitable for the purpose, regardless of manufacturing costs. From the spring of 1915 onwards, however, there was a move to concentrate production on the larger and more efficient undertakings. At the same time efforts were made to promote specialization and the division of labour. In 1915 the manufacture of rifles was spread over a number of different firms each of which specialized in an individual part, final assembly being carried out at the government factory at Saint-Etienne.[58] By the beginning of 1917, a protracted war seemed inevitable, and thereafter a number of new, specialized armaments factories were built.

By degrees scarcity of labour created a bottleneck in the armaments industry. During the first weeks of war, unemployment had still been a major problem. Immediately after mobilization 25 per cent of all workers (in terms of the pre-war labour force) had been

57. Fontaine, L'industrie française pendant la guerre, pp. 40ff.

58. R. Pinot, Le Comité des Forges de France au service de la nation (Août 1914–Novembre 1918), Colin, Paris, 1919, pp.192ff.

called up, and 40 per cent were unemployed; i.e. little more than a third were in employment.[59] Those particularly affected were building workers, printers and workers in luxury and other non-essential trades. Unemployment persisted in these branches even after September 1914, by which time the armaments industry was already short of skilled labour. In November, a central labour exchange was set up in Paris to cater for the unemployed and at the same time recruit workers for the munitions industry and agriculture; in addition, the Ministries for War and Agriculture ran their own special exchanges for the recruitment of munitions and farm workers.

However, the armaments industry concentrated primarily on recovering the skilled workers it had lost to the armed forces and on preventing any further call-up of men in this category. Before the war large-scale deferments had not been envisaged. In accordance with a plan prepared in 1912, 11,000 skilled workers liable for military service were to be placed in the reserved category, 7,600 of these being earmarked for the government munitions factories. The total number of employees (including those not liable for military service) in both public and private sectors of the industry was to be between 45,000 and 50,000. By August 1914 this mobilization programme was proceeding more or less according to plan,[60] but already in the following month the armaments industry was accorded absolute priority over the armed forces. Industrialists were entitled to secure the release of skilled workers from the army by submitting lists of names or stating their overall requirements; they could also visit army depots and engage work-people from among the new recruits. By the end of 1915 about half a million skilled workers had left the forces to return to their jobs. Such men, though not enjoying full legal rights, were paid the same wages as civilians, contrary to the wishes of some industrialists who felt that as conscripts they should be employed exclusively on a semi-military basis.[61]

On the whole, mobilization was effected with extreme ruthlessness. Not until later did the government decree that fathers of six or more children might be temporarily released and that men

---

59. Fontaine, *L'industrie française pendant la guerre*, p. 62.

60. See Reboul, *Mobilisation industrielle*, vol. I.

61. See W. Ovalid and C. Picquenard, *Salaires et Tarifs. Collections collectives et gréves*, Presses Universitaires de France, Paris, 1928.

having lost several brothers or sons in the war might be excused front line service. Women, juveniles, foreign workers and prisoners of war were increasingly to take the place of those who had been killed in action or were still serving. Immediately after the outbreak of war, as a result of mobilization and the economic crisis, employment in industry reached a nadir, but it soon picked up. In September it was rising steadily and, by the beginning of 1917, industry was employing on average almost the same number of workers – if not the same number of skilled men – as before the war.

A further bottleneck in the production of armaments was the restricted capacity of heavy industry. The coal and iron industries had been virtually eliminated by the invasion. More than three-quarters of the pre-war capacity of the mining, iron and steel industries lay either in the occupied regions or within the battle zone. Once the fronts had been stabilized the remaining capacity was expanded and put to more intensive use. In the north, mines, coke ovens and steelworks, some of them actually within range of the German guns, were started up again. Hydro-electric power was expanded to take the place of coal.[62] But none of this was enough to offset production losses, and the French economy remained heavily dependent on the import of industrial staples. Of the coal, coke and pig iron consumed in 1917, nearly two-fifths was imported. Hence, simply by controlling imports, the government was able to exercise a reasonably effective control over industry.

At the outset, armaments policy came within the province of the War Ministry. Later (in May 1915) the department within the ministry primarily responsible for dealing with the armaments industry, the Sous-Secrétariat d'Etat de l'Artillerie,[63] was given a large measure of autonomy, and in December 1916 a separate Ministry of Munitions was set up. Its first chief was Albert

62. During the war the capacity of the hydro-electric power stations rose from 479,000 kw to 930,000 kw. Thus, in the exploitation of hydro-electric power, France ranked third after the U.S.A. and Canada; see R. Blanchard, *Les forces hydro-électriques pendant la guerre*, Presses Universitaires de France, Paris, 1924, p. 109.

63. While a 'Sous-Secrétariat d'Etat' was officially subordinate to a ministry, its chief, in effect, enjoyed the same authority as a minister; see P. Renouvin, *Les formes du gouvernement de guerre*, Presses Universitaires de France, Paris, 1925.

Thomas, a politician and right-wing socialist, who had previously been in charge of the Sous-Sécrétariat de l'Artillerie. In September 1917 Thomas was succeeded by an industrialist named Loucheur.

TABLE 10

FRANCE: PRODUCTION IN HEAVY INDUSTRY, 1913–18

	1913		1915		1917	
	Million tons	Index	Million tons	Index	Million tons	Index
Coal, coke	40·8	100	19·5	48	28·9	71
Pig iron	5·2	100	0·6	12	1·7	33
Steel	4·7	100	1·1	23	2·2	47

SOURCE: A. Fontaine, *L'industrie française pendant la guerre*, Presses Universitaires de France, Paris, pp. 194, 372, 375.

The High Command never played any special role in French armaments policy[64] and even the civilian authorities took a back seat, leaving most of the actual organization to the armaments manufacturers who subdivided the industry into regional groups or 'consortia'. So far as can be ascertained, it would seem that production priorities were largely determined by informal agreements, reinforced by a generous prices policy on the government side. Additional levers consisted in the release from military service of skilled workers for the benefit of factories engaged on armaments contracts and, with mounting scarcity, in the control and allocation of essential imports. From 1916 onwards the Comité des Forges, the employers' federation of the iron and steel industry, was entrusted by the government with the control of pig iron imports and, later, of steel imports. It was not till July 1918 that France's domestic pig iron production was centrally administered and allocated in accordance with the demands of the war effort.[65] As early as November 1918 the Ministry of Munitions was re-designated Ministry of Reconstruction, a rapid removal of war-time restrictions being regarded as the first prerequisite for economic recovery.

Russia

Russia was, in every respect, exceedingly ill-armed for war.[66]

64. See Bruneau, *Le rôle du Haut Commandement.*
65. See Pinot, *Le Comité des Forges de France.*
66. See Z. O. Zagorski, *State Control of Industry in Russia during the War,*

Industrialization in that country was still in its infancy. In 1913 big industry – a foreign body in a gigantic agrarian economy – was confined to a few centres, primarily Moscow and St Petersburg. Factory workers, excluding miners and employees in government factories, numbered some 2–3 millions, as opposed to 27 million agricultural workers. In the autumn of 1914 industrial plant in the western provinces (Poland's engineering works and textile, coal and iron ore industries, and the iron works, rubber and textile factories of the Baltic provinces) was in so far as possible dismantled and removed to the interior to save it from the advancing Germans. Obviously only a small part of the productive capacity could be preserved in this way, a great deal of material being lost in transit or else abandoned for lack of transport.[67]

In the first year of war an armaments policy was virtually non-existent. The czarist government confined itself strictly to the role of customer to the armaments industry, while the industrialists confined themselves no less strictly to their role of businessmen. The absence of controls meant easy money from the sale of corruptly won government contracts and from over-pricing. Conversely, little or nothing was done to boost production. It soon transpired that the armed forces were inadequately equipped with weapons and munitions, even in relation to the productive capacity of Russian industry. In the late spring of 1915, after a series of defeats in the field, the Russian government was jolted into some semblance of action by the dismal military outlook and by mounting criticism from the middle classes regarding the conduct of the war. In May it set up a Military Supply Commission consisting of civil servants, members of the Duma and representatives of private industry. Three months later similar commissions were created with responsibility for defence, fuel supplies, transport and

Yale University Press, Newhaven, 1928; Ja. M. Bukšpan, *Voenno-chozjajstvennaja politika. Formy i organy regulirovanija narodnogo chozjajstva za vremja mirovoj vojny 1914–1918 gg*, Moscow/Leningrad, 1929; K. N. Tarnoskij, *Formirovanie gosudarstvenno – monopolističeskogo kapitalizma v Rosii v gody pervoj mirovoj vojny (na primere metallurgičeskoj promyšlennosti)*, Moscow,1958. My chapters on Russian economic and financial conditions rely to a great extent on information supplied by Dr Heiko Haumann of the University of Freiburg, as also on his criticism.

67. See R. Claus, *Die Kriegswirtschaft Russlands bis zur Bolschewikischen Revolution* Schroeder, Bonn/Leipzig, 1922, pp. 67ff.

food supplies. In appointing these bodies the government went some way towards meeting the demands of the middle classes, who wanted a say in wartime policy. However, the competence of these new committees did not extend beyond the traditional administrative framework: they did not intervene either in the allocation of manpower and raw materials, or in the organization of production, or in cooperation between firms.

Even as the government was taking its first hesitant steps towards an armaments policy, the private sector was demanding the full mobilization of industry on a basis of personal responsibility. A concerted drive for victory, it was maintained, would involve a clean break with bureaucratic incompetence and the climate of speculation and corruption, while leaving intact the private basis of armaments production. Beginning in May 1915, 'War Industry Committees' were set up as self-governing organs of industry, with a headquarters in St Petersburg and with regional and local branches. In July the War Industry Committees resolved to coopt elected workers' groups to demonstrate that all classes were united in a common cause. But this scheme was boycotted by the overwhelming majority of workers. For the first time the Bolsheviks, who rejected all participation in the war being waged by the ruling classes and hence had called for the boycott of the War Industry Committees, had gained a signal political victory.[68] The government and big industry for their part harboured certain reservations about the War Industry Committees: the government rightly feared the political aspirations underlying the movement as a whole, while the established armaments firms had no particular desire to tamper with the old system which ensured not only good contacts with the procurement agencies, but also large profits. The backbone of the War Industry Committees consisted of men who, like their counterparts in Germany or the western bourgeois democracies, were genuinely concerned with technical efficiency, and also of representatives of small and medium-sized industrial undertakings which could not, by themselves, obtain either armament contracts, or the labour and materials with which to execute them. In the end even the government was bound to seek ways and means of increasing armaments production. A compromise was

68. See Central Committee of the C.P.S.U. institute of Marxism Leninism, ed., *Geschichte der Kommunistischen Partei der Sowjetunion*, 6 vols, Progress Publishers, Moscow, vol. II, pp. 631ff.

therefore reached whereby the War Industry Committees were awarded between 5 and 15 per cent of all official armaments contracts for distribution among their members in accordance with the latter's productive acpacity. Nevertheless, right up to the very last relations were never easy between the War Industry Committees and the Defence Council representing the government's armaments policy, a body with a decentralized organization of its own. After February 1917 the aim of the bourgeois provisional government was a central economic administration on the western model, but in fact the economy was no longer controlled by the state, but rather by the Soviets which had established themselves as an ancillary government.

Even had the administration of the war economy been more efficient, it would have been difficult, given the limited industrial potential, to attain any large-scale increase in armaments production. Nevertheless the armaments industry succeeded in materially raising output, albeit against a background of general economic decline. In the metal, chemical and leather industries there was a substantial increase in the number of persons employed. Petrograd became the centre of the armaments industry, with 403,000 workers (1917), primarily in the metal industry, as compared with 194,000 before the war. In all, production of weapons and munitions rose from 43,000 tons in 1913 to 397,000 in 1916; from 1915 onwards the iron and steel industry was engaged almost exclusively on government contracts. After civil requirements had been cut back, productive capacity came up against the limits imposed by shortage of skilled labour, the decline of the basic industries (coal, iron and steel) and the disorganization of the transport system. Had the Allied governments regarded the war as a common cause, the Russian peasant armies (by 1917 15 million soldiers had been mobilized) would have had their industrial base, not in Russia, but in the more advanced industrial countries of the Western Alliance. In fact, however, Russian imports declined steeply during the war, and Allied shipments of arms remained relatively insignificant. In 1916 Russia imported war materials to a total value of 318 million roubles, or 20·5 million pounds sterling, i.e. 2·3 per cent of Russian or 1·4 per cent of British war expenditure in the equivalent fiscal year.[69]

69. See P. N. Apostol, M. W. Bernatzky and A. M. Michelson, *Russian Public Finance during the War*, Yale University Press, Newhaven, 1928, p. 143;

As a result of the country's low economic efficiency, the war effort soon brought about a state of total prostration which in turn helped to hasten the demise of the old regime. After the February Revolution of 1917 the new government sought to initiate a 'bourgeois' armaments policy with the participation of such organized workers' groups (Mensheviks and Social Revolutionaries) as supported the war. But talk of integration no longer had any appeal for the great majority of the workers, peasants and soldiers. They followed the lead of the Bolsheviks who, from August 1914 onwards, had consistently refused to have anything to do with either the war or the war effort.

United States

Prior to 1914 the United States had possessed no munitions industry worthy of note. Industrially, armaments were unimportant by comparison, not only with the later war years, but also with the then output of the European countries, these having already been engaged in an arms race well before hostilities began.[70] During the period of America's neutrality, between 1914 and 1916, a not inconsiderable armaments industry came into

Zagorski, *State Control of Industry*, p. 35; E. V. Montagu, *Studies in British Financial Policy, 1914–1925*, Macmillan, London, 1952, p. 101. For a systematic treatment see B. Bonwetsch, *Kriegsallianz und Wirtschaftsinteressen. Russland in den Wirtschaftsplänen Englands und Frankreichs 1914–1917*, Düsseldorf, 1973.

70. R. D. Cuff, *The War Industries Board Business–Government Relations during World War I*, Johns Hopkins Press, Baltimore/London, 1973. B. M. Baruch, *American Industry in the War. A Report of the War Industries Board*, Government Printing Office, Washington, 1921; G. B. Clarkson, *Industrial America in the World War: The Strategy behind the Line, 1917–1918*, Houghton-Mifflin, Boston/New York, 1923; J. M. Clark, *The Cost of the World War to the American People*, Yale University Press, Newhaven, 1931; *Munitions Industry. Final Report of the Chairman of the United States War Industries Board to the President of the United States, February 1919*, printed for the use of the Special Committee on Investigating the Munitions Industry, Government Printing Office, Washington, 1935. R. B. Kester, 'The War Industries Board, 1917–1918. A Study in Industrial Mobilization', in *The American Political Science Review*, 34, 1940; P. A. C. Koistinen, 'The "Industrial-Military Complex" in Historical Perspective: World War I', in *The Business History Review*, 41, 1967; R. D. Cuff, 'Bernard Baruch, Symbol and Myth in Industrial Mobilization', ibid., 43, 1969.

being in response to Allied demand. The firm of J. P. Morgan acted as the central purchasing agency for the Allied governments but had, of course, no administrative powers on American soil. High prices and large profits sufficed to interest big corporations such as Dupont in the production of armaments on a strictly commercial basis. Indeed, so substantial were the profits that, even before declaring war at the end of 1916, the government imposed a special tax on war profits.[71] In April 1917, therefore, it found itself relatively well-placed for industrial mobilization. The industry had acquired technical expertise through producing armaments for the Allied governments, and had introduced a great deal of new production plant, most of which had already been written off.[72]

After her entry into the war, America had at her disposal a vast economic potential, but not the institutions or the plans for its conversion into military strength. Almost every industrialist was pressing for arms contracts, partly because of the profits, and partly in the anticipation that activities not essential to the war effort would sooner or later be suspended by the government. On the other hand, the army and navy were inexperienced in questions of industrial mobilization and were, moreover, fully occupied in organizing themselves to cope with the tremendous numerical increase in the armed forces. The consequent hiatus was to be filled by the War Industries Board whose task was to coordinate the requirements of army, navy and Allies and to plan industrial production in accordance with wartime priorities. The W.I.B. was set up in July 1917, almost concurrently with other wartime agencies such as Hoover's Food Administration, the National War Labor Board, the War Labor Policies Board, the War Trade Board and the War Finance Board, the latter being responsible for subsidies to essential undertakings. At first the W.I.B. acted only in an advisory capacity to a cabinet committee, the Council of National Defense. This arrangement proved impracticable and in March 1918, the War Industries Board was reorganized as a supreme federal authority with executive powers immediately answerable to the President of the United States.

71. See S. Ratner, *Taxation and Democracy in America*, Science Editions, New York, 1967.
72. Between 1914 and 1916 the Dupont chemical concern alone expended 220 million dollars, or more than three times its pre-war capital, on new plant; see Clark, *The Cost of the World War*, pp. 262ff.

The staff of the W.I.B. and its numerous subsidiary committees was recruited primarily from the business world. Its chairman was Bernard Baruch, a well-known Wall Street financier, and there were also a number of other tycoons who entered government service for the duration in return for a token salary – the 'dollar-a-year' men. In addition, army and navy officers were seconded to the W.I.B. on which they represented the interests of the armed forces *qua* 'consumers' of war materials. As a counterpart to the government administration and the official industrial lobby, a number of War Service Committees were set up which represented the various branches of the munitions industry. The W.I.B.'s planning of requirements led to some inter-departmental bickering with the military procurement agencies but, since there was no fundamental clash of interests, these conflicts were settled with comparative ease, nor did the services ever show any sign of wishing to control the industry. While the army and navy possessed a few factories of their own, neither they nor anyone else ever envisaged large-scale armaments production organized on a military basis. Somewhat more problematical was the administration's relationship with industry. The chief planning instrument in armaments policy was the classification of all contracts and individual concerns in accordance with degrees of priority, which in turn determined the allocation of raw materials and transport. Hence any downgrading of priority inevitably entailed financial loss for the firm concerned. In such cases the official industrial lobby, as well as an unofficial lobby consisting of industrialists within the W.I.B. itself, sought to protect the sector at risk.[73] This official and unofficial lobbying was exceedingly effective. For example, it forced the government to share out armaments contracts among as many firms as possible so as to keep them in being, although the original intention had been to concentrate production in a few new and efficient plants. As may be demonstrated from this and other instances, the supposed impartiality of the tycoons-turned-civil-servants was questionable. Often a manager of a leading corporation would be head of the W.I.B. committee responsible

73. For an interesting case-study, see an article by R. B. Cuff, in which he investigates the activities of George N. Peek, an agricultural machinery manufacturer, as a member of the War Industries Board; R. B. Cuff, 'A "Dollar-A-Year Man" in Government: George N. Peek and the War Industries Board', *Business History Review*, 41, 1967.

for his own particular branch of industry, thus arousing the suspicion of an inadmissible connection between public office and private interest. At the beginning of 1918 a draft bill was tabled whereby it was proposed to abolish the dollar-a-year men and replace them exclusively with full-time civil servants paid out of public funds; but it did not obtain a majority vote.

Munitions prices were negotiated between the W.I.B. and industry, not on the basis of each supplier's costs, but at a flat rate for all suppliers alike. Prices were fixed so high that even marginal firms made a worthwhile profit, while firms with better production facilities earned correspondingly more. As a result of the rising price of armaments, the government found itself in an unpleasant predicament. Even during the period of neutrality the price level had risen substantially. When the United States entered the war, speculative demand pushed up the price index fourteen points in one month.[74] Eventually the government felt compelled to intervene and, in September 1917, fixed various basic prices (iron ore, coal, coke, pig iron, copper, freight); the following month prices were fixed for a number of intermediate products. Maximum prices also applied to deliveries to civilian consumers and Allied governments.

How efficient, then, was America's armaments policy? Lloyd George, never sparing of criticism in his *Memoirs*, was notoriously unenthusiastic about the armaments of his allies: there were, he says, no braver men than those in the American forces, but 'the organization at home and behind the lines was not worthy of the reputation which American businessmen have deservedly won for smartness, promptitude and efficiency'.[75] This criticism is manifestly unfair for, after all, on her own showing, Britain obtained from the U.S.A. during the course of the war 926 million rounds of small arms ammunition, 31 million shells, 1·2 million rifles, 569,000 short tons of powder and explosives (a quantity equal to some fifty months' projected output under the Hindenburg Programme), 42,000 trucks, 3,400 aero-engines, 1,400 gun carriages, 866 planes. The Russian government received from America via

74. The index of wholesale prices (1913–14=100) rose from 156 in March 1917 to 170 in April 1917. See P. W. Garrett, *Government Control over Prices*, War Industries Board Price Bulletin, no. 3, Government Printing Office, Washington, 1920.

75. Lloyd George, *War Memoirs*, vol.V, p. 3068.

Great Britain 553 million rounds of small arms ammunition, 970,000 rifles and 24,500 machine guns.[76] However, there was undeniably a remarkable discrepancy between America's industrial might and her low output of heavy weapons: not a single tank of U.S. origin appeared on the battlefields of Europe, and it was only after the war had already been decided that American guns and aircraft entered service.[77] The U.S. army in Europe obtained its light and medium artillery from France, its heavy artillery from Britain, and its aircraft from both those countries. The fact of the matter is that American munitions production was planned for the long term, and the Allies achieved victory before America's wartime industrial potential was fully realized.

Three and a half years went by before the Allies reached agreement about a joint military command with Foch as Generalissimo; the final, decisive impulse was given by the German spring offensive of 1918.[78] Behind the lines, economic cooperation proved even more difficult.[79] During the first two years of hostilities, the war economies of the Allies operated independently of each other, little more being achieved than a limited exchange of goods and services, and that predominantly on a commercial basis. Prior to America's entry into the war, Britain was the economic hub of the alliance and any demand for economic cooperation meant in practice that Britain was expected to provide her Allies with industrial goods, shipping space and credits.

In August 1914 the Commission Internationale de Ravitaillement was set up in London with the object of coordinating armaments contracts placed with British firms by Allied governments. The first countries to be represented were Britain and France,

76. *History of the Ministry of Munitions*, 12 vols, 1921–22, vol. II, section 3, p. 8.

77. See G. A. Lincoln, W. Y. Smith and J. B. Durst, 'Mobilization and War', in S. E. Harris, ed., *American Economic History*, McGraw-Hill, New York, 1961, p. 220.

78. See Herzfeld, *Der Erste Weltkrieg*, pp. 111, 351ff; P. Renouvain, *La crise européenne et la première guerre mondiale*, 5th ed., Presses Universitaires de France, Paris, 1969, pp. 548ff, 555ff.

79. No systematic analysis of inter-Allied economic cooperation has yet been undertaken. From the French viewpoint, see E. Clémentel, *La France et la politique economique interallié*, Presses Universitaires de France, Paris, 1931. For a work of International scope, but relating only to shipping, see A. Salter, *Allied Shipping Control. An Experiment in International Administration*, Clarendon Press, Oxford, 1921.

subsequently delegates arrived from Belgium, Italy, Japan, Portugal, Romania, Russia and Serbia; the U.S.A. sent observers in 1917, but was not a formal party to the agreement. Despite this comprehensive participation, the Commission was of small economic importance, for in the first place munitions played no particular part in the exchange of goods, and in the second links with the main partners, France and Russia, were soon officially established independently of it. From July 1915 onwards, French armament orders by-passed the Commission, and went direct to the British Ministry of Munitions. After 1915 all Russian purchases, both in Britain and in the United States, were passed through the British government in accordance with a bilateral Anglo–Russian agreement. This agreement, officially termed 'good offices' by the British, meant in fact widespread powers of control since Russian purchases, even outside Great Britain, were largely financed by British credits. After America's accession, Russia concluded a similar bilateral agreement with that country. During the first months of the war Allied governments competed vigorously for supplies in neutral countries, particularly the U.S.A., with the result that prices rocketed and delivery dates could not be kept. At a meeting between the French, Russian and British Finance Ministers in Paris in February 1915 it was decided to coordinate purchases from neutral countries. Subsequently J. P. Morgan and Co. acted as joint agent for the Western Allies in the U.S.A. and, under the terms of the Anglo–Russian agreement, also handled Russian purchases there. Apart from the activities of these coordinating bodies, inter-Allied exchange was conducted in the early part of the war exclusively on a commercial basis.

Shipping constituted a bottleneck from the very outset. Before the war a large proportion of French and Russian trade with other countries on the European continent was carried by rail. Its redirection to Great Britain and overseas involved, aside from other difficulties, an enormous expansion of sea-borne trade which could only be effected with the help of the British merchant fleet. Normally some 850 British vessels operated on the French and Italian account and of these no less than 250 were employed in transporting coal to France. The British government enabled its Allies to fix long-term charters with British ship-owners, and made available, at controlled freight rates (blue-book rates) requisitioned tonnage for certain cargoes of military importance. For the rest, however, the Allies had to pay the high freight rates obtaining on the free market; e.g. in the thirteen months from April 1915 to May 1916, the rate for coal from Newcastle to the French Channel ports rose from 22 francs per ton to 63 francs.[80] Special treaties governed shipments to Russia which were arranged at the British end in the same way as British shipments. Up to 250 vessels were engaged in this trade.

Since the Allies' export trade had greatly diminished as a result of the concentration of their industries on munitions production, their exports were insufficient to meet freight charges and the cost of imports from Britain and third parties. Accordingly finance emerged as a third sphere of cooperation. Britain supplied her allies with munitions, coal, iron, steel and other essential goods and services on credit. At the same time her worldwide creditor position enabled her to place at their disposal foreign currency to finance their foreign purchases and to stabilize their exchange rates vis-à-vis third parties. The details of this financial cooperation will be discussed later in connection with financial and monetary policy.

Despite these various agreements, there was little evidence of economic solidarity within the alliance. Britain clearly rated her own civil and military requirements higher than shipments to the Allies. For a long time the British government was inclined to give industry and the shipping companies a free hand in the exploitation both of neutral markets and of the Allies' need for armaments. Shipments to the Allies were regarded not so much as a self-evident contribution to the common cause, but rather as a gesture of voluntary cooperation. At the end of 1916, Lloyd George weighed this policy in the scales and found it wanting.[81] Rightly, he saw inadequate economic support as one of the main reasons why the fronts in Italy, the Balkans and the east had not, as expected, eased the pressure on the principal theatre of war in northern France. Serbia and Romania had all but been eliminated from the conflict, Italy could only be kept in the war by means of increasing military and economic aid, while Russia was showing signs of complete economic prostration. Russia's geographical isolation, the collapse of her transport system and wartime economic organization, and the reluctance of the Allies to provide

80. Clémentel, *La France*, p. 70.
81. See Guinn, *British Strategy and Politics 1914–1918*.

support, all combined to accelerate an economic decline of which the ultimate cause was the excessive demands made on the country by the war.

Under the stress of the economic and military situation, steps were taken during the second half of the war to improve inter-Allied economic cooperation. This first made itself felt in the sphere of shipping. The old system, improvised rather than organized, functioned perfectly well as long as there was enough shipping space for all. But when, in the summer of 1916, these conditions ceased to obtain, the French and Italian governments complained that Britain had promptly sought to cut down the shipping space allotted to her allies. Conversely Britain suspected that her allies were insufficiently rigorous in the control of shipping within the areas under their jurisdiction. After the intensification of the submarine campaign had finally persuaded the Allies of the need for a coordinated transport policy, proposals were put forward for an inter-Allied clearing-house to determine priorities independently of individual national interest and as equitably as the common war effort would allow.

The Inter-Allied Shipping Committee was set up at the beginning of 1917, but this experiment miscarried, largely because the committee was not armed with the necessary executive powers. Not until November 1917 was it agreed in principle to pool the national merchant fleets and employ them in accordance with common economic priorities. This led to the creation of the Allied Maritime Transport Council (A.M.T.C.) which likewise had no executive powers but nevertheless functioned quite satisfactorily as a coordinating body. After each country had submitted its import programme, the A.M.T.C. established priorities in the light of available shipping-space and worked out transport plans, whereupon the national agencies revised their requisitions accordingly.

Shipping control turned on Great Britain's obligation to continue, despite her own difficulties, to make shipping space available for the imports of her allies. Apart from military cargoes, these comprised mainly coal and food for Italy and France and food for the Belgian civilian population; the latter shipments, which were the subject of special treaties, were exempted from the Allied blockade. By this time Russia was already out of the war. The rapidly growing U.S. merchant fleet, at first almost wholly employed on the conveyance of the American army and its supplies, would later have been fully integrated into the A.M.T.C. had not the Armistice supervened. The Allied transport problem was to some extent alleviated by the chartering of neutral merchant vessels, mainly on the British account, thus securing a fleet of some half a million gross tons which was made the direct responsibility of the A.M.T.C. In most of these transactions, then, Britain was essentially the 'seller', the other Allies the 'buyers', and hence the British government, though it never flexed its muscles in public, occupied a dominant position on the A.M.T.C. The real test of inter-Allied cooperation based on equal rights would have come only with the full integration of America's new merchant fleet.

Joint control of shipping-space necessarily implied decisions on national import programmes and hence it was obvious that these should not be determined on an *ad hoc* basis but rather coordinated from the outset. Accordingly, coordinating agencies were set up on the pattern of the A.M.T.C.: for grain in March 1918, for other foodstuffs in September and for munitions just before the Armistice, whose advent anticipated a similar arrangement for raw material imports.

Armaments policy: its preconditions and consequences

A comparison of wartime economic policy in the various countries reveals some noteworthy similarities. The economic consequences of a major war had nowhere been anticipated. During the early weeks vast armies were mobilized, while the economies continued to function as in peacetime. This discrepancy between military and economic mobilization sooner or later led to 'munitions crises' – in Germany and France within a few weeks of the outbreak of war, and in Britain, where military mobilization was more leisurely, within a few months. After this initial phase the national economies were mobilized in earnest and restraints placed on civilian demand. Germany, despite her initial lead (the same does not apply to the other Central Powers), was ultimately bound to be the loser in the arms race; indeed, her fate was already sealed on the first day of hostilities, for the totality of her war aims meant that her adversaries would fight to the bitter end. While the immediate incentive behind Germany's request for an armistice was provided by the military impasse, this in turn was linked with economic prostration both in the armaments industry and in the field of civilian supplies.

In the factories men who had been called up were replaced by juveniles, women, prisoners of war and more or less voluntary foreign labour, so that overall employment figures showed no great change: in 1913 7·4 million male and female workers were employed in German industry as against 6·6 million in 1918, corresponding figures for Britain being 8·4 million and 8·5 million. Above all the burden came to be shouldered increasingly by women; in the industrial labour force in Germany the proportion of women rose from 22 per cent (1913) to 35 per cent (1918), and in Britain, from 26 per cent (July 1914) to 35 per cent (July 1918).[82] This correspondence is remarkable in as much as the institutional conditions under which the women were recruited were very different.

Alongside the change in the composition of the labour force an important development is discernible in the reorganization of production processes. By comparison with civilian requirements the needs of the military were relatively homogenous; the long production runs favoured standardized production methods, as did the employment of numerous semi-skilled workers. To what extent the change in the employment structure and production processes was of lasting consequence over and above the particular circumstance of the war is still an open question. But a number of observations would suggest a conservative estimate. During the war there was a widespread fear among skilled workers and trade unions in Britain that the armaments policy would result in a permanent levelling of industrial production and industrial labour – a fear which, in the event, proved to be unfounded. When armaments production ceased, the proportion of women to the total number of wage earners again declined: in 1921 as in 1911 the average for British industry was some 30 per cent.[83] A similar

82. Wage earners and proportion of women, for Germany from G. Bry, *Wages in Germany 1871–1945*, Princeton University Press, 1960, pp. 193ff; for Great Britain, from G. D. H. Cole, *Trade Unionism and Munitions*, Clarendon Press, Oxford, 1923, p. 186.

83. In 1911 30 per cent of a total of 18.3 million wage-earners were women, in 1921, 29 per cent out of a total of 19·4 million; see B. R. Mitchell, *Abstract of British Historical Statistics*, Cambridge University Press, 1962, pp. 60ff.

process took place in Germany.[84] A longer perspective is needed if anything positive is to be said on structural changes in the field of production resulting from the Great War: we should have to isolate the trends that persisted after 1918 and determine the extent to which they were already distinguishable before 1914.

Economic history is now increasingly turning its attention to the socio-economic changes which were introduced by the interaction of industry and state during the First World War and which were, indeed, of long-term significance, even though the majority of direct controls were dismantled immediately after the Armistice. These changes, in themselves indisputable, have in broad terms been subjected to two opposing interpretations. Even during the war Lenin spoke of transition from the 'monopoly' stage of capitalism to the 'state monopoly' stage.[85] By this he meant the stage at which large corporations increasingly made use of the state apparatus to solve economic problems, especially in the field of armaments, where the contradiction between the interests of the individual capitalist and the combined interests of the capitalist class could not be resolved by the 'operation of the market'. Whether planning was primarily the responsibility of industry's own federations, of the civil ministries or of the military is, in the Marxist view, relatively unimportant; for instance, the military, though occupying a dominant position in Germany, were dependent on, and acted in concert with, big business.[86] On the liberal side, the fact of structural change is duly recognized but, in diametrical opposition to the Marxist interpretation, its distinctive character is seen as a growing tendency to harness the economy to non-economic, national or social goals. This view is epitomized in the term 'war socialism' so common at that time.

84. The proportion of women in paid employment in 1907 was 35 per cent and in 1925, 37 per cent; see W. Hoffmann, F. Grumbach and H. Hesse, *Das Wachstum der deutschen Wirtschaft seit der Mitte des 19 Jahrhunderts*, Springer Berlin/Heidelberg/New York, 1965, pp. 205, 210. The difference, compared with the British figure is perhaps attributable to the greater importance of the agricultural sector.

85. See more especially V. I. Lenin, *State and Revolution*, Lawrence & Wishart, London.

86. The influence of big industry on the Supreme Command and on the War Ministry has been very strongly stressed, in particular by historians in the German Democratic Republic. It has also been noted by G. Feldman, *Army, Industry and Labor in Germany 1914–1918*, Princeton University Press, 1966.

Now 'war socialism' is, of course, a term well calculated to mask certain essential features of the war economy. Long before historical studies had provided circumstantial evidence of the influence exerted by industry, the colossal profits earned between 1914 and 1918 had revealed that, in wartime, the basic capitalist structure of industry and society tended, if anything, to come more clearly into focus. No secret was made of these war profits; an early and still very readable comparative study of the subject, based on published material, appeared during the final phase of the war.[87] From this we learn that by 1915 profits were moving ahead impressively and that as the war went on a number of corporations had little difficulty in achieving profits several times greater than those of the pre-war years. These results were arrived at after ample allowance, in the form of substantial write-offs and transfers to reserves, had been made for the transitory nature of wartime business. Krupp's, for example, used this procedure to reduce their 1916/17 gross profit by nearly 50 per cent and were thus in a position to prove to what must have been an astonished public that the company had actually suffered a setback by comparison with the previous year.

TABLE 11

WAR PROFITS. PUBLISHED NET PROFITS OF VARIOUS ARMAMENTS CONCERNS IN GERMANY, AUSTRIA, FRANCE (MILLIONS OF MARKS, KRONEN, FRANCS)

	Pre-war average	1914/15	1915/16	1916/17
Krupp	31·6	33·9	86·5	79·7
Deutsche Waffen- und Munitionsfabrik	5·5	8·2	11·5	12·7
Kölner Pulverfabriken	4·3	6·5	14·5	14·7
Rheinmetall	1·4	3·5	9·9	15·3
Skodawerke	5·6	6·4	9·4	18·2
Waffenfabrik Steyr	2·7	6·7	17·7	18·3
Schneider (Creusot)	6·9	9·2	10·8	11·2
Hotchkiss	—	—	2·0	14·0

SOURCE: R. Fuchs, *Die Kriegsgewinne der verschiedenen Wirtshaftszweige in den einzelnen Staaten an Hand statitischer Daten dargestellt*, diss, Zurich, 1918, pp. 85, 105, 110.
    The pre-war average relates to the last two or three pre-war years.

87. R. Fuchs, *Die Kriegsgewinne der verschiedenen Wirtschaftszweige in den einzelnen Staaten, an Hand statistischer Daten dargestellt*, diss., Zurich, 1918.

Similarly the profit for the year 1916/17 amounting to 11 million francs announced by Schneider & Cie (Creusot) was arrived at after transfers to special reserves of no less than 48 million francs.[88] Profits of this order were achieved not only by firms immediately concerned with the production of war material (arms, munitions, and powder and explosives), but also by those engaged in basic industries (mining, iron and steel, chemicals), and in branches of manufacturing such as leather and motor vehicles. On the Allied side, the greatest profits were made in shipping. Life was endurable even for those who did not reap the benefit of the war boom; when, in Great Britain, the railways were requisitioned or, in Germany, textile firms had to curtail production for want of raw materials, the owners were indemnified. While there is a lack of representative studies on income distribution, it would seem highly probable that the upward trend in profits was general. More recent studies based on a critical examination of source material have provided detailed confirmation of what was already indicated by the magnitude of the war profits, namely the great extent to which government decisions depended on business interests. These findings point, not so much to the harnessing of big business to the machine of state, as to the reverse.[89]

88. ibid., pp. 87ff, 111.
89. Of late this has also found expression outside Marxist historiography in the theory of 'Organized Capitalism'. See H. A. Winkler, ed., *Organisierter Kapitalismus. Voraussetzungen und Anfänge*, Vandenhoeck & Ruprecht, Göttingen, 1973.

5

Food Supply in Wartime

The obverse of the massive armaments drive was general impoverishment. It has been estimated that, in the final phase, the war accounted for something like half the national output,[1] correspondingly less being left to maintain the standard of living of the population. Food supply provides a particularly clear example of the extent to which civilian requirements were subordinated to armaments and similarly of the extent to which the normal day-to-day existence of millions of people in Europe depended on the functioning of the world market. Before the First World War, Western Europe imported 26 millions tons of grain each year, while annual exports from the big grain exporting countries in Eastern Europe and overseas amounted to 27 million tons.[2] A breakdown by regions, however, reveals the varying degree to which the European belligerents were dependent on the world market. After decades of free trade Britain, more than any

1. On Germany: K. Roesler, *Die Finanzpolitik des Deutschen Reiches im Ersten Weltkrieg*, Dunker & Humblot, Berlin, 1967. On Britain: E. V. Morgan, *Studies in British Financial Policy, 1914–1925*, Macmillan, London, 1952. On Russia; P. Studenski, *The Income of Nations. Theory, Measurement, and Analysis: Past and Present*, New York University Press, 1958.

2. See League of Nations, *Agricultural Production in Continental Europe during the 1914–18 War and the Reconstruction Period*, Geneva, 1943.

other country, was dependent on imports for her food supplies.[3] Four out of every five slices of bread eaten in the British Isles were made of foreign flour. In order to compete with his counterparts on the Continent and overseas the British farmer had concentrated on livestock, so that the country's 'self-sufficiency quota' was higher in the case of meat, fats and milk; but this also necessitated the importation of animal feeds from abroad. In terms of calorie value, an average of 35 per cent of the food consumed came from home production.

TABLE 12

PRODUCTION AND EXPORT OF GRAIN BEFORE THE FIRST WORLD WAR (AVERAGE 1909–13, MILLIONS OF TONS)

	Production	Imports (+) or Exports (−)
Western Europe	73·8	+26·3
Eastern Europe	108·6	−13·2
North America	121·5	− 6·4
Southern exporting countries	14·7	− 7·5

SOURCE: League of Nations, *Agricultural Production in Continental Europe during the 1914–18 War and the Reconstruction Period*, Geneva 1943, pp. 58ff.

Western Europe: European countries including and to the west of Sweden, Germany, Switzerland, Italy. North America: U.S.A., Canada. Southern exporting countries: Argentina, Uruguay, South Africa, Australia, New Zealand.

Ever since the Great Depression a policy of protective tariffs had insulated German agriculture against the world market.[4] In 1913, 35 per cent of all wage-earners were still employed in agriculture, forestry and fisheries.[5] Germany regularly produced more

3. See S. J. Hurwitz, *State Intervention in Great Britain. A Study of Economic Control and Social Response, 1914–1919*, Columbia University Press, New York, 1949.

4. See F. Aereboe, *Der Einfluss des Krieges auf die landwirtschaftliche Produktion in Deutschland*, Deutsche Verlags-Anstalt, Stuttgart/Berlin/Leipzig, 1927; A. Skalweit, *Die deutsche Kriegsernährungswirtschaft*, Deutsche Verlags-Anstalt, Stuttgart/Berlin/Leipzig, 1928. More recently, M. G. Plachetka, *Die Getreide-Autarkiepolitik Bismarcks und seiner Nachfolger im Reichskanzleramt*, diss, Bonn, 1969.

5. See W. Hoffmann, F. Grumbach and H. Hesse, *Das Wachstum der deutschen Wirtschaft seit der Mitte des 19.Jahrhunderts*, Springer, Berlin/Heidelberg/New York, 1965, pp. 204ff.

than enough for domestic requirements of potatoes, rye and sugar-beet. Indeed the latter crop was very strongly export-oriented, some 40 per cent of production finding its way abroad. The country was 90 per cent self-sufficient in milk, milk products, meat and bread cereals of all kinds, 60 per cent in fats and eggs, and 40 per cent in fish.[6] These products may be reduced to a common denominator by expressing them in terms either of calories or of money values. Either way, Germany is shown to have been self-sufficient to the extent of about 90 per cent on the average.[7] This percentage relates only to final products and takes no account of the fact that in several respects German agriculture was dependent on imported inputs. An increase in agricultural production without a corresponding increase in the area under cultivation called for ever more intensive use of the soil, this being possible only if artificial fertilizers were liberally applied. In 1913 German agriculture as a whole used some 8 million tons of artificial fertilizers (superphosphates, basic slag, nitrate, sulphate of ammonia) or nearly six times as much as in 1890. Roughly one-third of these products (nitrate, raw phosphatic materials, sulphur) was imported. Stock-farming, while using home-produced grain, potatoes and sugar-beet for concentrated feeds, also depended heavily on foreign sources of supply: imports of barley feed, bran, maize and oilcake amounted in all to over 6 million tons a year and, like imported artificial fertilizers, accounted for about one-third of total consumption. Indeed, German stock-farming, as Aeroboe has graphically if not altogether accurately put it, had two legs on German and two legs on foreign soil.[8] A third but no less important factor was the dependence of German agriculture on foreign labour, nearly a million foreign seasonal workers being employed, notably on the large estates in the east.

Despite industrialization, France was still an important agricultural country whose domestic production of nearly all foodstuffs

6. Averages for corn 1909/10 to 1913/14, for animal fats 1912/13, from Skalweit, *Die deutsche Kriegsernährungswirtschaft*, pp. 10ff. All other data from Hoffmann, Grumbach and Hesse, *Das Wachstum*, pp. 301ff 307, 329, 630ff.

7. Monetary values based on Hoffmann, Grumbach and Hesse, *Das Wachstum*, pp. 520, 524, 646ff, 656ff. Calories from Skalweit, *Die deutsche Kriegsernährungswirtschaft*, p. 8.

8. Aeroboe, *Der Einfluss des Krieges*, p. 23.

was more or less equal to requirements.[9] Before the war, Italy's imports and exports of foodstuffs were about evenly balanced in terms of monetary value. In calorie terms, however, there was an import surplus,[10] since the foodstuffs she obtained from abroad – primarily bread cereals from south Russia – were of high calorie value by comparison with her exports of fruit, vegetables and wine. Before the Great War, the Habsburg Monarchy had comprised within its frontiers areas of underproduction of foodstuffs as well as areas of overproduction.[11] Grain and other farm products from the Hungarian half of the Empire were exchanged for industrial goods from the Austrian half. This exchange was protected, vis-à-vis the world market, by a common tariff on foreign goods. Thus Hungarian agriculture had an assured market for its products in Austria and, given an average harvest, could supply virtually all Austria's import requirements. Before 1914 Russia was the largest exporter of agricultural products in the world, the mainstay of her foreign trade being grain of which 11 million tons, out of an annual production of some 75 million, were exported.[12]

In none of these countries had any realistic plans been made for feeding the army and the civilian population in case of war. True, German agricultural interests had, from the end of the nineteenth century, been stressing amongst other things the importance to a war economy of a policy of self-sufficiency and protective tariffs, but in this they were largely motivated by considerations of internal politics. It would seem that, before 1914, German agricultural policy had been little influenced by any thought of a war economy, nor was there particular reason to make provision for a high degree of self-sufficiency in the food sector so long as calculations were based on a short war.[13] It was only after the event that the

9. See M. Augé-Laribé, *L'agriculture pendant la guerre*, Presses Universitaires de France, Paris, 1925.

10. See R. Bachi, *L'alimentazione e la politica annonaria in Italia*, Laterza, Bari, 1926.

11. See H. Loewenfeld-Russ, *Die Regelung der Volksernährung im Kriege*, Hölder-Pichler-Tempsky, Vienna, 1926; and G. Gratz and R. Schüller, *Der Wirschaftliche Zusammenbruch Österreich-Ungarns. Die Tragödie der Erschopfung*, Hölder-Pichler-Tempsky, Vienna, 1930.

12. See League of Nations, *Agricultural Production*, p. 65; and E. Nolde, *Russia in the Economic War*, Yale University Press, Newhaven, 1928.

13. See L. Burchardt, *Friedenswirtschaft und Kriegsvorsorge. Deutschlands wirstchaftliche Rüstungsbestrebungen vor 1914*, Boldt, Boppard, 1968.

government came to interpret the policy of self-sufficiency and protective tariffs as a wise, far-sighted measure. In Austria–Hungary the government placed its faith in Hungary's agricultural surpluses. In Great Britain food supply was primarily an import problem and hence, on the rare occasions before 1914 when wartime policy came up for discussion, it was not regarded as a problem at all. For no one doubted either the ability of the navy to keep open Britain's sea routes, or the ability of the export industry to earn the foreign currency needed to pay for imported food. The mistake shared by all concerned was to assume that the war would be a short one; in the event, the war necessitated state control and structural changes in the system of world food supplies to an extent that would have been almost inconceivable before 1914.

The Central Powers

After the outbreak of war, agriculture in Germany was ruthlessly subordinated to the requirements of the armed forces and the munitions industry.[14] Farmers and agricultural labourers were called up, to be replaced by women, juveniles and, during the early months, by unemployed industrial workers. Prisoners of war were also increasingly employed on the land until, in 1918, they numbered some 900,000 or roughly the equivalent of the foreign seasonal workers in peacetime. Under the Auxiliary Service Law of December 1916, agriculture was declared an essential occupation, but this did nothing to offset the effective shortage of manpower which, indeed, was making itself felt throughout the whole economy. The military requisitioned not only men but also horses and fodder; agriculture was left with ever fewer and increasingly ill-fed draught animals. In the case of fertilizers, Germany's monopoly of potash ensured ample supplies, but phosphates and nitrogen were scarce, despite the newly built nitrogen fixation plants. Since German industrial capacity was largely devoted to armaments production, there was a shortage, not only of agricultural machinery, but also of the fuel to run it.

Under the circumstances Germany's relatively high degree of self-sufficiency in foodstuffs before the war soon proved deceptive,

14. See Aeroboe, *Der Einfluss des Krieges;* and Skalweit, *Die deutsche Kriegsernährungswirtschaft.*

since agricultural production could not nearly be maintained. There was a general reduction in the area under cultivation, more especially corn-land, most of which was turned over to grass. In some cases, however, arable was simply left fallow for want of labour, seed and fertilizers. On average the corn harvests during the war were some 20 per cent lower than during the last few years of peacetime. Farmers did what they could to preserve their live-stock, at least so far as numbers went, but milk yields and dead-weights dropped appreciably. The decline in agricultural produc-tion, like the decline in food imports, was most marked in the final years of the war, thus compounding the general misery.

The speed with which an initial surplus can turn into a scarcity, and the irrelevance of a country's peacetime self-sufficiency to its war economy is amply demonstrated by the sugar industry. When war broke out there appeared to be more than enough sugar. Accordingly, at the end of 1914, the authorities recommended that the area under sugar-beet cultivation be reduced and, in the occu-pied areas of Belgium and Poland, they actually prohibited the crop. By the following harvest the area in Germany had contracted by a third and, since the yield per hectare had also diminished, sugar production fell within a year by some 40 per cent, i.e. the proportion exported before the war. At the same time, however, consumption had risen appreciably: faced with a general food shortage, the population had turned increasingly to sugar, par-ticularly in the form of jam and artificial honey. Next, it was pro-posed to increase production again, the yield per hectare being relatively high in terms of food value. But these plans were foiled by the lack of labour and fertilizers upon which this demanding crop was particularly dependent. For the rest of the war sugar remained in short supply. As early as 1915 a ban was placed on the use of beet as fodder and in 1916 there followed the introduction of sugar rationing and the inevitable creation of a distribution agency in the shape of the Imperial Sugar Office. During the last year of the war sugar production was further impeded by transport problems and lack of coal for the factories and refineries. Thus, in the end, Germany was only too glad to be able to extort 67,000 tons of sugar from the occupied Ukraine.

The authorities were unable to prevent the drop in the overall level of agricultural production and, indeed, it was these same authorities who, by their conduct of the war, had brought things

to such a pass. Nor did success always crown their direct intervention in production: for example their endeavour to achieve a
drastic simplification of the food supply system that would allow
for greater freedom of action in the nutritional field. It was proposed to restrict production not only of beer and spirits, but also
of meat, in favour of bread cereal, potatoes and root crops which
provided a higher nutritional value at the same cost. The cut-backs
in brewing and distilling presented relatively few problems. Before
the war, the distillation of alcohol from potatoes and grain had
been an industry of some magnitude. Between 1909 and 1913 a
yearly average of 2·5 million tons of potatoes and 0·4 million tons
of grain had been distilled into alcohol, about half of which went
into potable spirits, while the rest was used for technical purposes.
In anticipation of an early end to hostilities, there seemed at first
no reason to alter this state of affairs; indeed, because sugar stocks
were believed to be ample, the use of sugar beet and cane sugar
for distilling was actually encouraged. The adverse effects of this
policy on food supplies did not become apparent until the spring
of 1915 when production of potable spirits was drastically reduced
and distillation from grain halted altogether. From 1916 onwards
the distribution of alcohol became the responsibility of the Imperial Spirits Office. Thenceforward only the military authorities
were permitted to obtain spirituous liquor which ceased to be
available to the civilian population. Although the output of alcohol
for industrial purposes continued at a high level, overall production fell from 3·8 million hectolitres in 1913/14 to 2·4 million
hectolitres in 1917/18. Before the war the brewing of beer accounted for some 1·7 million tons of barley a year. The rationing of
malt to the breweries in the spring of 1915, which coincided with
the restrictions on distilling, led to a fall in production. Initially
fixed at 60 per cent of pre-war consumption, allocations had dropped by the end of the war to 15 per cent in Bavaria and 10 per cent
in the rest of Germany. Actual output fell somewhat more slowly,
to about a third of peacetime production, because wartime beer
was brewed with a progressively lower wort content; towards the
end it is reputed to have borne only a very remote resemblance to
the pre-war product.

'The effects of the war on the agricultural sector,' so Aeroboe
writes, 'manifested themselves primarily in a reduction of arable,
in the encroachment of fallow on arable, and in the transformation

of arable into permanent pasture.'[15] In fact this was just the opposite of what the government had intended, namely, the gearing of
stock-farming to the amount of fodder the country was capable of
producing, with the possibility of even further reductions of stock
in favour of grain and potatoes. Soon after the outbreak of war,
a ban was placed on the use of bread cereals for cattle feed; later
the ban was extended to potatoes and sugar-beet, the intention
being to prevent farmers from offsetting the absence of imported
feeds with home-grown foodstuffs. But the government's prices
policy militated directly against this, for after October 1914 grain
prices were fixed while meat prices continued to rise unchecked.
In other words, the government was virtually putting a premium
on the expansion of stock-farming and encouraging the circum-
vention of the feeding stuff regulations. In an attempt to cut down
stock-farming more effectively, the government issued a compulsory slaughtering order in respect of pigs that came into force at
the beginning of 1915. Over and above normal slaughterings, this
operation claimed perhaps 2 million victims – no very drastic
measure considering that in 1913 the country's pig population had
numbered some 27 million.[16] Nor did this order prove particularly
effective, the less so, no doubt, because pigs alone were involved
and farmers were able to turn to sheep and cattle instead. One
unlooked-for side effect of the prices policy became apparent after
the imposition of price controls on milk, when farmers turned to
meat, rather than milk production. Before long milk was unobtainable outside the black market except in cases of urgent need.
A characteristic of wartime food control was that the fixing of
individual prices occurred, not in accordance with a coherent plan,
but only when these were seen to have risen to an inordinately high
level. Hence the higher a price rose and the later it was controlled,
the higher would be the somewhat arbitrarily fixed price. It was
only with the setting up of the Food Control Office in May 1916
that any account was taken of the repercussions of price fixing on

15. See Aeroboe, *Der Einfluss des Krieges*, p. 84.
16. See ibid., pp. 50, 88, and Skalweit, *Die deutsche Kriegsernährungswirtschaft*, p. 97. Estimates of compulsory slaughterings vary between 1·6 and 2·5
million. The relevant literature tends to attribute too much importance to this
operation which has been described as 'a notable example of the errors to which
any system of planning is liable'; see G. Stolper, K. Häuser and K. Borchardt,
Deutsche Wirtschaft seit 1870, 2nd ed., Mohr, Tübingen, 1966, pp. 75ff.

production and supply, whereupon an attempt was made to re-adjust the relative prices of agricultural products. But by then the farmers had already begun to circumvent the official prices policy by concentrating more and more on the black market. Here, supply was no longer determined by official food priorities, but by the purses and preferences of the well-to-do.

The discrepancy between supply and demand brought about a rapid rise in food prices. It is true that as early as August 1914 urban and rural districts had been empowered by law to fix prices for articles in daily use. But these official retail prices only proved reasonably effective if a rise had been due to a temporary local shortage, itself the result, say, of hoarding by housewives or of transport difficulties in the early phase of mobilization. As time went on, however, the wholesalers sent their goods wherever they could obtain the best fixed prices, and boycotted any town which had imposed low prices in the interests of the consumer. In order to attract to their own localities the ever-diminishing supply of goods, towns vied with each other in the matter of maximum prices until finally the system was abolished altogether.

A new phase began when, in October 1914, the Bundesrat announced the introduction of general price controls, starting at producer level and applying initially to bread cereals. The government, which had introduced this policy in response to public opinion, had at first prevaricated, clearly realizing that they were embarking on something very different from the short-term legislation of August 1914 which had been directed against local-ized instances of over-pricing. It would seem that what finally convinced them was the Allied practice of using German price rises to gauge the effectiveness of the blockade. By the end of 1914 maximum prices had already been introduced for potatoes, sugar and feedingstuffs and, the following year, a whole series of items were added to this list, including butter and fish in October, milk, pork, fruit and vegetables in November. Despite their importance to the food programme, beef and mutton did not become subject to price controls until relatively late, in March 1916. Eventually the scheme embraced every conceivable kind of food from cattle on the hoof to acorns and horse chestnuts. Out of consideration for the producers, controlled prices were several times raised during the final years of the war.

The repercussions of the maximum prices policy on output have already been discussed in connection with production policy. As regards supplies, the fixing of individual maximum prices unfailingly resulted in the instant disappearance from the market – the licit market, that is – of the commodities concerned. Having studied prices, the farmer would turn to whatever form of production seemed most profitsble, e.g. to pig and cattle feeds, when maximum prices had been fixed for corn and potatoes. Or again, his reaction might be to circumvent the official distribution system and sell food illegally at higher prices. For example, 61,000 pigs a week were brought to the official markets before maximum prices were fixed in November 1915 and only 17,000 after that date. Hence sooner or later maximum prices were bound to be followed by direct state control.

Like all other controls, the organization of wartime food supplies did not follow any preconceived plan but rather the demands of the moment. Rationing began with the introduction of food cards for bread and flour in January 1915. Its implementation was entrusted to local associations each of which covered several urban and rural districts. Alongside these, but at national level, machinery was set up for collection and distribution, its function being to coordinate food supplies in the various regions and especially to ensure their movement from the country to the towns. Typical instruments of control were the Imperial Offices which were responsible for specific products. Each of these offices consisted of an administrative department and a commercial department. The administrative department exercised managerial functions, while the commercial department took care of the purchase, storage and sale of its own particular commodity. In theory the commercial departments were corporations subject to civil law and, for the most part, with limited liability; in practice, they represented a new type of 'war corporation' whose capital was put up partly by the producers and traders, and partly by public bodies at national, state and local association level. The commercial department of the Imperial Cereals Office, set up in 1915 as the first controlling authority, had evolved out of the Prussian War Cereals Corporation which had been founded as early as November 1914. Again, after the introduction of a new control, an existing cartel would sometimes be entrusted with the duties of a commercial department, e.g. as in the case of alcohol. On paper, then, wartime food administration corresponded approximately to the raw materials control (War Raw Materials Department and War Raw Materials Corporations).

At national level, food supply was the responsibility of the Ministry of the Interior which, in this capacity, administered the various Imperial Offices as well as the Central Purchasing Corporation, the agency responsible for food imports. In May 1916 the Ministry of Food was created as a separate authority under the former provincial administrator, von Batocki. The new ministry was set up to combat the rapid deterioration of the food supply situation. A 'food dictator', or so it was felt, was needed to pursue an effective food policy and to take the place of the multiplicity of agencies which, in this sphere, were duplicating each other's work if not actually competing against one another. But in fact the creation of the Ministry of Food made things worse rather than better. This was not, of course, due to organizational problems, although it is worth noting that the continued existence of competing authorities, in the shape of the Prussian Ministries and the military, stood in the way of a centralized food policy. While partly attributable to the intensification of the Allied blockade, the worsening food situation was chiefly the result of the increasing handicaps to which agriculture was subjected by the war. The position in regard to labour, draught animals, fertilizers, machinery and fuel steadily deteriorated and production suffered accordingly.

After the introduction of general rationing in 1916 the weekly entitlement per person was approximately as follows: 3·5 kg. potatoes, 160–220 g. flour (partly as bread), 100–250 g. meat, 60–75 g. fats, ·7 litres milk, 200 g. sugar, 270 g. 'spread' containing sugar (jam, artificial honey), 1 egg (when available), 120 g. fish. In fact these rations – unquestionably below subsistence level – were by no means always obtainable. The food crisis reached its peak in the winter of 1917/16 when a poor harvest combined with transport difficulties led to a breakdown in the provisioning of the larger cities. The swede, a vegetable execrated ever after, frequently took the place of bread and potatoes as the chief staple. In Berlin and Leipzig, the reduction of the bread ration in April 1917 was followed by the most serious strikes hitherto experienced in the war, strikes which developed into massive demonstrations for 'bread and peace'.

A disagreeable side effect of the food shortages was the steady decline in quality. As early as the beginning of 1915 nearly all bread contained potato flour and was known as 'K bread' (K for *Krieg* – war, or *Kartoffel* – potato). Milk was often adulterated by the producers or middlemen and the consumers dared not complain for fear of losing their ration altogether. Unscrupulous traders took advantage of the general state of want to place on the market an almost inexhaustible variety of worthless substitute foods whose only resemblance to the genuine article was their shape and colour: 'meat soup cubes' made of flavoured brine, 'egg substitute' made of ground maize or powdered potato with yellow colouring, and so forth. When in March 1918 substitute foods became subject to compulsory registration and licensing, more than 11,000 such products were already on the market.

TABLE 13
GERMANY: WARTIME RATIONS AND PEACETIME CONSUMPTION
(PEACETIME CONSUMPTION = 100)

	July 1916 to June 1917	July 1917 to June 1918	July 1918 to December 1918
Meat	31	20	12
Fish	51	—	5
Eggs	18	13	13
Lard	14	11	7
Butter	22	21	28
Cheese	3	4	15
Rice	4	—	—
Pulses	14	1	7
Sugar	49	56–67	80
Vegetable fats	39	41	17
Potatoes	71	94	94
Flour	53	47	48

SOURCE: Estimates made by W. Bach of food supplies in Bonn, cit. from W. Zimmermann, *Die Veränderungen der Einkommens- und Lebensverhältnisse der deutschen Arbeiter durch den Krieg*, Deutsche Verlags-Anstalt, Stuttgart/ Berlin/Leipzig, 1932, pp. 456ff.

Food controls did not affect the whole population alike; far from it. The armed forces were not included in the general scheme and, indeed, the forces' procurement agencies competed with the civilian War Corporations. Those engaged in agriculture enjoyed a specially favoured position in regard to food supplies. 'Self-suppliers' were in any case officially entitled to above-average rations and in practice they did even better. Producers could legally supplement their official rations with foods that did not fall within the controls because they were not available either regularly or in sufficient quantity, e.g. garden produce. There were also many unofficial and illegal ways of circumventing the regulations, since the government neither could nor would keep a strict check on rations in the rural areas. While it is just possible that the townsman might not have begrudged his country cousin this preferential treatment, what really galled him was the tremendous expansion of the black market. Anyone with enough money and the right connections could do a great deal to better his official rations. In 1918, according to reliable estimates, 'about one-eighth to one-seventh of grain, flour and potato output, one-quarter to one-third of milk, butter and cheese production, and one-third to one-half of egg, meat and fruit production passed through the hands of black marketeers at insane prices, sometimes as much as ten times the peacetime price'.[17] These quantities eluded the system of controls which, by official admission, was no longer able to ensure enough for normal subsistence as the war drew to a close. With the connivance of the central authorities, the armaments industry circumvented the official system to obtain extra rations for its workers, while Local Associations also bought food on the clandestine market at prices in excess of the official maximum. The disintegration of the controls was clearly cumulative: the less the authorities were able to guarantee minimum subsistence, the greater was the tendency to infringe the regulations, and this in turn reduced the official rations. Two main factors underlay this development: the general proliferation of profiteers, and the greed of the farming community, notably the big land-owners of east Germany who continued up to the very end to pit their political influence against the government's consumer-oriented food policy.

Germany's industrially less advanced allies were of no help in the sphere of food supplies. Indeed, they had their own problems.[18]

17. W. Zimmermann, *Die Veränderungen der Einkommens und Lebensverhältnisse der deutschen Arbeiter durch den Krieg*, Deutsche Verlags-Anstalt, Stuttgart/Berlin/Leipzig, 1932, p. 441.

18. On Austria-Hungary, see Loewenfeld-Russ, *Die Regelung der Volksernährung*, Gratz and Schüller, *Der wirtshaftliche Zusammenbruch Österreich-Ungarns*. (In an appendix Schüller quotes an exchange of letters between the Austrian and Hungarian Prime Ministers, Stürgkh and Tisza, which gives a vivid impression of food supply difficulties.) On Bulgaria: G. T. Danaillow,

In Hungary the 1914 grain harvest was particularly disappointing, being nearly one-third less than normal and hence barely sufficient for the Kingdom's requirements of bread cereals and seed. True, the failure of the harvest could not, at this juncture, be blamed on the war; nevertheless, the outbreak of hostilities meant that Austria could no longer turn to foreign suppliers as she would otherwise have done had the Hungarian harvest failed to come up to scratch. Moreover, though the first wartime harvest in 1915 was better than the previous year's, it was still below the peace-time average, while subsequent yields dropped appreciably owing to wartime conditions. After the commencement of hostilities only limited supplies could be imported from abroad and, by the end of the first year of war, stocks in the hands of the producers and wholesalers had already been expended to make good the 1914 shortfall. After the outbreak of war food prices rose steeply. In November 1914, a system of maximum prices on the German pattern was introduced for cereals. At the beginning of the following year, government grain controls were established, though administered separately in either half of the Empire. Ever diminishing food resources gave rise to violent friction which perpetuated the old rivalries between the two. Although never easy in Hungary, the food situation remained substantially better than in Austria. In 1916, Hungarian grain production per head of population amounted to some 203 kg. and in Austria to some 72 kg.[19] Nevertheless, in 1916 Hungary supplied no more than 100,000 tons of grain and flour to Austria, as against 2·1 million tons yearly before the war, and deliveries of other foodstuffs were likewise drastically reduced. The Hungarian government saw to it that, wherever possible, it was Austria that bore the brunt of the food shortages. While the Kingdom did, indeed, introduce rationing, the official scale was higher than the Austrian,[20] and controls were less rigidly

---

Les effets de la guerre en Bulgarie, Presses Universitaires de France, Paris, 1932. On Turkey: A. Emin, Turkey in the World War, Yale University Press, New Haven, 1930.

19. Based on harvest and census returns in Gratz and Schüller, Der wirtschaftliche Zusammenbruch Österreich-Ungarns, pp. 44ff, 152.

20. E.g. in Hungary, in 1917, the daily flour ration was 400-500 g. for the self-suppliers and 233 g. for town-dwellers, as compared to 300-366 and 200 g. respectively in Austria. See Loewenfeld-Russ, Die Regelung der Volksernährung, p. 62.

enforced. But the government's principal beneficiaries were the big land-owners who demanded enormous quantities of feedingstuffs in the hope of coming through the war with their herds intact. Hungarian pigs, or so it was wryly said in Austria, meant more to them than Austrian human beings. Again, within the two halves of the Empire there were national rivalries which militated against a unified food policy. The Czechs in Austria, like the Croats in Hungary, opposed state control – in any case unpopular among the rural population – on national grounds.

During the war, deliveries of food between the Central Powers remained surprisingly low. Bulgaria supplied her allies with tobacco (if that may be accounted a food), Turkey exported olive oil to Germany, while Austria–Hungary supplied Bulgaria and Turkey with sugar amounting to 18,000 tons.[21] The blockade cut the Central Powers off from overseas imports, besides restricting the export trade of their neutral neighbours. Foreign trade with the neutrals was never completely suppressed, however; up till the end Scandinavia, Holland and Switzerland were important suppliers of highly nutritious foods (meat, fats, fish, milk, cheese). And above all, the Central Powers continued to have access to Romania whose pre-war exports of some 3·3 million tons of grain a year placed her among the most important exporters of agriculture produce.[22] After the outbreak of war Romanian grain and oil became a trump card in the political gambling game between the Central Powers, the Allies and the Romanian government. In December 1915, by the terms of a preliminary agreement, the Central Powers received 550,000 tons of grain while a later agreement, in March of the following year, provided for the supply of a further 1·4 million tons. Of this, 850,000 tons had in fact been delivered when Romania entered the war. After the occupation, when the country was virtually at the mercy of the Central Powers, a further 2·2 million tons of food, including 1·9 million tons of grain, were exported, approximately equal quantities going to Germany and Austria–Hungary, and a more modest amount to Bulgaria and Turkey.[23] In 1919 the Central Powers placed great hopes on the 'bread truce' with the Ukraine. Though the results

21. See ibid, pp. 368-76.
22. See G. Ionesco-Sisesti, *L'agriculture de la Romanie pendant la guerre*, Presses Universitaires de France, Paris, 1929, p. 16.
23. See ibid., p. 59.

never came up to expectations, the occupation authorities nevertheless managed to squeeze some 400,000 tons of foodstuffs, chiefly grain and sugar, out of the exhausted country.[24] In the other occupied territories, particularly Serbia, any surplus was claimed by the armies of occupation. Belgium and northern France themselves needed to import large quantities of foodstuffs and special agreements were concluded with the Allies to allow food for the civilian population to pass through the blockade.[25]

The Allies

Great Britain

At a very early stage Great Britain began to experience difficulties over sugar, two-thirds of which had been imported from Germany and Austria–Hungary before the war.[26] August 1914 saw the creation of the Royal Commission on Sugar Supplies, a body that was given exclusive control of imports and distribution. The commission bought the sugar in the overseas producing countries and allocated it to individual refineries and wholesalers on the basis of their average pre-war market share. This aside, food supplies in the first two years of war were little affected. Up till the end of 1916 imports of foodstuffs remained at about 90 per cent of the pre-war level, such reductions as there were being attributable to the diversion of shipping for military purposes. The U-boat, despite the launching of the 'unrestricted' or 'intensified' campaigns in the early part of 1916 and of 1917, did not as yet constitute any appreciable menace. Nor did domestic agriculture at first experience any difficulties. By the beginning of 1915 an average of 16 per

24. H. Loewenfeld-Russ, op. cit., pp. 395–403.

25. See P. Collinet and P. Stahl, *Le ravitaillement de la France occupée*, Presses Universitaires de France, Paris, 1928; and A. Henry, *Le ravitaillement de la Belgique pendant l'occupation allemande*, Presses Universitaires de France, Paris, 1924.

26. On British food policy, see W. Beveridge, *British Food Control*, Oxford University Press, 1928; and T. H. Middleton, *Food Production in War*, Clarendon Press, Oxford, 1923. These accounts provided much of the material for the relevant chapters in: Hurwitz, *State Intervention in Great Britain*; and M. Olson, *The Economics of Wartime Shortage. A History of British Food Supply in the Napoleonic War and in World Wars I and II*, Duke University Press, Durham, 1963.

cent of agricultural workers in England and Wales had joined the armed forces, but at times of cultivation and harvest their places were largely filled by workers from other occupations as well as by women and juveniles. Thanks to the weather, the harvest of 1915 was, in fact, better than average.

Thus there was in effect no food shortage, but the public was becoming increasingly discontented over rising prices. In June 1915 and June 1916 retail food prices were respectively 33 per cent and 61 per cent higher than in July 1914. By July 1915 wages had risen by a mere 5 to 10 per cent, and, twelve months later, by 15 to 20 per cent, so that in real terms food had become somewhat dearer.[27] The reasons for the price rises were; on the one hand, mounting freight rates and the shortage of supplies and, on the other, wartime inflation which also led, amongst other things, to a rise in the demand for foodstuffs in money terms.

TABLE 14
UNITED KINGDOM: IMPORTS OF FOODSTUFFS, 1913–18

	Million tons	Index (1913 = 100)
1913	18·3	100
1914	16·7	92
1915	17·0	93
1916	16·3	89
1917	13·8	75
1918	11·9	65

SOURCE: W. Beveridge, *British Food Control*, Oxford University Press, 1928, pp. 354ff.
Foodstuffs include cattle feed.

The initial incentive for a government food policy was provided in the early autumn of 1916 by the poor harvest, largely due to bad weather, and by the transport difficulties which were already becoming acute even before the unrestricted submarine campaign. In October 1916 another authority was set up along the same lines as the Commission on Sugar, namely the Royal Commission on Wheat Supplies which was subsequently responsible, not only for wheat, but for all forms of cereal. Through these two commissions the state controlled two-thirds of the country's food imports by

27. See A. Bowley, *Prices and Wages in the United Kingdom 1914-1920*, Clarendon Press, Oxford, 1921, pp. 35, 106.

weight and about three-quarters in terms of calorie value. Moreover the Board of Trade had a virtual monopoly of refrigerated meat imports, most of which went to the army.[28] Initially, however, government intervention was confined to imports. The distribution of foodstuffs was left to existing trade channels, and domestic production was also exempt from controls.

Not until the change of government in December 1916 was a new food policy initiated on the basis of rigid import control, enhanced production and regulated distribution. It was not an easy decision for the government. Shortly before leaving office in November 1916 the Asquith administration had admitted on principle the need for centralized control. In December 1916 Lloyd George created the Ministry of Food as the visible expression of a reorientation of food policy. But it was the U-boat blockade that provided the real incentive for concrete measures.

Although the proportion of foodstuffs to total imports rose slightly (from 40 to 42 per cent), food imports between 1916 and 1917 fell by 2·5 million tons and, between 1917 and 1918, by a further 1·9 million tons. By 1917 food imports had fallen to three-quarters and by 1918 to about two-thirds of pre-war levels. These, like all other imports, were strictly controlled and the bodies responsible for administering them formed the nucleus of the inter-Allied import control agencies on which, from April 1918, the European neutrals were also represented. The government purchased the grain harvest in the producing countries, organized transport, and conveyed the goods to the consumers by means of a comprehensive distribution network. One of the first consequences of centralized control was concentration on the North Atlantic: grain and meat were imported for preference from the U.S.A. and Canada in order to shorten voyages and thus economize on vessels. True, such of the Australian wheat harvest as was available for export was purchased, but most of it was stored *in situ* for want of shipping space. When supplies from Germany and Austria–Hungary dried up, sugar was at first imported mainly from the Netherlands East Indies and later from Cuba. The financing of U.S. imports presented little difficulty for, since America's entry into the war in April 1917, her government had granted the necessary credits. Another effect of import control was to enable the authorities to give precedence more rapidly than the

28. See Beveridge, *British Food Control*, p. 114.

market might have done to whatever food imports they deemed most essential. Thus, in 1917 priority had been given to bread cereals, whereas in 1918 these constituted a smaller proportion of total imports because home production had risen in the meantime; in their stead large weights of ham and bacon were shipped from the U.S.A.

The most cogent answer to import restrictions was the expansion of home production. As a consequence of its close integration into the world economy, British agriculture had specialized in animal husbandry which, as a 'finishing industry' yielded better profits than arable farming. With the decline in imports this specialization suddenly lost its value for, given equal inputs, the cultivation of cereals could feed more people than livestock rearing. At the end of 1916, the government overtly committed itself to the encouragement of cereals cultivation with the trenchant slogan 'back to the seventies'. Within the shortest possible time, i.e. by the harvest of 1918, some 7·5 million acres of grazing land were to be ploughed up – nearly as much, that is, as had been turned over from arable to grass between 1870 and 1914 under the influence of increasing dependence on world supplies. A wave of patriotic fervour sustained the cereals policy and helped to overcome not only the initial resistance of the farmers who feared for their future profits, but also the difficulties attendant upon the relatively unfavourable price of grain. Out of consideration for the mood of the workers, the government did not wish to raise grain prices although this would have boosted their cereals policy. Rather than have recourse to the price mechanism, they chose to rely on direct controls. A decree of January 1917 empowered the government to determine, through local committees, what land in any given area should be ploughed up. For the most part their decisions were accepted and recourse was seldom had to the ultimate sanction of denying the farmer the use of his land.

This policy had come too late to influence the 1917 wheat harvest, for the country's main crop was winter wheat; nevertheless, in the spring of 1917 some 2·5 million acres were turned over to potatoes and oats. At first the ploughing up of grassland for the 1918 harvest proceeded somewhat slowly because of the shortage of labour, horses and machinery but, thanks to favourable weather in the late autumn, winter and spring, the targets were nevertheless achieved. Farmers had sown a substantial acreage with winter wheat in the expectation that newly ploughed land would be available in the spring of 1918 for other crops, with the result that the 1918 wheat harvest was appreciably better. By comparison with 1916 the area under cultivation for the 1918 harvest had increased by 7·5 million acres to a total of some 31·25 million. In this way about three-quarters of the arable area, which had been turned over to grass during the fifty years preceding the war, had reverted to its previous state.

In 1918 production of grain and potatoes was some 40 per cent above the average for the years 1904–13. Taking into consideration the drop in livestock production, there was still a rise in food production of some 24 per cent reckoned in terms of calorie value. Such comparisons as were made went to show that the yield per acre on the newly ploughed up land was very much the same as on the old arable.

This rigorous process involving the reorganization of agriculture and the boosting of production was only possible because, within the general framework of the war economy, priorities had been determined accordingly. The agricultural sector was allotted additional labour for ploughing up, sowing and harvesting, and provided with extra horses, machinery, seed and fertilizers. The government mobilized thousands of prisoners of war, released serving soldiers and recruited women for work on the land. Tractors, rarely seen hitherto, were produced in increasing numbers and located in central depots. Seed and fertilizers were given specific priorities vis-à-vis munitions production. In 1916 and 1917 the British economy was able to mobilize substantial resources for the agricultural sector, despite the claims of the armaments industry, and herein lies the vital distinction between German and British food policy.

A further 2·5 million acres were to be ploughed up for the 1919 harvest, but these plans were upset by the German spring offensive of 1918. In agriculture, as in other branches of the economy, all able-bodied workers were called to the colours to help contain the enemy's final thrust. Increased production was subordinated to this end and, indeed, proved unnecessary since the autumn brought victory to the Allies.

The first steps towards food control consisted in regulation of imports and state intervention in home production. The systematic organization of food distribution to the consumer did not begin

until some months later. Faced with the complexity of a centralized distribution system that would control supplies to every
single consumer and thus entirely replace the market mechanism,
the Ministry of Food first experimented with 'voluntary rationing'.
Under this procedure, the housewife was expected to restrict herself to a voluntary ration scale to be announced from time to time
by the Ministry. The first programme, of February 1917, envisaged
a weekly ration of four pounds of bread, two and a half pounds of
meat and three-quarters of a pound of sugar. The basic idea was
to substitute meat (nearly all of which was home-produced) for
the bread, i.e. grain (nearly all of it imported) normally consumed.
But because of the cost, this was something that only wealthier
households could afford. Even in normal times the poorer classes
could not possibly have afforded the proposed meat ration, whereas they consumed a correspondingly larger quantity of bread. In
the case of agricultural workers, ten to fourteen pounds was not
uncommon. 'The sugar ration of three-quarters of a pound,
corresponded to a reasonably reduced average consumption, but
its announcement caused discontent among those who through
faulty distribution were unable to get any sugar at all.'[29] Hence
voluntary rationing proved a failure. Nor were the overriding
problems – price rises and inadequate distribution – solved in the
initial phase of the new policy. By June 1917 retail food prices had
doubled as compared with July 1914.

Price fixing and rationing were not generally introduced as
central instruments of the government's food policy until the
summer of 1917 when a new Food Controller was appointed.
Maximum prices for certain essential foods first came into force
in September 1917, after which the scheme was continuously extended until, towards the end of the war, it embraced practically
all foodstuffs. From the outset, price fixing was linked with the
state control of every aspect of supply, from production or importation to consumption. The wholesale and retail trades continued
to act as the distributive machinery, but under government direction and on fixed margins. Considering that the system was now
divorced from any mercantile function, it was perhaps unneces-
sarily cumbrous and could have dispensed with a number of

29. See A. Bowley, *Prices and Wages in the United Kingdom 1914-1920*,
Clarendon Press, Oxford, 1921, p. 35.

middlemen. But the government deemed it important not only to retain what were well-tried distributive channels and to avoid unduly disrupting them, but also to safeguard commercial interests.

Rationing is not necessarily a corollary of price fixing, if, for example, the distributive machinery can provide the required quantity at a given price. This was the policy adopted in the case of bread which, as a staple food, had to be readily available. Indeed consumption was actually encouraged by subsidizing bread prices. Such restrictions as there were applied, for example, to the use of wheat for brewing, feeding livestock or any kind of industrial purpose.

There were also regulations for millers and bakers concerning the admixture of other kinds of flour. In this way, despite occasional bottlenecks, bread remained unrationed up till the very end, unlike other important foodstuffs, all of which were eventually subject to rationing.

A certain amount of experience had already been gained in the sphere of sugar distribution. Initially, rationing was carried out at trade level: wholesalers and retailers were allotted quotas calculated as a percentage of their pre-war sales, a procedure which led to a great deal of injustice because of wartime shifts of population to the armaments centres. Thus, a trader might receive a quantity of sugar disproportionate to the number of his customers, whereas in a new centre of population the commodity might be almost unobtainable. Moreover, retailers were given no instructions as to how their customers should be rationed. Often they adopted the simple and profitable, if highly asocial, method of doling out their sugar in proportion to a customer's total purchases. Despite numerous complaints, this system was not changed until the introduction of general food control. In June 1917 a new rationing scheme was adopted, this time based on the individual household. Each householder was to register with the retailer of his choice who would thenceforward be his permanent source of supply. The retailer in his turn would register with a specific wholesaler, whereupon both would receive allocations in accordance with the number of their registered customers. Considerable administrative work was involved if the new system was to be operative by the end of the year. But registration, having been completed, proved of great use when rationing was extended to other foodstuffs.

Though there were alarming reports to the contrary, the country's food supplies were initially proof against the worst onslaughts of the unrestricted U-boat campaign. Prices rose, but most foodstuffs were still within the reach of even the poorer classes. It was only at the end of 1917 that the food crisis began, one of its manifestations being the long shopping queues for butter, margarine and tea, and at a later date, for butcher's meat. In London there would sometimes be a queue of up to 3,000 outside a single shop. A few local Food Committees tackled the queue problem by extending the registration scheme recently introduced for sugar to other scarce foods, retailers being instructed to sell specific items only to registered customers. At the end of December this scheme was universally enforced by the Ministry of Food. In January 1918 it was decided to issue ration cards as well. Thus, the customer, while still having to register, also had to tender the appropriate ration card when purchasing a commodity in short supply, while the trader was required to produce counterfoils as evidence of the amounts supplied. This additional measure was aimed at a better control of distribution as affecting the customer and, more especially, the trader. In February 1918 ration cards were issued for meat and in July ration books for all types of food in short supply. The scheme was an immediate success and virtually put a stop to the queues outside the food shops. Overall, rations were no larger than before but they were better distributed. People could count on receiving their prescribed rations irrespective of whether they shopped early or late.

Compared with the averages for the years 1909–13, the *per capita* consumption of butter, fresh meat and sugar had fallen substantially by 1918, in each case by roughly 40 per cent. Milk consumption had dropped by about a quarter. On the other hand consumption of bread, potatoes, lard, margarine and ham had risen appreciably, thus largely compensating for the decline in a few important foodstuffs. There were more staple foods and, from the summer of 1918, heavy workers were granted generous supplementary rations in the form of American bacon and ham. Though nutrition was below the pre-war standard, rations were nevertheless adequate and, more important still, could be maintained. From a comparison made by the Ministry of Food in 1918, Britain emerges more favourably than Germany or even neutral Holland. Not only were supplies better, but circumstances favoured more equable distribution. As in Germany, soldiers and farm workers were given preferential treatment, but they constituted a smaller proportion of the total population. From this viewpoint Britain's dependence on imports might seem, paradoxically enough, to have been an

TABLE 15

UNITED KINGDOM: WEEKLY *per capita* CONSUMPTION OF
ESSENTIAL FOODSTUFFS

	lb	Index (1909–13 = 100)	
	1909–13	1917	1918
Flour	4·28	110	112
Butcher's meat	2·04	82	62
Bacon and ham	0·34	106	135
Butter	0·31	65	55
Margarine	0·11	218	200
Lard	0·11	73	136
Potatoes	3·67	105	143
Sugar	1·46	68	64

SOURCE: W. Beveridge, *British Food Control*, Oxford University Press, 1928, p. 311.

advantage so far as her food policy was concerned. For obvious reasons, imports were easier to control than the more elusive home production. But in the final count, Britain's higher nutritional level may be attributed to the superiority of her general resources and system of priorities. Despite the extent of its war effort, the British government was able to earmark a sufficiency, not only of shipping space for food imports, but also of factors of production for domestic agriculture, whereas German agricultural production collapsed under the burden of the rigorous militarization of the national economy. Nor were controls and rationing unknown in those countries where, in more normal times, agriculture had adequately supplied the home market and even been an important exporting sector.

France

In France agricultural production declined drastically as a result of the call-up, the occupation of the northern part of the country and the shortage of fertilizers and machinery. The 1917 wheat harvest was the poorest on record, being 40 per cent below the pre-war level, while sugar production, largely located in northern France, was even harder hit. On average the wartime grain harvests were 2·6 million tons, the potato harvests 1·9 million tons, and the sugar-beet harvests 2·5 million tons below the pre-war level.[30] As a result France inevitably became a major importer of foodstuffs. In accordance with the general import programme jointly agreed by the Allies at the end of 1917, France imported 639,000 tons of foodstuffs a month, of which wheat accounted for 275,000 tons.[31] Nevertheless food became scarce and prices rose. In October the government intervened in the case of grain, and in April 1916 price controls were extended to a range of other basic foods. However, these measures did nothing to stabilize the price level; rather, maximum prices were continuously adjusted to the inflationary trend. For instance, the pre-war price of wheat was somewhere between 23–5 francs per 100 kg., in 1915 the price was fixed at 30 francs and by 1918 it had been raised to 75 francs. State monopolies, controlling the entire supply channel from producer to consumer, were created for sugar in 1916 and for grain in 1917. Indeed sugar, flour and bread were the first foods to be individually rationed, and from June 1918 ration cards were made compulsory throughout France. The bread ration, the basis of food control, was initially fixed at 400 g. a day for normal consumers and 600 g. for workers in agriculture and heavy industry; in 1918 both scales had to be reduced by 100 g.

Italy

In Italy the outbreak of war in 1914 raised a number of short-term food problems because imports of grain from Romania and South Russia had been cut off. But this crisis was soon surmounted.[32] Other sources of supply were found and it was even possible to increase imports; the decline in home production caused by the war never exceeded 10 per cent and thus gave no cause for alarm.

30. See Augé-Laribé, *L'agriculture pendant la guerre*, pp. 53-63.

31. P. Pinot, *Le contrôle du ravitaillement de la population civile*, Presses Universitaires de France, Paris, 1925, p. 287.

32. See Bachi, *L'alimentazione*. There is a brief résumé in L. Einaudi, *La condotta economica e gli effetti sociali della guerra italiana*, Laterza, Bari, 1933, pp. 179-96.

Not until the crisis of 1917 did the grain harvest show a 30 per cent drop as against the pre-war level. By comparison with, say, France, this setback was nevertheless a tolerable one; on the other hand, there was scarcely margin enough in Italy to cut down consumption. True, army rations were lower than those of the other Allies, but they were still higher than the normal consumption of the majority of industrial and agricultural workers. Hence, those who were hardest hit by restrictions on consumption were the masses, whose standard of living had been abysmally low even before the war. This difficult situation was, indeed, taken into account in framing inter-Allied shipping and import policy. The final import programme of July 1918 guaranteed Italy an absolute minimum of some 4 million tons of foodstuffs, three-quarters of it in the form of grain. In fact, food imports in 1918 were about 40 per cent higher than before the war. In Italy, as in almost all other countries, controls were first applied to prices. In March 1916 maximum prices, which had hitherto applied only to goods requisitioned for the armed forces, were extended to various staple foods. The same year saw the beginnings of a central control which was to cover everything from compulsory purchase to the individual rationing of consumers. In 1917 ration cards, or *tessere*, were made obligatory, first for bread and later for other foods; up till June 1921 these continued to determine the standard of living of the lower classes. The provisioning of the industrial centres proved to be the main problem. In Milan the daily ration was fixed at 200 g. a day for normal consumers and 400 g. for workmen. Country people were very much better fed because 'self-suppliers' were able to evade government controls.

Russia

Even Russia, which before the war had been the granary of Europe, experienced food supply difficulties, For this, inadequate distribution rather than insufficient production was to blame.[33] As

33. On Russian food control, see A. N. Antsiferov, A. D. Bilimovich, M. O. Batshev and D. N. Ivantsov, *Russian Agriculture during the War*, Yale University Press, Newhaven, 1930; S. S. Demosthenov, N. V. Dolinsky, P. B. Struve, K. I. Zaitsev, *Food Supply in Russia during the World War*, Yale University Press, Newhaven, 1930; and A. M. Anfimov, *Rossijskaja derevnja v gody pervoj mirovoj vojny (1914–favral' 1917 g.)*, Moscow, 1962.

in all the other belligerent countries, agriculture suffered as a result of the call-up. 15 per cent of all able-bodied men were mobilized in 1914, and 36 per cent in 1916. Since there had been a considerable amount of hidden unemployment in agriculture before 1914, however, the effect of mobilization was not as drastic as, for instance, in Germany or France. Not until 1916 did the shortage of manpower become a problem of any magnitude, and then the main sufferers were the big estates which were dependent on hired labour, whereas smallholdings, as family concerns, were able to carry on. The wartime grain harvests were approximately 10 per cent lower than the pre-war average and, like the drop in the number of livestock, gave little cause for concern. Since exports of foodstuffs, notably grain, almost ceased during the war, the overall level of supplies must necessarily have improved. The real problem consisted in the fact that food was not reaching the towns. The imbalance between town and country in the matter of supplies is plainly discernible in the price trend; for instance, by the spring of 1917 the price of wheat, as compared with the pre-war average, had risen by 231 per cent in the producing areas and by 808 per cent in the industrial areas. If we remember that over the same period the wages of industrial workers had risen by no more than 100 per cent, we may gain some idea of the hardships involved. Indeed, from the spring of 1915 onwards, food shortages led to strikes in industrial areas.[34]

Of the multiplicity of factors which influenced the supply of foodstuffs, two in particular stand out. There was a general tendency among rural producers to hold back supplies. This 'withdrawal from the market' had a wholly rational economic basis. In the exchange of agricultural and industrial products the peasants were now getting decidedly the worst of the bargain; whereas the price of agricultural products had more or less trebled by the autumn of 1916, those of shoes, textiles and implements – in so far as such things were obtainable at all – had risen even more dramatically. Since, in exchange for the foodstuffs which they brought to market, the peasants could obtain only a few industrial products at exorbitant prices and of indifferent quality at that, a better alternative seemed to be to consume more and more of their own produce. That the terms of exchange between agriculture and

34. See S. Kohn and A. F. Meyendorff, *The Cost of the War to Russia*, Yale University Press, Newhaven, 1932.

industry had become ever more one-sided is evident from the growing amounts of cash hoarded by the peasants, forced savings which were imposed by the absence of goods.[35] Such food supplies as came on the market were first tapped by the state to meet military requirements, while the towns had to make do with what was left over.

A further reason for the huge disparity between town and country in the matter of prices and supplies was the general disorganization of the transport system. As a result of transport difficulties, themselves caused by the military's excessive demands on the inadequate railway network, St Petersburg, Moscow and other centres of consumption were isolated from the agricultural producing areas in the south and south-east. Moreover, the administration contributed to the disintegration of the economy in individual regions when, shortly after the outbreak of war, it introduced controls on the export of grain from areas having a surplus. These regional embargoes, intended to facilitate the procurement of foodstuffs by the military, also served the interests of a number of provincial administrations who could thus lay the responsibility for the food problem on other provinces. Once the central government had come to realize the disadvantages to the war economy of economic fragmentation, they embarked on an uphill and largely unsuccessful struggle against regional self-interest. In the centres of consumption, moreover, prices were forced up by middlemen whose position had been enormously strengthened by the regional fragmentation of the markets. Traders of all kinds, mills, sugar refineries and even banks – which had climbed on to this bandwagon with great alacrity – exploited the food shortages to make profits far in excess of the pre-war norm.[36]

National food policies and the world economy

The war in Europe brought about substantial changes in the world's food supply and even, in some cases, a direct reversal of the trends prevailing before 1914. In Britain the real decline in

35. On this point see P. N. Apostol, M. W. Bernatzky and A. M. Michelson, *Russian Public Finance during the War*, Yale University Press, New Haven, 1928.

36. S. S. Demosthenov, N. V. Dolinsky, P. B. Struve, and K. I. Zaitsev, *Food Supply in Russia*, pp. 369ff.

imports was partially compensated for by a considerable rise in home production, an achievement which, however, cancelled out the trend of the past forty-four years towards increased dependence on foreign supplies. Conversely, France and Italy succeeded in partially offsetting the drop in their own agricultural production by importing large quantities of foodstuffs from Canada and the U.S.A. The Central Powers, and Germany in particular, were hit, not only by their exclusion from the world market, but also by the steep decline in home production due to the war. Though Russia disappeared from the world market as a supplier, the internal disruption of her economy nevertheless gave rise to serious food problems.

As has been shown in the case of individual countries, agricultural production on the Continent of Europe fell steadily throughout the war.[37] According to League of Nations estimates the Continental grain harvest in 1919 was some 33 per cent lower than in peacetime, a decline for which the reduction in the area under cultivation and the lower yield per acre were equally responsible. The supply of animal products also dropped by about 33 per cent over the same period, as compared with only about 20 per cent in numbers of livestock. This disparity confirms what has already emerged from a consideration of individual countries, namely that farmers sought to maintain their herds intact throughout the war.

In the overseas grain-producing countries – the United States and Canada in the northern hemisphere and Argentina, Uruguay, South Africa, Australia and New Zealand in the southern hemisphere – production tended to rise during the war years. The only exception was 1916 when harvests were universally poor. In this connection it would seem pertinent to review once again the national food policies of individual countries. The drastic deterioration in the food situation both of the Allies and of the Central Powers in this particular year was due not only to war conditions but also, and quite manifestly, to the more fortuitous failure of the harvest all over the world. Nor, in other years, did a rise in output automatically connote a rise in the volume of exports. In 1917 and 1918 the exports of the southern producers showed a marked decline, even as compared with the pre-war level. The exports of the northern producers (U.S.A. and Canada) also fell by compari-

37. League of Nations, *Agricultural Production*, pp. 52ff, and tables in appendix.

son with the first years of the war, but were nevertheless above the peacetime level. This is a further statistical illustration of the 'concentration on the North Atlantic' mentioned above. Shortage of shipping space meant that the Allies transferred their foreign trade to North America at the expense of more distant suppliers.

TABLE 16
GRAIN PRODUCTION AND GRAIN EXPORTS, 1909–19
(MILLIONS OF TONS)

	North America		Southern exporting countries	
	Production	Export	Production	Export
1909–13	121·5	6·4	14·7	7·5
1914	124·5	9·8	16·8	6·5
1915	152·3	15·7	17·5	7·3
1916	120·5	16·6	10·7	7·7
1917	138·6	12·9	17·6	4·1
1918	132·8	11·1	15·6	5·8
1919	118·5	12·9	16·5	9·1

SOURCE: League of Nations, *Agricultural Production in Continental Europe during the 1914–18 War and the Reconstruction Period*, Geneva, 1943, pp. 58ff.
North America: U.S.A., Canada. Southern exporting countries: Argentina, Uruguay, South Africa, Australia, New Zealand.

European wartime demand resulted in an enormous export boom for the overseas suppliers. The U.S.A. exported wheat to the value of 142 million dollars in 1913 and 505 million dollars in 1918.[38] In some cases, as in Argentina in 1917, rising prices created an increase in the value of exports, even when the volume of exports was falling.[39] The export boom had far-reaching consequences which will be discussed elsewhere. On the one hand rising agricultural incomes produced a multiplier effect in the economies of the exporting countries generally; on the other hand, there were disadvantages to the consumer in those countries, for he was having to compete with the Allies' virtually insatiable monetary demand. The exporting countries' reaction to this was to impose controls

38. See US Department of Commerce, Bureau of the Census, ed., *Historical Statistics of the United States. Colonial Times to 1957*, Government Printing Office, Washington, 1961, p. 546.
39. See H. J. Williams, 'Latin America's Foreign Exchange and International Balances during the War', *Quarterly Journal of Economics*, 33, 1918/19, pp. 436ff. The price of grain rose from 10 U.S. dollars per 100 kg in July 1914 to 19 U.S. dollars in June 1917.

on foreign trade. Argentina, for instance, placed a temporary export embargo on wheat and imported that commodity from Australia.[40]

The rivalry between export and consumer interests was particularly marked in the neutral countries of Europe, some of which were already traditional exporters of foodstuffs: Denmark and Holland of meat and dairy products, and Norway of fish. Belligerents on both sides were their customers and as such combined political coercion with economic incentives. These supplies, however, declined, for the foreign trade of the European neutrals was increasingly subjected to Allied control which adversely affected *inter alia*, both agriculture and fisheries. Hence the food situation in the neutral countries was not dissimilar to that obtaining in the belligerent countries. In the course of the war the price of bread in Sweden rose by nearly 100 per cent, of dairy products, eggs and margarine by 175 per cent, of meat by more than 400 per cent, whereas nominal wages went up by only about 100 per cent.[41] It is hardly surprising, therefore, that the neutral governments, though never intervening as vigorously as the belligerents in the field of food supplies, should also have evolved their own food policies comprising maximum prices, direct rationing, and controls on foreign trade.

40. See ibid., p. 437.
41. See H. Westergaard, ed., *Sweden, Norway, Denmark and Iceland in the World War*, Yale University Press, Newhaven, 1930, pp. 17 and 21.

were indirect dealings possible because the warring countries and a number of neutrals had more or less openly suspended the gold standard.

The conversion of bank notes into gold was prohibited in Russia on 27 July, in Germany on 4 August and in France on 5 August 1914. Even before the war this facility had not been available in Italy where the lira had been kept close to parity by interventions on the part of the central bank and the state. On the outbreak of hostilities, Germany and Russia likewise banned the export of gold. In view of her strong creditor position, France at first restricted, but did not prohibit, the export of gold, and it was not until July 1915 that an official ban was imposed. The manner in which Britain went off the gold standard was both pragmatic and unobtrusive. In theory, the legal convertibility of Bank of England notes into gold persisted throughout the war. However a series of regulations made it increasingly difficult for the public to avail itself of this right. The private export of gold also remained legal throughout, but in practice this too was greatly restricted: firstly, because the Bank of England refused to cooperate in gold transfers between private individuals; and secondly because high wartime insurance charges meant that arbitrage dealings in gold in the form of bullion shipments were no longer an attractive proposition. After 1917 exports of gold were further affected by general controls on foreign trade and shipping space. It was not until April 1919, when these wartime controls had been lifted, that an official ban was temporarily placed on the export of gold.

It has often been suggested that the gold standard was 'kept flying' by the United States under the guidance of the newly created (1913) Federal Reserve System. But in fact, after her entry into the war, America introduced certain modifications: from September 1917 onwards the export of gold was authorized only under special licence and in June 1917 the Federal Reserve Act was amended to enable the banking system greatly to increase the supply of paper money by reducing the gold reserve requirement. Thus, the United States, like Great Britain, abandoned the gold standard in practice while maintaining its outward and legal form. After the outbreak of war a succession of neutral states followed the lead of the belligerents by suspending legal convertibility and placing an embargo on gold shipments. From 1915 the main problem facing the neutrals was not so much a drain as an influx of gold. A number of countries (Denmark, Holland, Norway, Sweden and Spain) either restricted or temporarily prohibited its import.

Officially, individual states were at pains to maintain the semblance of a gold standard in respect of their national currencies. Their currency laws avoided any visible departure from the gold standard and the central banks further endeavoured, with the support of their governments, to maintain if not increase their gold reserves although, after the suspension of legal convertibility a gold reserve was not really needed.[2] Gold from current production increased the reserves of the Russian Central Bank and the Bank of England, the latter having been accorded sole purchasing rights to South African and Australian gold production. At the outbreak of war the Banque de France held very substantial gold reserves and, moreover, possessed a kind of gold mine of its own in the shape of large private hoards which it was able to mobilize by appealing to French patriotic sentiment. In Germany the Reichsbank was likewise able to draw upon large private hoards and obtained further supplies of gold by means of confiscations in the occupied territories of Belgium, Romania and Russia. Even in wartime there were still some international gold movements, both within the systems of alliances and between belligerents and neutrals, but in the main a country's import surpluses were financed by bilateral credit agreements rather than by the transfer of gold as hitherto. This explains the apparent paradox whereby, despite Britain's vast import surpluses during the war, the Bank of England could show on balance an accrual of gold. The central bank reserves, to all intents and purposes devoid of function, came to symbolize a fictitious gold standard to which, for a variety of reasons, governments and banks continued to cling. In the first place, the war was regarded as no more than a temporary interruption, after which normal relations would immediately be resumed, hence it seemed desirable that the appropriate institutions and forms should in so far as possible be left intact. In the second place, the outward stability of the currency continued throughout the war to be universally regarded as a symbol of economic efficiency. From the point of view of rational economics, this might appear questionable, but it was not without psychological

2. On the individual central banks see League of Nations, *Memorandum on Currency and Central Banks. 1913–1924*, 2 vols, Geneva, 1925.

importance. Thirdly, it was hoped that a substantial gold reserve would so impress the neutrals (and potential suppliers) that they would continue to accept a currency, in reality weakened by wartime inflation, at an exchange rate as close as possible to the official parity. Indeed the neutrals were largely under the illusion that, after the termination of hostilities, all the belligerents would once more stabilize their currencies at the pre-war parity.

Despite this carefully maintained façade, there was, in effect, no gold standard during the Great War. It was obvious that, after the currency crisis of July/August 1914, the warring parties would not be able to return to the gold standard, either within their own respective camps or vis-à-vis the neutrals. Internally, the money supply was enormously increased in the interests of war finance, a measure that was, of course, only feasible if the legal convertibility of notes remained in suspense. Externally, payments in gold were ruled out by the enormous import surpluses which could not in any circumstances be offset by the transfer of gold. The cumulative deficits on merchandise account for the five years 1914–18 amounted to 62·1 billion francs in France, 2·1 billion pounds in Britain, 31·6 billion lire in Italy, and 4·5 million roubles in Russia (up to and including 1917). Germany's import surplus, also at current prices, amounted to a total of 15·3 billion marks for the period August 1914 to November 1918, and that of Austria-Hungary (1914–17 inclusive) to some 11 billion kronen.[3] Thanks to their export surpluses, the neutrals' position in respect of gold remained very strong throughout; but here, in what remained of the world economy outside the warring camps, the intrinsically feasible restoration of the gold standard was frustrated by the absence of a currency strong enough to take the lead. The pound, as a controlled wartime currency, had ceased to play that role. Gold itself was no substitute since a number of neutral nations were opposed to an excessive influx of the metal. Before the war the gauge of a currency's quality had been its convertibility at all times into gold. But conversely the monetary quality of gold lay in its convertibility at all times into any other currency. During the war, however, this was no longer the case. In the absence of a

3. For the Allies, see League of Nations, *Memorandum on Balances of Payments and Foreign Trade Balances 1910–1924*, 2 vols, Geneva, 1925, vol. II. In respect of the Central Powers see Brown, *The International Gold Standard*, vol. I, pp. 52ff.

universal yardstick the various 'hard' neutral currencies tended to fluctuate, not only in relation to the wartime currencies, but also in relation to each other.[4] Wherever the influence of the warring parties extended the gold standard was replaced by two competing exchange control systems with administered parities. In the neutral money markets there emerged a complex of free exchange rates.

TABLE 17

FOREIGN TRADE (MERCHANDISE ACCOUNT) OF THE EUROPEAN ALLIES, AT CURRENT PRICES

		1910/13	1914	1915	1916	1917	1918
France	Exports	6·5	4·9	3·9	6·2	6·0	4·7
(billion	Imports	8·0	6·4	11·0	20·6	27·6	22·3
francs)	Balance	−1·5	−1·5	−7·1	−14·4	−21·6	−17·6
Gt Britain	Exports	474	431	385	506	527	501
(million	Imports	611	601	753	851	994	1,285
pounds)	Balance	−137	−170	−368	−345	−467	−784
Italy	Exports	2·3	2·2	2·5	3·1	3·3	3·3
(billion	Imports	3·5	2·9	4·7	8·4	14·0	16·0
lire)	Balance	−1·2	−0·7	−2·2	−5·3	−10·7	−12·7
Russia	Exports	1·5	1·0	0·4	0·6	0·5	—
(billion	Imports	1·2	1·1	1·1	2·8	2·0	—
roubles)	Balance	+0·3	−0·1	−0·7	−2·2	−1·5	—

SOURCE: League of Nations, *Memorandum on Balances of Payments and Foreign Trade Balances, 1910–1924*, 2 vols, Geneva, 1925, vol. II.
The values for Russia relate only to exports crossing the Empire's western borders.

The currencies of the belligerent countries were also traded in the neutral markets, sometimes at a substantial discount as compared with the official rate, with the result that there was a dual exchange rate for war currencies. If, for reasons of prestige, a government wanted to bring the value of its currency on the neutral, uncontrolled markets into line with the official rate, it would have to intervene to support that currency. In fact this sometimes happened, but there were limits to the practice, since the first priority

4. Compare, for example, the fluctuations of the various belligerent and neutral currencies against the Swiss franc, in C. Blankart, *Die Devisenpolitik während des Weltkrieges* (*August 1914–November 1918*), Füssli, Zurich, 1919. Brown, *The International Gold Standard*, records fluctuations against the dollar.

for foreign exchange was the need to finance essential imports (both public and private).

On the Allied side the chief currency problem consisted in maintaining the parity of the pound in relation to the dollar, for the pound in its turn buttressed the currencies of the other European Allies.[5] After the outbreak of war, the exchange rate of the British pound was initially high because fugitive capital was pouring into London from various other countries. But gradually this situation began to change as a result of official armaments buying in the United States, the growing civilian import surplus and the war credits granted by Britain to her Allies. From the summer of 1915 the foreign exchange problem was in the main a dollar problem. In 1915 Britain transferred to the U.S.A. gold to a total of 328 million dollars, a third of which was shipped across the Atlantic while the remainder came from British holdings in Canada. Further shipments followed, but it was clear that equilibrium in the balance of payments could not be maintained solely by gold movements, even had this been desirable. Large transfers of gold served neither the interests of the British who wanted to husband their gold reserve, nor those of the Americans who feared a strong inflationary surge. Accordingly the balance of payments was brought into equilibrium largely by movements of capital.

In the summer of 1915, at the instigation of the government, a consortium of private British banks negotiated a credit of more than 50 million dollars, and the Bank of England was instructed to purchase dollar securities held by British nationals. From August 1915 the government began to intervene in the foreign exchange markets in order to stabilize the parity of the pound in relation to the dollar, the requisite dollars being obtained by the sale of Treasury Bills in New York. In October 1916 a joint Anglo–French loan of over 500 million dollars was floated in the United States, half of it (the equivalent of some 50 million pounds) falling to Britain. As from the end of 1915 the British government systematically acquired private holdings of marketable dollar securities in order to sell them in America.[6] This operation resulted

5. Besides the study already mentioned by W. A. Brown, see more particularly E. V. Morgan, *Studies in British Financial Policy, 1914–1925*, Macmillan, London, 1952.

6. In January 1917 the British government was given powers to call in this paper, if necessary against the holders' wishes.

in the repatriation of a sizeable number of American securities and it was due in large measure to this that the U.S.A. moved from a net debtor to a net creditor position. Despite this supporting operation the British government was to experience difficulty from the autumn of 1916 onwards in finding the necessary foreign exchange. An aggravating factor was the advice given in November of that year by the Federal Reserve Board to American financial institutions, warning them that, from a banking point of view, it would not be sound policy to accept many of the belligerents' long-term loans, since there could be no certainty of their being redeemed. The foreign exchange problem was solved only with America's entry into the war, after which the necessary dollar credits were made available by the U.S. Treasury. By the end of the war the British government was in credit with her allies to the extent of some 7 billion dollars, whereas her debts amounted to some 4 billion dollars, most of which was owing to the U.S.A., though there were also smaller sums in respect of Canada, Japan, the European neutrals and the Latin-American countries.[7] In addition, there had been substantial liquidations of short-term and long-term foreign investments, some through the agency of the government and some on private initiative.

Both France and Russia sought to attach themselves to the dollar-sterling bloc.[8] In order to finance the country's import surpluses the Banque de France sold all the gold that had flowed in immediately after the outbreak of war (over 400 million francs), and also transferred a further 160 million francs of its earlier gold holdings to Great Britain, Spain and the U.S.A. But in the long term the French found it even harder than the British to stabilize the exchange rate and to finance import surpluses solely by surrendering gold. As early as 1914 the government and the Banque de France had begun to sell Treasury Bills abroad. However, this course placed a strain on the country's creditworthiness and hence was little more than a stopgap. Though in 1914 France had been a major international creditor, much of her foreign investment was in Russia and had been immobilized by the war. The French

7. See Morgan, *Studies in British Financial Policy*, pp. 320ff.

8. See H. Truchy, *Les finances de guerre de la France*, Presses Universitaires de France, Paris, 1926; and P. N. Apostol, M. W. Bernatzky and A. M. Michelson, *Russian Public Finance During the War*, Yale University Press, New Haven, 1928.

government therefore sought to extend inter-Allied cooperation from the military to the financial field. In February 1915 agreement was reached in principle on financial cooperation between the three main Allies, and in April France for the first time received a substantial credit from Britain. To finance its import surpluses the Russian government first had recourse to those assets, amounting in all to some 500 million roubles, which it held abroad, principally in France when the war broke out. In December 1914 it sold gold to the value of 8 million pounds to Britain. By the beginning of 1915 disposable assets abroad were exhausted and, although the Russian government was subsequently to make repeated transfers of gold to foreign countries, it relied thereafter largely on borrowings, for the most part from Great Britain.

These early Allied borrowings from Britain laid the foundations for a complex and comprehensive system of inter-Allied war credits. The formal basis for future inter-Allied cooperation in the financial field was laid down at a conference of finance ministers held in February 1915. The Allied governments agreed to collaborate closely in matters such as the granting of credit to the lesser Allies, the floating of joint foreign loans and the establishment of close liaison between central banks. Thereafter collaboration was sustained by means of regular consultations. Until the entry of the United States into the war Britain acted as the Allies' banker, a role she traditionally assumed in European wars. France, too, granted credits, if on a smaller scale, to Russia, Serbia, Belgium and Greece. Altogether, inter-Allied war credits had risen by 1 April 1917 to 4·3 billion dollars, 88 per cent of these having been granted by the British and 12 per cent by the French governments. The main recipients were Russia (48 per cent of the total amount), Italy (16 per cent), France (13 per cent), British Dominions and colonies (13 per cent) and Belgium (7 per cent). The remainder was shared out between Greece, Portugal, Romania and Serbia.[9]

In view of their own foreign exchange problems, the British government and the Bank of England could maintain their role of bankers to the alliance only by placing an extremely severe strain on the country's international creditor position. However, in consequence of the close cooperation agreed upon in February 1915, the Bank of England received a measure of support from the

9. See H. G. Moulton and L. Pasvolsky, *War Debts and World Prosperity* The Brookings Institution, Washington, 1932.

central banks of France, Russia and (to a lesser extent) Italy, which handed over gold worth a total of 983 million dollars.[10] British war credits were not tied to purchases in Britain, being also intended to help the Allies finance their import surpluses vis-à-vis third parties. The Russian government, for example, spent in the United States nearly half of the monies lent by Britain.[11] Nevertheless, in neutral money markets difficulty was experienced in tying in the exchange rates of the continental European Allies with the dollar-sterling bloc. In New York, in August 1915, the franc was quoted at 8 per cent, the lira at 17 per cent and the rouble at 28 per cent below their pre-war parities. Thereafter it proved possible to stabilize the franc at this level, but the lira and the rouble continued to fall.

After America's accession and the beginning of the second phase of the war, Britain and France continued to make loans available that were, if anything, higher than during the appreciably longer first phase. But America's war credits soon put those of the European Allies into the shade. Thenceforward America gradually became the alliance's most important financier. It was a role that inevitably devolved on her, for the Allied foreign exchange problem was essentially one of import surpluses vis-à-vis the United States. From the outbreak of war up till 1 April 1917 Allied purchases of U.S. goods amounted to some 7 billion dollars. Finance for these imports came from the following sources: exports to the U.S.A., 1·6 billion dollars; sales of gold, 1·1 billion dollars; liquidation of short-term U.S. foreign debts, 500 million dollars; repatriation of American securities and other investments from foreign holders, 1·4 billion dollars; credits, 2·4 billion dollars.[12] After America's entry into the war, the European Allies' import surpluses were mainly financed by U.S. government loans. Between 1917 and the Armistice Allied imports of armaments and other merchandise from the U.S.A. amounted to 10·3 billion dollars; over the same period the Allies received from the American government credits totalling 7·1 billion dollars.[13] American credits were usually

10. In formal terms, what was involved was not a sale, like earlier inter-Allied gold transfers, but a loan for the period of the war credits.

11. Apostol, Bernatzky and Michelson, *Russian Public Finance*, p. 312.

12. Estimates by Morgan et al., cit. Brown, *The International Gold Standard*, vol. I, p. 65.

13. Moulton and Pasvolsky, *War Debts*, pp. 42, 426.

granted as part of the Allies' purchasing programmes and hence were tied to specific purposes and were not intended to be used for the stabilization of exchange rates in the money markets of third countries.

Great Britain and the United States each, for a time, acted as bankers to the alliance, but the effect in either case was very different. For Britain, credits proved a burden since most of the recipients wanted dollars, not pounds. Hence she had to turn to the United States to refinance the credits she had granted. America, on the other hand, was in effect financing her own exporters, thus promoting her agriculture and industry; moreover, widespread prosperity meant that there was no difficulty in raising the necessary funds within her own boundaries. In this way war credits helped to consolidate the country's economic primacy.

TABLE 18
INTER-ALLIED GOVERNMENT DEBTS AT THE TIME OF THE ARMISTICE
(MILLIONS OF DOLLARS)

Debtors	Creditors			Total
	U.S.A.	Great Britain	France	
Great Britain	3,696	—	—	3,696
France	1,970	1,683	—	3,653
Russia	188	2,472	955	3,615
Italy	1,031	1,855	75	2,961
Belgium	172	434	535	1,141
Others	21	570	672	1,263
	7,078	7,014	2,237	16,329

SOURCE: H. G. Moulton, L. Pasvolsky, *War Debts and World Prosperity*, Brookings Institution, Washington, 1932, p. 426.

Besides the U.S.A., Great Britain and France, other Allies were also creditors but for smaller amounts. 'Others' in the above table includes Serbia, Romania, some of the British Dominions, Greece, Portugal and Cuba.

Currency problems did not loom so large for the Central Powers which were in any case cut off from the world market by the blockade. Within the economic area still accessible to Germany and her allies trade relations became increasingly dependent on bilateral negotiations at government level, and the significance of money as a universal means of exchange dwindled accordingly. Within the alliance, Germany and Austria–Hungary found themselves compelled to give economic support to Bulgaria and, more especially, to Turkey.[14] Although Austria–Hungary helped to supply the other allies, she in her turn was dependent on German aid. Settlements in respect of these various transactions were put off until after the war. Trade with neighbouring neutrals inevitably resulted in export surpluses among the latter who, by the end of the war, held considerable quantities of Reichsbank notes and other mark securities.

Foreign trade relations of a rather specialized kind consisted in exploiting the occupied territories, but here the very fact of compulsion meant that there were no foreign exchange problems. What imports remained available to the Central Powers depended primarily on the Allied blockade. Though on occasion the financing of import surpluses was difficult, it did not constitute a crucial bottleneck. However, the Central Powers were not able to maintain for their currencies the fiction of a fixed parity with gold in the neutral money markets. In New York, as early as December 1914, the mark and the krone had already suffered falls, and by November 1916 they were standing at 26 per cent and 41 per cent respectively below their pre-war parities.[15] In 1918 Turkish paper money, issued at par three years previously, stood at a discount of some 80 per cent against coin in the domestic market.[16] Nevertheless, despite the depreciation of currencies and fluctuations in exchange rates, wartime governments maintained a reasonably effective control over their currencies which therefore enjoyed a better reputation than the position really warranted. Neither the internal value of money nor the rates of exchange between currencies had felt the full impact of wartime inflation. To some extent this was due to strict controls at home and abroad, and partly also to the public's continuing confidence in the value of money. Most people anticipated that, when peace returned, both the internal and external value of money would be restored to the pre-war level, pending which they were perfectly prepared to hold large quantities of bank notes and other monetary assets. In this way monetary problems had been merely deferred, not solved, and hence the Armistice

14. See A. Emin, *Turkey in the World War*, Yale University Press, New Haven, 1930; G. T. Danaillow, *Les effets de la guerre en Bulgarie*, Presses Universitaires de France, Paris, 1932.

15. Brown, *The International Gold Standard*, vol. I, p. 49.

16. Emin, *Turkey in the World War*.

did not at first bring any alleviation. Rather, the situation was aggravated.

War Finance

The collapse of the gold standard was brought about by the massive war effort of the leading trading nations. Even before 1914 the arms race had led to an enormous rise in European military expenditure, enormous, at least, by the scale of the day. According to German estimates – in each case calculated at the par rate of exchange – defence expenditure for the year 1913 amounted in Germany to 503 million dollars, in Russia to 488 million dollars, in Britain to 355 million dollars, in France to 316 million dollars, and in Austria–Hungary to 172 million dollars. This meant that the population had to bear a charge *per capita* of 8 dollars in France, 7·8 dollars in Britain, 7·4 dollars in Germany, 3·3 dollars in Austria–Hungary, and 2·8 dollars in Russia.[17] The proportion of armaments expenditure to national income on the eve of the war amounted in Germany to 3·5 per cent, in Britain to 3·6 per cent and in Austria–Hungary to about 4 per cent.[18] Russia engaged in even higher armaments expenditure: some 6 per cent of national income.[19]

During the Great War the public expenditure of the belligerents rapidly reached a level vastly higher than anyone had known before. Everywhere the first war budgets were substantially in

17. See Reichsarchiv pub. *Kriegsrüstung und Kriegswirtschaft*, vol. I: *Die militärische, wirtschaftliche und finanzielle Rüstung Deutschlands von der Reichsgründung bis zum Ausbruch des Weltkrieges*, with appendices, 2 parts, Mittler, Berlin, 1930. part II, (appendices), p. 540.

18. For Germany: war expenditure and net national product from W. Hoffmann, F. Grumbach and H. Hesse, *Das Wachstum der deutschen Wirtschaft seit der Mitte des 19.Jahrhunderts*, Springer, Berlin/Heidelberg/New York, 1965, pp. 261, 723, 825ff. For Britain: War expenditure from E. V. Morgan, op. cit., National income at factor cost from P. Deane and W. A. Cole, *British Economic Growth 1688–1959*, 2nd ed., Cambridge University Press, 1967, p. 330. For Austria-Hungary: War expenditure from Reichsarchiv pub., op. cit., part II (appendices), p. 530. National income from estimates by Fellner and Gürtler, cit. from N. Gross, *Industrialization in Austria in the Nineteenth Century*, diss., University of California, Berkeley, 1966, p. 195. (Arms expenditure amounts to 3·7 per cent of Fellner's estimate of national income and to 4·1 per cent of Gürtler's.)

19. War expenditure from Apostol, Bernatzky and Michelson, op. cit., p. 66.

excess of peacetime budgets – and this was only a beginning. In the years that followed, total war involved a continuous rise in public expenditure. Compared with the first, the final war budget represented an increase of 505 per cent in Germany, 448 per cent in France, 562 per cent in Britain and (up to 1916) 315 per cent in Russia. The growth in public expenditure was the result both of the war itself and of the associated inflation, but it is almost impossible to ascertain precisely how great was the war expenditure (as distinct from total public expenditure) in each individual country. If by war expenditure in the broader sense we mean all expenditure arising out of the war, then four items are deserving of special mention: actual military expenditure; war-related expenditures by civil authorities (e.g. transport and the administration of controls); subsidies including interest on the national debt; and, fourthly, credits to Allies. Only the first two items are economically relevant in the sense of there having been a corresponding absorbtion of goods; from the fiscal aspect, however, all four items are of equal importance.

In those days, only a part of defence expenditure was itemized in the budget. In Great Britain and the United States expenditure on the armed forces, on war credits and on debt servicing (which for the most part concerned debts newly incurred) was shown as such, but not war-related expenditure incurred by the civil authorities. In France, military expenditure and debt servicing are shown as defence expenditure. In addition there were special accounts (*dépenses recouvrables* and *comptes spéciaux*) which largely consisted of war expenditure by the civil authorities and in loans to allies. A number of items of war expenditure might also be included in 'civil' expenditure. In Germany and Russia the financing of the war was effected by means of special budgets: in Germany, an extraordinary budget and in Russia, a special war budget which existed alongside the ordinary and extraordinary parliamentary budgets. There were both fiscal and political reasons for this particular form of accounting. It was customary, indeed *de rigueur*, for special budgets to be covered by the creation of credits, as opposed to the ordinary budget, which was covered by taxation. Thus it was possible to make a show of adhering to

National income from P. Studenski, *The Income of Nations, Theory, Measurement and Analysis: Past and Present*, New York University Press, 1958, p. 148. Calculated on this basis, the exact proportion is seen to be 5·8 per cent.

conventional financial practice even if, in the end, no more than a small fraction of public expenditure was met by taxation. Since, moreover, neither the extraordinary nor the war budget was subject to parliamentary control, governments actually incorporated part of their 'normal' expenditure in the war budget.

TABLE 19

PUBLIC EXPENDITURE DURING THE FIRST WORLD WAR
(BILLIONS OF MARKS, FRANCS, POUNDS, ROUBLES OR DOLLARS)

			War expenditure	Debt servicing	War credits	Civil expenditure
			Share (per cent)			
	Public expenditure during the war					
Germany	1914–18	159·0	83	15	—	2
France	1914–18	170·5	79	11	—	10
Great Britain	1914–18	10·6	62	7	16	16
Russia	1914–16	35·5	76	6	—	18
U.S.A.	1917–19	34·8	54	2	26	17

SOURCES: K. Roesler, *Die Finanzpolitik des Deutschen Reiches im Ersten Weltkrieg*, Duncker & Humblot, Berlin 1967, pp. 197ff; G. Jèze, *Les dépenses de guerre de la France*, Presses Universitaires de France, Paris, 1926, p. 22; E. V. Morgan, *Studies in British Financial Policy, 1914–1925*, London, 1952, p. 101; P. N. Apostol, M. W. Bernatzky, A. M. Michelson, *Russian Public Finance during the War*, Yale University Press, New Haven, 1928, pp. 73–220; C. Gilbert, *American Financing of World War I*. Greenwood, Westport, Conn., 1970, pp. 68ff.

Details concerning the war expenditure of individual countries tend to vary widely, since findings depend entirely on the way it is distinguished from civil expenditure – whether, that is, debt servicing and war credits are counted as war expenditure, and whether account is taken of the heavy cost, in the first years of peace, of demobilization and other wartime legacies. Moreover, government accounting in wartime was not always meticulous and hence it is sometimes difficult to reconstruct reliable figures. All comparisons hitherto drawn between the war expenditure of the belligerents have dispensed with detailed individual estimates on the pretext that the whole increase in expenditure was due, directly or indirectly, to the war. Thus, in the case of every country, war expenditure has been defined as the difference between total public expenditure and a notional 'peacetime' budget corresponding to public expenditure during the last year of peace, the assumption being that the latter item would have remained constant had there been no war. Though it may have serious drawbacks, this method has the beauty of simplicity and recommends itself to anyone who, without too much tedious research, wishes to establish comparisons and place a figure on the sum total of the world's wartime expenditure. It is with these reservations in mind that one such table is reproduced below. Here, credits to Allied countries are subsumed under war expenditure, while credits received have been deducted therefrom to avoid duplication. What emerges is war expenditure totalling 209 billion dollars at current prices, or 82 billion dollars at 1913 prices. Conversion into constant prices is always a problem and in this case is deserving of further scrutiny. In terms of approximate order of magnitude the findings would seem acceptable; a detailed study of Germany's war finances confirms that the scale of war expenditure in money terms was largely attributable to the rise in prices.[20]

TABLE 20
WAR EXPENDITURE DURING THE GREAT WAR (1914–19)
(BILLIONS OF DOLLARS)

	'Normal' public expenditure	'War expenditure'	War expenditure at 1913 prices
France	5·0	28·2	9·3
Gt Britain	4·7	43·8	21·2
Remainder of Empire	5·9	5·8	1·8
Italy	2·9	14·7	3·2
Russia	5·9	16·3	5·4
U.S.A.	2·9	36·2	17·1
Other Allies	3·3	2·0	(−0·3)
Allies	30·6	147·0	57·7
Germany	3·3	47·0	19·9
Austria–Hungary	5·4	13·4	4·7
Bulgaria, Turkey	1·4	1·1	0·1
Central Powers	10·1	61·5	24·7
All belligerents	40·7	208·5	82·4

SOURCE: H. Mendershausen, *The Economics of War*, Prentice-Hall, New York, 1941, p. 305.
'Other Allies' denotes Belgium, Greece, Japan, Portugal, Romania, Serbia. In terms of constant prices the war expenditure of these countries was, on balance, clearly more than offset by Allied loans.

20. K. Roesler, *Die Finanzpolitik des deutschen Reiches im Ersten Weltkrieg*, Duncker & Humblot, Berlin, 1967, pp. 197ff.

In principle, the problems of war finance were the same in every country. The 'modern' method of financing the war through the medium of central banks – a method practised throughout the conflict – betrays a characteristic rhythm, namely the creation of money alternating with the absorption of purchasing power.[21] The government obtained cash from the central bank in exchange for its own short-term liabilities. This paper would be either renewed or redeemed out of revenue obtained by the state from taxation or longer loans. The sale of War Loans or other government paper outside of the central bank meant, just as did increased taxation, the absorption of the purchasing power of private individuals, except that it left an accumulation of assets in private hands which could be turned into purchasing power after the war. The creation of money by the state unleashed an inflationary impulse which was at first largely concentrated on the armaments industry, but later transmitted itself to the economy as a whole by way of the multiplier effect. At first additional demand was met by the utilization of unemployed capital and labour, but once full employment had been attained (as happened in most countries roughly in the spring of 1915), state and private interests found themselves competing for the limited productive capacity available. Hence the absorption of private purchasing power by taxation and loans served two purposes. First, it slowed down the price rise, itself undesirable on several counts. Second, and more important, war finance acted as a monetary regulator. By the absorption of purchasing power, private demand was curbed and it was precisely this – the adaptation of the economy from peacetime to wartime production – that was the whole purpose of wartime economic policy. The less the state succeeded in regulating money demand by reducing private purchasing power, the more it was compelled to resort to direct controls. Theoretically if is possible to imagine two models: in the case of the first the state attracts the desired real resources solely by means of harsh taxation; in the second case, that of an inflationary economic policy, money gradually loses its function as a medium of exchange,. while the allocation of factors of production and the distribution of goods are increasingly handled by central command. Convinced liberals

21. The theory of war finance is dealt with in a number of readily available sources. E. g., see A. C. Pigou, *The Political Economy of War*, rev. ed., Macmillan, London, 1940.

thought the first model practicable, whereas the second came a good deal closer to reality, as will be demonstrated below with references to Germany, France, Britain, Russia and the United States.[22]

TABLE 21
NATIONAL BUDGET; 1914–18

		1914	1915	1916	1917	1918	1914–18
Germany	Expenditure	8·8	25·8	27·8	52·2	44·9	159·0
(billions of	Income	2·5	1·8	2·1	8·0	7·4	21·8
marks)	Deficit	6·3	24·0	25·7	44·2	37·0	137·2
France	Expenditure	10·4	22·1	36·8	44·7	56·6	170·6
(billions of	Income	4·2	4·1	4·9	6·2	6·8	26·2
francs)	Deficit	6·2	18·0	31·9	38·5	49·9	144·5
Gt Britain	Expenditure	560	1,560	2,200	2,700	2,580	9,590
(millions	Income	230	340	570	710	890	2,730
of pounds)	Deficit	330	1,220	1,630	1,990	1,690	6,860
Russia	Expenditure	5·7	11·7	18·1	—	—	35·5
(billions of	Income	2·9	2·8	4·0	—	—	9·7
roubles)	Deficit	2·8	8·9	14·1	—	—	25·8
U.S.A.	Expenditure	—	—	0·7	2·1	13·8	16·6
(billions of	Income	—	—	0·7	1·1	4·2	6·0
dollars)	Deficit	—	—	—	1·0	9·6	10·0

SOURCES: K. Roesler, *Die Finanzpolitik des Deutschen Reiches im Ersten Weltkrieg*, Duncker & Humblot, Berlin, 1967, pp. 197ff; G. Jèze, *Les dépenses de guerre de la France*, Presses Universitaires de France, Paris, 1926, p. 22; E. V. Morgan, *Studies in British Financial Policy, 1914–1925*, London, 1952, p. 101; P. N. Apostol, M. W. Bernatzky, A. M. Michelson, *Russian Public Finance during the War*, Yale University Press, New Haven, 1928, pp. 73–220; C. Gilbert, *American Financing of World War I*, Greenwood, Westport, Conn., 1970, pp. 68ff.

22. To obviate tiresome repetition, the list has been left incomplete although, of course, a study of the wartime financial policy of Italy or Austria-Hungary would be equally rewarding. On Italy see L. Einaudi, *La guerra e il sistema tributaria italiana*, Laterza, Bari, 1927, summed up in L. Einaudi, *La condotta economica e gli effetti sociali della guerra Italiana*, Laterza, Bari, 1933; F. A. Répaci, *La finanza Italiana nel ventento 1913–1932*, Einaudi, Turin, 1934; F. A. Répaci, 'Il costo finanzario in Italia della prima guerra mondiale', in *Studi in Onore di Gaetano Pietra*, Cappelli, Rocca San Casciano, 1955. On Austria-Hungary, see, G. Gratz and R. Schüller, *Der wirtschaftliche Zusammenbruch Österreich-Ungarns*, Hölder-Pichler-Tempsky, Vienna, 1930;

Germany

In the German Empire the first steps towards financial mobilization had already been taken during the final decade of the nineteenth century.[23] Hence, when war came, the necessary legislation was conveniently to hand and on 4 August 1914 it was placed on the statute book. The desire to adhere to the gold standard at least ostensibly, and hence to make as few amendments as possible to the Bank Law of 1875, involved having recourse to a somewhat complicated makeshift. Thus special banks of issue, the so-called 'loan banks', under the administration but legally independent of the Reichsbank, were brought into being with powers to issue their own bank notes (loan bank notes) against collateral in the form of goods and securities. The use of appropriate interest rate differentials enabled these new institutions to take over the function of creating cash for private industry, thus giving the Reichsbank greater freedom to concentrate on war finance. Most of the terms of the Reichsbank Law, more especially the provisions relating to reserve requirements, though formally retained, were rendered meaningless in practice by two amendments. For its cash reserves, the Reichsbank was permitted to use not only gold but also the paper money issued by the new loan banks and, for the balance of its liquid assets, could hold government Treasury Bills as well as trade bills up to an unrestricted amount.[24] This meant that there was no longer any restriction on the creation of money by the state, and the Reichsbank's holding of Treasury Bills increased as rapidly as did the number of notes in circulation.

Financial mobilization, like all the other economic preparations for war, was based on the premise of a short war financed exclu-

A. Popovics, *Das Geldwesen im Kriege*, Hölder-Pichler-Tempsky, Vienna, 1925. Information on the financial policy of the other belligerent countries may be found in the relevant national monographs published in the Carnegie series.

23. W. Lotz, *Die deutsche Staatsfinanzwirtschaft im Kriege*, Deutsche Verlags-Anstalt, Stuttgart/Berlin/Leipzig, 1927; Roesler, *Die Finanzpolitik des deutschen Reiches*; R. Andexel, *Imperialismus – Staatsfinanzen, Rüstung, Krieg. Probleme der Rüstungsfinanzierung des deutschen Imperialismus*, Akademie-Verlag, Berlin, 1968.

24. The term 'Treasury Bill' was used in this context because of its analogy to the trade bill and was intended to perfect the 'camouflage'; previously the only short-dated paper had been Treasury Bonds without interest.

sively by borrowings. There had been no preparation whatever for the kind of war-oriented fiscal policy demanded by a protracted conflict. In February 1915 Helfferich took over the Imperial Treasury; in presenting his budget for 1915/16 he confirmed that the intention was to find the means for waging the war 'almost exclusively' by borrowings: i.e. the 'temporary expedient' of loans from banks of issue which would then be regularly funded by War Loans. The financing of the war was based expressly on the expectation that, when peace came, the enemy would have to foot the bill. 'The instigators of this war have brought upon themselves the leaden weight of billions; it is for them, not us, to drag it with them for decades to come.'[25] Hence in formulating its fiscal policy, the government set its sights very low. Taxation was to cover only 'ordinary' expenditure unrelated to the war, and also the interest on the National Debt. But even this proved difficult enough. In the 1915/16 budget, tax increases could only be avoided because a final payment was still outstanding from the defence contribution (a non-recurring levy imposed in 1913), and also because even 'normal' military expenditure was largely absorbed into the extraordinary budget. In its next budget the government was unable to avoid imposing new taxes which were in any case being demanded on socio-political grounds by the German Socialist Party and by public opinion in general. That the big profiteers should enrich themselves unpenalized by taxation had become intolerable.

From the start the German fiscal system was ill-equipped to cope with war finance because income tax, which in Britain had proved simple to operate and exceptionally productive, was the preserve of the Federal States and internal politics precluded any change. Before 1914 Imperial taxes consisted of customs dues and excise duties, these last applying mainly to non-essentials such as coffee, liquor and tobacco, i.e. precisely those sources of revenue which, because of the blockade and the economic decline, could only yield diminishing returns. But in 1917 an excise duty was levied on coal which was still in plentiful supply. No one appeared to be worried by the fact that the Empire inevitably paid the coal tax itself, in as much as it was the chief purchaser of industrial goods, and such war expenditure could, of course, always be foisted on to the extraordinary budget. Of longer-term significance was the general turnover tax introduced in 1916 (first called the

25. Cit. from Roesler, *Die Finanzpolitik des deutschen Reiches*, pp. 71ff.

'turnover of goods stamp'). Initially the rate was ·01 per cent of turnover and, from 1918, ·05 per cent. The tax applied to all paid work, with the exception of the wholesale trade and the liberal professions. A special tax of 10 per cent was also introduced for a number of luxury goods.

A war profits tax applying to corporations was announced in December 1915 and introduced the following June. Critics opined that this long incubation period had given the profiteers ample opportunity to salt away their gains.[26] The new tax, at first conceived as a non-recurring levy, was imposed on profits made since the outbreak of war in so far they exceeded the average of the five years preceding the war. Excess profits were taxed on a sliding scale ranging from 10 to 50 per cent. In February 1917, when collection had already begun, the rate went up to 60 per cent. A new war profits tax, introduced in 1918 in respect of profits made since June 1916, envisaged a standard rate of 60 per cent with concessions only in respect of 'low' excess profits of under 1 million marks. In the case of individuals the war profits tax was initially levied on the increase in their fortunes between 1913 and 1916, and hence surplus incomes which had been consumed escaped taxation. Subsequently the war profits tax on the individual was no longer confined to an increase in assets but was also extended to income in excess of his assessment for Federal State income tax for 1913. This Imperial tax was calculated on a sliding scale up to a maximum of 50 per cent. Besides the war profits tax there was also a wealth tax rising to ·05 per cent on assets in excess of 1 million marks.

Now, as before the war, all Imperial taxes were collected by the finance departments of the individual states. However, in 1918 one step at least was made towards the standardization of the financial system, with the creation of the Imperial Financial Court as a supreme tribunal in questions of Imperial taxation. This development and the 'invention' of a general turnover tax, were among the few enduring results of the financial policy pursued during the war.

In all 44 per cent of ordinary revenue was provided by excise and stamp duties, 42 per cent by the defence contribution and war profits tax and 14 per cent by various levies, e.g. on the profits of the Reichsbank and the loan banks. From the viewpoint of rigorous fiscal policy, the main shortcoming was the kidglove treatment

26. ibid., p. 73.

of company profits and private incomes. The war profits taxes were inadequate in many respects: not only were they imposed too late but, being applicable only to *changes* in income and profit, they exempted, by their very nature, large profits and incomes in so far as these were the same as they had been in peacetime. Moreover the manner in which the imposts were levied and collected afforded the profiteers ample opportunity to conceal their gains. In extenuation, the Imperial government pleaded the custom whereby taxes on assets were the preserve of the Federal States and further argued that, since far-reaching changes were undesirable in the exceptional circumstances of the war, any comprehensive reform of public finance must be postponed until its conclusion. Up till the end, fiscal policy was based on the constant hope that, after the war had been won, the cost would be borne by the enemy. On top of this, there was the reluctance (predictable enough in view of the power structure), to do anything that would arouse the concerted opposition of industry. Taxation more or less covered ordinary expenditure so that there could be little or no formal objection to existing fiscal policy. But since, during the war, government expenditure was largely dealt with by way of the extraordinary budget, the overall significance of taxation was relatively small. In the five fiscal years covering the war, revenue from taxation met at most some 14 per cent of Imperial expenditure. Hence the absorption of purchasing power remained essentially the function of the loan banks.

The main burden of raising revenue was borne by War Loans, nine in all, which were floated in March and September of every year, beginning with the autumn of 1914. The terms were in all cases similar, namely a return of 5 per cent on an issue price approximately at par. By pre-war standards the yield was attractive. Moreover each loan was launched to the accompaniment of much patriotic propaganda. There were no conversion rights as in Britain nor, in view of the similar terms of each issue, would this have served any purpose. The chief subscribers were the public, since the savings banks purchased comparatively small amounts for their own account, and the commercial banks even less. An appreciable proportion of the first issue (some 20 per cent) was taken up by the public with the help of credit facilities provided by the loan banks against collateral, but later, in view of the generally high level of liquidity, this practice ceased.

Up to the fourth War Loan (March 1916) the proceeds of the loans were in each case greater than the short-term debt outstanding on the final subscription date. From the fifth War Loan onwards (September 1916) the proceeds failed to keep pace with the rapidly increasing total National Debt. On the other hand, considerable numbers of Treasury Bonds without interest were sold on the open market, outside of the Reichsbank. This has been put down to the divergence of personal and corporate incomes. While real wages and salaries were falling, many concerns were making huge profits but could not, because of general shortages and the centralized control of real resources, invest their money in fixed assets on working capital and hence necessarily turned to government securities. Here they showed a preference for short-term forms of investment which could be rapidly liquidated after the end of the war and of wartime controls.

Because of this uneven development in the field of savings, not only was there a change in the composition of the National Debt so far as loans and Treasury Bonds were concerned, but the War Loans themselves gradually lost their 'popular' character. The proportion of small subscriptions of 2,000 marks and less dropped from 16·5 per cent to 8·2 per cent between the first and ninth War Loans, whereas the proportion of large subscriptions in excess of 1 million marks rose from 19·5 per cent to 33·6 per cent over the same period. For the time being the open-market disposal of short-term Treasury Bonds served, as did the War Loans themselves, to immobilize surplus purchasing power; but since the public now held assets which could be rapidly run down for cash, these measures made the eventual problem of mopping up the surplus all the greater.

At the end of the last fiscal year of the war (1918/19) the Imperial debt had reached 156·1 billion marks, an increase of 150·7 billion marks since March 1914. Of the total debt 40 per cent was short-term, half of which again (some 30 billion marks) was held by the Reichsbank. It has not been possible to discover how the remainder was apportioned as between the rest of the banking system and the public, though it is clear that the latter accounted for the major part.[27]

27. There are a few figures for the end of December 1918: Treasury Bonds at the Reichsbank, 27·2 billion marks; 'Loan banks' holdings of War Loans, 0·9 billion marks; War Loans held by the Prussian savings banks which ac-

France

After France had declared war the Banque de France placed an advance of 2·9 billion francs at the government's disposal against short-term Treasury Bonds. [28] This transaction, as also a corresponding increase in the bank's note issue, had already been provided for in 1911, under an agreement concluded between the central bank and the state against the possibility of mobilization. The ceiling put on the government's short-term indebtedness to the central bank had to be raised several times, finally attaining 27 billion francs in 1919.

At first the French government relied exclusively on borrowing, a course justified in December 1914 by the Finance Minister, M. Ribot, on the grounds that a country already hard hit by the war could not be asked to bear a still heavier tax burden. The use of taxation to meet the cost of the war was postponed until victory had been won. In fact, at this juncture the government was doling out with both hands the money newly created by the central bank and thus helping to generate war profits so huge as positively to invite fiscal intervention; but this the government failed, or perhaps had no wish to see. It was not until the middle of 1916, nearly two years after the outbreak of war, that the authorities departed from this policy and introduced higher taxation, on the grounds that current revenue should at least cover the interest on the National Debt. But once again the liquidation of actual war expenditure was put off until after the war. The French pre-war fiscal system was undoubtedly antiquated and was based on the principle of an individualism so extreme that any fiscal interference, or even official inquiries into a person's financial circumstances were regarded as an infringement of civil liberties. Consequently, indirect taxation accounted for a large part of the revenue, while direct taxation was confined for preference to concrete taxable objects such as land, urban property and commercial undertakings. In July 1914, just before war broke out, the

---

counted for 76 per cent of all deposits in German savings banks, 8·5 billion marks; total negotiable securities (trade bills and Treasury Bonds) held by commercial banks making returns, 16·0 billion marks. See Roesler, *Die Finanzpolitik des deutschen Reiches*, pp. 143, 210, 214, 219.

28. See Truchy, *Les finances de guerre*.

Assembly had voted a general tax on incomes at the very modest rate of 2 per cent. Its introduction had been planned for 1915 but was then postponed until the following year because of wartime conditions. Either traditional opposition to taxation was too strong, or fiscal policy was not pursued with sufficient energy; whatever the case, the new tax yielded a total of no more than some 0·9 billion francs over the three years 1916 to 1918. During the war, despite price rises, the old direct taxes brought in on average the same amount as before, i.e. a total of 4·1 billion francs for the period 1914–18. A war profits tax was introduced in 1916 as a special levy and, as in Germany, was conceived as a tax on profits in excess of normal peacetime profits. Initially it had been based on a flat rate of 50 per cent but from 1918 was calculated on a sliding scale ranging from 50 to 80 per cent. In 1917 and 1918 this tax yielded a total of 0·8 billion francs and thus can hardly have succeeded in effectively siphoning off what were quite abnormal profits. Measured against the target set in 1916, fiscal policy was inadequate. In 1918 interest on the National Debt exceeded income by 230 million francs, in other words the government had to borrow still more money to pay the interest on the existing debt. In all, 15 per cent of government expenditure was met by taxation, a proportion similar to that in Germany.

The first French War Loan was not floated until November 1915. This relative tardiness as compared with other countries was justified on the grounds that a government loan had been issued in July 1914 and that the difficult economic circumstances in the first year of war made another flotation impossible. Three further War Loans followed in 1916, 1917 and 1918. These took the form of *rentes perpétuelles* (undated stocks) which meant that the government was not bound to a fixed redemption date but might, after the elapse of a certain time, elect to redeem them. Even on the first War Loan, the yield of 5·7 per cent was relatively high. In all, War Loans brought in 24·1 billion francs. The French government depended for its funds largely on the sale of short-term Exchequer Bonds to the public. Besides the usual short-term *Bons du Trésor*, a new class of bond, *Bons de la Défense Nationale*, with a currency of three to twelve months, were placed on the market in September 1914. At first conceived purely as a means of bridging finance, these *Bons de la Défense Nationale* met with such an enthusiastic reception from the public that the government adopted them as a permanent medium of war finance. Short-term paper recommended itself to the government by its relatively low interest rate (from 3·5 to 5 per cent, depending on the state of the market) and, more especially, by the ease with which it could be sold. Its popularity with the public may be attributed to its ready negotiability, more particularly since bank deposits had been frozen in consequence of various moratoria. From February 1915, medium-term bonds – *Obligations de la Défense Nationale* – were placed on offer with a currency of between five and ten years, but the public preferred short-dated paper. A substantial portion of state indebtedness also arose from external borrowings, the main purpose of which was not, however, to cover the budget, but to acquire foreign currency. From 1914 to 1918 inclusive, a total of 130 billion francs was obtained by internal credit operations.[29] Of these, 42 per cent (55 billion francs) came from short and medium bonds, 25 per cent (32 billion francs) from foreign credits, 19 per cent (24 billion francs) from War Loans, 13 per cent (17 billion francs) from credits from the Central Banks, and 1 per cent (1·3 billion francs) from miscellaneous sources, including the government loan of July 1914.

Britain

The problem that overshadowed Great Britain's monetary and financial policy at the end of July and the beginning of August 1914 was that of the international liquidity crisis; itself produced by the tensions immediately preceding the war, its effect was, of course, felt most strongly in London as the financial centre of the world.[30] Thus the means of financing of the war were, so to speak, brought into being almost by accident. On 1 August 1914 the Bank of England asked for and was given authorization, customary at times of crisis, to exceed the fiduciary issue prescribed by the Bank Act of 1844. This gave the Bank more latitude for support operations, at the same time enabling it to provide funds in anticipation

29. ibid., p. 139. – Calculations of borrowings do not cover exactly the same period as that of the budget deficit. Hence borrowings for 1914–18 are shown as lower, and for 1919 as higher, than the budget deficit.

30. See Morgan, *Studies in British Financial Policy.* Also to be recommended are two earlier accounts: F. W. Hirst and J. E. Allen, *British War Budgets*, Oxford University Press, 1926; and J. Stamp, *Taxation during the War*, Oxford University Press, 1932.

of war spending. Additional funds were obtained by placing Treasury Bills on the open market and by the issue of currency notes in denominations of 10s. and £1. In November 1914 the first War Loan was floated to fund short-term debt, and the same month saw the presentation of the first war budget (as a supplement to the existing 1914–15 budget) which imposed a number of tax increases. On this occasion Lloyd George, then still Chancellor of the Exchequer, announced the government's intention of meeting at least a portion of the rising expenditure by means of taxation.[31] His successor, McKenna, in presenting the budget for 1916/17, formulated the principle that taxation should cover not only normal, peacetime expenditure but also interest payments on, and the management and prescribed redemptions of, the National Debt. This has been described as 'one of the strangest principles ever laid down in the history of public finance',[32] but whatever the case, it was a policy rather more harsh than that of most of the belligerents. Taxes rose with each succeeding budget. There were three main sources of revenue – income tax, which had already before the war proved both lucrative and capable of expansion, sundry indirect taxes, and the newly introduced excess profits duty.

Income tax   During the war the standard rate of income tax was progressively raised from 6·25 per cent to 30 per cent. This, combined with super-tax, meant that higher incomes were eventually subjected to a rate of rather more than 50 per cent.

Indirect taxes   One revolutionary innovation was McKenna's introduction of import duties in 1915, a measure which brought to an end Britain's time-honoured tradition of free trade. These duties had a dual function: firstly they provided funds for the Exchequer, and secondly they restricted imports, thus saving foreign currency and shipping space. In addition, the authorities relied on indirect taxation in the form of the traditional excise duties. The duties on alcohol, tobacco, tea and sugar were increased, while new taxes were imposed on petrol, mineral waters, matches and cider.

31. See D. Lloyd George, *War Memoirs*, 6 vols, Nicholson & Watson, London, 1933–36, vol. I, pp. 117ff.
32. Morgan, *Studies in British Financial Policy*, pp. 92–93.

Excess profits duty The Munitions of War Act of July 1915 provided for a tax on profits, the munitions 'levy', which applied to all 'controlled establishments'. This was followed in September by a similar tax, the excess profits duty, which applied to firms other than controlled establishments. The standard rate of profit was fixed at the owner's choice, either as the average of the last pre-war years, or at 6 to 7 per cent on the capital employed in 1914, with allowances for subsequent investment. Excess profits duty, initially levied at 50 per cent, had risen by 1918 to 80 per cent. In 1917 the munitions levy was merged with excess profits duty. Despite the introduction of new taxation and increases in existing taxes, revenue lagged well behind expenditure and the deficit continued to grow right up to the time of the Armistice. In all, revenue from taxes in the five fiscal years 1914/15 to 1918/19 covered about 28 per cent of government expenditure. Nor, judging by the pronouncements of Lloyd George and McKenna, had the government expected anything better.

The spearhead of the attack on private spending was the policy of debt creation. By 1917 three major War Loans had been floated, later to be followed by medium bonds. Loans offered the usual combination of commercial inducement and patriotic appeal; in this, the British government was even more concerned than other governments with presenting its new flotations in a commercially attractive form. Even the first War Loan of November 1914 offered a return of 4 per cent, whereas before the war a rate of 3·25 per cent had been customary for government paper. The rate for the second War Loan (June 1915) rose to 4·5 per cent and for the third (January 1917) to 5·3 per cent. Hence the cost of the National Debt increased appreciably, the more so since subscribers were entitled to convert their holdings into the latest and most attractive issue and, naturally enough, made full use of this facility. This was a completely new principle in borrowing policy and was only justifiable on the propagandist grounds that the government wanted the reception of the issue to be as impressive as possible. For the same reason, the Bank of England offered generous credit facilities to buyers on the occasion of each loan. Hence the absorption of purchasing power was nothing like as considerable as it could and should have been.

By the beginning of 1916 the government had begun to find its borrowing policy too expensive. Having regard to the wartime fall in the value of money, real interest rates were, it is true, negative, but it was generally anticipated that after the war rates would be at a lower level. Accordingly, the government went over to medium bonds (three to five years) which it hoped to fund on favourable terms after the war. First issued in December 1915, medium-dated paper was unable to compete successfully with the War Loans. As from October 1917, therefore, National War Bonds were issued whose rate of interest corresponded to the latest War Loan and which, in the absence of other investment opportunities, could be readily absorbed by the market in large quantities. A considerable proportion was taken up by the banks which thereby became one of the mainstays of war finance. Between March 1914 and March 1919 the internal debt rose in all by 5·5 billion pounds to 6·1 billion pounds. Of this, 23 per cent (1·4 billion pounds) was short-term. A floating debt of this order gave cause for general alarm. The average rate of interest payable amounted to 4·65 per cent against 3·25 before the war and in absolute terms, interest payments, at 224 million pounds, exceeded an entire pre-war budget.

Russia

At the end of July 1914, the government of Russia embarked on the monetary preparations needed for financing the war.[33] The National Bank's obligation to exchange gold for bank notes was suspended, the export of gold prohibited, and the Bank empowered to discount Treasury Bills up to any amount. Its note issue was raised from 300 million to 1,500 million roubles, further increases being authorized as required; in March 1917, bank notes to the value of 9·9 billion roubles were in circulation.

Before 1914 the Russian financial system still displayed many of the features of the old regime and hence was hardly adequate as a basis upon which to finance the war. In the last pre-war budget the state alcohol monopoly provided as much as 26 per cent of total revenue, and the state railways a further 24 per cent, while a mere 8 per cent was yielded by the various direct taxes on trade and

33. See A. L. Sidorov, *Finansovoe polozenie Rossii v gody pervoj mirovoj vojny, 1914–1917*, Moscow, 1960, and Apostol, Bernatzky and Michelson, *Russian Public Finance.*

industry, urban property, and agriculture; plans to merge these latter taxes into a general tax on incomes, though already in existence, had not yet been implemented.

When, in August 1914, an Imperial ukase officially imposed prohibition for the duration of the war, it was not so much the consumption of alcohol that was affected, but rather the country's most important source of revenue, since illicit liquor by its very nature went untaxed. The general disorganization of the economy and the decline in foreign trade involved a further substantial loss of income, so that in 1914 total revenue was 15 per cent and in 1915 17 per cent below the 1913 level. To make good the losses, or at least balance the parliamentary budgets, existing customs dues, excise and stamp duties and various direct taxes were several times raised. This – and to an even greater extent the inflationary upsurge of prices – raised the tax revenue for 1916, at least in money terms, above the pre-war level. The most important fiscal reforms, conceded at the eleventh hour by the czarist regime, came too late to help finance the war. A general tax on the incomes of companies and individuals – voted in the Duma as early as 1907 – was finally introduced in 1916, as was an excess profits tax. Income tax was on a sliding scale with a top rate of 12 per cent. Contrary to the original intention, the existing direct land taxes remained in force since at first the fiscal authorities were reluctant to lose these well-tried sources of revenue. The excess profits tax, at the relatively modest rate of 20 per cent, was to apply equally to companies and individuals.

As in Germany, revenue from taxation more or less met 'normal' expenditure, in this instance Parliament's ordinary and extra-ordinary budgets; the military estimates were financed by borrowing. Since war expenditure in Russia never attained the same level as in other countries (principally because of her premature withdrawal from the conflict) taxation covered, in a purely accounting sense, a relatively large proportion of public expenditure, namely some 27 per cent (roughly comparable with Britain). However, this calculation is purely theoretical. A substantial proportion of ordinary revenues derived from duties on imports, almost exclusively armaments, and from the profits of the railways, which mainly carried government traffic. The government simply transferred money from one pocket into another, i.e. from the war budget to the ordinary budget. In this way there was an improvement in the *proportion* of spending to revenue, but not in the absolute amount by which purchasing power was absorbed.

A serious shortcoming of Russian war finance was its inability to induce the public to take up a sufficient quantity of government paper. The first War Loan, yielding 5·3 per cent, was floated in October 1914. Subscriptions totalled 466 million roubles, far too little to fund the Treasury Bonds then outstanding. There were six further War Loans, of which the last, the Freedom Loan, was floated in March 1917 by the new bourgeois government amidst a blaze of publicity; yields gradually rose to 5·9 per cent. In all the War Loans brought in 11·4 billion roubles, a considerable sum in absolute terms, but paltry by comparison with the rapid growth of the total National Debt.

At the outbreak of the October revolution the National Debt amounted in all to 52·9 billion roubles – an increase, that is, of 39·4 billion roubles since the beginning of the war. No less than 35 per cent (13·8 billion roubles) of this increase was attributable to central bank credits, 33 per cent (12·9 billion roubles) to War Loans and medium-term debt, 12 per cent (4·9 billion roubles) to Treasury Bills sold on the open market, and 20 per cent (7·8 billion roubles) to foreign loans.[34] Russia's relative lack of success in her borrowing policy was due in part to the somewhat unsophisticated banking system and in part to the fact that, at least up till the end of 1916, the peasants were hoarding a considerable amount of cash (instead of buying government paper). It has been estimated that perhaps half of the total notes in circulation were absorbed by these hoards. The Kerensky rouble alone, it seems, failed to gain public confidence.[35]

United States

The wartime financial policy of the United States had already been initiated before their entry into the conflict. 'Armed neutrality' resulted in a rise in public expenditure and, to adjust revenue accordingly, various tax increases were introduced in September 1916.[36] From April 1917 onwards, in accordance with universal

34. ibid., pp. 321ff.

35. See M. Dobb, *Soviet Economic Development since 1917*, rev. ed., International Publishers, New York, 1968, pp. 71ff.

36. See C. Gilbert, *American Financing of World War I*, Greenwood, Westport, Conn., 1970.

practice, short-term Treasury Certificates of Indebtedness were issued to provide for future war expenditures. A total of 22 billion dollars was involved, of which more was taken up by banks than by the public.

Income tax, which yielded 16 per cent of revenue in 1916 and 59 per cent in the war budgets of 1917–20, was the mainstay of the government's fiscal policy. From 1917 to 1919, altogether 29 per cent of public expenditure was met by taxation. Hence it would seem that America's financial policy was somewhat more successful than that of Britain. This was not, of course, due to exceptionally harsh taxation, but rather to the country's late entry into the war and to a timely Armistice.

In the United States, too, the main task of absorbing private purchasing power fell to War Loans. The first of these, the Liberty Loan, was floated in May 1917, and was followed by four more loans, including the Victory Loan of April 1919, all of them being issued in accordance with normal market practice. The yield, which rose gradually from 3·5 per cent to 4·75 per cent, was in keeping with the relatively low interest rates prevailing in the United States and hence was less than the yield on the European War Loans. Thanks to a smooth running banking system and to the large amount of money held by the public, the loans found a ready market. In all, the five War Loans brought in 21·4 billion dollars. From 1918, the mobilization of small savings was effected by the issue of medium-term War Savings Certificates of low denominations. Net of repayments, these brought in 0·8 billion dollars. Between June 1916 and June 1919 the American National Debt rose overall by 24·3 billion dollars. 75 per cent of this sum (18·1 billion dollars) was held by the commercial banks, 6 per cent (1·6 billion dollars) was redeemed, and only 1 per cent (175 billion dollars) remained as a floating debt with the Federal Reserve Banks.[37]

Inflation

During the First World War both the theory and practice of war finance were seen very largely in budgetary terms. The sole object was to meet rising public expenditure as expediently as possible. The fact that the absorption of purchasing power by means of a

37. ibid., p. 229.

combination of taxes and loans could be a politico-economic regulator was not taken into consideration, if indeed it was recognized at all.

In every case tax revenue met only a small proportion of war expenditure and a country would sometimes spend more on transfer payments alone than it received by way of taxation. In the main, war expenditure was met by deficit financing. Attention has often been drawn to the anomaly whereby a government may compel the population to take up arms, yet dares not lay a finger either on property or on incomes. But fundamentally this was in accord with the logic of the system, as was the fact that in general the National Debt was tricked out to appeal to lenders. The real economic burden of the war was coincident with the war itself; it was borne either by current production or by disinvestment (consumption of stocks, running down of productive equipment) or by contributions from abroad (import surpluses). Thus loans did not project the *real* burden into the future as was frequently supposed during the war. But they did affect the way in which the burden was shared out between individuals: the cost of the war was borne in the first instance by the state's creditors who were subsequently to be reimbursed by the taxpayers as a whole. According to Pigou, it was this sharing out of the burden between individuals that constituted the real, psychological benefit of financing the war by way of loans. The great mass of taxpayers failed to see that in the final count it was they who would have to bear the cost of the war and generally believed that the enemy, once beaten, would foot the entire bill. Thus the population as a whole remained unaware of exactly how much the war was currently costing.[38] We may, however, suppose that there was another reason for financing the war out of loans. During the Great War income inequalities were becoming ever more extreme: on the one hand, impoverishment, on the other vast profits. In wartime a productive fiscal policy must involve the progressive taxation of incomes and property, as has already been seen in the case of Great Britain and the U.S.A.; in more normal times, on the other hand, the burden of taxation could be spread out more evenly over the population by means of excise and stamp duties.

A special problem was the practice of passing on taxes; to do so under conditions of wartime inflation was by no means difficult

38. See Pigou, *The Political Economy of War.*

and readily produced a vicious spiral. The taxes a manufacturer paid to the state one day he recovered the next by increasing the price of his armaments. Where taxes were wholly passed on to the state, the increased revenue shown in the budget was matched by a corresponding increase in its own expenditure. This effect was particularly in evidence in the case of, for instance, the coal tax in Germany and certain excise duties and transport taxes in Russia. Although in these circumstances no effective transfer of purchasing power was achieved, a larger proportion of expenditure was being met out of revenue. Thus the ratio of fiscal revenue to government expenditure is not a reliable guide to the efficacy of taxation policy.

Among the belligerents, inflationary war finance combined with the centralized control of their economies gave rise to a glut of purchasing power in private hands. Since there were only limited opportunities for consumption or investment, firms and individuals inevitably held larger amounts of money and other liquid assets than they really wanted. This resulted in constant inflationary pressure whose intensity, since prices were kept artificially low, is generally measured by the rise in note circulation and the short-term floating debt placed outside of the central banks. As compared with the pre-war figure (late 1913) note circulation had, by the end of 1918, risen in Germany by 1,141 per cent, in France by 532 per cent, in Italy by 504 per cent, and in Britain by 1,154 per cent.[39] Concurrently with the increase of cash in circulation, central and commercial banks considerably expanded their deposit business. The inflationary rise in prices was highly embarrassing for governments from the viewpoint both of public morale and of the ever-mounting cost of state purchases. During the war, therefore, all countries introduced price controls, mainly for foodstuffs, but also for other commodities. While these controls did nothing to damp down the inflationary spiral *per se* they served to turn 'open' inflation into a less visible, 'suppressed' inflation. In as much as the price indexes of the various countries included controlled prices, they ceased to reflect the full pressure of inflation. This qualification should be borne in mind when considering Table 22 below; here it is shown that by and large

39. See League of Nations, *Memorandum on Currency and Central Banks, 1913–1924*, 2 vols, Geneva, 1925, vol. I, pp. 120ff.

prices rose during the war to twice their pre-war level and in some countries actually quadrupled.

The price indices reveal the combined effect of inflationary pressure and government controls. *Ceteris paribus*, the greater the proportion of controlled prices included in the index and the earlier the introduction of price controls, the stronger, statistically speaking, the curb on price rises, since in general governments fixed a particular price at the level it had reached at the time of intervention. If, for example, the trend in Germany, when compared with that in Britain or the United States, appears more favourable than her monetary and financial policy and general economic situation would seem to warrant, this may be attributed to the wider scope of her price controls and their relatively early introduction.

TABLE 22
INDEX OF WHOLESALE PRICES (1913 = 100)

	1914	1915	1916	1917	1918	1919
Germany	106	142	153	179	217	415
France	102	140	189	262	340	357
Gt Britain	100	127	160	206	227	242
Italy	96	133	201	299	409	364
Canada	100	109	134	175	205	216
India	100	112	128	147	180	198
Japan	95	97	117	149	196	239
U.S.A.	98	101	127	177	194	206
Sweden	116	145	185	244	339	330

SOURCE: *Monthly Bulletin of Statistics of the League of Nations*, cit. from J. M. Keynes, 'A Tract on Monetary Reform', *Collected Writings*, vol. IV, Macmillan, London, 1971, p. 3.

It is a remarkable fact that the depreciation of money should have affected every country throughout the world. Both the dollar and the yen lost approximately half their internal purchasing power and the Swedish krona as much as two-thirds, although these currencies had no difficulty in maintaining their parity in relation to gold; indeed, in Sweden the price of gold actually tended to fall. After the war the varying rates of inflation made it somewhat difficult to find a new and acceptable basis for international parities, the more so since it was no longer possible, because of price controls, to deduce from the movement of the internal price level the actual extent to which money had depreciated in value. The United States, Japan and a number of neutrals continued to adhere to the old parity in relation to gold. After a laborious process of deflation, Britain joined the gold bloc on the basis of her pre-war parity. On the Continent, where wartime inflation had been more severe, the economic and political problems of the post-war period produced a further inflationary impulse, with a consequent depreciation of currencies. The governments of Belgium, France, Italy and Portugal, as well as those of a number of east and south European countries, mopped up excess purchasing power by moderate inflation and eventually stabilized their currencies at levels varying between 25 per cent (Italy) and about 1 per cent (Estonia and Latvia) of their pre-war parity. In Germany, Austria, Poland, Russia and Hungary, the currency got completely out of control as a result of hyperinflation. Here, as the necessary prerequisites for stabilization, the old discredited currencies were completely discarded and new units introduced.[40] In retrospect it is clear that the various stabilization measures in no instance yielded a viable exchange rate – one, that is, taking due account of price movements and economic changes since 1913. Thus, too great a strain was placed on adjustment mechanisms whose real function was the equilibration of the balance of payments: the resultant 'over-' and 'undervaluation' of individual currencies contributed materially to the instability of the international exchanges during the twenties.

40. See League of Nations, *The Course and Control of Inflation. A Review of Monetary Experience in Europe after World War I*, Geneva, 1946.

7

The Labour Movement between Integration and Revolution

August 1914

The epoch-making significance of the Great War derives from the fact that it destroyed the multilateral capitalist world economy, at the same time ushering in the period of rivalry between the capitalist and socialist economic systems. The Russian October Revolution and the triumph of the revolutionary labour movement under the circumstances of a world war permanently changed the international economy. This is what lends particular importance to the history of the labour movement within the general context of economic history.

Before 1914 it was generally held that, in the developed industrial countries, the social classes lived alongside if not in opposition to each other as though they were separate nations. When war broke out, the attitude of the working class was in doubt.[1]

1. A great deal has been written about the Second International; readers are advised to refer to the outstanding and well annotated bibliography by George Haupt: *La Deuxième Internationale 1889–1914. Etude Critique des Sources. Essai Bibliographique*, Mouton, Paris/La Haye, 1964. A readily available German account may be found in J. Braunthal, *Geschichte der Internationale*, 2 vols, Dietz, Hanover, 1961–63. A work entirely devoted to the problem of the International and the war is G. Haupt, *Der Kongress fand nicht statt. Die Sozialistische Internationale 1914*, Europa-Verlag, Vienna/Frankfurt/Zurich,

Governments were not sure whether they would have to force the workers to join the war by wholesale oppressive measures, or whether the ideological ties of patriotism and nationalism would be strong enough to induce them and their organizations to participate voluntarily. Indeed, there were some grounds for doubt since the Second International had more than once stressed that it was the duty of the workers of all countries to defend the international solidarity of the working class against the onslaughts of imperialism and nationalism. Latterly, in response to mounting tension in Europe, the Extraordinary Congress of the Second International, which met in Basle in 1912, had unanimously agreed to a manifesto calling upon the peoples to resist war with all the means at their disposal.[2] In July 1914 the workers' organizations in Germany, France, Britain, Italy, Austria–Hungary and Russia called for demonstrations against the impending war, and the masses obeyed. But when it came to the point, when the dreaded declarations of war had been made, this opposition collapsed. The workers' parties adopted the official version of a just and 'defensive' war, and endorsed war credits while acknowledged leaders of the labour movement such as Emile Vandervelde in Belgium and Jules Guesde and Marcel Sembat in France became members of bourgeois war cabinets. There were two notable exceptions: in the Duma war credits were opposed by the Mensheviks and Bolsheviks, and in the Skuptshina, the Serbian parliament, by two socialist deputies.

In so far as such mental attitudes are still ascertainable today, it would seem that, in approving the war, the leaders of the labour movement were acting in concert with the masses. Although there was some opposition, it counted for little in the face of momentary war hysteria and militant defensiveness. The decision of August

---

1967. For a short survey, see also W. Abendroth, *Sozialgeschichte der europäischen Arbeiterbewegung*, Suhrkamp, Frankfurt, 1965.

2. The relevant resolutions can be readily found in O. H. Gankin and H. H. Fisher, eds, *The Bolsheviks and the World War. The Origin of the International*, collected documents, Stanford University Press, 1940, reprint, 1960. The Basle Manifesto is regarded as the final and definitive expression of the International's attitude to war. However, as Georges Haupt has recently shown, the leaders of the Second International had begun as early as 1913 to disassociate themselves from this document which it was their intention to revise at the congress to be held in Vienna in August, 1914. See Haupt, *Der Kongress fand nicht statt*.

1914 reveals that, long before the war and despite rising social tension, there had been a marked tendency on the part of the workers to integrate with bourgeois society and its institutions.

Before 1914 the larger legal trade union organizations had, to an even greater extent than the workers' parties, pursued a policy of gradual improvement within the existing capitalist system. If, as in Germany, they did not officially disassociate themselves from a Marxist-revolutionary programme, the intention was to strengthen their members' ideological cohesion rather than to encourage concrete revolutionary action. The decision taken by the workers' parties in August 1914 sanctioned the continuance, war or no war, of a non-revolutionary policy of self-interest. The purpose of the trade unions' strategy was to safeguard their members' interests and, perhaps in return for their cooperative attitude, to achieve institutional improvements – an aim particularly dear to the German organizations. But for the historian there still remains the unpalatable fact that, by inner conviction, most of the leaders of the labour movement, both in the unions and in the parties, were in the final analysis more strongly committed to nationalism than to international proletarian solidarity.

Trade unions during the war

Germany

At the outbreak of war the German trade unions had 2·5 million members.[3] Despite these impressive numbers, they had still not secured the official recognition of employers and government. Some sections of small and medium industry and certain of the handicrafts trades had, under pressure of circumstances, consented to recognize the unions and conclude wage agreements, but in big industry the monarchical attitude still prevailed. Not only the Imperial and state governments, but also the judiciary, were fully convinced that it was their duty to protect the employer's 'assets'.

3. This number only includes the Free Trade Unions. See P. Umbreit, *Die deutschen Gewerkschaften im Kreig*, Deutsche Verlags-Anstalt, Stuttgart/ Berlin/Leipzig, 1928, p. 161. At that time there were some 21 million wage earners, of whom 7·4 million were industrial workers. From W. Zimmermann, *Die Veränderungen der Einkommens und Lebensverhältnisse der deutschen Arbeiter durch den Krieg*, Deutsche Verlags-Anstalt, Stuttgart/Berlin/Leipzig, pp. 285, 350.

The ban on association had, of course, been lifted since the founding of the Empire, and the Reichstag had thrown out the notorious 'Prison Bill' of 1899 by a narrow majority. But an elastic interpretation of the penal law combined with bureaucratic chicanery enabled strikes and general union activities to be dealt with scarcely less severely than at the time of the Socialist Law.[4]

The outbreak of war put an end, at least for a time, to this sharply defined polarization of trade unions on the one hand and employers and state on the other. But there had already been informal contacts between the government and the unions from which it had transpired that, in case of war, the unions would range themselves behind the government, while the government for its part would tolerate the unions and not, as right wing circles had originally intended, suppress them by force.[5] On 2 August 1914, at a plenary conference of trade union leaders, an irreversible decision was taken to support government policy. No longer was there any question of the political strikes which had previously been mooted within the international labour movement as an anti-war measure; thenceforward the unions expressly renounced industrial strikes also. From a passive acceptance of official war policy, the unions rapidly switched to active cooperation. On the ideological plane they disseminated the official line of a 'defensive war' and came perilously close to identifying the imperialist war with trade union interests. This view was plainly expressed in an article attacking the social democratic Left, published in December 1915 by the central organ of the trade unions. The article read:

> The policy of 4 August 1914 accords with the most vital union interests. It ensures that enemy invasion is kept at bay; it safeguards us against the partition of German territory and the destruction of flourishing branches of industry; it safeguards us against the fate of an unhappy outcome to the war which would saddle us for decades with a burden of war damages. This policy, it seems to us, safeguards not only the sphere of industry and

4. See Umbreit, *Die deutschen Gewerkschaften im Kriege*, pp. 13ff.
5. See G. Feldman, *Army, Industry and Labor in Germany 1914–1918*, Princeton University Press, 1966; J. Kocka, *Klassengesellschaft im Krieg. Deutsche Sozialgeschichte 1914–1918*, Vandenhoeck & Ruprecht, Göttingen, 1973; and W. Richter, *Gewerkschaften, Monopolkapital und Staat im Ersten Weltkrieg und in der Novemberrevolution*, Tribune, Berlin, 1959. For a useful earlier work, see Umbreit, *Die deutschen Gewerkschaften im Kriege*.

raw materials at home, but also the import of the raw materials necessary to our production and the export and sale of our manufactures abroad. It sets at naught our enemies' strategic and economic plans to subdue us, and guarantees German labour freedom of development and a free world market. The trade unions must in all circumstances abide by the policy of 4 August 1914, nor can they warn too earnestly against attempts to thwart the policy of the present faction.[6]

On the practical plane the trade unions engaged in broadly based activities of a more or less socio-political character. They assisted the unemployed, helped to implement government food policy, associated themselves with the Imperial Labour Registration Office, the labour exchange set up in August 1914, and promoted the recruitment of women, juveniles and foreign workers for the munitions industry. True, these activities might benefit individual workers but above all they connoted support for the government's wartime economic policy and the assumption of some of its burdens. The unemployment benefits paid by the unions, for instance, enabled the Imperial government to delay tackling the problem of massive unemployment that confronted it in the early days of the war. It was only in December 1914, as a result of pressure from the unions, that the government 'advised' municipalities to set up welfare organizations for the unemployed, with the prospect of state assistance in exceptional cases.

The trade unions wished to create what they described as 'work communities' in which employers and workpeople would together agree socio-political measures, possibly with state participation. These work communities, it was hoped, would, as it were, compensate for the industrial truce by securing for the unions the official recognition of the employers, an aim for which they had long been striving. However it is typical of what, despite the industrial truce, was still to a great extent a reactionary social climate that these work communities were at first viable only in trades which had been subject to wage agreements before the war, and which lay outside the mainstream of industry: for instance printing, building and joinery, painting, brewing and tailoring. The trade unions' proposal of 1914/15 to create a 'central work community' at national level was turned down by the employers' associations. From the outset the industrial truce was a very one-sided affair. By giving their assent to official policy, both military

6. Cit. from ibid., p. 175.

and economic, the unions had secured for themselves virtually no advantages beyond the preservation of their formal legality.

The high rate of unemployment at the beginning of the war, no less than the renunciation of strike action, helped to undermine the workers' bargaining position economically and, by extension, politically. But with the coming of the war boom all this changed. Not until June 1915, however, did unemployment fall below the pre-war average for the Empire,[7] though even before that date there had been an acute shortage of skilled workers in the centres of the munitions industry such as Berlin. In these circumstances skilled workers could, without recourse to industrial disputes, at least improve on their standard wage by exploiting the competition for labour among armaments firms. To this the majority of employers reacted by demanding that the industrial truce be supplemented by a law binding the employee to his place of work. However, even among employers this demand did not go uncontested, for a number of them realized that any ban on mobility would put an undue strain on the willingness of the unions and, above all, of the workers themselves, to cooperate.

There is a certain, if not complete, similarity between on the one hand, the 'hard' and 'soft' lines in social policy and, on the other, the 'extreme' and 'moderate' lines adopted in the pursuit of war aims – an aspect elaborated more especially by Marxist historians.[8] Advocates of both lines were to be found in the civil as well as in the military administrations. Von Falkenhayn, for example, the Chief of General Staff, was strongly in favour of the direction of labour, while the official advisers to the Prussian War Ministry, Sichler and Tiburtius, came out strongly against it. The arguments put forward in their 'Report on the Deferment of Men Liable for Call-up', written for the Factories Division of the General War Department, repay quoting at length:

> On the home front, too, the workers are presently serving their country by carrying on their trades with the utmost goodwill. In this they are encouraged and urged on by their trade

7. See F. Hesse, *Die deutsche Wirtschaftslage von 1914 bis 1923*, Fischer, Jena, 1938, pp. 478ff.

8. See W. Gutsche, 'Erst Europa – und dann die Welt. Probleme des Kriegszielpolitik des deutschen Imperialismus im Ersten Weltkrieg', *Zeitschrift für Geschichtswissenschaft*, 12, 1964. Also J. Kuczynski, *Darstellung der Lage der Arbeiter in Deutschland von 1900 bis 1917/18*, Akademie-Verlag, Berlin, 1967.

unions. Any legal or military compulsion applied to labour would have a crippling and disastrous effect on that good will and on the cooperative attitude of the unions. The allusion to compulsion in the form of military discipline, so splendidly exemplified in the armed forces, is a misreading of the fundamental distinction between service in defence of one's country, in which everyone works only for the common weal without thought of personal advantage, and capitalist labour relations, in which the performance of the worker provides the employer with a return on his capital. As a result of historical developments, these relations are regarded by the workers – whether rightly or wrongly is perhaps not ascertainable in time of war – as a state of hostilities, and to intervene in such a way as to compel one side by *government directives* to perform a task, for which the other receives maximum *remuneration* from that same government, would be regarded by the workers no less than by other sections of the population as bias in favour of the employer and would, moreover, undermine the confidence placed in the military administration by classes that are of crucial importance to the prosecution of the war.[9]

An early and typical example of cooperation between employers' associations and trade unions, along the lines of the foregoing report to the Prussian War Ministry, may be found in the Berlin metal industry where, in February 1915, the unions consented to restrictions on the mobility of labour. A worker who wanted to move to another firm had to obtain permission in the form of a 'discharge certificate' from his current employer. If this was refused he could appeal to an arbitration committee on which the employers' association and the metal workers' union were equally represented. In practice, the committee generally arrived at a compromise whereby the worker remained in his job but at a higher wage. The employers were perfectly satisfied with this arrangement, since it effectively kept down rises occasioned by the competition for labour. Even Borsig, who had first advocated rigorous compulsory service for workers, later expressed his approval of cooperation with the unions. Less easy to understand is the consent of the latter which, in this instance, surrendered one of the workers' essential rights. The Berlin agreement shows just how much official recognition meant to the trade unions.

9. R. Sichler and J. Tiburtius, *Die Arbeiterfrage, eine Kernfrage des Weltkrieges*, Deutsche Verlags-AG, Berlin, pp. 13ff. Italics as in original. Also Feldman, *Army, Industry and Labor*, pp.75ff.

At the end of 1916, the introduction of the Patriotic Auxiliary Service Law revived the controversy over compulsory service and mobility, this time as a matter of principle and on a nationwide plane. The 'military dictatorship' of Hindenburg and Ludendorff ushered in a new phase of extremely close cooperation between heavy industry and the Supreme Army Command which, immediately after taking over the reins in August 1916, put forward the Hindenburg Programme with the object of effecting a massive increase in armaments production. A few days later the Supreme Army Command demanded universal compulsory service for men and women between fifteen and sixty, declaring this to be absolutely essential to the programme. This demand had already been discussed with the representatives of industry. It may be said without exaggeration that heavy industry saw in the Supreme Army Command a powerful guarantor of its interests, and to that extent the 'hard' line in official social policy had asserted itself. On the other hand, experience had shown how important was the cooperation of the unions in the implementation of wartime economic policy. Not only were they of help in countless individual cases, but above all they, and they alone, were in a position to act as a buffer between wartime policy and the growing war-weariness of the masses. It was these political considerations that persuaded the Imperial government to maintain at all costs its relations with the unions and social democracy. At bottom even Ludendorff, although not prepared to make the political, economic and social concessions necessary to that end, subscribed to this policy when he stipulated that the proposed compulsory service law should receive broad assent in the Reichstag. For the trade unions this provided a useful lever vis-à-vis the government and, on the political plane, lent strength to the representations of the parliamentary social democratic faction.

The Patriotic Auxiliary Service Law was passed on 2 December 1916 with the majority of the Social Democrats voting in favour, secure in the knowledge of union support. The law provided for industrial conscription in the case of all males aged between seventeen and sixty. A ban was placed on mobility to the extent that a worker might only change jobs on the strength of a discharge certificate from his current employer; however, the law expressly cited the prospect of higher wages as legitimate grounds for moving to another firm. By way of a concession to organized labour, provision was made, in firms with a minimum of fifty work-people, for permanent 'workers' committees' which may be regarded as the immediate forerunners of the works councils. Their mandate was defined as follows:

> It is incumbent upon the Workers' Committee to promote good relations both within the labour force and with the employer. It is to bring to the notice of the employer, and give an opinion upon, the petitions, requests and complaints of the labour force relating to wages and other working conditions, to the organization of the firm and to its welfare arrangements.[10]

Even today there is still no consensus of opinion over the advantages and disadvantages to the workers and unions of the Auxiliary Service Law. The trade unions had at last attained their goal – official recognition by employers and the state. The new arbitration committees and workers' committees provided not only favourable opportunities for day-to-day union work but also for indoctrinating the workpeople, a task they performed so effectively that – much to the chagrin of the trade union leaders – they became breeding grounds for revolutionary activity. This law gave official sanction to wage claims and mobility, even in the case of workers on temporary release from the armed forces. So far-reaching were its implications, however, that after a while big industry and the Supreme Army Command contemplated abolishing it and reverting to the *status quo ante*.

On the other hand, those in the unions who championed the Auxiliary Service Law had to admit that it was first and foremost a coercive measure and they vindicated their cooperation, not on the grounds of its success, but rather as being a lesser evil when compared with what, in their view, was the only alternative, namely undisguised military dictatorship. But above all, in consenting to the Auxiliary Service Law, the unions had not only endorsed the policy of industrial truce; they had also publicly declared themselves for the existing regime at a time when the opposition of the working people to the war was already becoming plainly audible. Cooperation between unions, employers and state

10. National Auxiliary Service Law, para. 12, cit., from Umbreit, *Die deutschen Gewerkschaften im Kriege*, pp. 242ff. The text of this law is also quoted by R. Armeson, *Total Warfare and Compulsory Labor*, Nijhoff, The Hague, 1964, pp. 137–40; and by G. Feldman, *Army, Industry and Labor*, pp. 535–41.

was further consolidated when Alexander Schlicke, chairman of the Metal Workers' Union, joined the War Bureau as union representative. Faced with the alternative of supporting the old order or placing themselves at the head of a revolutionary movement, the trade union leaders opted for the former. In this way they ensured that their organization continued to enjoy legality and recognition; membership, which had declined rapidly up till the end of 1916, started to pick up again and by 1918 was higher than before the war. Now was the time to mobilize this potential for the democratic restructuring of the economy, society and the state – but the opportunity was missed.

The growing discontent of the working population with wartime policies manifested itself in sporadic outbreaks of open resistance in the spring of 1917. The causes of this development may be attributed largely to the steady deterioration in the standard of living, to the generally intolerable conditions arising out of the war, and to the demand for ever greater sacrifices. After the 'turnip winter' of 1916–17, the standard of living deteriorated to a quite unprecedented degree. From the very beginning there had been political opposition to the war[11] and the longer the conflict lasted, the more ground was gained by the left wing, both in the party and in the unions. One important indication of the change of mood at the base was the increase in strike activity. In August 1914 there were no strikes at all; already in 1915 an average of 1,000 workers were on strike each month, and in 1916, 10,000.[12]

The beginning of 1917 was marked by food riots in a number of towns and by strikes in the North Rhine–Westphalian munitions industry. In his Easter message of 7 April 1917, Wilhelm II made some vague promises of post-war electoral reform, but the political effect of this half-hearted pledge was completely overshadowed by an official announcement, eight days later, to the effect that the bread ration was to be cut. In Berlin and Leipzig the workers struck in protest, but bread was not their only concern. In Leipzig they demanded, besides better supplies of foodstuffs and coal, the conclusion of a peace without annexations, the ending of the state of emergency, the abolition of the Auxiliary Service Law, freedom of the Press and of assembly and, finally,

11. See Carl E. Schorske, *German Social Democracy 1905–1917. The Development of the Great Schism*, Harvard University Press, Cambridge, Mass., 1955.
12. See Kuczynski, *Darstellung der Lage der Arbeiter*, p. 249.

universal and equal suffrage throughout the Empire. The qualitative difference between economic and political strike action was equally plain to the opposite side, namely the state and the employers. General Groener, head of the War Bureau, at first betrayed a certain sympathy for the workers' economic demands which, after the privations of the winter, seemed to him comprehensible, but when the political nature of the strikes became evident, his response was a harsh demand for the militarization of the munitions workers. This was considered too extreme a measure, not only by the government but also by the industrialists who feared that its application would be economically disadvantageous, even though in other respects they were calling for a 'hard' line.

Thenceforward there was an unbroken succession of protest strikes. June and July 1917 saw a great wave of strikes, centred mainly on the Ruhr and Upper Silesia. In Berlin, in January 1918, 400,000 workers struck for a peace without annexations or contributions, while Kiel, Hamburg, Halle and Magdeburg were the scene of similar actions. On average 50,000 workers were on strike each month in 1917 and 100,000 in 1918.[13] For the most part these actions, at least the larger ones, were forcibly broken either by conscripting the workers for military service, or by court martialling or militarizing them. But none of these methods succeeded in suppressing political resistance. The naval mutiny in the summer of 1917 plainly demonstrated that even the armed forces were not excluded from the social struggle.

The division of the nation into a war party and a peace party had been a reality since the strikes of April 1917; the rift was irrevocable and was growing wider every day. On the one hand there was the success of the Patriotic Party, founded in September 1917 by the Supreme Army Command in conjunction with heavy industry, which demonstrated that a large section of the German bourgeoisie could still be organized into a movement in favour of imperialism and militarism.[14] On the other there was the craving for peace of the masses under the political leadership of the Independent Social Democrats who, in April 1917, had formed their own party. The breadth of the movement can be gauged from the fact that, along with the Spartakus Group, both the former

13. ibid.
14 See Feldman, *Army, Industry and Labor*, p. 431.

'Centrists' and large sections of the party apparatus went over to the Independent Social Democratic Party of Germany (U.S.P.D.). The uncompromising demand for peace was a bond that united even those who did not support the revolutionary programme of the Left. Renouvin, when considering the inner tensions which manifested themselves in much the same guise in all the belligerent states, advances the hypothesis that governments may prosecute a war even in opposition to the great majority's desire for peace, so long as social institutions continue stable.[15] In Germany people had evidently reached the limits of their endurance. As we know, the rift in the nation continued beyond the Armistice. The vanquished imperialists closed their eyes to the inevitability of their military defeat and instead took refuge in an intensified struggle against the class enemy.

Britain

There is a widely held belief that in Great Britain the social climate prior to 1914 was more peaceful than in Germany. But in so far as this assumes an absence of class contradictions and class struggles it is erroneous. Neither the unions' share in economic growth nor their political rights had been presented to them on a platter, but had been earned in the course of dogged disputes.[16] Though the *embourgeoisement* of many sections of the working class cannot be overlooked there was, on the other hand, a solid, if numerically not very important, 'left wing' tradition. The view of a socially peaceful Britain is correct in as much as the ideological spectrum was constricted and the class struggle waged rather more pragmatically. In the main the trade union movement was patently reformist, lacking as it did the Marxist-revolutionary veneer which was still to some extent maintained by the German unions as a result of their connection with social democracy. On the other hand British ruling circles were free of the those ultra-reactionary draconian elements found in Germany among the Junkers and the big industrialists.

After the outbreak of war, the trade union leaders succeeded

15. See R. Renouvin, 'L'opinion publique et la guerre en 1917', *Revue d'Histoire Moderne et Contemporaine*, 15, 1968, p. 23.

16. See E. Hobsbawm, 'Trends in the British Labour Movement since 1850', *Labouring Men. Studies in the History of Labour*, Basic Books, New York, 1964, p. 328.

without much opposition in bringing the masses into line with government policy.[17] In conjunction with the party, they proposed the industrial truce already mentioned, supported recruitment for the armed forces and later cooperated with the employers and the state in the mobilization of industry. Nevertheless, there was a measure of conflict. The first major trial of strength between the unions on the one hand and the employers and the state on the other occurred over the question of dilution.[18] This problem has already been touched on in connection with wartime economic policy; essentially it hinged on the employers' intention to replace skilled workers who had joined the forces with unskilled labour, principally women, and at the same time standardize and mechanize production processes. This development was not peculiar to Britain. It was also taking place in Germany and France without arousing any serious opposition. In Britain it became a problem of the first order because the skilled worker saw in rigid demarcation according to trade and skill an essential means of insuring his status and income against the economic risks inherent in the capitalist system. Since the craft unions were the mainstay of the trade union movement, dilution inevitably became a central issue of union policy. Later the question of dilution was to become bound up with the more general questions of worker participation and control, fields which were no longer the exclusive preserve of the skilled craftsmen.

After a great deal of bargaining between employers and workers, punctuated by strikes, the Shells and Fuses Agreement was concluded at the beginning of March 1915. By its terms the unions accepted dilution, while for their part the employers promised that skilled workers would suffer no material loss from the reorganization of production, that the terms would be valid only for the duration, that after the war the old conditions would be restored and, above all, that the unions would be permitted to participate in the implementation of dilution in the various factories. Having regard to their initial demands, the unions had made concessions without any *quid pro quo* worth mentioning; but from the outset

17. See S. J. Hurwitz, *State Intervention in Great Britain. A Study of Economic Control and Social Response, 1914–1919*, London, 1949.

18. See also G. D. H. Cole, *Trade Unionism and Munitions*, Clarendon Press, Oxford, 1923; and the official account in *History of the Ministry of Munitions*, 12 vols, 1921–22.

they had been in a poor bargaining position, for the employers, in calling for maximum increases in munitions production, had had the support, not only of the government, but also of public opinion.

It was not long before the classic theme of union policy – the struggle for higher wages and a better standard of living – became a crucial issue along with the controversy over dilution. On the outbreak of war the unions had renounced an active wages policy both on patriotic grounds and because they believed that the war and the concomitant price rises would be of short duration. But as it gradually became apparent that price rises had come to stay, employees necessarily reverted to an active wages policy to combat the steady deterioration in their standard of living. Among the industrial disputes that followed, the strike on the Clyde acquired national importance.[19] Here, within a comparatively narrow compass, was a concentration of iron and steel industries, shipyards, engineering and chemical works, textile mills and mines. Glasgow, the heart of this industrial complex, was also a considerable seaport. With the new armaments contracts came a brisk wartime boom which attracted numerous workers from other parts of Britain. It also had its drawbacks, namely rising prices and a housing shortage. Shortly before the outbreak of war the workers had submitted wage claims which they had withdrawn following the industrial truce, only to revive them at the beginning of 1915 under the pressure of the rising cost of living. In February the engineers, the most important group in the munitions industry, came out on strike. It was a wildcat strike, not recognized by the trade union organizations, but supported by most of the shop stewards. The *ad hoc* strike committee composed of workers and shop stewards remained in being after the strike was over and constituted itself a permanent organization known as the Clyde Workers' Committee. Thus in one sense the wage dispute assumed a political complexion and from then on the committee viewed the policies both of the government and of the official unions with equal mistrust.

19. On this strike, see the references given in the two previous notes and also J. Cunnison and W. R. Scott, *The Industries of the Clyde Valley during the War*, Clarendon Press, Oxford, 1924; B. Pribicevic, *The Shop Stewards' Movement and Workers' Control 1910–1922*, Blackwell, Oxford, 1959, and J. Hinton, *The First Shop Stewards' Movement*, Allen & Unwin, London, 1973.

As a result of the dispute over dilution and the revival of industrial action, the government felt that more vigorous intervention was called for. In February 1915 an advisory committee was set up and in March, largely as a result of its recommendations, the unions and the government concluded the Treasury Agreement which confirmed the arrangements already worked out between unions and employers. However it went beyond the Shells and Fuses Agreement in that the unions undertook to suspend restrictive practices of all kinds (among which was the 'go slow'), once more confirmed their renunciation of strikes as an industrial weapon in factories essential to the war effort, and agreed to the principle of compulsory arbitration in wage disputes, either by courts on which they had equality of representation or by government committees. At the request of the largest of the unions, the Amalgamated Society of Engineers, the government promised that there would be a supplementary agreement controlling employers' profits, whereby the advantages deriving from more intensive use of labour and from the abandonment of traditional procedures would benefit the state rather than the individual employer.

The new coalition government of which, as Minister of Munitions, Lloyd George was one of the leading members, at once set about tightening up the provisions and extending the scope of its labour policy. The legal basis for this was provided by the Munitions of War Act, passed at the beginning of July 1915 after the briefest of debates. As has already been mentioned in another context, this act had two main features: firstly, it created a system of 'controlled establishments' in which the state was given far-reaching rights of intervention in the affairs of the workers and also – at least on paper – of the owners. Secondly, it tied the worker to his place of work. Any operative employed in the armaments industry who wanted to move to another firm had first to obtain his employer's permission. If this was refused without good reason the man was entitled to appeal to the Munitions Tribunal. The only way in which a worker could circumvent this requirement was to allow six weeks to elapse between jobs, but there were few who could afford to forego their wages for so long. Worse still, higher wages and better working conditions were not, under the Act, adjudged sufficient grounds for a change of employment, nor in practice were they recognized as such by the tribunals.

Thus the restrictions imposed on a worker's freedom of movement were more rigid than, for example, those laid down by the German Auxiliary Service Law of December 1916. Although the unions were opposed to the 'leaving certificate' system, they were not prepared to make it a pretext for an open breach with the government.

At first the Munitions of War Act was no more than a declaration of intent, and it was not so much its promulgation that gave rise to dispute as its subsequent enforcement. In practice compulsory arbitration proved to be unworkable if resisted by the workers. It was put to the test as early as July 1915 when the South Wales miners came out on strike, not only against the employers, but also against the government whose mediation offer they had rejected. In view of the impossibility of sending 200,000 miners to prison, the government gave way and agreed to most of their demands. During the subsequent course of the war the government was similarly at pains to settle wage disputes in the munitions industry by means of nominal concessions rather than confrontations.

Dilution was exceedingly unpopular with the large majority of workers in the armaments industry, and the agreements concluded by the unions in March 1915 were already in jeopardy. The dispute over dilution acquired a more general character after various measures, each as unpopular as the next, had been lumped together in the Munitions of War Act. Upon its implementation, new conflicts arose out of the workers' demands for the control of dilution. Finally, pressure from the unions led to the relaxation of the leaving certificate regulations in the autumn of 1915, while in 1917 the mounting opposition of the workers induced the government to abolish all restrictions on their freedom of movement.

An area of conflict more or less foreign to the unions' habitual sphere of activity was compulsory military service. In August 1914 Britain was the only one of the great powers to enter the war with a system of voluntary enlistment. The unions supported the official recruiting campaign as part of their policy of cooperation. Indeed, everything went smoothly so long as the Asquith government and, in its early stages, the new coalition government adhered to the principle of a volunteer army. That the situation was changing became apparent when the supply of volunteers began to dry up. True, during the first six months of 1915 an average of 20,000 men were still coming forward each week, but the War Office estimated that 30,000 – a figure later stepped up to 35,000 – recruits were needed to make good losses and permit the expansion of the army as planned. The effect of this shortfall was to bring over influential politicians, Lloyd George among them, to the 'compulsionist' camp. For all practical purposes the way was paved for conscription when in July 1915 a National Register was set up, originally with the intention of providing a survey of the number and qualifications of persons available for service in industry and the armed forces. The following month a Cabinet Committee investigating national resources in men and materials reached the conclusion that the proposed target of 70 divisions was not attainable on a voluntary basis. According to the committee, the choice was between tailoring military plans to the potential intake of volunteers and introducing compulsory military service. As a concession to the anti-compulsionists, the government made a final attempt in October 1915 to exploit to the full the possibilities of voluntary enlistment. This took the form of the Derby Scheme, so called after Lord Derby who had been entrusted with its administration. On the basis of the National Register, all men between the ages of eighteen and forty-one were required to report. This did not mean an immediate call-up, but allocation to the reserve. Able-bodied and, on principle, single rather than married, men, in so far as they were not indispensable to the munitions industry, were to come forward by age-groups, beginning with the youngest. The Derby Scheme was accompanied by patriotic appeals from the King, the government and even the trade unions, and was not unsuccessful. By the middle of December 1915 over two million men had been attested. But measured against the ambitious hope of a 100 per cent response, the ultimate result was not very impressive. Of the 2·2 million unmarried men who were to be conscripted, little more than half anticipated the call-up. This cleared the way for the compulsionists. The Military Service Act affecting single men was passed in January 1916 and put into effect in March. Two years later, after the military had stepped up their demands, the bill was extended to married men. The only M.P.s to vote against the Second Military Service Act were twenty-seven 'old Liberals', under Sir John Simon, and ten left wing Labour representatives.

If the unions accepted general military conscription, it was on the tacit understanding that skilled workers would as a rule be regarded as indispensable and hence exempt. Indeed, this had initially been the intention of the government which did not wish to jeopardize armaments production. But after the enormous losses of the Somme offensive, and with armaments production apparently assured, the government decided in the autumn of 1916 to increase the rate of call-up. This marked the beginning of dogged skirmishing between the unions and the military over the recognition of this or that operative as a skilled worker. In November 1916 the wrongful conscription of a Sheffield mechanic led to a local strike, thus providing the unions with a pretext for demanding a full-scale investigation. The government gave way and, before the month was out, had introduced the 'Trade Cards Scheme' whereby the unions were accorded powers to decide whether or not a man qualified as a skilled worker and hence was exempt from military service. Skilled workers were issued by their unions with 'trade cards' stating that they were in a reserved occupation.

The Trade Card Scheme did not long survive the change of government that took place in December 1916. The following April the scheme was unilaterally terminated by the authorities, and the unions were compelled to forfeit the powers that had been conferred on them. However, in view of the mounting social tension evidenced by the strikes in the munitions industry in May 1917, the government still shrank from actually calling skilled workers to the colours, and the matter was left in the air. But a turning-point came with the German offensive in the spring of 1918. Faced with a powerful resurgence of patriotism, the unions gave way, thus enabling the government to call up skilled workers from essential industries in order to help repulse this final thrust.[20]

There was a limit at which trade union cooperation ceased, namely compulsory national service. In June 1915 Lloyd George declared that the state must have the right to direct a man to the front or to industry, whichever it deemed to be in the best interests of the general weal.[21] This, in effect, was a demand for national

20. See P. Guinn, *British Strategy and Politics 1914 to 1918*, Oxford University Press, 1965, pp. 280ff.
21. *The Times*, 4 June 1915, cit., from Hurwitz, *State Intervention in Great Britain*, p. 104. See also D. Lloyd George, *War Memoirs*, 6 vols, Nicholson & Watson, London, 1933–36, vol. III, pp. 1350ff.

service, albeit hedged about by clauses. Out of consideration for the unions the government at first contented itself with organizing national service on a voluntary basis through the medium of the War Munitions Volunteers Scheme of June 1915. In practice this scheme signified little because the munitions volunteers who came forward were for the most part already employed in essential industries. While the Munitions of War Act of July 1915 did not impose national service, the clause relating to leaving certificates meant that munitions workers were bound to their place of employment. This clause was opposed by the unions who repeatedly called for its annulment. At the end of 1916 national service again came up for discussion and in November the Asquith cabinet actually passed a formal resolution to lay the appropriate draft legislation before Parliament.[22] But once again Lloyd George shied away from the prospect of trade union opposition, and instead introduced a voluntary system, this time on a somewhat broader basis. The new National Service Scheme applied to all men between the ages of eighteen and sixty-one, and subsequently also to women, whereas the earlier War Munitions Volunteer Scheme had comprised skilled workers only. In all, 270,000 men and women registered under the National Service Scheme but, as with its predecessor, most of the volunteers were already in essential occupations. The increasing demands of the military on the nation's manpower combined with the war-weariness of large sections of labour left little scope for voluntary effort. In June 1918 the government made a final attempt to introduce a form of general national service by calling on all skilled workers who had been exempted from military service to register on a voluntary basis under the existing Munitions Volunteer Scheme, on pain of forfeiting their exemption. In practice this would have meant abandoning the voluntary scheme of June 1915 in favour of general national service, a measure which had from the start been energetically combated by the unions. On this occasion, too, their opposition was so violent that the government quietly shelved the project.

Although the unions endeavoured to safeguard their members' interests and were by no means always complaisant in their dealings with government and employers, their policy was viewed with increasing mistrust by the workers. As in all other countries,

22. See Guinn, *British Strategy and Politics 1914 to 1918*, p. 177.

there was good reason for this. The war had brought about a drastic deterioration in the workers' position and, while they and their organizations were subjected to restrictions for the sake of King and country, the control of industry remained all too clearly in the hands of the employers who expected and obtained substantial profits in return for their contribution to the war economy.

In the vacuum thus created between the workers and the official trade unions there arose a spontaneous labour movement which came to be known, after its chief protagonists and the principle item on its platform, as the 'Shop Stewards' Movement' or 'Workers' Committee Movement'.[23] Before the war the shop stewards had been the unions' spokesmen in the factories. British trade unions were primarily organized on an occupational basis, in accordance with their aim of pursuing a policy of wage differentials as between trades. As a rule a number of unions functioned in the same factory, and the shop stewards, as intermediaries between their own organizations and the workers, had the task of recruiting members, collecting subscriptions and notifying the local union branch of shop floor problems. This intrinsically humdrum function gained in importance during the war when, alongside general wages policy, industrial problems such as the fixing of piece rates, the change-over to war production and, above all, dilution, began to loom large. Since they were constantly grappling with these questions, the shop stewards acted as a ready-made catalyst for a spontaneous labour movement.

The demand for workers' committees and workers' control which attained such significance in this spontaneous labour movement may be traced back to the pre-war period and, not fortuitously perhaps, to the industrial region of Clydeside already referred to. The Clyde was a traditional stronghold of the left wing in the British Labour Movement. This faction, primarily represented by the Socialist Labour Party, wanted to organize the workers by factories and branches of industry, starting at production level, thus postulating a socialist democracy in which industry would be directly controlled by the workers. The scheme was not

23. See W. Kendall, *The Revolutionary Movement in Britain 1900–1921*, Weidenfeld & Nicolson, London, 1969; Pribicevic, *The Shop Stewards' Movement*; Hinton, *The First Shop Stewards' Movement*; G. D. H. Cole, *Workshop Organization*, Clarendon Press, Oxford, 1923; and Cunnison and Scott, *The Industries of the Clyde Valley*.

unlike syndicalism but, whereas the latter never had much of a following in Britain, industrial unionism, i.e. the principle of factory organization and the demand for workers' control, gained a certain footing among the workpeople and the minor functionaries of the traditional unions, although the Socialist Labour Party itself never grew to any size.

In the course of negotiations with employers and the government in the spring of 1915 the unions had been accorded joint consultation rights in the implementation of the dilution programme. In order to put these rights into effect, joint armament committees were set up in April and May 1915 at centres of the munitions industry such as Glasgow, Newcastle and Leeds. The workers' representatives on these committees did not simply confine themselves to dilution or other 'labour questions' in the traditional sense of the term, but also evolved plans for the participation of workers and their unions in the management of the state munitions factories. The armament committees were regarded by G. D. H. Cole and other trade unionists as forward-looking experiments in the joint control of industry, which would bring about a qualitative change in the capitalist relations of production. These hopes were based on a brief phase of experimentation when the status of the armament committees had yet to be officially defined and Lloyd George, in speaking of economic policy generally, used such terms as 'control' and 'nationalization'. But from the outset the employers' representatives on the armament committees opposed every attempt to involve the latter in the management either of private concerns or of the new government munitions factories. These plans were in any case doomed, for in the summer of 1915 the new Ministry of Munitions abolished the regional armament committees in favour of its own strictly centralized organization whose establishment was enlarged to cover the whole country. The unions, and more notably the Amalgamated Society of Engineers, raised little or no objection. The idea of workers' control in the comprehensive sense of the term was more or less foreign to them, nor did they realize until it was too late that the armament committees had provided an opportunity of exerting influence not only upon dilution but on the munitions industry as a whole.

Hence the demand for workers' control was put forward, not by the official unions, but rather by spontaneous workers' committees, themselves reminiscent of the early beginnings of the Socialist Labour Party. The first of these committees evolved out of the strike committee which, in February 1915, had organized the Clydeside engineers' strike. When the strike was over, the Clyde Workers' Committee constituted itself a permanent organization with the object of tackling the numerous shop floor problems arising out of the change-over to munitions production. Here a major issue was dilution which, on the strength of previous agreements and the Munitions of War Act, employers were preparing to introduce on a grand scale in the summer of 1915. After some hesitation the Clyde Workers' Committee accepted dilution on principle, but at the same time demanded that the state take over the munitions industry and that the workers be accorded full rights of co-determination in production matters. A visit by Lloyd George to the Clyde in December 1915, intended to pour oil on troubled waters, ultimately did more harm than good. The government rejected co-determination and, without co-determination, the workers rejected dilution. But when it came to the point, the Clyde Workers' Committee proved to be as helpless as the trade unions the year before. Their anti-dilution tactics stood condemned as prejudicial to munitions production at a time of national emergency and, under threefold pressure from state, employers and public opinion, resistance gradually crumbled away. In several factories the shop stewards signed agreements which were more or less consistent with the position adopted by the unions. The workers were given a say in the implementation of dilution, but none at all in the management of the factories. In March 1916 a fruitless strike and the consequent deportation of the leading members of the Clyde Workers' Committee finally broke what resistance remained. All things considered, the downfall of the Clyde Workers' Committee was hardly surprising. The demand for workers' control meant nothing less than a fundamental revision of the capitalist relations of production, something that could no more be achieved by sporadic resistance than by the well-meaning scheme evolved earlier by the workers' representatives on the armament committees.

Despite this setback, the dispute on the Clyde helped to promote the cause of workers' control. It gave wide publicity to the Clydeside workers' demands which were taken up at national level by the Shop Stewards' Movement. This movement gained a foothold in the metal industry, the most important branch of the munitions industry, and later in mining; Sheffield now joined Glasgow as a centre of the labour movement's left wing. The setback on the Clyde had taught the left wing to take a long-term view. Intermittent negotiations with the government over workers' control were seen to be ineffective and were rejected for that reason. When in 1917 the government subsequently offered the workers a drastically modified form of co-determination on what were known as the Whitley Committees, the shop stewards turned down the proposal. Instead they directed their efforts towards building up an organization with a broad mass base that was intended ultimately to overcome the capitalist system. From 1917 onwards they held regular conferences at national level.

The strength of the Shop Stewards' Movement lay in its close contacts with the workers. It was better able than the unions, bound as they were by their undertakings to the government, to devote itself to the numerous problems of the shop floor and consistently to promote labour interests such as wages and exemption from military service. This practical work lent immediacy to the demand for workers' control. On the other hand there was a latent weakness in the movement, namely the discrepancy between its long-term goals and the actual social conditions. The left wing of the labour movement, under the influence of the Russian Revolution, came increasingly to believe that a union-oriented policy alone could never achieve workers' control which, on the contrary, called for a political struggle. Though the leaders of the Shop Stewards' Movement made approaches to the newly formed Communist Party, there was no formal link-up. However, the mass of workers refused to follow them along this path, the more especially since the recrudescence of the general wage question – which was also the province of the trade unions – now eclipsed many of the problems arising out of the war. Hence the Shop Stewards' Movement was unable to assert itself as an independent movement, although its demands continued to provide inspiration for British trade unionism.

Wage levels and wage differentials

The unions were never a political counterpoise, but rather might be described as junior partners in the formulation of official economic policy. Nor were they equipped for the role of a politically decisive factor, even had such an opportunity arisen. The British trade unions were avowedly 'reformist' and in Germany, too, a discussion of union strategy some years before had led to the conclusion that the organizations should confine themselves to economic and social questions and steer clear of the political struggle. The war was to show that such distinctions were factitious. By assenting to the war, the unions adopted a position which prevented them from safe-guarding their members' concrete material interests. Despite all their efforts and a few isolated institutional achievements, the position of the workers as a whole deteriorated drastically during the war. To substantiate the foregoing we must now consider the trend in wage levels and wage differentials.

Germany

In the decades preceding the Great War, real wages in Germany rose slightly; thus from the nineties onwards the working class participated to some extent in the 'Imperial upsurge'.[24] This prolonged phase of growth was interrupted at more or less regular intervals by crises. One of these occurred in 1913 when the rate of growth of the net national product at constant prices fell off, and unemployment rose by almost 3 per cent.[25] With the outbreak of war the crisis became more acute. General mobilization was hardly conducive to orderly economic activity and, even when it was completed, a gloomy view was taken of business prospects outside of the few industries specializing in armaments. Unemploy-

24. See G. Bry, *Wages in Germany 1871–1945*, Princeton University Press, 1960. From the Marxist viewpoint: J. Kuczynski, *Darstellung der Lage der Arbeiter in Deutschland von 1900 bis 1917/18* (*Die Geschichte der Lage der Arbeiter unter dem Kapitalismus*, Vol. IV), Akademie-Verlag, Berlin, 1967. Both rely to some extent, but not exclusively, on Zimmermann, *Die Veränderungen der Einkommens– und Lebensverhältnisse.* For the history of the previous period see also A. V. Desai, *Real Wages in Germany 1871–1923*, Clarendon Press, Oxford, 1968.

25. See W. G. Hoffmann, F. Grumbach and H. Hesse, *Das Wachstum der deutschen Wirtschaft seit der Mitte des 19. Jahrhunderts*, Springer, Berlin/Heidelberg/New York, 1965, p. 828; Kuczynski, *Darstellung der Lage der Arbeiter*, p. 315.

ment rose to over 20 per cent,[26] while the decline in business activity alone meant lower earnings for many who kept their jobs. On top of that, the situation in the labour market led many firms to reduce their wage rates. Hardest hit were the women; in September 1914 their average daily wage was approximately 15 per cent less than it had been in March.[27] But in certain trades men also suffered a considerable loss of earnings.[28] Wages were adversely affected, not only by high unemployment, but also by the industrial truce whereby the unions had renounced industrial action. From January to July 1914 there had been, on average, 170 strikes a month; in August 1914 there were no strikes at all, and from September to December the monthly average was 6. With social peace in view, the government frowned on the exploitation of unemployment and of the industrial truce for the purpose of depressing wages. A general directive was issued to the effect that army contracts should be awarded only to those firms which did not pay less than standard rates; but this directive had little force since at that time standard minimum rates were far from being the norm.[29]

The lowering of wages at the beginning of the war hit the workers particularly hard because there was simultaneously a marked rise in the cost of living. Retail prices immediately soared, an abnormal movement that was attributable to widespread panic buying. The shops were invaded by people anxious to lay in stocks of food and other articles in daily use. Traders improved the shining hour by charging whatever the market would stand. In Berlin, to give but one example, the price of a pound of flour rose in one day from 25 to 40 pfennigs and a pound of salt from 11 to 60 pfennigs – this, at a time when a man's hourly wage was between 40 and 80 pfennigs, according to his trade.[30] The wave of panic buying and its exploitation by the profiteers came as no surprise to the govern-

26. On employment see F. Hesse, *Die deutsche Wirtschaftlage von 1914–1923* Fischer, Jena, 1938.

27. Bry, *Wages in Germany*, p. 200.

28. For a survey of individual branches, see Kuczynski, *Darstellung der Lage der Arbeiter*, p. 328.

29. By the end of 1913 wage agreements were in force in respect of 1·3 million workers. See Umbreit, *Die deutschen Gewerkschaften im Krieg*, p. 33.

30. Prices from A. Skalweit, *Die deutsche Kriegsernährungswirtschaft*, Deutsche Verlags-Anstalt, Berlin/Leipzig/Stuttgart, 1927. Wages from Kuczynski, *Darstellung der Lage der Arbeiter*, p. 371.

ment. The emergency legislation, which had been kept in mothballs until promulgated on 4 August 1914, included a maximum prices law. This empowered local and district councils in time of war to fix maximum prices for 'articles in daily use, notably foodstuffs and forage of all kinds, as also unprocessed natural products, and heating and lighting fuels'.[31]

The maximum prices now imposed by the local authorities, combined with a drop in panic buying, forced down some of the more inflated prices to acceptable levels. However a decentralized maximum prices policy proved wholly ineffectual in the face of the subsequent inflation which, though not so spectacular as the huge price rises of the early days, nevertheless eroded the value of money all the more steadily and surely. Wartime inflation was due, not to a temporary shortage such as might be brought about by private hoarding or distribution difficulties, but rather to a fundamental discrepancy between diminishing supplies and the continuing high level of demand. This relationship has already been mentioned in the chapter on war finance: from the outset the state withdrew from the economy both manpower for the armed forces and materials of all kinds for their equipment, but failed to pursue a consistent fiscal policy that would have brought about a corresponding reduction in private demand. In October 1914, maximum prices were imposed for grain and applied not only to retailers, but also to producers and wholesalers. It was only under pressure from public opinion, however, that the government, albeit slowly and reluctantly, extended its maximum prices policy to other essential goods.

From the beginning of 1915, mobilization combined with the armaments boom led to a noticeable drop in industrial unemployment which, overall, had fallen to its pre-war level by April of that year. In the essential industries and in agriculture there were already complaints about a shortage of labour, and such unemployment as thereafter remained was due to various obstacles to mobility. As demands on the munitions industry increased and ever more men were called to the colours, shortage of manpower came to be the crucial bottleneck in the war economy. Full employment brought a further rise in money wages, and it may be supposed that the resumption of industrial disputes in 1915 and 1916 also helped to accelerate the process. But neither the level

31. See Skalweit, *Kriegsernährungswirtschaft*, p. 116.

of money wages nor their rate of increase kept pace with the rising cost of living, with the result that the real position of the working class grew noticeably worse from year to year.

Wage trends entered a third phase with the introduction of the Hindenburg Programme, mentioned earlier in this book, and the Patriotic Auxiliary Service Law. Total economic mobilization gave yet another powerful stimulus to inflation, for the government was pumping more money than ever before into the armament sector. The inflationary stimulus communicated itself to civilian demand while at the same time output for civilian needs was ruthlessly cut back in the interests of the war effort. It is therefore correct to say that prices *and* wages rose; contrary to the expectations of many employers, the Auxiliary Service Law did not bring about a fall in wages. Indeed, by recognizing financial gain as sufficient grounds for a change of employer, the state actually placed the seal of official approval on wage rises. But, as before, wages continued to lag behind rising prices. It was only during the last year of the war that wages and the cost of living rose at the same rate, since government price controls were now more strongly reflected in the price index.

However, the cost of living index had long ceased to be a reliable guide to the true value of money. Large sections of the population were compelled, at least in so far as their means allowed, to supplement their rations by buying on the black market. Whereas in 1918 the cost of living was officially 200 per cent higher than before the war, reports issued by various authorities show that on the black market some prices had risen by 300 to 700 per cent. In September 1918 a man's average wage was 10·26 marks a day as against 4·84 marks in March 1914; in September 1918 a woman earned on average 5·41 marks a day as opposed to 2·27 marks in March 1914.[32] But in October 1918 the Berlin police chief reported that the black market price for a pound of butter was 24 marks and for an egg, 1·50 marks.[33] Account must be taken, not only of the inadequacy of the official price index which, for obvious reasons, did not include black market prices,

32. Average over twelve branches of industry, no account being taken of variations in the numbers of workers. See Zimmerman, *Die Veränderungen der Einkommens- und Lebensverhältnisse*, pp. 367ff. According to these figures the increase was 112 per cent for men and 138 per cent for women.

33. See Kuczynski, *Darstellung der Lage der Arbeiter*, p. 357.

but also of the deterioration in the quality of all consumer goods: textiles, foodstuffs, shoes, all came to the normal consumer in the form of some kind of substitute. The war had visited upon the people tremendous impoverishment, thinly veiled by the hectic activity in the munitions industry and an inflationary war boom. There were, however, differences in the degree of distress, differences between the armament and the civil sector, between men and women, between skilled and unskilled workers.

There is nothing surprising about the wage differentials between trades. Any industry essential to armaments was overwhelmed with orders. Munitions manufacturers used high wages as a bait to lure workers away from their competitors and from other sectors, for wage costs could be passed on to the customer, i.e. the state. With the launching of the Hindenburg Programme, the procurement agencies no longer negotiated fixed price contracts but instead worked on a basis of cost plus a profit margin of so much per cent; thus every wage increase actually benefited the employer since it automatically increased his profits. That this would trigger an explosive wage–price spiral was perfectly clear to the authorities, but no official wage controls were possible so long as employers refused to countenance any control of profits. On the other hand, non-essential industries were compelled by a shortage of raw and other materials to curtail production and hence were in some cases over-manned. For this reason, it was relatively difficult to push through wage increases, and so money wages lagged far behind the rising price level. According to figures issued by the Imperial Statistics Office between 1914 and 1918, nominal wages for men in war industries (metal, engineering, chemical, electrical) rose by 142 per cent, in civil industries (food stuffs, textiles, clothing, printing) by 68 per cent. The armaments boom expanded the wages hierarchy and unseated some sections of the former 'workers' aristocracy'. In 1914 the wages hierarchy was headed by the printers with an average daily wage of 6·50 marks and in 1918 by the electrical workers with a daily wage of 13·46 marks. Those who remained at the lower end included textile workers, with a daily wage of 3·64 marks in 1914 and 6·47 marks in 1918. Whereas some of the glitter from the employers' war profits rubbed off on to the specialists in the munitions factories, thus putting them in a position to buy on the black market, the Lusatian weavers were earning between 26 and 33 marks a week, and it is difficult to imagine how they could subsist on this wage. The munitions workers were regarded with a certain envy, particularly by the dispossessed middle class of white collar workers who accused them of profiteering. On the other hand, workers in the heavily populated centres of the munitions industry were particularly hard-hit by rising prices and the housing shortage, so that even here there can hardly have been any real improvement in living standards.

The traditional differences in status that had obtained between skilled and unskilled, adults and juveniles, men and women, tended to lessen as the war proceeded. Skilled workers who had been called to the colours were replaced by semi-skilled workers, notably women and juveniles. These changes in the composition of the labour force had, for background, the restructuring of production processes. Increasing standardization and mechanization meant that factory work became increasingly subdivided into skilled tasks such as preparatory work, supervision and maintenance on the one hand, and simple (and correspondingly monotonous) operations on the other. Thus, less skilled employees, in particular women and juveniles, were not confined to unskilled tasks but, as semi-skilled mass-production workers, were responsible for a large part of the factory's output, which in turn implied a relative improvement in earnings potential. According to figures for 1918 in respect of six Rhineland munitions and explosives factories, a semi-skilled worker earned on average 19 marks a day, while a skilled worker earned only 12 marks. An explanatory note points out that production was mainly dependent on semi-skilled chemical workers whose relatively high daily earnings were based on piece rates and danger money, whereas the skilled workers, being mostly engaged in craft activities, were paid by the hour. However, there were exceptions to this trend, particularly in the case of highly skilled, much sought-after specialists. At Krupp's, for example, the wages of skilled workers rose more rapidly than those of the unskilled.[34] According to figures for industry in Bavaria, the wage differential between skilled and unskilled workers diminished in the civil industries and increased in the war industries.[35]

34. See Zimmerman, *Die Veränderungen der Einkommens- und Lebensverhältnisse*, pp. 382–92.

35. See Bry, *Wages in Germany*, p. 204.

The wage differential between men and women was steadily eroded. In the course of the war, women's average daily earnings rose by 138 per cent (from 2.27 marks to 5.41 marks), and those of men by 112 per cent (from 4.84 marks to 10.26 marks). The steeper rise in women's average earnings was mainly due to the fact that shortage of manpower gave them access to sectors, such as the metal industry, that offered a better rate of pay, whereas before the war they had been typically engaged in lower-paid occupations: for instance textiles and clothing. But social discrimination had by no means ceased. Now as before women earned on average only about half as much as men. They did not emerge from the status of unskilled workers with its concomitant insecurity, nor did they receive equal pay for equal work. In March 1914 women's wages in the metal industry were 37 per cent of those of men, in the chemical industry 46 per cent, and in the textile industry 63 per cent; in September 1918 the corresponding figures were 51 per cent, 55 per cent and 66 per cent.

As a result of wartime inflation, white collar workers in both public and private sectors found themselves, like the working class, in drastically reduced circumstances. According to figures produced by the Imperial Statistics Office, the real income of officials fell during the war to 70 per cent of the pre-war level in the case of the junior grades, and to 55 per cent and 47 per cent respectively in the case of the middle and senior grades.[36] The percentages vary because certain cost of living bonuses were paid at a flat rate on the assumption that senior officials were less hard-hit than those at the lower end of the earnings scale. In the private sector the wages of white collar workers also lagged noticeably behind the rising price level, more so on the commercial than on the technical side. The traditional deference of white collar workers towards their employers, whether private or public, meant that they were less able to defend their own interests than many of the workers whose special skills were in demand in the munitions industry. In an objective sense, i.e. in terms of their material circumstances, many of these white collar workers were moving closer to the proletariat, whereas their social aspirations depended on keeping as great a distance as possible between themselves and

36. See A. Günther, *Die Folgen des Krieges für Einkommen und Lebenshaltung der mittleren Volksschichten Deutschlands*, Deutsche Verlags-Anstalt, Stuttgart/Berlin/Leipzig, 1932.

the lower classes. The awareness of being 'déclassé' precluded solidarity; the anger of the dispossessed middle class was directed, less against the war and its instigators than, for example, against the munitions workers who, thanks to their skills and their militancy, were somewhat better able to maintain their real earnings. It was of small comfort to the white collar workers that, on average, they were still appreciably better-off than the mass of the workers.

Britain

In the summer of 1914 the wages of industrial workers in Britain varied between 20s. in the textile industry and 40s. in the metal industry.[37] Within the various trades wages might differ widely depending on qualifications: in the building trade, for example, unskilled workers earned 26s., skilled workers 40s. At the lower end of the scale farm wages were rather less than 20s. a week, including payments in kind. In the years immediately preceding the war, the nominal level of wages rose slightly but failed to keep pace with rising prices, so that real earnings tended to fall. During the summer of 1914 the unions in a number of important trades had recourse to industrial action in order to obviate a further drop in real earnings.

This development was interrupted by the war for, as in other countries, organized labour in Britain agreed to abstain from industrial action in the interests of munitions production; on 24 August 1914, the unions and the Labour Party issued a joint statement to this effect.[38] Their undertaking had already been anticipated in practice: the hundred strikes in progress at the beginning of August 1914 had dwindled to twenty by the end of the month. The relevant statistics for the second quarter of 1914 show 250,000 workers on strike and 5 million lost working days, against 21,000 and 160,000 respectively for the fourth quarter.[39] In some places the trade unions' industrial truce aroused little enthusiasm but rarely met with overt opposition.

37. See A. Bowley, *Prices and Wages in the United Kingdom 1914–1920*, Clarendon Press, Oxford, 1921.

38. Reproduced in G. D. H. Cole, *Trade Unionism and Munitions*, Clarendon Press, Oxford, 1923, p. 52. Also in Hurwitz, *State Intervention*, pp. 240ff.

39. See ibid., p. 241.

Partly because of the economic crisis following the outbreak of war, and partly because of the moderation of the unions, wages did not rise during the early months of the conflict. Nor for their part did the employers, like many of their German opposite numbers, take advantage of the situation to depress piece-rates and time-rates. However, reduced business activity in certain sectors meant a substantial loss of earnings for piece-workers, since the 'freeze' applied to piece-rates but not to income. In the cotton industry the operatives' average weekly wage in August 1914 was some 30 per cent lower than in peacetime and in December their earnings were still some 10 per cent below the pre-war average.

From the summer of 1915 onwards rising prices compelled the unions to demand wage increases, or rather to revert to the demands that had been held in abeyance since August 1914. According to official estimates, food prices at the beginning of 1915 were 20 per cent, and consumer prices generally 10 to 15 per cent higher than in July 1914; hence real earnings had declined appreciably. In their wage negotiations the unions had set their sights comparatively low, for their chief concern was to keep pace with the cost of living rather than secure a share in the rapidly increasing armaments profits. Instead of percentage increases in time and piece-rates, therefore, they often agreed 'war bonuses' at a flat rate for all workers in one trade. The increases secured in 1915 and 1916 were too modest to reduce the gap between earnings and the rising level of prices, but in the last two years the gap narrowed. Increasing pressure from the workers brought about a steeper rise in wages both in absolute and relative terms, whereas prices rose more slowly because official price controls were now gradually taking effect. However earnings did not catch up with prices until after the war.

Wage trends varied widely from trade to trade. Both the government and the employers paid relatively high wages to essential workers in order to obviate the risk of industrial disputes and hence of production stoppages; they also wanted to attract additional labour. The wages of metal workers, miners, railwaymen and dockers rose by between 80 and 100 per cent, more or less at the same rate as the cost of living. In other trades, earnings lagged far behind price rises. In the cotton industry, for example, wages at the end of 1917 were nominally a little more than 20 per cent above the pre-war level.[40] During the final year of war piece-rates were raised on several occasions but since shortage of raw materials also necessitated short-time working, effective earnings actually dropped in certain cases. Nevertheless in terms of profitability the cotton industry was admirably placed, for the change-over to a sellers' market permitted employers to achieve a substantial increase in profits despite falling production and correspondingly fewer goods for sale.

During the war wage differentials based on skill diminished noticeably. This was due to the upgrading of unskilled workers, especially women, as a result of dilution, and even more to the widespread practice of awarding wage increases in the shape of a flat rate cost of living bonus. Between July 1914 and July 1918, the wages of skilled workers in engineering rose by about 70 per cent and those of unskilled workers by some 110 per cent. According to Bowley, the wages of unskilled workers during the war rose overall by something like 100 to 125 per cent, while those of skilled workers rose by less than 100 per cent;[41] though not derived from a representative random sample, these figures are nevertheless based on a thorough knowledge of the statistical material. Even agricultural workers, who in 1914 were at the lower end of the earnings scale, were better able to maintain their real wages than many industrial workers.

One noticeable trend was the relative improvement in women's as compared with men's wages. Here the decisive factor was the invasion by women of traditionally male occupations, above all in the munitions industry. Moreover, especially where women's wages were concerned, the state deemed it advisable to intervene in the interests of industrial peace. In October 1915 the minimum wage for women munition workers who had taken the place of men was fixed at £1 a week; initially this applied only to state-owned factories but, from February 1916 onwards, was extended to all controlled establishments. Women engaged in skilled work were to receive the same rate as a skilled man doing the same job. This minimum wage set standards which extended beyond the munitions industry to the traditional female occupations. Never-

40. On wages and profits in the cotton industry, see more especially H. D. Henderson's monograph, *The Cotton Control Board*, Clarendon Press Oxford, 1922.
41. See Bowley, *Prices and Wages*, p. 100.

theless, the principle of equal pay for equal work was not realized. Means of circumventing it were provided not only by the imprecise wording of the regulations but also by the fact that, as a result of the general trend towards automated production, no exact parallel could be drawn between the older and newer plants. On average, women's wages in industry as a whole were some 150 per cent higher in the autumn of 1918 than they had been before the war, having risen from some 14s. to the region of 35s., but this did not mean parity with men's wages. In April 1918 women munitions workers employed by the state earned on average 23 to 39 per cent less than the men; taking a cross-section of industry as a whole, the difference was even greater, since the traditionally female occupations still remained at the lower end of the earnings scale.

Prior to 1914 wages differed considerably from region to region. Wage agreements at national level were first introduced before the war in the iron and steel and the coal industries. In engineering and shipbuilding, on the other hand, such agreements were worked out strictly at regional level with the result that there were wide disparities: for example the weekly wage of a skilled turner in engineering varied between 24s. in Cornwall and 46s. in London.[42] In addition to such anomalies within the same trade, there were also differences arising out of the individual industrial structure of each region. Inter-regional wage differences were not so much nominal as real, being attributable in part to the supply of cheap labour in the rural areas and in part to differences in the cost of living: food prices, and in particular rents, were lower in small towns and in the country. During the war conflicting influences were at work on these anomalies. On the one hand, official wages policy, supported by the unions, aimed at eliminating them (the trend was towards wage agreements at national level; in the later phase of the war inter-regional price differences were likewise becoming less marked as a result of official prices policy). On the other hand, differences in industrial structure meant, of course, that inter-regional differences in average incomes still persisted. These last became even more marked, since the largest wage increases were recorded in the centres of the munitions industry. It should also be noted that, contrary to the general trend, wage increases in individual sectors varied considerably in respect of

42. See H. Wolfe, *Labour Supply and Regulation*, Clarendon Press, Oxford, 1923, p. 235.

identical jobs, particularly in iron and steel and in metal working; in the period July 1914 to July 1918, wages of skilled workers in individual centres rose by anything between 50 per cent plus and nearly 100 per cent.

In Britain, too, a downward trend in the real standard of living of the working population between 1914 and 1918 cannot be disregarded, but distress never reached the same catastrophic proportions as in Germany. The thesis has, indeed, been advanced that there was a tendency towards the levelling out of working class conditions, not only 'from above' as a result of the relatively steep fall in the wages of skilled labour, but also 'from below' as a result of the decrease in the incidence of extreme pauperism.[43] One argument in favour of this is the relatively steep nominal rise in wages that took place at the lower end of the scale. Before the war, a family of two adults and three children with an income of 23s. a week was regarded as being on the poverty line.[44] Wages were so low at the time that many working class families lived below this minimum, even in cases where the breadwinner followed a respectable trade and was constantly employed. In so far as some exceptionally low wages rose more quickly than the cost of living, the number of families living below the poverty line decreased. A further argument turns on continuity of employment. Work was plentiful in the munitions industry and unemployment virtually disappeared. From the spring of 1915 the number of people receiving public assistance declined so noticeably that there was talk of a 'workhouse exodus'.[45] Both arguments are, of course, based on what were no more than marginal improvements. By no means all low wage earners enjoyed a disproportionately large nominal rise: in the cotton industry, for example, wages, which in 1914 were at the very bottom of the scale, rose exceptionally slowly. While it is perfectly true that the workers who remained at home enjoyed continuity of employment, this was clearly only because millions of their fellows were serving in the forces; hence the 'improvement' was a distinctly specious one.

43. See E. Abbott, 'English War Statistics of Pauperism', *Journal of Political Economy*, 33, 1925; A. Bowley, *Some Economic Consequences of the Great War*, Thornton Butterworth, London, 1930.

44. See A. Bowley, *Prices and Wages in the United Kingdom 1914–1920*, Clarendon Press, Oxford, p. 162.

45. Abbott, *English War Statistics*, p. 17.

The development already noted in the case of Germany and Britain holds good in a wider context.[46] Among the belligerents but also in many neutral countries, inflation caused real wages to fall, a nadir being reached in 1917. Thereafter the unions succeeded, or appeared to succeed, in maintaining real wages; as a result of state controls, prices rose more slowly than before while the threat of strike action led to the award of higher money wages. This nominal adjustment during the final year of the war was, of course, fictitious since only limited supplies were available at controlled prices. The scarcity of goods and hence the actual drop in real wages manifested itself all the more clearly in the black market. According to a study conducted by the International Labour Office, wage differentials steadily diminished during the course of the war and the gap between skilled and semi-skilled workers (particularly women), narrowed.[47] For this, two reasons are adduced: firstly, wage increases adjusted to the rising cost of living were frequently based on a flat rate and hence the income rise in the lower wage groups was relatively steeper; secondly, changes in production methods, e.g. mass production, enabled semi-skilled workers – here again, mainly women – to move up into better-paid jobs.

The Second International and the socialist revolution

As is evident from the example of the German and British labour movements, the trade unions did not lightly come to terms with their bourgeois governments; they endeavoured to safeguard the interests of the workers and were prepared to engage in limited conflicts. It would be inappropriate to speak of a 'betrayal' of the workers' cause. But viewed objectively, the unions were the prisoners of their own strategy having already, long before the war, committed themselves to improvements *within* the system. In the opinion of those who, even after August 1914, continued to adhere to the socialist tradition (or at any rate found their way

46. International Labour Office, *Fluctuations des salaires dans différents pays de 1914 à 1921*, Geneva, 1922.

47. International Labour Office, *Fluctuations des salaires dans différents pays de 1914 à 1925*, Geneva, 1926. This study comprises more countries than the above-mentioned work but goes into no more detail in regard to the individual war years.

back to it), and who were fighting *against* the capitalist system, the leaders of the right wing majority in the labour movement were moving dangerously close to the ruling bourgeois governments. After the labour movement's big organizations, once the pride of the Second International, had drawn in their horns, confining themselves to the promotion of their interests within the system, small minorities were all that remained to uphold the socialist tradition and wage a determined struggle against the capitalist system and above all against the imperialist war.

In Germany, the faction within the S.P.D. (German Socialist Party) opposed to the war and the party's official policy of industrial truce, rallied round the left wing under the leadership of Karl Liebknecht and Rosa Luxemburg, Franz Mehring and Klara Zetkin.[48] When the war credits were being voted in the Reichstag on 4 August 1914, the left still conformed to party discipline, but they made no secret whatever of the split over the question of the industrial truce. The turning-point came when, on 3 December 1914, Karl Liebknecht voted against the second War Credits Bill. This faction formed itself into the International Group (renamed 'Spartakus Group' in January 1916) which, after the party had split in 1917, became one of the mainstays of the new Independent Socialist Party. Another and quite separate group of anti-war socialists, calling themselves the International Socialists of Germany, rallied round the left wing social democrat Julian Borchardt and his periodical *Lichtstrahlen*. Despite their common goal, there was a certain amount of friction between the two groups.[49]

In France the periodical *La Vie Ouvrière*[50] formed the rallying

48. See Schorske, *German Social Democracy*. Useful, if somewhat narrow in conception as regards method and content is H. Wohlgemuth, *Burgkrieg, nicht Burgfriede! Der Kampf Karl Liebknechts, Rosa Luxemburgs und ihrer Anhänger um die Rettung der deutschen Nation in den Jahren 1914–1916*, diss., Dietz, Berlin, 1963.

49. For numerous documents, see *Die Zimmerwalder Bewegung. Protokolle und Korrespondenz*. H. Lademacher, ed., 2 vols, Mouton, The Hague/Paris, 1967. Also letter from Liebknecht to Borchardt in Wohlgemuth, *Burgkrieg*, pp. 280ff. On the '*Lichtstrahlen-Gruppe*', see also A. Rosmer, *Le mouvement ouvrier pendant la guerre. De l'union sacrée à Zimmerwald*, Libraire du Travail, Paris, 1936, p. 250; N. Lenin and G. Sinoviev, *Gegen den Strom. Aufsätze aus den Jahren 1914–1916*, Verlag der Kommunistischen Internationale, 1921.

50. See Rosmer, *Le mouvement ouvrier*, pp. 209–16. Alfred Rosmer was

point for various militant trade unionists and socialists who were opposed to the *Union Sacrée*. In November 1914, as a protest against the nationalist policy of the Confédération Générale du Travail, Pierre Monatte resigned from the committee, only to be immediately called up.[51] The opposition did not permit themselves to be discouraged by the close liaison between the government and the leaders of the labour movement's right wing. Thereafter Merrheim represented the oppositional minority in the committee, while his Metal Workers' Union became the spearhead of the anti-war faction. In honour of May Day 1915 and in defiance of the censor, the union's organ, *L'Union des Métaux* published the opposition's slogan 'This war isn't our war'.

Whereas in France opposition to the war first manifested itself among the ranks of the trade unions, in Britain it was the unions who were the most determined advocates of the Labour Party's war policy.[52] Of the affiliated socialist parties, the Fabian Society, of intellectual rather than political significance, was the only one to be uncompromisingly in favour of war. The majority of Independent Labour Party members were anti-war and, in a manifesto of August 1914, the I.L.P. disassociated itself from the Labour Party's war policy. Ramsay MacDonald who, with Keir Hardie and Philip Snowden, was one of the leading members of the I.L.P., resigned the chairmanship of the Labour Party in favour of Arthur Henderson, an active member of the trade union movement. Although the I.L.P. was no more a Marxist party after 1914 than it had been before that date, Karl Liebknecht himself

---

himself a member of this group, along with Pierre Monatte, Marcel Martinet, Alphonse Merrheim, Amédée Dunois, Henri Guilbeaux, Daniel Renoult and Martov, the Russian socialist. See also R. Wohl, *French Communism in the Making, 1914–1924*, Stanford University Press, 1966, pp. 58–62; A. Kriegel, *Aux origines du communisme français, 1914–1920*, 2 vols. Mouton, Paris/The Hague, 1964.

51. See Rosmer, *Le mouvement ouvrier*, pp. 177–81.

52. See C. F. Brand, *British Labour's Rise to Power. Eight Studies*, Stanford University Press, 1941; C. F. Brand, *The British Labour Party. A Short History* Stanford University Press, 1964; G. D. H. Cole, *A History of the Labour Party from 1914*, Routledge, London, 1948. At the time the Labour Party was an umbrella organization without individual members. It comprised the trade unions, the Independent Labour Party and the Fabian Society; when war broke out, the British Socialist Party was suing for membership, which was granted in 1916.

was to testify that, together with its brothers in Russia and Serbia, this party had 'saved the honour of socialism amidst the frenzied slaughter of the peoples'.[53] The British Socialist Party, a Marxist organization, was divided over the question of participation in the war. While the majority was 'uncompromisingly anti-war',[54] a minority, under the founder, Henry Hyndman, proved to be resolute nationalists, and in 1916 they left the party.[55]

The decisions of August 1914, had in effect, brought about the dissolution of the Second International. After throwing in their lot with their respective governments, the chief workers' parties were cut off from one another by the battle lines. Vandervelde, the last president of the Second International, joined the Belgian government; the International Socialist Bureau, which removed from Brussels to The Hague in December 1914, became no more than a shadow of its former self. The initiatives undertaken with so much optimism at the beginning of the war by the neutral socialist parties invariably foundered on the same problem: having rallied to their governments, the workers' parties and trade unions, though able to agree within their respective military alliances, so that there was no shortage of 'socialist' conferences in either of the belligerent camps, could not bridge the gulf dividing them from the 'enemy'. Hence the task of safeguarding the internationalism of the labour movement remained the responsibility of the oppositional minorities.

Besides conducting the political struggle at home, these minorities endeavoured to pick up the broken threads of international relations. From the unremitting efforts of socialists and opponents of the war there arose the 'Zimmerwald Movement' which, during the conflict, represented the true International of the labour movement.[56] The first conference, from which the movement

53. Letter written in December 1914 to the editor of the *Labour Leader*, cit., from Wohlgemuth, *Burgkrieg*, p. 253.

54. Cole, *History of the Labour Party*, p. 20.

55. See C. Tsuzuki, *H. M. Hyndman and British Socialism*, Oxford University Press, 1961.

56. For a general survey, see A. Reisberg, *Lenin und die Zimmerwalder Bewegung*, Dietz, Berlin, 1966. A history of the Zimmerwald Movement still remains to be written. Two important collections of documents are: O. H. Gankin and H. H. Fisher, eds., *The Bolsheviks and the World War*; and Lademacher, ed., *Die Zimmerwalder Bewegung*. There are several well-known accounts of the Zimmerwald Movement written by active participants and

derived its name, took place in September 1915 at the invitation of Swiss and Italian socialists in the little village of Zimmerwald near Berne.[57] The goal to which they were pledged was opposition to the war. Socialists of patriotic persuasion had not been invited. One of the moral climaxes of the conference was a joint declaration by the French and German delegates:

> In as much as we disassociate ourselves from the industrial truce, in as much as we remain true to the class struggle which constitutes the foundation for the building of the Socialist International, we, the German and French socialists and trade unions, stand shoulder to shoulder with our countrymen in the struggle against this fearful destiny and the genocide which degrades mankind.[58]

But despite their common desire for peace, no one could agree on the course to be pursued. A left wing group ranged itself behind Lenin's programme which in the meantime had come to be regarded as the classic exposition of the Marxist strategy and tactics to be employed against the imperialist war: namely strict political demarcation and organizational separation from the patriotic, 'opportunist' trend in the labour movement; revolutionary mass operations against the war; and, finally, the transformation of the imperialist war into a civil war against the ruling classes.[59] Implicit in Lenin's programme were two uncomfortable

which are therefore of a documentary nature: A. Balabanoff, *Die Zimmerwalder Bewegung 1914–1919*, Hirschfeld, Leipzig, 1928, reprint., Verlag Neue Kritik, Frankfurt, 1969; J. Humbert-Droz, *Der Krieg und die Internationale. Die Konferenzen von Zimmerwald und Kienthal*, Europa-Verlag, Vienna/Frankfurt/ Zurich, 1964; Rosmer, *Le mouvement ouvrier* – a second volume appeared twenty-three years later – *De Zimmerwald à la Révolution russe*, Mouton, Paris/The Hague, 1959. A concise account which, however, hardly does justice to the Zimmerwald left, may also be found in J. Braunthal, *Geschichte der Internationale*, vol. II, Dietz, Hanover, 1963.

57. The whole affair was somewhat picturesque. Robert Grimm, the Swiss organizer, assembled the delegates in the Berne Volkshaus and, in order to shake off agents and spies, conveyed them from there to Zimmerwald in four carriages. When the inhabitants of Zimmerwald later discovered exactly what the 'friendly tourists' had been up to, they solemnly protested against the 'abuse' of their village. See Humbert-Droz, *Der Krieg und die Internationale*, pp. 128ff.

58. H. Lademacher, ed., *Die Zimmerwalder Bewegung*, vol. I, pp. 175ff; Gankin and Fisher, eds., *The Bolsheviks and the World War*, pp. 328ff.

59. The 'left faction' of the conference is generally held to comprise those

conclusions – uncomfortable not only for the governments and their 'social-patriotic' coalition partners, but also for the socialist delegates. The first was the abandonment of the Second International which, after August 1914, remained no more than a shadow of its former self and in Lenin's view was in effect extinct since the responsible organizations had gone over to the camp of the ruling classes; hence the oppositional minorities must combine to form a Third International to carry on the revolutionary struggle of the working class. The second was the revolutionary defeatism of Lenin who stated quite unequivocally that on the international plane it was impossible to determine which was the lesser evil for socialism – the defeat of the Allies or that of the Central Powers; but from the viewpoint of the Russian proletariat, the least of evils was the defeat of czarism.[60] The defeat of 'one's own' government, so Lenin averred, was virtually a prerequisite if the revolution was to be expedited.

The left did not succeed in obtaining a majority for their resolution at the Zimmerwald conference. The main divergence turned on the question of a split: whereas the left regarded a split as a prerequisite for determined action, most of the delegates wanted just the opposite, namely to increase their influence within the labour movement's existing organizations and thus ultimately acquire some influence over the latter's policy. Merrheim, the representative of the French revolutionary syndicalists and one of the spokesmen for the majority at the conference,[61] never tired

---

delegates who presented drafts for a resolution and a manifesto of the left; besides the Bolsheviks (Lenin and Zinoviev), these included the delegate of the Latvian Social Democrats (Winter), the delegate of the Polish Social Democratic opposition (Radek), the delegates from Sweden and Norway (Högland and Nerman) and a Swiss delegate, Platten. But there was never any very clear delimitation; a few of the delegates were 'left' and yet were not held to belong to the 'faction', e.g. Berta Thalheimer, a friend of Rosa Luxemburg's and Klara Zetkin's. Cf. Lademacher, ed., *Die Zimmerwalder Bewegung*, pp. 43–180; Lenin and Sinoviev, *Gegen den Strom*, pp. 277–90.

60. See V. I. Lenin, 'Der Krieg und die russische Sozialdemokratie', *Ausgewählte Werke in zwei Bänden*, Dietz, Berlin, 1959/60, vol. I, pp. 679–86 (written in September/October, 1914).

61. The majority which combined against the programme of the left was not, like the latter, a close-knit faction. Besides the French (Merrheim, Bourderon), and Italian delegations, it counted among its spokesmen members of the German delegation (the group round Ledebour, who stood midway between Liebknecht and the 'Centrists').

of emphasizing that the struggle for the masses must be conducted and won within the existing unions, however reactionary these might currently be. Consequently most of the delegates were not in favour of any fundamental secession or reorientation on the part of the opposition, least of all a split in the International, or rather, the founding of a new and revolutionary Third International. The conference ended with a fiery anti-war manifesto. This unmasked the propaganda which declared the war to be a generally defensive one, condemned the policy of cooperation pursued by parties and unions, demanded that nations be given the right of self-determination, called for an immediate peace without annexations or reparations and proclaimed a class struggle against the war. At the same time, however, the terms of the manifesto were sufficiently non-committal to permit of a large measure of anti-war solidarity; despite pressure from the left, it contained no open challenge to the 'opportunists', nor did it tie down the socialist parties to any definite line of action. In the interests of a united front, the left associated itself with the manifesto but in a supplementary declaration expressed its disagreement with the final points mentioned above. It was generally agreed that co-operation and an exchange of opinions between oppositional minorities be institutionalized. To this end an International Socialist Committee was set up, its task being to maintain contacts with the various parties and groups and to make preparations for a new conference. Thus its function was similar to that of the International Socialist Bureau of the Second International.

Seen in historical perspective, the problems of a movement which, both chronologically and politically, stood midway between the Second and Third Internationals, were already becoming clearly defined. Opposition to imperialist governments like the demand for peace, brought together left wing 'revolutionaries' – the nucleus of the future Third International – and 'pacifists' whose prime concern was peace rather than revolution and who still adhered firmly to the traditions of the Second International, hoping to rectify the nationalist volte-face of August 1914 by changes at the top.

The course of the second conference of the Zimmerwald Movement, held in April 1916 in the village of Kienthal in the Bernese Oberland, was also determined by a confrontation of 'revolutionaries' and 'pacifists'. Although the 'social-patriotic' leaders of the workers' parties in individual countries, like the International Socialist Bureau, in no way did justice to the restraint shown by the Zimmerwald Conference (and, indeed, having tried and failed to play down the movement, launched a violent attack upon it) the majority of the delegates at Keinthal balked at a split in the International. The prevailing opinion continued to be that the opposition should agitate and gain influence within existing organizations and thus bring about a change of course. The Zimmerwald left, although still in the minority, succeeded in improving its position: 'The second Zimmerwald conference indubitably represents a *step forward*.'[62] This optimism was well-founded, for the majority (whose composition differed materially from that of the first conference) was drawn together less by a positive programme of its own than by prevarications and reservations in respect of the Bolshevist programme, and hence the Zimmerwald Movement's dynamic was now plainly the preserve of the left. Moreover, revolutionary propaganda was beginning to take effect among the masses, a process which could only reinforce the position of the left wing. Assuming as they did that time was on their side, the left found it easier to support a resolution which, in accordance with the wishes of the majority, omitted all mention of a split or of revolutionary action. On one point the Kienthal resolution was more concrete than that of Zimmerwald – namely, in demanding that socialists in all countries should vote against war credits and resign from bourgeois governments; this was patently a concession to the increasing importance of the left. All in all, the confrontation within the Zimmerwald Movement was more plainly in evidence at Kienthal than at Zimmerwald. While the main resolution was unanimously accepted, many delegates qualified their assent with provisos.[63] In fact the majority opinion at Kienthal was not far removed from that of the 'Centrists' after the latter had carefully disassociated themselves from the jingoism of the early weeks of the war; however, Lenin and the Bolsheviks regarded the 'Centrists' as little better than 'social-patriots'. The third conference of the Zimmerwald Movement, held in Stockholm in August 1917, was already overshadowed by

62. Lenin and Sinoviev, *Gegen den Strom*, p. 354.

63. The peculiar impression made on the conference by these partial retractions has been described by A. Balabanoff in her memoirs, *Erinnerungen und Erlebnisse*, Laubsche Verlagsbuchhandlung, Berlin, 1927, p. 131.

the Russian Revolution which ushered in a new phase of the labour government.

The Russian October revolution inevitably came as a surprise to all those who had expected the first socialist revolution to take place in the most advanced industrial country, or at least at the heart of the international labour movement as represented by the Second International; in either case, Russia was peripheral to the mainstream. Yet this superficial paradox should not blind us to the fact that, even before the Great War, a revolutionary situation of tremendous dynamism was developing in Russia: seen objectively, the centre of the revolutionary movement had been shifting towards Russia ever since the beginning of the twentieth century.[64]

By comparison with western Europe, industrialization in Russia was of very recent date but for that very reason it displayed some extremely modern features. In particular the concentration of industry in a few major undertakings centred on St Petersburg and Moscow has been repeatedly adduced as a decisive factor in the class conditions and the class consciousness of the workers: in a large factory, the polarization of capital and labour was so well defined, if only in a purely quantitative sense, as to be immediately evident. While at least some sections of industry could be described as thoroughly up-to-date from a technological viewpoint, social attitudes were distinctly reactionary.[65] Elementary rights, which the workers of western Europe had won for themselves in the nineteenth century, were still denied to Russian workers when war broke out in 1914. Under the threat of revolution implicit in the October Manifesto of 1905, the government had made a number of concessions, including freedom of association and assembly, but these were largely rescinded when the relevant legislation was introduced in 1906. A trade union could not be set up without official authorization, which might be arbitrarily refused; a total ban was imposed on central organizations comprising several trade unions. In general czarism's response to the failure of the

64. On events leading up to the revolution (with a bibliography relating to its subsequent history), see D. Geyer, *Die Russische Revolution. Historische Probleme und Perspektiven*, Kohlhammer, Stuttgart, 1968; and M. Ferro, *La Révolution de 1917. La chute du tsarisme et les origines d'octobre*, Aubier, Paris, 1967. According to the western calender, the February revolution took place in March and the October revolution in November, 1917.

65. See W. Grinewitsch, *Die Gewerkschaftsbewegung in Russland. Erster Band: 1905-1914*, Verlagsgesellschaft des ADGB, Berlin, 1927.

1905 revolution was an intensification of reactionary measures; thus the Coalition Law was so broadly interpreted as virtually to place a ban on coalition. Almost the whole of the trade union movement was forced into illegality. Not only was the labour movement plagued by legal restrictions, but labour disputes were attended by open and often brutal intervention on the part of the executive, the military and the police. Even though the political rivalry between the old regime and the liberal aspirations of the bourgeoisie was becoming ever more pronounced, czarism lent its unconditional support to the employers in the socio-political sphere in order to make them a bulwark against labour unrest. Massive official intervention on the side of the employers had the unexpected effect of rapidly investing all industrial disputes with a political quality, irrespective of the motive behind them; wage disputes and revolutionary action went hand in hand. Parallel to the polarization of capital and labour, Russian peasant society had a dynamic peculiar to itself – a dynamic that was wholly revolutionary and derived from incomplete agrarian reform.[66] Initially the unsolved agrarian question had provided a political basis for the Social Revolutionaries but when, in the summer of 1917, the latter shrank from a radical solution, the Bolsheviks took over the revolutionary potential presented by the peasantry.[67]

The year 1912 marked the beginning of a tremendous wave of strikes whose orientation became increasingly political until, in the summer of 1914, they were deliberately aimed at creating a new revolutionary situation. When Poincaré arrived in St. Petersburg on a state visit in July 1914 some 200,000 of the city's workers were out on strike. Just how 'revolutionary' the situation was in the summer of 1914 is a moot point. Soviet historians incline to the view that things were heading straight for a socialist revolution when the war intervened; western historians think it conceivable that the social conflicts could have been canalized into a bourgeois-liberal reform movement.[68] Whatever the case, history has pre-

66. Cf. Geyer, *Die Russische Revolution. Historische Probleme und Perspektiven*, p. 27.

67. This development is stressed, for instance, by J. Carmichael, *Die Russische Revolution*, Rowohlt, Reinbek, 1967, p. 127–37. For detailed information on the Socialist Revolutionaries, see O. H. Radkey, *The Agrarian Foes of Bolshevism. Promise and Default of the Russian Socialist Revolutionaries, February to October, 1917*, Columbia University Press, New York, 1958.

68. See also the debate conducted in the *Slavic Review*, 23, 1964 and 24,

cluded its ever being put to the test. The revolutionary movement was temporarily checked by the war which thus provided the old regime with one last breathing space. Strikes, barricades and street demonstrations became a thing of the past. On 2 August (20 July in the Russian calendar), the day war was declared on Germany, a vast throng came out to greet the czar. 'It was,' writes Alexandra Dumesnil, 'undoubtedly the only day of his reign on which he was really popular.'[69] According to Rodzianko, the President of the Duma, workers in St Petersburg, who were out on a strike and demonstrating against the regime, at once declared themselves ready to fight for their country.[70] But to all appearances the wave of nationalism did little more than ruffle the surface. It is said that the peasants, who after all had to bear the main brunt of the war, were far from sharing the general enthusiasm.[71] In the provinces, reservists demonstrated with red flags, revolutionary songs and cries of 'Down with the War!' So serious were some of the disturbances that loyal troops had to be called out to deal with them.[72] In St Petersburg, Moscow and a number of other industrial centres, anti-war demonstrations similarly flawed the image of unalloyed patriotism.[73]

In the long term the war intensified the polarization processes already present before 1914.[74] Wartime economic policy increased the political importance of the bourgeoisie although, from the social point of view, no real harmonization between public and private interests was ever achieved. Far from being alleviated, tensions increased: the old regime viewed with mistrust the bourgeoisie's demand for power in return for its contribution to

1965: L. Haimson, 'The Problem of Social Stability in Urban Russia, 1905–1917'; A. P. Mendel, 'Peasant and Worker on the Eve of the First World War'; T. H. Lane, 'The Chances for Liberal Constitutionalism'; L. Haimson, 'Reply'. For Lenin's estimate of the situation, see amongst others, Lenin, *Der Krieg und die russische Sozialdemokratie*.

69. A. Dumesnil, 'Les milieux ouvriers russes et la déclaration de guerre en 1914', *Revue de l'Histoire de la Guerre Mondiale*, 12, 1934, pp. 233ff.

70. See M. Hellman, ed., *Die russische Revolution 1917*, Munich, 1964, p. 47.

71. This is stressed by, for instance, M. Hellmann, ed., *op. cit.*, p. 30.

72. See Dumesnil, 'Les milieux ouvriers russes', p. 234.

73. See Institute of Marxist Leninism, ed., *Geschichte der Kommunistischen Partei der Sowjetunion*, Central Committee of the C.P.S.U., 6 vols, Progress Publishers, Moscow, vol. II, pp. 538ff.

74. See L. Haimson, 'The Problem of Social Stability, in Urban Russia, 1905–1917', *Slavic Review*, 23, 1964, pp. 17ff.

the war effort. For their part, the middle classes mistrusted the autocratic regime which, after the reverses in the summer of 1915, they openly repudiated for its obvious incapacity to harness the country's total resources to the demands of power politics. Although bourgeois opposition to the old regime became more clearly defined during the war, its protagonists were unable to bridge the gulf that divided them from the industrial proletariat and the lower strata of the peasantry. It seems doubtful whether the mass of workers and peasants had any knowledge at all of the tensions within the ruling classes. From a worm's eye view, the difference between czarism and leaders of the bourgeois opposition, such as Guchkov and Milyukov, may have appeared uncomfortably small.

The significance of the labour movement, and above all its revolutionary determination, declined after the outbreak of war. One of the reasons adduced for this, besides the superficial wave of patriotism just mentioned, was the imprisonment and banishment of revolutionary cadres, notably from among the ranks of the Bolsheviks. A further contributory factor was the drafting to industrial centres of new and politically uneducated workers, not only to replace men who had been called up but also to meet the increasing demand for armaments. However, the setback was no more than temporary. After only a few months it became apparent that the war had strengthened rather than sapped the revolutionary movement. Between April and August 1915 a great wave of strikes demonstrated the extent to which dissatisfaction had already spread amongst the masses. The first strikes were predominantly economic: the deterioration in the standard of living, rising prices, housing shortages and, last but not least, the contrast between the drop in real wages and the huge wartime profits were obvious causes for dissatisfaction. From October 1915 political motives came to play an increasingly important role alongside economic motives; as had happened before 1914, the executive's sharp reaction contributed materially to the politicization of the strikes: the government which, since the spring of 1915, had been viewing the strikes with some concern, reacted with a peculiar combination of repressive force and political fatalism. In the end, revolution came to be regarded as more or less inevitable by the very people who most feared and hated it.[75]

75. See also the collected documents edited and annotated by M. Cherniav-

During the war the revolutionary movement was primarily the concern of the industrial workers, above all those in the big industrial centres of Moscow and St Petersburg; even before 1914 the metal workers in the latter city had been regarded as constituting the vanguard of the revolution. But it would be wrong to assess the importance of the movement by the number of its active protagonists which, in relation to the total population, was undoubtedly small. In the first place the revolutionary movement mustered the active, politically committed sections of the population which were, moreover, concentrated in the centres of political power; and in a country where political controversy did not normally penetrate to large sections of the population this was a factor of some importance. In the second place, considerable dissatisfaction was building up among the peasants both at home and in the forces, even though at first neither group was politically conspicuous. The failure to solve the agrarian problem was aggravated by the enormous battle casualties which affected the peasant population most of all.[76] As the events of 1917 were to show, the land-hunger and craving for peace felt by the peasants both in and out of uniform constituted a political potential that could be readily mobilized in a crucial situation.

The question of the significance of the Bolsheviks to the development of the revolutionary movement in Russia itself is notoriously controversial. Whereas non-Marxist authors contend that after August 1914 the Bolshevist cadres were broken up by the police and that, being in exile, the Central Committee under Lenin had only limited opportunities for action,[77] Soviet historiographers attribute to the Bolsheviks a leading role in the workers' labour disputes and political actions.[78] However, no one denies that the outbreak of the bourgeois revolution in March 1917 took the

---

sky, *Prologue to Revolution. Notes of A. N. Iakhontov on the Secret Meetings of the Council of Ministers, 1915*, Prentice-Hall, Englewood Cliffs, 1967.

76. Up till February 1917 it was estimated that 8 million had been killed, wounded, missing or taken prisoner; see Geyer, *Die russische Revolution. Historische Probleme und Perspektiven*, p. 55.

77. See e.g., G. Katkov, *Russia 1917. The February Revolution*, Longman, London, 1967, pp. 28ff.

78. See Institute of Marxist-Leninism, ed., *Geschichte der Kommunistischen Partei der Sowjetunion*, vol. II, pp. 592–650.

Bolsheviks as much by surprise as all the other participants.[79] Even after the revolution, the Bolsheviks were indisputably in the minority; the provisional government was set up by the former bourgeois opposition who were later joined by right wing social- ists, while in the Soviet the Social Revolutionaries and Menshe- viks predominated. Nevertheless, within a few months the Bolshe- viks had come to power, the bourgeois February revolution having been followed by the Socialist October revolution. This develop- ment cannot simply be ascribed to the Bolsheviks' tactical skill or to unhappy coincidence. Rather it points to the social fact that the new dual regime of provisional government and Soviet was incapable of resolving the conflicts which had led to the first revolution. The leaders of the Social Revolutionaries and the Mensheviks tended for the most part to follow the line which the 'progressive bloc' had already pursued in opposition to the old regime and continued to pursue in the provisional government, namely more efficient conduct of the war and, in the social sphere, modest socio-political concessions to safeguard the system. This programme conveniently ignored social realities in that it prom- ised no definite issue to any of the questions which were preoccupy- ing the masses (ending the war, agrarian reform, the condition of the urban proletariat). Even before March 1917, the exponents of the progressive bloc had been regarded as a force 'which neither knew, nor took cognizance of, the people, its impulses and aspirations . . . which was no closer to that same people than your imperial bureaucrat or high-ranking soldier'.[80] They were in even less of a position to provide a satisfactory solution when revolution had made the masses more demanding and more conscious. By associating themselves with this line, the Social Revolutionaries and Mensheviks gambled away their political potential. In the summer of 1917 the Bolsheviks were the only party to take up the demands of the workers, peasants and soldiers and to uphold

79. This has since been confirmed by Soviet historians; see Geyer, *Die rus- sische Revolution. Historische Probleme und Perspektiven*, p. 57. There is no point in providing here a blow by blow account of the February and October revolutions, more especially since this is readily available elsewhere; see R. V. Daniels, *Red October, The Bolshevik Revolution of 1917*, Scribner, New York, 1967; and W. H. Chamberlin, *Die Russische Revolution 1917–1921*, vol. I, Europäische Verlagsanstalt, Frankfurt, 1958.

80. Geyer, *Die russische Revolution. Historische Probleme und Perspektiven*, p. 65.

them with any consistency. Hence the fact that power eventually accrued to them was not without historical logic.

The immediate effect of the two Russian revolutions was to strengthen the revolutionary movements in the belligerent countries. However, the historian is faced with difficult problems of demarcation. Besides the example of the Russian February revolution, a number of wholly independent factors were at work at the beginning of 1917, 'the year of crisis'; the protraction of the war and the deterioration in the food situation and in living conditions generally had given rise in all countries to a widespread war-weariness which, at various focal points, flared up into overt resistance to the conflict. These 'autonomous' factors should not be under-estimated; at the same time it is clear that the change of course taken in 1917 by the labour movement in the belligerent countries cannot be understood without reference to developments in Russia. At bottom, the February revolution was not unwelcome to the bourgeois parliamentary governments and the 'social patriots' of the West; they hoped that, after the dissolution of the reactionary czarist regime, the Entente might present itself with greater credibility as a democratic alliance against Central European despotism. However their joy over this ideological consensus was unmistakably mingled with fear that the revolution might impair Russia's war effort. On the other hand, the left wing of the labour movement found it easier to acclaim a revolution which, though it could by no means be described as proletarian, consistently and from the start championed those demands which were already pointing the way beyond the bourgeois revolution, namely the creation of workers' councils and the immediate cessation of hostilities. In Germany, Rosa Luxemburg's response to the news from Russia was little short of rapturous and the fact that the revolution exerted an influence on the masses is evident not least from the anxious pronouncements made by representatives of the ruling classes.[81] In France, news of the Russian revolution coincided with the great wave of refractoriness which, in the spring of 1917, shook the munitions industry and the armed forces. On 1 May Merrheim's traditionally left wing trade union organ, *Union des Métaux*, published the peace slogan of the

81. See L. Stern, *Der Einfluss der Grossen Sozialistischen Oktoberrevolution auf Deutschland und die deutsche Arbeiterbewegung*, Rütten & Loening, Berlin, 1958.

Petrograd Soviet, 'Down with war! Long live the Russian revolution!' and the soldiers took up the cry.[82] In Italy the revolution evoked a particularly strong response. The front page of the central organ of the Socialist Party, *Avanti!*, carried daily and detailed reports of the Russian revolution. '*Fare come in Russia*' ('Do as they do in Russia') was a slogan often heard on the lips of Italian socialists.[83] Even the British labour movement, which traditionally held aloof from the Marxist-revolutionary line, was lastingly influenced by the Russian revolution.[84] As in France and Germany, news of the revolution irrupted just as a country-wide wave of strikes was about to begin. The demand for an immediate armistice without annexations or contributions was compatible with the pacifist tendencies in the party and the unions, and the left wing called for workers' and soldiers' councils on the Russian model.

In retrospect, then, not only the revolutionary initiatives but also the demarcation lines are plain to see. Nowhere outside Russia was the labour movement able to force a government to sue for peace. The war was brought to an end only by the total military and economic prostration of the Central Powers.

The split in the International, already presaged at the conferences of Zimmerwald and Kienthal, was accelerated by the Russian revolution. Quite soon after the February revolution Lenin believed the time had come to break with the Zimmerwald majority. By now the revolutionary wing of the international labour movement had a firm base in Russia, whence it was to devote itself to building up the Third International. In this the Zimmerwald pacifists were a hindrance rather than a help, more especially since they and the 'Centrists' had drawn so close together as to be almost indistinguishable. Hence Lenin's axiom: 'The Zimmerwald morass must no longer be tolerated. There can be no question of maintaining half-hearted connections with the chauvinist International of Plechanov, Scheidemann and co. for

82. See R. Wohl, *French Communism in the Making, 1914–1924*, Stanford University Press, 1966, pp. 87ff.

83. H. König, *Lenin und der italienische Sozialismus 1915–1921. Ein Beitrag zur Gründungsgeschichte der Kommunistischen Internationale*, Böhlau, Cologne/ Graz, 1967, p. 19. The fact that the Russian revolution evoked an exceptional response in Italy is also confirmed by Braunthal, *Geschichte der Internationale*, vol. II, p. 130.

84. See S. Graubard, *British Labour and the Russian Revolution, 1917–1924*, Harvard University Press, Cambridge, Mass., 1956.

the sake of the Zimmerwald "Kautskyites". We must immediately break with this International. We should remain with Zimmerwald *only* for purposes of information.'[85] True, a third conference was held by the Zimmerwald Movement in Stockholm in August 1917, side by side with a socialist conference which the International Socialist Bureau had at long last convened,[86] but neither school of thought exerted any influence on the subsequent course of events. By the summer of 1917 the international labour movement had split into two separate schools, represented on the one hand by the 'social patriotic' socialist majority in western and central Europe and, on the other, by the Bolsheviks. In February 1919 the right wing constituted (or rather, reconstituted) itself in Berne under the old title as the Second International. A month later the communist Third International was solemnly inaugurated in Moscow. Hard on the heels of the split in the umbrella organization, there followed the split in the labour parties and trade unions of individual countries.

85. V. I. Lenin, 'Die Aufgaben des Proletariats in unserer Revolution (Entwurf einer Platform der proletarischen Partei)', *Ausgewählte Werke in zwei Bänden*, vol. II, Dietz, Berlin, 1959, p. 40 (italics in original).

86. H. Meynell, 'The Stockholm Conference of 1917', *International Review of Social History*, 5, 1960.

8

War Aims and
the Peace

With the outbreak of war the liberal-capitalist world economy disintegrated and the structural changes wrought by the conflict left little hope of its reconstruction on pre-war lines. But this disintegration was due not so much to the working of economic laws as to political action. Neither the declared war aims of the belligerents nor the peace terms that were ultimately imposed were calculated to restore international economic links; rather, both in theory and in practice, they tended ever more towards autarky. The war aims programmes are of interest to the economic historian mainly because they sought to combine a measure of economic interdependence with the demands of power politics.[1] In both belligerent camps efforts were made to replace the multilateral world economy of the pre-war period with large economic groupings having a structure determined by power politics.

1. In his bibliography Gunzenhäuser (of the Stuttgart Weltkriegsbibliothek) lists some 2,300 works on the peace negotiations as also a considerable number on the war aims debate on both sides: M. Gunzenhäuser, *Die Pariser Friedenskonferenz 1919 und die Friedensverträge 1919–1920. Literaturbericht und Bibliographie*, Bernard & Graefe, Frankfurt, 1970. Despite this apparent superfluity of books, an economic-historical analysis of war aims and the peace treaties still remains to be written.

Central Europe

Plans based on the *Mitteleuropa* concept first took shape in Imperial Germany soon after the consolidation of the Empire in the eighteen-eighties. Fritz Fischer has shown that the orientation of the Imperial government, like that of the pressure groups and of public opinion, oscillated between a 'world policy' and a '*Mitteleuropa* policy' in a well-defined rhythm determined by economic fluctuations.[2] Industrial expansion provided an impulse towards a 'world policy', while there was a swing of the pendulum towards *Mitteleuropa* whenever overseas political or economic expansion encountered resistance, as happened during the last four pre-war years. A 'central Europe' under German domination was to be the political and economic basis upon which Germany could take a stand against competing 'world empires': the U.S.A., Great Britain and Russia. In these plans, economic interests were associated with those pseudo-economic arguments which, though couched in economic terms ('*Lebensraum* for the growing population'), were at bottom economically meaningless and at best served to divert internal conflicts to other fields. In the event, her aspirations to world power status grounded on *Mitteleuropa* were instrumental in deciding Germany to embark on a preventive war.

The outbreak of war sparked off a general controversy in official and unofficial circles alike on the subject of war aims. Pressure groups, individual industrialists and bankers, political

2. See F. Fischer, *Krieg der Illusionen. Die deutsche Politik von 1911 bis 1914*, Droste, Düsseldorf, 1969. More specifically on the Central European idea: H. C. Meyer, *Mitteleuropa in German Thought and Action 1815–1945*, Nijhoff, The Hague, 1955; Z. Jindra, 'Über die ökonömischen Grundlagen der "Mitteleuropa" Ideologie des deutschen Imperialismus', K. Obermann, ed., *Probleme der Ökonomie und Politik in den Beziehungen zwischen Ost- und Westeuropa vom 17. Jahrhundert bis zum Gegenwart*, Rütten & Loening, Berlin, 1960. Since then a great deal has been written on German war aims. The most recent discussion was sparked off by the important treatise (following several preliminary articles) by F. Fischer, *Der Griff nach der Weltmacht. Die Kriegszielpolitik des kaiserlichen Deutschland 1914/18*, 3rd ed., Droste, Düsseldorf, 1964. Fritz Fischer and his school have developed these theses and have made a close study of various specific questions. For a discussion, see W. Schieder, ed., *Erster Weltkrieg. Ursachen, Entstehung und Kriegsziele*, Kiepenheuer & Witsch, Cologne/Berlin, 1969. A synthesis of Marxist positions may be found in: F. Klein, ed., *Deutschland im Ersten Weltkrieg*, 3 vols, Akademie-Verlag, Berlin, 1970.

parties and nationalist agitation societies, as well as the Imperial government itself, put forward programmes all of which, even the more 'moderate', were indubitably aggressive. The first organization to produce a war aims programme was the Pan-German League. The nub of that programme, formulated in August 1914, was a central Europe which 'together with the territorial spoils of war won by Germany and Austria-Hungary, will form a large, uniform economic area'.[3] Germany's spoils of war were described in grandiose terms: in the west, annexation of Belgium, the French iron-ore district of Longwy-Briey and the Channel coast as far as the Somme, occupation of a fortified line from the Somme estuary to Verdun, and the conversion of Toulon into a German naval base on the Mediterranean. The population of the above territories was to be evacuated and replaced by German citizens from within the Empire and elsewhere. In the East, Russia was to be driven back to the frontiers she had occupied before the time of Peter the Great. This meant the annexation of the Polish frontier districts and of Russia's Baltic provinces as a 'strategic bulwark' and 'settlement area'. It was further envisaged that the German-controlled Central European Federation should comprise the following nominally independent member states: Austria–Hungary, Bulgaria, Romania, Netherlands, Switzerland, Denmark, Norway, Sweden and Finland. Germany's colonial possessions, with the addition of French and Belgian territories, were to be attached to the Central European Federation. The Pan-German League was no negligible entity. Originally it had been a petty-bourgeois nationalist agitation society, but the nature of its aims had made it the platform for influential and extreme right wing business circles, especially big land-owners and leaders of heavy industry. Both groups had found a repository for their own particular interests in the Pan-German programme. In the case of heavy industry, the emphasis was on the annexation of the French iron ore districts, the control of Belgium and the acquisition of the Belgian Congo. The land-owners wanted to expand eastwards so as to lend added weight to the agrarian sector in the German economy and in the political sphere as a whole.

By means of skilful propaganda, heavy industry and the Junkers succeeded in securing a broad base for the Pan-German programme and thus in presenting their particular interests in a

3. Cit. from Fischer, *Der Griff nach der Weltmacht*, p. 120.

patriotic and 'national' guise. At the end of September 1914 the Pan-German League organized a rally of the 'producer-classes', at which representatives of industry, agriculture, the crafts and commerce pledged their support to the Pan-German annexationist policy. This rally marked the beginning of uninterrupted cooperation between the League and the representatives of business interests. In March 1915 the leading business federations produced a joint war aims programme largely based on that of the Pan-Germans. In May this programme was laid before the Chancellor in the form of a joint petition from the Central Federation of German Industrialists, the Industrialists' League, the Landowners' League, the German Farmers' League, the Imperial Small Traders' League and the Christian Farmers' Societies. This lobby was later joined by the Hanseatic League, representing mercantile interests. Lest it might appear that the war was being waged solely to secure mining concessions and export markets, the Pan-German League organized a war aims rally of the intelligentsia in June 1915. Nearly 1,200 signatures (including those of such prominent academics as Dietrich Schäfer, Friedrich Meinecke and Otto Hintze) were appended to a resolution which evinced an annexationism no less extreme than that of the business federations. From this endeavour was born the 'Independent Committee for a German Peace', which has rightly been described as 'a centre of annexationist propaganda'.[4]

Side by side with German industry's official war aims programme, which was based on Pan-German demands, petitions were also submitted to the government by individual industrialists and bankers who had formulated programmes of their own: Krupp, Rathenau (A.E.G.), Stinnes, Thyssen, Gwinner (Deutsche Bank), to name only the more important. Some of the demands made by the leaders of the coal, iron and steel industry were even more excessive than those of the Pan-Germans. Thyssen drew attention to southern Russia (the Donets Basin, the Crimea and the Caucausus whose iron and manganese ore was of interest to his company), and went on to point out that access to Persia via Russia and Asia Minor would make it possible to threaten the

4. See K. H. Schädlich, 'Der "Unabhängige Ausschuss für einen Deutschen Frieden" als ein Zentrum der Annexionspropaganda des deutschen Imperialismus im ersten Weltkrieg', F. Klein, ed., *Politik im Krieg 1914–1918*, Akademie-Verlag, Berlin, 1964.

British Empire.[5] In the main, Krupp's demands agreed with those of the Pan-Germans, but he introduced an exotic note into the war aims controversy by including the distant territory of New Caledonia in whose nickel ore the Krupp combine was interested.[6] In the programmes formulated by Rathenau and Gwinner, on the other hand, we may discern the somewhat aloof attitude adopted towards heavy industry's rabid annexationism by the export-oriented manufacturing sector and its associated banks.[7] Rathenau and Gwinner placed the emphasis on central Europe as a customs union rather than as an association of states. They recommended that, in the west, there should be a settlement with France which was to join the customs union, while in the east, autonomous nation states should be created in what were then Russia's western provinces. This programme of 'indirect' rule (economic hegemony and semi-autonomous satellite states) was expressly intended as a less conspicuous and at the same time a more stable alternative to the 'direct' expansion advocated by the Pan-Germans. On the colonial question, the 'moderate' view was largely in accord with the Pan-German. Rathenau's and Gwinner's advocacy of 'indirect' rule could only be regarded as representing a minority opinion in business circles, since all the large employers' federations supported the Pan-German demands. However, the 'moderate' view commended itself for internal political reasons because, unlike the Pan-German programme, it was acceptable to the liberal bourgeoisie and the social democratic right wing.

The Imperial government's stance in the war aims debate, as represented by the Chancellor, Bethmann Hollweg, has been described as a 'policy of the diagonal', in other words the endea-

5. See also W. Treue, *Die Feuer verlöschen nie. August Thyssen-Hütte 1890–1926*, Econ, Düsseldorf/Vienna, 1966, pp. 182ff. Indeed, these war aims of Thyssen's show him to be 'an industrialist who thought in terms of large economic areas and wished to initiate a new order in the interests of the economy as such, without any regard for traditions and actual circumstances' (p. 183).

6. Krupp's memorandum, written in November 1914 and submitted to the Chancellor in July 1915, quoted in full by W. Boelcke, *Krupp und die Hohenzollern in Dokumenten*, Athenaion, Frankfurt, 1970.

7. On the two factions in big business see especially W. Gutsche, 'Erst Europa – und dann die Welt. Probleme der Kriegszielpolitik des deutschen Imperialismus im Ersten Weltkrieg', *Zeitschrift für Geschichtswissenschaft*, 12, 1964; J. Kuczynski, *Darstellung der Lage der Arbeiter in Deutschland von 1900 bis 1917/18 (Die Geschichte der Lage der Arbeiter unter dem Kapitalismus*, vol. IV), Akademie-Verlag, Berlin, 1967.

vour to steer a middle course between the Pan-Germans and the moderates. Central to the government's official war aims memorandum of 9 September 1914 (the 'September Programme') was the demand for an economically unified central Europe: 'The aim should be the founding of a central European economic union by means of joint customs agreements. . . . This union, which must inevitably stabilize Germany's hegemony over central Europe, would probably not have a joint constitutional executive, and its members, though ostensibly enjoying equal rights, would in fact be under German leadership.'[8] To this extent the September Programme corresponded to the views of the moderate lobby in the war aims controversy. At the same time the programme contained a sop to Pan-German aspirations in the west by calling for the annexation of Longwy-Briey and parts of Belgium. The formulation of war aims in respect of Russia, like the discussion of the colonial question, was put off till a later date. Thus, without antagonizing the moderate lobby, the door was kept wide open for all manner of annexationist speculation over conquests in both east and west.

Throughout the war, German war aims proved relatively constant and were little influenced by the ups and downs of the military situation. The prolongation of hostilities did little to induce a more conciliatory mood in the Pan-German lobby. Rather, their attitude would seem to have hardened, particularly as a result of the move to the right occasioned by the change in the Supreme Army Command in August 1916. In May 1917 almost the same groups as had put forward the war aims programme of March 1915 – namely, the federations representing German business interests both large and small, along with various agitation societies – issued a public appeal which culminated in the demand: 'Only a peace with reparations, an increase in power and the acquisition of territory can lastingly ensure our people its national existence, its position in the world and the freedom to develop its economy.'[9]

For reasons of domestic and foreign policy, the government continued to pursue a course more in line with the moderate lobby.

8. Cit. from F. Fischer, *Krieg der Illusionen, Die deutsche Politik von 1911 bis 1914*, Droste, Düsseldorf, 1969, p. 769.

9. Cit. from F. Fischer, *Der Griff nach der Weltmacht, Die Kriegszielpolitik des kaiserlichen Deutschland 1914/18*, 3rd ed., Droste, Düsseldorf, 1964, p. 437.

In 1916/17 these divergencies from the Pan-German programme were such as to lead to open conflict between the government and the Third Supreme Army Command. But whereas in the past historiographers have laid much emphasis on this conflict, depicting it as a straight fight between Bethmann Hollweg and Hindenburg-Ludendorff, there now seems reason to suppose that there was at bottom a certain objective community of interests. In the first place, official war aims were invariably formulated in terms so vague that they could also be interpreted in an annexationist sense, a case in point being the Central Powers' 'peace proposals' of December 1916. In the second place, even the 'moderate' position adopted by the government was so aggressive as to be wholly unacceptable to the Allies; no less than the Pan-German programme, it postulated the total victory of the Central Powers.

If *Mitteleuropa* commended itself as an economic concept central to Germany's internal war aims discussion, it was because the various schools of thought could interpret it according to their own lights and give it whatever concrete substance they chose. For the same reason *Mitteleuropa* was a suitable focal point for the coordination of war aims among the Central Powers.[10] The military partnership between Germany and Austria–Hungary provided the basis for the international *Mitteleuropa* movement which, as a result of alliances and of military developments up till the end of 1915 (and the conquest of Serbia), tended very strongly in a southeasterly direction – the so-called 'Berlin–Baghdad Line'. Friedrich Naumann's book, *Mitteleuropa*, which appeared in 1915, caught the mood of the day and generated a veritable wave of enthusiasm. However, when the Central Powers actually got down to negotiations, the concept proved much more difficult of realization than had been supposed. In Austria–Hungary, Bulgaria and Turkey there was latent resistance to a Central Europe in which Germany aspired to hegemony – a hegemony which she would undoubtedly attain because of her economic superiority. Hence 1916 is regarded as the year in which the *Mitteleuropa* idea reached its apogee.

10. On Central Europe, besides the literature already mentioned, see also the study by G. Gratz and R. Schüller, *Die äussere Wirtschaftspolitik Österreich-Ungarns. Mitteleuropäische Pläne*, Hölder-Pichler-Tempsky, Vienna, 1925. On the Turkish alliance: V. Trumpener, *Germany and the Ottoman Empire*, Princeton University Press, 1968; F. G. Weber, *Eagles on the Crescent. Germany, Austria and the Diplomacy of the Turkish Alliance 1914–1918*, Cornell University Press, Ithaca, 1970.

Thereafter national particularism emerged more clearly. At the Brest–Litovsk and Bucharest peace negotiations there could be no doubt that the dream was fading. In each case the talks were long-drawn-out, not only because the vanquished found it difficult to accept the rigorous peace terms, but also because the victors could not easily reach mutual agreement over their own particular national interests and their claims to the common 'spoils'.

In December 1917 the Soviet government opened the Brest–Litovsk peace talks with a programme specifically intended as a basis for a general peace in all theatres of war, a peace, moreover, 'without annexations and reparations'.[11] In this, the programme bore a certain resemblance to Wilson's demand for 'peace without victory' and accorded with the desire for peace of the masses, not only in Russia but in all belligerent countries.[12] With an eye to popular feeling, the representatives of the Central Powers did not dare to repudiate this programme outright, but instead made certain reservations which, in effect, kept the door open for annexations and reparations. When the peace terms were actually formulated in January 1918, it was clear that the annexationist war aims of the Pan-Germans had prevailed. At the negotiations the extreme right was represented primarily by the Supreme Army Command which, however, cannot be held wholly responsible for what transpired. The representatives of the German Foreign Ministry, though ostensibly more moderate than the military, demanded annexations which fundamentally were no less extensive, while Germany's allies, by introducing their own particular interests, added to, rather than alleviated, the severity of the peace terms. The treaty, signed in March 1918, brought Finland, the Baltic provinces, Poland and the Ukraine, as well as Kars, Ardahan and Batum in the Caucasus, within the Central Powers' sphere of

11. See J. W. Wheeler-Bennett, *Brest-Litovsk. The Forgotten Peace, March 1918*, Macmillan, London, 1956 (first pub. 1939). For a recent work based on a comprehensive study of the archives, see W. Baumgart, *Deutsche Ostpolitik 1918. Von Brest-Litovsk bis zum Ende des Ersten Weltkrieges*, Oldenburg, Vienna/Munich, 1966. However, Baumgart's work becomes detailed only in respect of events from the spring of 1918 onwards (after the peace negotiations). See also Baumgart's comparative study, confined largely to the political sphere, 'Brest-Litovsk und Versailles. Ein Vergleich zweier Friedensschlüsse', *Historische Zeitschrift*, 210, 1970.

12. G. Schulz, *Revolutionen und Friedensschlüsse 1917–1920*, 2nd ed., dtv, Munich, 1969, p. 110.

influence – either by 'direct annexation' or as 'temporarily' occupied zones or as 'independent' satellite states. Already in February 1918, while negotiations with Soviet Russia were still proceeding, the Central Powers had concluded a separate peace with their Ukrainian 'puppet government'.[13] The Reichstag debate on the Treaty of Brest–Litovsk betrayed how broad was the political basis of annexationism. Only the Independent Social Democrats voted against the treaty, while the Social Democratic majority abstained, a move that suggested a disquieting convergence with the political line of the Supreme Army Command. Notwithstanding the peace treaty, the Central Powers continued to advance in the region of the Don, the Kuban and the Caucasus during the summer of 1918 and when, in August, Germany concluded bilateral supplementary treaties with Soviet Russia the terms were even harsher: not only were Esthonia and Livonia formally detached from the Russian union of states, but reparations amounting to 6 billion marks were demanded. The directors of the Reichsbank took advantage of this opportunity to request part-payment in gold as a means of increasing its reserves against the note issue – an ingenious contribution to the interdependence of economics and politics.[14] No secret was made of the fact that at Brest-Litovsk the prime concern was not self-determination but grain, ore, coal and mineral oil. While the talks were still in progress fierce disputes broke out not only between the allied governments but also between competing private interest groups over the distribution of the economic spoils. German and Austro–Hungarian interests clashed in the Ukraine, as did German and Turkish interests in the Caucasus. In the summer of 1918 German industrialists and bankers made comprehensive plans for the economic penetration of Russia, heedless of the fact that both there and in Germany economic difficulties precluded their early realization.

During the peace negotiations with Romania, Pan-German expansionist aspirations were to some extent kept within bounds by political considerations, namely the susceptibilities of Ger-

13. See Wheeler-Bennett, *Brest-Litovsk*, p. 316.

14. See W. Baumgart, *Deutsche Ospolitik 1918. Von Brest-Litovsk bis zum Ende des Ersten Weltkrieges*, Oldenburg, Vienna/Munich, 1966, pp. 298ff. In fact the Soviet Union paid, in two instalments, a sum of 560 million in gold and roubles. The gold presumably came out of the Romanian central bank reserves which had been evacuated to Russia to save them from the Germans, only to be impounded by the Russians after the revolution.

many's allies and the balance of power in the Balkans. As a component of *Mitteleuropa* Romania was to be opened up to economic exploitation, but to this end her productive capacity was to be maintained in so far as possible. Under the terms of the Peace of Bucharest, the Central Powers secured control over Romania's oil wells, grain exports and railways. The exploitation of the oil wells was vested in a monopoly (the Mitteleuropäische Erdölgesellschaft) in which the German Empire was to have a 56 per cent interest, Austria–Hungary 24 per cent and Romania 20 per cent. Germany and Austria–Hungary received pre-emptive rights to Romanian grain exports for a period of seven years. Both in form and content the Romanian peace-terms corresponded more or less to the 'indirect' expansion advocated by those who wished to see a German *Mitteleuropa* founded primarily on economic hegemony. Although reducing Romania to little more than a political and economic colony of the Central Powers, the treaty was considered moderate in Germany and was, after the event, to be criticized for undue leniency by the majority of the extremists in the war aims controversy. This criticism found unexpected support in the Deutsche Bank which, though otherwise no doubt favouring 'indirect' expansion, saw in the creation of a state oil monopoly a threat to its own 'traditional' private interest in Romanian oil.[15]

At this point it might be pertinent to consider the *Mitteleuropa* concept in terms of its economic viability. In examining the war aims controversy we have already seen which particular private interests were involved. Heavy industry wished to acquire raw material deposits and production plant – not in the sense of their being placed under German jurisdiction but rather of their passing into private German ownership. The big land-owners, desirous of increasing the economic and political importance of Germany's agricultural sector, wished to acquire land either for themselves, or in order to deflect the 'resettlement movement' from their own doorsteps to the vast territories in the east. The big exporting industries (electrical goods, chemicals, metal working) hoped that the abolition of customs duties in Europe would result in better sales. The big banks wished to see their 'spheres of influence' politically safeguarded, and protected against foreign competitors.

15. On the Deutsche Bank's oil interests in Romania, see F. Seidenzahl, *100 Jahre Deutsche Bank. 1870–1970*, Frankfurt, 1970.

The *Mitteleuropa* concept, embroidered and popularized by countless ideologists, served as a convenient screen for these various interests. But all attempts to give it concrete economic shape failed and, indeed, were bound to fail in view of its inherent contradictions, a defect it shared with the war aims controversy as such. The acquisition of land in the east – the bait with which heavy industry secured the Junkers' assent to the seizure of plant and raw materials in the west – would, in the long run, inevitably have retarded German industrial development. This clash of interests became even more apparent at inter-governmental level. Without protective tariffs, Austrian industry could not hold its own against its more powerful German competitors, nor could the Junkers east of the Elbe compete with the Hungarian farmers. Neither government could abandon the interest groups concerned, even had it wished to do so. During the wartime Austro–German discussions on *Mitteleuropa*, these difficulties were much in evidence.

The concept appeared more than ever questionable when proffered as an alternative to economic integration. Though important to the German economy, the area concerned was by this time in no way adequate to its needs. During the last years before the war the countries generally subsumed under *Mitteleuropa* in the widest sense of the term (Europe with the exception of Britain, Russia, Spain and Portugal) took 50 per cent of Germany's exports and supplied 30 per cent of her imports.[16] Hence a German 'withdrawal' from the international economy to an internally unified but aggressively protectionist central European base was, in economic terms, of dubious viability. In the export field Germany had as much to lose through possible retaliatory measures overseas as she could hope to gain in *Mitteleuropa*. The provenance of imports into Germany and *Mitteleuropa* shows even more plainly that, under normal circumstances, neither was economically self-sufficient. Though the *Mitteleuropa* ideologists would have hesitated to admit as much, Germany had become part and parcel of the international economy. Better opportunities for economic growth were offered by integration into the world economy than by a Central European economic area protected by military power and customs tariffs. Mitteleuropa was not, indeed, a politico-

16. See League of Nations, *Memorandum on Balance of Payments and Foreign Trade Balances, 1910–1924*, 2 vols. Geneva, 1925.

economic but rather an ideological programme which provided a screen for various and competing private business interests and certain expansionist aspirations. Moreover, like *Lebensraum* or 'our own raw materials base', both supposedly advantageous if not actually vital to Germany, *Mitteleuropa* belonged to those pseudo-economic ideologies whose function, ever since the end of the nineteenth century, had been to deflect elsewhere the growing inner tensions of an industrial society.

TABLE 23

PERCENTAGE DISTRIBUTION OF GERMAN TRADE IN 1913
EUROPEAN COUNTRIES

	Exports	*Imports*
Gt Britain	14	8
Belgium, Netherlands	12	6
Austria–Hungary	11	8
Russia	9	13
France	8	5
Scandinavia	8	5
Switzerland	5	2
Italy	4	3
Balkans	2	1
Others	2	3
Europe	75	45

SOURCE: League of Nations, *Memorandum on Balances of Payments and Foreign Trade Balances, 1910–1924*, 2 vols., Geneva, 1925, vol. I, pp. 112ff, 142, 162.

Denmark, Finland, Norway and Sweden are subsumed under Scandinavia, and Bulgaria, Greece, Romania and Serbia under Balkans.

Versailles

At no time did the Allies produce an economic programme as coherent as the *Mitteleuropa* plans of the Central Powers.[17] Allied

17. Since the archives are not yet available for public inspection, Allied war aims have not been subjected to such thorough investigation as those of the Central Powers. For a general survey see A. J. P. Taylor, 'The War Aims of the Allies in the First World War', R. Pares and A. J. P. Taylor eds., *Essays Presented to Sir Lewis Namier*, Macmillan, London, 1956; W. W. Gottlieb, *Studies in Secret Diplomacy during the First World War*, Allen & Unwin, London, 1957; H. I. Nelson, *Land and Power. British and Allied Policy on Germany's Frontiers 1916–1919*, Routledge & Kegan Paul, London, 1963;

economic cooperation began in the spring of 1915 when the discussions included plans for the post-war period about which, however, no definite conclusions were reached. At the invitation of the French, a conference of Allied politicians met in Paris on 27 and 28 March 1916. Here the main subject of discussion was the French demand that the Allies should undertake not to conclude separate economic treaties with the Central Powers, thus complementing the Pact of London of 5 September 1914 which provided against the conclusion of separate peace treaties. Next, it was decided to convene an economic conference which would examine in detail inter-Allied economic cooperation in war and peace. This conference, by its very terms of reference a ripost to the *Mitteleuropa* plans, opened in Paris on 14 June 1916.[18] The chief results of its deliberations were agreement on closer cooperation in the blockade of the Central Powers, on the exchange of natural resources and on the protectionist measures to be adopted vis-à-vis German trade during the demobilization phase; further, a resolution, couched in general terms, on the long-term prospects of economic cooperation after the war.

The resolution was unanimously adopted but, beyond a general declaration of principles, it contained little in the way of definite agreements. The Allied governments gave no firm commitments respecting their future economic policy nor could anything else be expected in view of their divergent interests. French interests were primarily concerned with the recovery of Alsace-Lorraine; also with the Saar, whose coal-mines were regarded as a desirable complement to the iron ore of Lorraine.[19] The French government was further anxious to prolong the economic war beyond the armistice so as to sap Germany's economy and thus keep her politically in check. Britain, Italy and Russia regarded the French plans with some scepticism, not only because their interests were wholly different, but also because in peacetime their economies were closely interlinked with those of the Central Powers.

---

and B. Bonwetsch, *Kriegsallianz und Wirtschaftsinteressen. Russland in den Wirtschaftsplänen Englands und Frankreichs 1914–1917*, Düsseldorf, 1973.

18. See the official protocol: *Conférence économique des gouvernements alliés, tenue à Paris les 14, 15, 16 et 17 juin 1916. Programme, procès-verbaux des séance et acte de la conférence*, Imprimerie Nationale, Paris, 1916.

19. See P. Renouvin, 'Die Kriegsziele der französischen Regierung 1914–1918', W. Schieder, ed., *Erster Weltkrieg*.

The British government had entered the war in order to maintain the status quo in Europe.[20] But as the war proceeded, official wars aims changed with each shift in the country's internal power structure. Liberal imperialism, which had begun to assert itself in the Liberal Party from 1902, and in British policy generally from 1906, was concerned only with maintaining the existing structure, i.e. an Empire revolving round, and dependent upon, Great Britain. This was one reason, among others, for seeking a *rapprochement* with France. The influence of the new imperialism grew as the war went on and finally emerged triumphant in December 1916 under Lloyd George's premiership. Its view – an unprecedently radical one – of the Empire as a homogenous association no longer centred on Britain was based on the fact that British economic interests were showing an increasing tendency to move overseas. This, perhaps, explains why colonial imperialism experienced its final fling in Britain at a time when throughout the world it was already heading for a crisis. From Wilson's 'Fourteen Points' which demanded, *inter alia*, that in settling colonial questions account should be taken of the interests of the peoples concerned, it is clear that imperialism could no longer be taken for granted. In renouncing an imperialism centred on Europe, the new imperialism admitted as much: on the other hand, it was responsible for giving a renewed boost to territorial expansionism. Not without encouragement from the Dominions, it turned its eyes increasingly towards the German colonial empire and Turkey's possessions in the Near East.

At the time of the Allied Economic Conference Britain's war aims differed from those of the French not only in their regional structure but also in the extent of their realization. In June 1916 (at the time of Verdun!), a French occupation of Alsace-Lorraine, let alone the Saar, was still a somewhat remote possibility; and, even if France succeeded in acquiring these territories, their defence against a numerically and economically stronger neighbour would not only be a cause for grave anxiety but also call for long-term planning. From the British perspective, however, the Allied blockade had already ensured that Germany's economic and military presence was wholly confined to the Continent of

20. Besides the war aims literature already mentioned, see especially V. H. Rothwell, *British War Aims and Peace Diplomacy 1914–1918*, Clarendon Press, Oxford, 1971.

Europe; the German colonial empire (save for East Africa where the Germans were fighting a dogged if hopeless rearguard action) was in Allied hands, and Britain had gained a firm foothold in the Turkish possessions on the Persian Gulf. All that was needed to place the final seal on these *faits accomplis* was the military defeat of the Central Powers. Once overthrown, Germany could hardly continue to represent a political or economic threat outside of Europe.

Italy's war aims differed from those of her other allies in that they were concerned exclusively with Austria, and not with Germany. Indeed, it was not till after the Allied Economic Conference in August 1916 that Italy declared war on Germany (having been at war with Austria–Hungary since May 1915). Italy had close economic ties with Germany and, during the first months of the war, had continued to maintain a not inconsiderable volume of trade with that country via Switzerland. Hence it was not in Italy's interests that inter-Allied economic cooperation against Germany should continue into the post-war period.

The Russian government, too, regarded the long-term politico-economic proposals of the Paris Conference with a sceptical eye, and refused outright to commit itself to any specific foreign trade policy in respect of the post-war period.[21] It took the view that the permanent diversion of the country's foreign trade from Germany to the Allies would involve tremendous difficulties. In peacetime some 40 per cent of grain exports went to Germany. Among the Allies, the British market might perhaps present an alternative, but if Russian grain was to be competitive in that quarter, Britain would have to abandon imperial preference and also the most favoured nation clause in regard to Argentina and the United States. Such a radical revision of Britain's external trade policy was barely conceivable either in St. Petersburg or, for that matter, in London. Vague assurances at the conference to the effect that the Allies would, 'in so far as possible', indemnify each other for the loss of enemy markets, could hardly have satisfied the Russian government.

The conference in Paris was followed by regular inter-Allied consultations on economic matters, notably within the framework of the newly created Comité Permanent International d'Action

21. See E. Nolde, *Russia in the Economic War*, Yale University Press, New Haven, 1928.

Économique. Under pressure of circumstances, economic cooperation between the Allies actually progressed to the point of setting
up the inter-Allied organizations for centralized control in specific
fields, of which mention has already been made. There was, however, no consensus among the Allies over their long-term politico-
economic programmes. After the socialist revolution Russia
ceased to be a party to Allied cooperation but by that time
America had entered the war. Although she maintained close
economic ties with Britain, virtually none of her own interests
conflicted with those of the Central Powers. Hence, beyond
repudiating Germany's hegemonic aspirations in the shape of
Mitteleuropa, the Allies failed, right up to the Armistice, to agree
a common politico-economic programme. It was only during
inter-Allied discussions preceding the Peace Conference and, from
January 1919, at the conference itself, that the war aims of the
individual Allies were combined to form a 'consolidated' peace
programme which was thereupon imposed without more ado on
Germany and her partners.[22] The main object of the peace treaties
was comprehensive political reorganization. However both the
negotiations and the actual treaties raised a number of important
economic questions.

International trade and the colonial question

The general view, both during and after the war, was that economic
factors exerted considerable influence on political decisions.[23] It is
a view that accords more closely with the standpoint of present-
day left wing social democratic and Marxist historians than with,
for example, that of the bourgeois-conservative historiographers

22. A guide to the voluminous literature on the peace negotiations may be
found in the bibliography compiled by Gunzenhäuser, *Die Pariser Friedens-
Konferenz 1919*. As introductory works that are both lucid and informative, I
would still commend some earlier compilations in which economic questions
are also given their due: H. W. V. Temperley, ed., *A History of the Peace Conference of Paris*, 6 vols., Oxford University Press, 1920-24; J. B. Scott, ed.,
The Paris Conference. History and Documents, 6 vols, Columbia University
Press, New York, 1934-42. For a more recent account dealing mainly with the
politico-diplomatic aspect, see A. Schulz, *Revolutionen und Friedensschlüsse
1917-1920*, dtv, 2nd ed., Munich, 1969.
23. See also League of Nations, *Raw Material Problems and Policies*,
Geneva, 1946.

of the day, who explained the origins and causes of the Great War largely in terms of diplomatic imbroglios. Economic rivalries and the struggle for raw materials, with their concomitant system of discriminatory foreign trade practices and colonial preferences, were generally regarded as one of the causes of conflict before 1914 and hence also as a potential threat to world peace.

Wilson's Fourteen Points of 8 January 1918 took this view into account in calling for economic freedom of movement and an international review of the colonial question. To quote point three: 'The removal, as far as possible, of all economic barriers and the establishment of an equality of trade conditions among all the nations consenting to the peace and associating themselves for its maintenance.' Again, point five: 'A free, open-minded, and absolutely impartial adjustment of all colonial claims, based upon a strict observance of the principle that in determining all such questions of sovereignty the interests of the populations concerned must have equal weight with the equitable claims of the governments whose title is determined.'[24] Because of protectionist trends in the United States, Wilson soon found himself compelled to clarify point three. What was meant, he now said, was not, of course, universal free trade, but simply the equal treatment of all countries. Accordingly a country's tariffs might be high or low provided they applied to all trading partners alike.

Despite this substantial modification, point three was eventually swept under the carpet at the Peace Conference. So strong were protectionist trends that the Allied governments preferred not to commit themselves in respect of their future external trade policy. For the same reason there was no support for the Franco–Italian proposal that, in order to moderate the fight for raw materials, the Allies should abolish all import and export duties on industrial raw materials. In the end it proved impossible so much as to agree a text banning discrimination, let alone restrictive practices, in international trade. The stumbling block here proved to be the French, who wanted to continue the economic war against the Central Powers beyond the peace settlement. In politico-mercantile terms, all that the peace-makers' activities finally amounted to was the requirement that unilateral and most favoured nation rights be accorded to the Allies by Germany for five years and by

24. Cit. from *The Encyclopaedia Britannica*, Vol. XXXII, London/New York, 1922, p. 1084.

Austria, Hungary and Bulgaria for three years. By comparison with the original demand contained in the third of Wilson's Fourteen Points, this was indeed a sorry result.

The fifth point, dealing with the colonial question, fared no better. It was certainly no coincidence that the demand for an international settlement of the colonial question, one that would take into account the rights of oppressed peoples, originated in the United States whose form of imperialist expansion was predominantly indirect. For in no way did this preclude a combination of economic (i.e. *de facto* political) dependence and formal political independence, Central and South America being a case in point. By contrast Wilson's demands were hardly consonant with the colonial policy of the major European powers or with the nascent colonial aspirations of the British Dominions themselves.[25]

The peace treaties created the mandatory system, a special form of colonial dependency calculated to placate anti-colonial sentiment. Under this system the former German colonies and the Turkish territories in the Near East, instead of being ceded to the victorious powers as colonial possessions, were to be administered on behalf of the League of Nations and in the interests of the indigenous populations. A mandate might be one of three kinds, depending on a territory's state of development and the obligations of the mandatory. The most 'backward' territories were designated class C mandates and became an integral part of the mandatory power. Class B mandates, while enjoying a certain measure of institutional independence, were required to afford to all nations equal opportunities for economic activities within their borders. Territories classified as A mandates were those which, on principle, were capable of functioning as independent nations and needed no more than temporary 'guidance' by the mandatory powers. Thus, what had formerly been German south-west Africa was assigned to the Union of South Africa as a class C mandate, German East Africa to Britain as a class B mandate and Iraq, also to Britain, as a class A mandate. At bottom, what was involved was not so much the objective ability of the mandated territories to govern themselves as a compromise between the imperialist

25. See D. K. Fieldhouse, *Die Kolonialreiche seit dem 18. Jahrhundert*, Fischer, Frankfurt, 1965, pp. 208ff; H. D. Hall, 'The British Commonwealth and the Founding of the League Mandate System', K. Bourne and D. C. Watt, eds., *Studies in International History*, Longmans, London, 1967

powers' mercantile and expansionist interests on the one side and, on the other, anti-colonial sentiment, not least in the dependent territories.

The new frontiers

The peace settlement showed that the right of national self-determination, implicit in Wilson's Fourteen Points and expressly endorsed in his later statements, was incompatible with the realities of power politics; in the event, that right was plainly infringed on several counts. Here the determining factor was the political bias in favour of the consolidation and expansion of national power; only in exceptional cases were economic interests paramount, for instance, the French advance into the Saar, which led to the temporary neutralization of the territory and the transfer of its coal mines to France. In the Versailles peace terms, as previously in the formulation of Allied war aims, economic or pseudo-economic considerations featured much less prominently as an argument for territorial aspirations on the Continent than in Germany's war aims controversy, for instance, or in the peace settlements of Brest-Litovsk and Bucharest. The economic interests of the Allies were concentrated upon the colonies and war damages.

Nevertheless the new frontiers were, of course, of some economic interest. The economic significance of the territorial changes has already been discussed from the viewpoint both of Germany's economic efficiency and of the international allocation of resources. Under the terms of the Peace Treaty Germany ceded 13 per cent of her territory and, with it, 10 per cent of her population. The German economy thus lost large tracts of farmland (15 per cent of the area under cultivation), raw material deposits (75 per cent of her iron ore, 26 per cent of her coal and potash), and important industrial centres (the Lorraine iron industry, the Alsatian textile industry and part of Upper Silesia's heavy industry).[26] In Germany there was an immediate storm of protest, and even today it is still genereally assumed that the loss of territory left the country 'very much poorer'.[27] While in terms of total

26. See G. Stolper, K. Häuser and K. Borchardt, *Deutsche Wirtschaft seit 1870*, 2nd ed., Mohr, Tübingen, 1966, pp. 88ff.
27. ibid., p. 89.

national income this may be so, it is of little real significance; the transfer of Alsace-Lorraine to France diminished Germany's national income and increased that of France. But it is equally clear that, in terms of *per capita* income, Germany might well have grown richer, if only because the agricultural territories ceded in the east had acted as a brake on German economic development. If the division of the German economy into a 'modern' and a 'backward' sector in the pre-1914 period is seen as disadvantageous to growth,[28] so conversely the loss of backward regions must be regarded as tending to foster growth.

It is generally agreed that the new frontiers, besides signifying the redistribution of resources from one country to another, impeded the development of the international economy as a whole. As a result of tariffs and other, sometimes absurd, obstacles,[29] frontiers forthwith became economic as well as political. In the majority of cases, adaptation to a new national market proved difficult for the economy of the territories concerned. Before the war Bohemia's industries, for example, had enjoyed a large, protected market in the Danubian Monarchy, whereas the new state of Czechoslovakia found itself obliged to export under world market conditions, and this at a time when the other successor states were legislating against industrial imports in order to build up their own national industries. Within the Danubian Monarchy, German Austria had existed largely by providing public and private services in exchange for agricultural products and industrial goods. Hence, as a rump state, she was at first barely viable in economic terms. Now this is not to say that such an adaptation was impracticable, or that small states were necessarily condemned to economic stagnation (Switzerland being a case in point), but the adjustment of the economic structure to the new political circumstances was a slow and expensive process. Expense is, of course, no argument against aspirations to national independence or the redrawing of frontiers, although at one time it was often claimed

28. On this hypothesis, see for instance D. S. Landes, *The Unbound Prometheus. Technological Change and Industrial Development in Western Europe from 1750 to the Present*, Cambridge University Press, 1970. pp. 330ff.

29. For a time the successor states would not allow rolling stock to travel beyond their borders for fear of confiscation; this constituted a considerable impediment to goods traffic between countries; see E. Schultze, *Die Zerrüttung der Weltwirtschaft*, Kohlhammer, Berlin/Leipzig/Stuttgart, 1923, p. 132.

to be so, especially in Germany. To the countries concerned, the new frontiers may well have been worth the expenditure involved.

Reparations[30]

During the war both sides had intended to make their defeated adversary foot the bill. The German government repeatedly announced its intention of recouping its entire war expenditure from the enemy, an intention that was partially realized in the eastern peace treaties. For their part, the Allies agreed that reparations were to be demanded, but opinions differed as to the amount.[31] The terms of the Armistice of November 1918 contained only a somewhat vague allusion to 'compensation'. This was interpreted by the Americans, in accordance with various public statements made by Wilson, as compensation for damage caused by *unlawful* action by the Central Powers, notably the violation of Belgian neutrality. It was also held to cover loss of property suffered by private individuals as a result of warlike action by those powers, but not the general war expenditure of the Allies. America's European allies, however, based their case on the war-guilt of the Central Powers and, having regarded the war from the outset as an unlawful action, placed a broad interpretation on the term 'compensation' as signifying complete material indemnification. This standpoint corresponded almost exactly to the original German intention of making the enemy bear the total cost of the war.

30. There has recently been a new edition of the classic work on the reparations question: J. M. Keynes, 'The Economic Consequences of the Peace', (*Collected Writings*, vol. II), Macmillan, London, 1971 (first pub. 1919). A good guide to the exceedingly complex development of the reparations question up to 1924 is still provided by C. Bergmann, *Der Weg der Reparationen. Von Versailles über den Dawesplan zum Ziel*, Sozietäts-Druckerei, Frankfurt, 1926. An attempt impartially to assess the conflicting standpoints is made by E. Wüest, *Der Vertrag von Versailles in Licht und Schatten der Kritik: Die Kontroverse um seine wirtschaftlichen Auswirkungen*, Europa-Verlag, Zurich, 1962; and more recently, by P. Krüger, *Deutschland und die Reparationen 1918/19*, Deutsche Verlags-Anstalt, Stuttgart, 1972.

31. On this controversy, see also P. M. Burnett, *Reparations at the Paris Peace Conference. From the Standpoint of the American Delegation*, 2 vols, Columbia University Press, New York, 1940; P. Tillmann, *Anglo-American Relations at the Paris Peace Conference of 1919*, Princeton University Press, 1961.

It is not difficult to trace back the divergence of opinion in the Allied camp to economic interests. While America was prepared to accord her European allies a measure of compensation, her prime concern was to re-establish Germany as a trading partner, an aim that could only be delayed by a crushing burden of reparations. Some of her European allies, on the other hand, had suffered severe material damage and, moreover, in the context of the world economy, saw themselves as Germany's immediate rivals. Hence, even before the peace talks had begun, their respective governments had individually decided to claim substantial war damages.

Inter-Allied discussions having proved fruitless, the peace treaties omitted to specify either the total amount of reparations or the proportion to be paid by each of the Central Powers. Rather, they confined themselves to assigning sole guilt for the war to the enemy and deducing therefrom an as yet unlimited liability to damages. In accordance with the principle of joint responsibility, the claim for reparations was formally addressed to all the Central Powers, but in point of fact mainly to Germany, the only one of the vanquished nations capable of paying.

A special commission was to determine, by May 1921, the amount of the damage done by Germany and her allies, and hence the reparations due. Pending this decision, Germany was to make an advance payment of 20 billion gold marks which, in the nature of things, would mostly take the form of deliveries in kind from stocks and from current production. By May 1921 almost the entire German merchant fleet (2·2 million gross tons) had been handed over, along with 5,000 locomotives, 136,000 railway waggons, 130,000 articles of agricultural machinery, 135,000 head of cattle and 50,000 horses; in addition, 24 million tons of coal and 15 million tons of dyestuffs were supplied from current production. Germany's offer to take an active part in the reconstruction of Belgium and the north of France was turned down by the Allies. Estimates vary considerably as to the value of payments in kind. According to the Allies this amounted to 2·6 billion gold marks, a sum which was absorbed by occupation costs alone. They further valued at 2·5 billion gold marks the Saarland collieries made over to France and public property in the ceded territories. On the German side, however, reparations payments up till May 1921, including property confiscated abroad, warlike material surrendered and the waiving of Germany's claims on her former allies, were estimated somewhat unconservatively at over 37 billion gold marks.[32]

As we know, the Reparations Commission eventually fixed the reparations debt at 132 billion gold marks, an amount the German government was compelled to admit after receiving an ultimatum from London in May 1921. The Commission had based its calculations on what the Allied governments were demanding and, indeed, were bound to demand in view of the domestic situation in their respective countries. Whether Germany was able to pay such a sum, and whether unilateral payments of this order were in any way economically feasible, did not enter the discussion.

In Germany many attempts were made to prove that it would be impossible to raise the reparations which, it was alleged, would in any case bring down untold poverty on the country. The first of these took the form of a Note dated 13 May 1919 in which the German delegation informed the Allies in all seriousness that the demands for reparations, combined with the other terms of the Versailles Treaty, would condemn several million Germans to death by starvation.[33] Though at home, these assiduous efforts enjoyed huge success, they were received with rather more scepticism abroad. In fact, it was the payment, not the raising of the reparations, that presented the real economic problem. Unilateral transfers of the order envisaged, superimposed on the commercial traffic in goods and capital, could only impair the functioning of the international exchange mechanism. Thus for the Allies the economic advantages of reparations were doubtful in the extreme.[34]

32. Bergmann, *Der Weg der Reparationen*, pp. 100ff.
33. See Burnett, *Reparations at the Paris Peace Conference*, vol. II, p. 8; A. Luckau, *The German Delegation at the Paris Peace Conference*, Columbia University Press, New York, 1941, p. 243.
34. On this point, Schumpeter remarks that reparations, had they in fact been made in real terms in the form of export surpluses, would have meant, for the German economy, 'the industrial conquest of the better half of the world'. J. A. Schumpeter, *Konjunkturzyklen. Eine theoretische, historische und statistische Analyse des kapitalistischen Prozesses*, 2 vols, Vandenhoeck & Ruprecht, Göttingen, 1961, vol. II, pp. 723ff (note 10).

9

Decentralization of the International Economy

Europe

The decentralization of the international economy was one of the most momentous consequences of the Great War. The economic significance of Europe declined and, for a number of years, economic activity remained below the pre-war level. When the process of growth resumed, Europe had, relatively speaking, fallen behind various non-European countries, certain of which had in the meantime made notable advances. For the space of four years the economic potential of most of the European countries had been concentrated on the prosecution of the war, while private consumption and investment in non-essential industries had been largely held back in favour of armaments production and the expansion of the munitions industry. After the Armistice the work of reconstruction was burdened with a heavy legacy in death and devastation. At least 8·6 million people had lost their lives in the Great War.[1] If the rise in the wartime death rate is regarded as solely due to the war, civilian losses are seen to be almost as high as those in the armed forces.[2] In those areas of Belgium and northern France, eastern and southern Europe and northern Italy

1. European losses from M. Gilbert, *First World War Atlas*, Weidenfeld & Nicolson, London, 1970, p. 158.
2. See H. Mendershausen, *The Economics of War*, Prentice-Hall, New York, 1941, p. 307.

which had experienced the direct impact of the war, the land had been laid waste and large numbers of public and private buildings and industrial installations had been destroyed. Nor should shipping losses be forgotten: despite increased wartime building, the world's merchant fleet was 16 per cent smaller after the war than in 1914.[3] It is extraordinarily difficult to quantify the direct destruction in terms of money values. In his celebrated critique of the Peace Treaty, Keynes estimated that in the case of France material damage qualifying for reparations amounted to 800 million pounds, of Great Britain to 570 million, of Belgium to 500 million and of the remaining Allies (Italy, Greece, Romania, Serbia) to 250 million, making 2·1 billion pounds in all.[4] Neither Russia nor the Central Powers are included in this calculation, while estimates produced by the Allies themselves are very much higher than those of Keynes.[5] Damage totalling 130 billion gold marks was reported to the Reparations Commission. To this sum were later added demands for 95 billion gold marks in respect of pensions payments; as we have seen, claims amounting to 132 billion gold marks were admitted.

Though there might be disagreement as to the monetary value of the property destroyed, the consequences were all too plain. Wartime destruction, the wear and tear on plant and the running down of stocks meant that on average industrial production in Europe in 1920 was about one-third below 1913 levels; unlike Britain, where production was almost back to its pre-war level, continental countries were reporting a drop of 50 per cent and more.[6] And though in the field of arms and munitions standardization had led to increased productivity,[7] the average for industry

3. The total shipping tonnage of the European sea-faring nations fell from 36·5 million gross tons in June 1914 to 30·0 million gross tons in June 1919; see C. E. Fayle, 'Seaborne Trade', *History of the Great War*, by direction of the Historical Section of the Committee of Imperial Defence, 3 vols, Murray, London, 1920–24, vol. III, p. 469.

4. See J. M. Keynes, 'The Economic Consequences of the Peace', *Collected Writings*, vol. II, Macmillan, London, 1971. (First pub. 1919), pp. 71–85.

5. On the various estimates, particularly for France, see G. Jèze, *Les dépenses de guerre de la France*, Presses Universitaires de France, Paris, 1926, pp. 64–83.

6. See I. Svennilson, *Growth and Stagnation in the European Economy*, United Nations Commission for Europe, Geneva, 1954, pp. 304ff.

7. See A. S. Milward, *The Economic Effects of the World Wars on Britain*, Macmillan, London, 1970, pp. 33ff.

as a whole had probably fallen. In coal mining, for example, output per shift in 1913 was 1·1 tons in Britain, 0·9 tons in Germany and 0·7 tons in France; in 1920 it had fallen by 30 per cent. In the U.S.A. on the other hand, where output per shift had in any case been very high (3·3 tons), it rose over the same period by 10 per cent.[8] One direct consequence of the drop in productive capacity was a strong demand for imported foodstuffs and – exceptional in Europe – for industrial goods. In real terms, more foodstuffs and finished goods were imported during 1919 than before the war whereas, in line with reduced industrial activity, the import of raw materials had fallen to half the pre-war level.[9] Faced with lower productive capacity and a critical transport situation, demand in Europe turned primarily to the United States and Britain. Total continental imports for the two years 1919 and 1920 are estimated at 17·4 billion dollars, of which 12·4 billion dollars represent a surplus of imports over exports. By comparison with her continental neighbours, Britain had suffered less from the immediate effects of the war, but here too, pent-up demand resulted in a massive balance of trade deficit amounting to a total of 4·1 billion dollars for the two years 1919 and 1920.[10]

There were many who felt that wartime controls should be continued after the Armistice, since this would not only accelerate the reconstruction of Europe's economy and its reintegration into the international economy but might, in the long term, change the structure of the capitalist system. In June 1918 the British Labour Party launched its peace programme, 'Labour and the New Social Order', which called in general terms for the planning of production and distribution and, more specifically, demanded the nationalization of important key industries.[11] However, in none of the victorious industrial states did the advocates of a planned economy succeed in making any real headway. Governments and influential business interests both regarded the rapid dismantling of wartime controls as an essential prerequisite for economic reconstruction – save perhaps in Germany, where a plan for

8. Svennilson, *Growth and Stagnation*, p. 254.

9. League of Nations, *Raw Material Problems and Policies*, Geneva, 1946, p. 14.

10. League of Nations, *Europe's Overseas Needs 1919–1920 and How They Were Met*, Geneva, 1943, pp. 23ff.

11. See G. D. H. Cole, *A History of the Labour Party from 1914*, Routledge & Kegan Paul, London, 1948, p. 65.

organized capitalism, described by Rathenau, Moellendorf and others as 'common weal', was not without practical results. This difference may partly be attributed to the stronger *étatiste* tradition in that country whose industry, moreover, finding itself exposed to heavy anti-capitalist attack, was prepared to make cautious concessions if only to preserve the system as a whole.[12]

In the field of international economic relations, opposition to certain aspects of economic planning was not so unanimous. In view of the arduous task of reconstruction, the British, French and Italian governments were in favour of maintaining the inter-Allied economic organizations, at least for a transitional period, to help grapple with immediate post-war problems. In February 1919 a unanimous decision by the Allies led to the creation of the Supreme Economic Council whose mandate was to consider the economic measures to be adopted during the reconstruction period: i.e. material aid for reconstruction in devastated territories, the economic restoration of those countries most affected by the war and, finally, the organization of supplies to neutral and former enemy countries in so far as this would not prejudice Allied requirements.[13] For the better exercise of its mandate, the Supreme Economic Council was instructed to coordinate the work of existing inter-Allied economic organizations. But this, the formal apotheosis of inter-Allied economic cooperation was, at one and the same time, its effective demise. The abolition of national controls cut the ground from under the feet of inter-Allied organizations such as the Allied Maritime Transport Council. Completely deprived of all opportunity for direct intervention, they were reduced to making recommendations to the various governments. This of itself was enough to impair the efficiency of the international, or rather, inter-Allied organizations, quite aside from the fact that the United States were opposed on principle to the continuation of controls.

The American government shared the belief, then prevalent in industrial circles, that unhampered private initiative was best

12. For a critical review of this trend, see J. Kucyznski, *Studien zur Geschichte des staatsmonopolistischen Kapitalismus in Deutschland 1918 bis 1945* (*Die Geschichte der Lage der Arbeiter unter dem Kapitalismus*, vol. XVI), Akademie-Verlag, Berlin, 1965.

13. Cit. from League of Nations, *Raw Material Problems and Policies*, Geneva, 1946, p. 17.

calculated to expedite reconstruction and, further, that private international business contacts were generally conducive to peaceful understanding, whereas state intervention could only give rise to conflict. Underlying this idealistic view was the practical argument that, should inter-Allied cooperation continue, the United States would, by reason of their economic efficiency, inevitably become the 'great provider'. The Americans feared, not without justification, that inter-Allied cooperation was in effect tantamount to inter-Allied control of certain of their country's economic resources. The official standpoint was clearly set out in instructions issued in October 1918 by Herbert Hoover, with State Department approval, to the U.S. Food Administration in London:

> This Government will not agree to any programme that even looks like inter-Allied control of our economic resources after peace. After peace over one-half of the whole export of food supplies of the world will come from the United States and for the buyers of these supplies to sit in majority in dictation to us as to prices and distribution is wholly inconceivable. The same applies to raw materials. Our only hope of securing justice in distribution, proper appreciation abroad of the effort we make to assist foreign nations, and proper return for the service that we will perform will revolve around complete independence of commitment to joint action on our part.[14]

Inevitably this view prevailed since nothing could be done without the cooperation of the United States. Hence the two inter-Allied organizations set up to deal with economic problems in the demobilization period: namely the Inter-Allied Supreme Council for Supply and Relief and the Supreme Economic Council already mentioned, were restricted to purely coordinating activities that did not infringe national sovereignty. This produced at least one positive result conducive to the reconstruction of the international economy, in that differences among the Allies prevented the prolongation of the economic offensive against the Central Powers; hence the lasting division of the international economy into two hostile camps, seriously debated on both sides during the war, never came to pass. Whereas the French government hoped, by continuing economic discrimination, to keep Germany politically in check, the other Allies believed that nothing but economic

14. *Papers Relating to the Foreign Relations of the United States, 1918,* suppl., 1, vol. I, pp. 616ff, cit., from League of Nations, op. cit., p. 12.

disadvantages could accrue from such a course. The blockade, whose continuation after the Armistice was opposed primarily by the United States, was therefore relaxed and in 1921 was officially suspended.[15]

U.S.A.

The impoverishment of Europe during the war was in strong contrast to the prosperity of certain of the non-European countries. The latter enjoyed what was tantamount to a protective tariff against European competition because the leading industrial nations were concentrating entirely on war production and hence had withdrawn from the world market. Moreover, for some countries the war marked the beginning of a tremendous export boom since the European Allies were prepared to pay almost any price for raw materials, foodstuffs and industrial goods. By virtue of their economic structure and their relative proximity to western Europe, the United States were particularly favoured by this development. Even before 1914 the United States had been one of the leading industrial nations; indeed, in terms of coal and steel production, then often taken as the index of a country's industrial potential, America led the world. At the same time agriculture had retained its importance and, as a producer of wealth, came a close second to industry.[16] As an exporter the United States competed not only with the industrial nations of Europe but also with the non-industrial primary producers in the rest of the world: wheat, cotton and oil together accounted for over a third of American exports.

The outbreak of war and the concomitant disorganization of world trade initially exerted a depressive influence on America's foreign trade. Exports decreased in quantity and prices fell. In terms of value, total exports in 1914 were more than 15 per cent lower than in the preceding year. But before long the first crippling effects of the war gave way to a period of lively activity and the

15. On this see documentation in: S. L. Bane and R. H. Lutz, eds., *The Blockade of Germany after the Armistice, 1918–1919*, Stanford University Press, 1942; also J. A. Huston, 'The Allied Blockade of Germany, 1918–1919', *Journal of Central European Affairs*, 10, 1950.

16. U.S. Department of Commerce, Bureau of the Census, *Historical Statistics of the United States. Colonial Times to 1957*, Government Printing Office, Washington, 1961, pp. 140ff.

United States experienced a wartime export boom. Exports increased from 2·8 billion dollars in 1913 to 7·3 billion dollars in 1918. The proportion of exports which, before the war, had been somewhere between 5 and 6 per cent, amounted in the final war years to some 10 per cent, a level which, after the collapse of the wartime and post-war booms, was never to be attained again. Outside of Europe, America was the only industrial power worthy of note, and it was to her that the Allies inevitably turned for their additional wartime requirements. Again, there was a demand from non-European countries for industrial goods, most of which had previously been supplied by Europe. As a supplier of raw materials and foodstuffs, the United States were also in a favourable situation because, as shipping space contracted, the European Allies concentrated their demand on North America at the expense of more distant primary producing countries such as Australia and New Zealand.

The export boom centred mainly on arms and munitions, essential raw materials, foodstuffs and industrial goods. Shortly after the outbreak of war, the British government placed important contracts with American steel producers. France, and later, Italy followed suit with large orders. In 1914 there was no munitions industry to speak of in the United States. When the first Allied contracts came in, new plant was built for the production of munitions, arms and other war material, while the steel industry adapted some of its rolling mills to the processing of steel for shells. The strength of American industry lay firstly in its important heavy sector which, even before the war, had been one of the foremost in the world and, secondly, in its efficient application of modern production techniques.[17] All the belligerents needed weapons and munitions as urgently as they needed foodstuffs. In the first phase of the war U.S. exporters continued to supply both sides and, much to the chagrin of America's future ally, Britain, large shipments of canned goods and bacon found their way to the Central Powers via Copenhagen and Rotterdam. Subsequently,

17. See B. M. Baruch, *American Industry in the War. A Report of the War Industries Board*, Government Printing Office, Washington, 1921; *Munitions Industry. Final Report of the Chairman of the United States War Industries Board to the President of the United States, February 1919*, Printed for the use of the Special Committee on Investigating the Munitions Industry, Government Printing Office, Washington, 1935.

the United States more than made up for this at a time when the Allied armed forces and civilian populations were being increasingly compelled to have recourse to American food supplies. These shipments partially replaced the grain and meat previously supplied by Australia and New Zealand, countries which were now difficult of access because of the shipping situation; they almost entirely replaced Danish bacon after the blockade had partially inhibited exports from Denmark; and when wartime conditions prevented France from meeting her own grain requirements, American wheat again came to the rescue. Between 1913 and 1918 the value of American exports of wheat and flour rose from 142 million dollars to 505 million dollars, while over the same period meat exports rose from 68 million dollars to 668 million dollars.[18] In the foreign trade statistics shipments of war material are not distinguished from civil exports; nevertheless an approximate comparison may be made. Between 6 April 1917 and 30 November 1918, Allied purchases of armaments, grain and other commodities in the U.S.A. amounted in all to 6 billion dollars. In the two years 1917 and 1918 total U.S. exports were valued at 14·2 billion dollars.[19] Hence Allied government purchases represented a substantial slice of American exports.

The war boom brought a rapid rise in business profits. As early as 1915 net industrial profits were some 20 per cent above the pre-war level, and in 1918 as much as 120 per cent.[20] If we assume that industry had allowed for a generous measure of depreciation, these estimates are certainly conservative. A profits explosion of this order need not surprise us, for an inflationary boom generally entails a redistribution in favour of profits. Indeed, during the war the proportion of profits to national income showed a distinct rise, more especially the share of corporate profits, whereas the proportion of wages declined. This decline is all the more striking in that in the longer term, the proportion of wages has shown a tendency to rise. The vast majority of wage and salary earners did not derive much advantage from the war boom. Rising prices

18. U.S. Department of Commerce, Bureau of the Census, *Historical Statistics of the United States. Colonial Times to 1957*, Government Printing Office, Washington, 1961, p. 546.

19. ibid., p. 562; H. G. Moulton and L. Pasvolsky, *War Debts and World Prosperity*, Brookings Institution, Washington, 1932, p. 42.

20. See J. Viner, 'Who Paid for the War?', *Journal of Political Economy*, 28, 1920, p. 62.

caused real wages to fall below the pre-war level but since, on the other hand, employment increased, the total wage bill as compared with the pre-war period probably remained much the same in real terms.[21] Not only industrialists but also farmers profited by the war boom. The latters' gross profits rose from 6·2 billion dollars in 1913 to 13·5 billion dollars in 1918, while net incomes (after deducting all expenses, including employees' wages) rose over the same period from 3·9 billion dollars to 8·9 billion dollars.[22] In terms of the extent to which they themselves could benefit from the divergence of prices from costs, the farmers never again had it so good, even during the Second World War.

TABLE 24
U.S.A.: DISTRIBUTION OF INCOME, 1900–29
(PERCENTAGE SHARE OF NATIONAL INCOME)

	Wages and Salaries	Rents, Leases	Interest	Profits of partnerships	Profits of corporations
1900–09	55·0	9·1	5·5	23·6	6·8
1910–19	53·2	7·7	5·2	24·2	9·7
1920–29	60·5	7·6	6·2	17·6	8·2

SOURCE: U.S. Department of Commerce, Bureau of the Census, *Historical Statistics of the United States. Colonial Times to 1957*, Government Printing Office, Washington, 1961, p. 141.

From the viewpoint of the world economy, the war boom enormously strengthened America's international position. Her unique situation as a supplier of raw materials, foodstuffs and manufactured goods gave rise to substantial export surpluses so that the United States changed from a debtor into a creditor nation. According to conservative estimates, American private investment abroad rose from 3·5 billion dollars in 1914 to 7·0 billion dollars in 1919, whereas foreign investment in the U.S.A. declined from 7·2 billion dollars to 4 billion dollars over the same period.[23] According to a different estimate, America's private net creditor position after the Armistice was running as high as 3·7

21. See ibid; also W. C. Mitchell et al., *Income in the United States. Its Amount and Distribution 1909–1919*, Harcourt Brace, New York, 1921, p. 102.

22. U.S. Department of Commerce, Bureau of the Census, *Historical Statistics of the United States. Colonial Times to 1957*, Government Printing Office, Washington, 1961, p. 283.

23. C. Lewis, *America's Stake in International Investments*, Brookings Institution, Washington, 1938, pp. 606, 114.

billion dollars.[24] During the war American investors greatly strengthened their position in Canada and Latin America at the expense of British capital interests which had previously predominated there. In addition to this private foreign investment, the U.S. government had, by the end of the war, claims on Allied governments amounting to 7·1 billion dollars but it must be admitted that these were of limited benefit.[25]

TABLE 25
U.S.A.: PRIVATE FOREIGN INVESTMENT, 1914–24
(BILLIONS OF DOLLARS)

	1914	1919	1924
Europe	0·7	2·0	2·7
Canada	0·9	1·5	2·6
Latin America	1·6	2·4	3·7
Others	0·3	0·5	1·0
Total long-term foreign investments	3·5	6·4	10·0
Short-term foreign investments	—	0·5	0·8
Total foreign investments	3·5	6·9	10·8

SOURCE: C. Lewis, *America's Stake in International Investments*, Brookings Institution, Washington, 1938, p. 606.

The heading 'Others' includes Africa, Asia and Australia, as well as another heading 'International Investments' that cannot be itemized. The table gives minimum figures; neither direct nor portfolio investments could be included in their entirety.

The Far East

The industrial upsurge experienced by Japan during the First World War has often been regarded by Europeans as a by-product of U.S. expansion[26] although, of course, in absolute terms Japan's economic importance was comparatively small. When war broke out, the first phase of industrialization was just over.[27] The

24. H. B. Lary, *The United States in the World Economy*, Government Printing Office, Washington, 1943, p. 123. The disparity is not surprising since Cleona Lewis explicitly states that her estimates are minimum figures and do not include all direct and portfolio investments.

25. See Moulton and Pasvolsky, *War Debts and World Prosperity*.

26. See D. A. Demangeon, *Le déclin de l'Europe*, Payot, Paris, 1920.

27. See W. W. Lockwood, *The Economic Development of Japan Growth and Structural Change 1868–1938*, 2nd ed., Princeton University Press, 1968. For a compendium of this detailed study, see W. W. Lockwood, 'The Scale of Economic Growth in Japan, 1868–1938', S. Kuznets, W. E. Moore, J. Spengler eds,

country immediately threw in its lot with the Allies but the limited scope of its military operations made no great demands on domestic resources. From an economic point of view, Japan was hardly on a war footing. After weathering the crisis induced by the outbreak of war, the economy experienced a tremendous upswing which, just as in North America, began as an export boom and then, by way of the multiplier and accelerator effects, continued as a domestic boom. Japan's export industries were the main beneficiaries of the boom in the United States and of the withdrawal of European goods from the Asiatic markets. The chief exporter was the cotton industry which registered a vast increase in sales in its pre-war markets, China and the U.S.A. and, for the first time, succeeded in gaining a foothold in Australia, India, the Dutch East Indies and other south-east Asian countries. Prior to 1914 about a quarter of Japanese cotton production had been exported; during the war the proportion rose as high as 50 per cent. The silk industry was likewise able substantially to step up production and increase exports. Thus, unlike the U.S.A. and Canada, Japan experienced an indirect, derivative war boom. As a result of high transportation costs (whether by sea to western Europe or by the Trans-Siberian Railway) exports to the European Allies dwindled in importance by comparison with those to geographically less remote markets. In all, shipments of war material to Allied governments amounted to only 120 million U.S. dollars, or 4 per cent of Japan's total wartime exports. The boom in exports and in the shipping industry brought in its wake a tremendous upsurge in domestic investment and industrialization. Already before the war Japanese industry had begun to produce capital goods in addition to consumer goods, but for the most part requirements of iron and steel, machinery and ships had still been met from abroad. All this changed with the war, when demand for capital goods increased while in real terms imports of these items decreased as a result of wartime conditions. This exceptionally favourable market situation led to considerable expansion in the

Economic Growth: Brazil, India, Japan, Duke University Press, Durham, 1955. Of the earlier works appearing in the Carnegie Series, the following are also of use: G. Ogawa and K. Yamasaki, *The Effect of the World War Upon the Commerce and Industry of Japan*, Yale University Press, New Haven, 1929; U. Kobayashi, *The Basic Industries and Social History of Japan, 1914–1918*, Yale University Press, New Haven, 1930.

engineering, shipbuilding, chemical and iron and steel sectors. Indeed, towards the end of the war Japanese yards were actually building merchant vessels for the United States. Under the impetus of the boom, Japanese industry went a long way towards diversified production in the place of its earlier concentration on cotton and silk. Between 1914 and 1919 the number of factories rose from 32,000 to 44,000, the number of factory workers from 1·2 million to 2 million, and the gross value of industrial production from 1·4 million yen to 6·7 million yen.[28] At the same time, although the average size of concerns increased (according to the above figures from 37 to 46 employees), Japan maintained a 'dual' industrial structure. On the one hand, a few large concerns and government factories, on the other a multiplicity of small firms which owed their considerable powers of survival to the narrowness of their specialization.

As in the United States, the chief benefits of the war boom accrued mainly to capitalists. Money wages barely kept pace with the rising price level. Although labour productivity patently increased, the real wages of industrial workers during the war years remained on average the same as before, the 40 per cent rise in nominal wages being offset by a similar rise in the cost of living.[29] But since wages outside industry rose more slowly, the real wage level as a whole actually fell, despite the war boom. On the other hand, shipping and industrial undertakings recorded enormous profits, and companies were able to pay out as annual dividends up to 80 per cent of their paid-up capital. This unequal distribution of gains has been attributed primarily to the rigid class structure and the ample supply of labour. Because of demographic growth and surplus labour in agriculture, industry had a permanent 'industrial reserve army' on which to draw.

Japanese foreign trade gradually assumed a structure typical of industrial countries, namely a high proportion of exported manufactures and a high proportion of imported raw materials. After the war, however, Japan did not fit easily into the normal pattern of industrial countries and primary producers, because the structure of her foreign trade varied in accordance with the trading partner or, as is sometimes said, 'faced two ways'.[30] To the U.S.A.,

28. Lockwood, *The Scale of Economic Growth*, p. 156.
29. ibid., pp. 172ff.
30. ibid., pp. 131ff.

Canada and Europe, Japan exported various semi-manufactures, above all raw silk; also simple manufactured goods whose principal input was the country's most important 'natural resource', namely, cheap labour. To her Asiatic neighbours, Japan exported textiles and other industrial consumer goods, as well as unsophisticated machinery. In this latter field she competed with the United States and Europe, from both of which, however, she continued to import industrial equipment of an up-to-date and specialized nature.

TABLE 26

JAPAN: ANALYSIS OF FOREIGN TRADE IN 1913 AND 1918
(PERCENTAGE SHARES)

	Exports		Imports	
	1913	1918	1913	1918
Foodstuffs	10	11	17	11
Raw materials	8	5	49	51
Semi-manufactures	52	39	17	27
Finished Goods	29	44	17	10
Total (millions of dollars)	315	978	363	831

SOURCE: G. Ogawa, K. Yamasaki, *The effect of the World War upon the Commerce and Industry of Japan*, Yale University Press, New Haven, 1929, pp. 5ff.

The percentage figures do not quite add up to 100 because a non-itemized remainder ('Various') has been excluded. The totals have been converted at the par rate 1 yen = 49·8 cents, although in New York in 1918 the yen rose above the specie point.

Thanks to the war boom, Japan achieved huge surpluses in her balance of payments. The export surplus between 1914 and 1919, amounting to more than 3 billion yen, was larger than the total import surplus since the Meiji Restoration and the start of modernization. Consequently by the end of the First World War, Japan had become a net creditor.[31] This position offered a favourable opportunity for liquidating her foreign indebtedness – an opportunity that was not taken. The government hesitated to raise the necessary internal loan (the debts being mostly on public

31. Cf. Lockwood, *The Economic Development of Japan Growth and Structural Change 1868–1938*, 2nd ed., Princeton University Press, 1968. E. R. Reubens, 'Foreign Capital and Domestic Development in Japan', S. Kuznets, W. E. Moore, J. Spengler eds, *Economic Growth: Brazil, India, Japan*.

account, the new assets on private account). Of the foreign credits granted during the war to the European Allies and China for political purposes, a large part (owed by Russia and China) proved to be bad debt. In the main the export surplus was reflected in increasing currency reserves and holdings of short-term foreign securities, resources which were quickly exhausted in consequence of the unfavourable trend in the balance of payments during the twenties. By 1929, therefore, Japan had again become a debtor nation. On the other hand, direct investment by Japanese business concerns in China was of considerable long-term economic and political significance. As an exporter of capital as well as of goods, Japan took full advantage of the relative impotence of the Great Powers, preoccupied as they were with Europe, to consolidate her position in China, more especially in Manchuria. China's coal and iron ore industries and modern pig iron production plant came under the complete control of Japanese heavy industry, while Japanese influence also increased in the cotton industry.[32]

At this period China could hardly be said to have existed as a political entity, and the years following the fall of the Manchu dynasty in 1911 have been described as 'one of the most chaotic, confusing, and disunited periods' in Chinese history.[33] The President of the new republic, Sun Yat-sen, was succeeded after only five months in office by Yuan Shih-k'ai who, in 1915, sought to have himself proclaimed the founder of a new dynasty, but in this he was foiled, primarily by Japan, but also by rival warlords. Yuan's death in 1916 was followed by a turbulent period during which the various warlords competed for supremacy in Peking and in Canton. Japan attempted to exploit the situation by presenting China with the notorious 'Twenty-one Demands' which, had they ever been complied with, would have reduced her to the status of a Japanese protectorate. Nevertheless, Japan's influence continued to grow. Indeed, under the terms of the Treaty of Versailles, the German leaseholds in Shantung were accorded to

32. See Y. K. Cheng, *Foreign Trade and Industrial Development of China*, University Press of Washington, 1956; A. Feuerwerker, 'China's Nineteenth Century Industrialization: The Case of the Hanyehping Coal and Iron Company, Limited', C. D. Cowan, ed., *The Economic Development of China and Japan. Studies in Economic History and Political Economy*, Allen & Unwin. London, 1964.

33. F. Shurman, O. Shell, eds, *Republican China (China Readings*, vol. 2), Penguin Books, London, 1968.

Japan and not to China, despite the fact that the latter had formally joined the Allies in 1917 and thus could be accounted one of the victors. The indignation aroused by this *diktat* led to the creation in 1919 of the May Fourth Movement which is regarded as the precursor of the present anti-imperialist movement.[34]

In striking contrast to her political disorganization, China's economy, like that of Japan, enjoyed a considerable boom in the fields of exports and industrialization.[35] In addition to silk and tea, which made up about a third of pre-war exports, Chinese wool, hides and leather, vegetable oil and mineral ores were also in demand abroad. Although there continued to be an adverse balance of payments, the deficit was dwindling. The export boom, high freight rates, and the withdrawal of European goods from the world market, all favoured the growth of Chinese industry which, at the outbreak of war, was still in its infancy. The leading sector was cotton, a feature typical of industrial revolutions ever since England first set the pattern. Despite forced selling by the Japanese, the Chinese market for textiles was virtually inexhaustible. Between 1914 and 1920, the production of cotton yarn rose by 150 per cent, while the number of spindles almost doubled, from 1·1 million to 2·1 million.[36] Coal and steel production, the basis of heavy industry, was expanded, as was the consumer goods sector, while the railway network was enlarged.

Substantial profits were at once the consequence of, and the motive force behind, the war boom. The expansion of the home market, combined with exports of coal, iron ore and pig iron to Japan, enabled a number of firms to recover from chronic financial difficulties – among them, to everyone's surprise, the Hanyehping Company, by far the most important of China's coal and iron concerns. This firm's annual average loss of 1·2 million (Mexican) dollars for the period 1912–15 was converted into an average

34. See Chow Tse-Tsung, *The May Fourth Movement. Intellectual Revolution in Modern China*, 3rd ed., Harvard University Press, Cambridge, Mass., 1967.

35. See Y. K. Cheng, *Foreign Trade and Industrial Development of China*, University Press of Washington, 1956; J. Chang, *Industrial Development in Pre-Communist China. A Quantitative Analysis*, Aldine, Chicago, 1969. This work was preceded by a concise study: J. Chang, 'Industrial Development of Mainland China, 1912–1949', *Journal of Economic History*, 27, 1967.

36. J. Chang, *Industrial Development in Pre-Communist China. A Quantitative Analysis*, Aldine, Chicago, 1969, p. 119, Y. K. Cheng, op. cit., p. 51.

annual profit of 2·8 million dollars between 1916 and 1919; after the war, between 1920 and 1923, the company again found itself making losses averaging 2·1 million dollars a year.[37] Of greater importance than this temporary profits explosion was the change wrought by the boom in the structure of the business élite.[38] The old élite was an unreliable, conservative, often corrupt alliance of Confucian bureaucrats and occidentally-minded merchants of *compradores*.[39] Already undermined by the revolution, it was definitively ousted, after violent ideological and financial clashes, by a new class of industrialists and bankers which followed the Japanese model in combining 'technocratic efficiency' with a rigidly nationalistic orientation. There was besides, a separate and highly privileged business élite consisting of foreign merchants, industrialists and bankers, more especially in the Treaty Ports and in Manchuria, then under Japanese economic control. This pervasive economic presence of the imperialist powers was, of course, bound up with China's political dependence, and was to remain a characteristic feature of the Chinese economy until the revolution of 1949. It is also considered to be one of the main reasons why, despite undeniable progress during the Great War, China remained economically backward in certain important respects.

Even before the war the modern sectors of the Chinese economy had in many cases been controlled by foreign interests: foreign investment in China in 1914 is estimated at 1·6 billion U.S. dollars.[40] About one-third of the cotton industry was in foreign (Japanese and British) hands, and during the war Japanese capital

37. Feuerwerker, *China's Nineteenth-Century Industrialization*, p. 93. The expression of sums in Mexican dollars is not unusual. China had a silver currency and, besides the Chinese standard dollar, U.S. American dollars and Mexican dollars were also in circulation. The Haikwan *tael*, often found in statistics, was a unit worth 1,558 Chinese dollars and was mainly used for calculating customs dues.

38. See M. C. Bergère, 'La bourgeoisie chinoise et les problèmes de développement économique (1917–1923)', *Revue d'Histoire Moderne et Contemporaine*, 16, 1969.

39. For a detailed account, see A. Feuerwerker, *China's Early Industrialization. Sheng Hsuan Huai (1844–1916) and Mandarin Enterprise*, Harvard University Press, Cambridge, Mass., 1958.

40. For a detailed account see C. M. Hou, *External Trade, Foreign Investment, and Domestic Development: The Chinese Experience, 1840–1937*, Harvard University Press, Cambridge, Mass, 1965.

was able further to consolidate its already strong position.[41] The Hanyehping Company which, up till 1915, had enjoyed a monopoly of Chinese iron ore and iron production, had come completely under Japanese control as a result of supply agreements

TABLE 27
CHINA: PRODUCTION OF IMPORTANT BASIC MATERIALS
AND INDUSTRIAL GOODS, 1914–20

	Coal (thousand tons)	Iron ore (thousand tons)	Pig iron (thousand tons)	Steel (thousand tons)	Cotton yarn (thousand bales)	Index of industrial production (1914 = 100)
1914	7,974	505	130	56	534	100
1915	8,493	596	166	48	625	112
1916	9,483	629	199	45	667	119
1917	10,479	640	188	43	734	134
1918	11,109	999	158	57	800	138
1919	12,805	1,350	237	35	1,100	170
1920	14,131	1,336	259	68	1,333	200

SOURCE: J. Chang, *Industrial Development in Pre-Communist China. A Quantative Analysis*, Aldine, Chicago, 1969, pp. 60, 116ff.

and a financial tie-up. Thus a company which should have provided the basis for the independent industrialization of China became a supplier of raw materials and semi-manufactures to Japanese heavy industry. More than half its ore and pig iron production was sold to Japan and this at prices which, up till 1914, were below cost. Though, during the war, the company's prices were high enough to generate profits, they were still below the market level. The new mines and iron foundries (Anshan, Penchihu) which came into operation in Manchuria in 1915 were, as Japanese creations, integrated into Japanese heavy industry from the very start.[42] This foreign influence explains why, despite increased production of pig iron, domestic steel output stagnated; and, together with the lack of Chinese business enterprise, it also explains the absence of any capital goods industry worthy of mention, notwithstanding very favourable preconditions in the shape of heavy industry. This absence undoubtedly acted as a

41. Y. K. Cheng, op. cit., p. 51. The share of Japanese spindles increased from 21 per cent in 1915 to 26 per cent in 1920.

42. See Feuerwerker *China's Nineteenth Century Industrialization*.

brake on the process of industrialization, especially during the Great War when there was a drop in imports both of consumer and of capital goods. Because of these restrictions on its capacity, the consumer goods sector was unable to take full advantage of the openings presented by the war. It was not till after the Armistice that the pent-up demand for capital and consumer goods manifested itself in increased imports and simultaneously in a renewed, if short-lived, spate of industrialization. Industrial production which had gone up by 34 per cent between 1914 and 1918 rose by another 45 per cent between 1918 and 1920.

TABLE 28
CHINA: IMPORTS 1913–20

	Imports		Percentage share		
	(in millions of Haikwan taels)	Cotton goods	Iron, steel and other metals	Machinery	Total industrial goods
1913	570	19·3	5·3	1·4	40·4
1916	516	14·1	5·1	1·3	40·5
1920	762	21·8	8·3	3·2	47·0

SOURCE: Y. K. Cheng, *Foreign Trade and Industrial Development of China*, University Press of Washington, 1956, pp. 32, 35.

Latin America

Prior to 1914 the Latin American national economies fitted almost exactly into a two-sector model of the world economy in which industrial countries are contrasted with primary producers;[43] for they exported raw materials and food in exchange for European industrial goods, European capital and European population surpluses. After North America, Latin America and, above all Argentina, was a favourite area for British economic expansion. Typical of these economies was their specialization in individual staples: Argentina exported grain, meat and wool, as did Uruguay; Brazil exported coffee and rubber. In Chile, nitrate accounted for some 75 per cent of exports, while three-quarters of Mexico's exports con-

43. For some general aspects of Latin-American underdevelopment, see A. G. Frank, *Capitalism and Underdevelopment in Latin America*, Penguin, London, 1971; C. Furtado, *Economic Development of Latin America. A Survey from Colonial Times to the Cuban Revolution*, Cambridge University Press, 1970.

sisted of minerals (gold, silver, lead and copper).[44] For the national economies of Latin America, this concentration on primary goods entailed all the usual disadvantages: a tendency for their terms of trade to deteriorate, an undesirable exposure of the domestic economy to fluctuations in world demand and, not least, economic and political dependence on the European and U.S. capital interests which controlled the most important export sectors. Just before the First World War efforts were accordingly made to diversify both production and exports. But if, as is often the case nowadays, the road to economic development is seen as a choice between 'export-led growth' and development focused on import substitution, then that choice had not yet been made in Latin America in 1914. Three innovations must be considered as responsible for the pattern of subsequent economic growth. In the first place the export sectors were increasingly entering upon the stage of processing agricultural products: meat extract factories, meat refrigeration plants, mills and sugar factories were built for the most part with foreign capital. While this trend improved the export performance of the agrarian producer, it simultaneously increased his economic dependence on the foreign investor.[45] In the second place, various countries such as Peru and Mexico discovered that in mineral oil they had a new staple with an expanding market; shortly before the war, oil had already moved up behind copper as Peru's second most important export commodity.[46] Thirdly, we should cite, as a particularly successful example of industrial import substitution, the Brazilian cotton industry whose expansion had been favoured by the protective tariff of 1879.[47] The 'one million spindle mark', a kind of milestone in the development of mechanized cotton spinning, was

44. G. Wythe, *Industry in Latin America*, 2nd ed., Columbia University Press, New York, 1949, p. 7.

45. *Frigoríficos* were erected in Argentina from 1882, first with British capital and, from 1907, also with U.S. capital; in Uruguay from 1904, see Wythe, *Industry in Latin America*, pp. 80, 131.

46. See L. S. Rowe, *Early Effects of the War upon the Finance, Commerce and Industry of Peru*, Oxford University Press, New York, 1920.

47. On this subject, see the monograph by S. J. Stein, *The Brazilian Cotton Manufacture: Textile Enterprise in an Underdeveloped Area, 1850–1950*, Harvard University Press, Cambridge, Mass., 1957. This had previously appeared in shortened form: S. J. Stein, 'Brazilian Cotton Textile Industry, 1850–1950', S. Kuznets, W. E. Moore, J. Spengler eds, *Economic Growth: Brazil, India, Japan*.

reached by Brazil in 1909 (India 1876, Japan 1898, China 1912). The cotton industry was the first manufacturing industry to achieve any economic importance not only in Brazil but also, though of course on a smaller scale, in Columbia, Ecuador, Peru and Venezuela.[48]

Initially the outbreak of war underlined the disadvantages of a single-sector national economy, as may be plainly seen from what happened in Chile.[49] In peacetime her nitrate had largely been destined for the fertilizer industry overseas but when shipping movements were brought to a standstill by the presence of naval units belonging to both belligerents, there were many who took a gloomy view of immediate prospects. Moreover, believing that the war would be of short duration, they in no way anticipated the subsequent war boom. Initially it seemed that the pessimists had been proved right: a large number of plants suspended operations but even so, much of the nitrate still being produced had to be stockpiled. As a result the government found itself compelled to provide support for this distressed sector. But more than anything else the story of Chilean nitrate illustrates the danger to society of too narrow an export base. Before the war, some 50,000 workers had been employed in the nitrate fields. The crisis put most of them out of work and, since no other form of employment was available in the north, thousands of workers were transferred to the central and southern provinces where they either forced down the already low agricultural wages or else had to be maintained by the state. It was not until the summer of 1915, after the transition to a protracted war of attrition in Europe, that the outlook changed. A keen demand developed for Chilean nitrate which, for the most part, now found its way to the powder and explosives industry rather than to agriculture. Generally speaking, once the crisis of the first months of the war had been overcome, staples such as grain, meat, rubber and coffee were similarly in demand.[50]

In the course of time, however, it proved possible to meet only part of European requirements; from 1916 onwards, we may dis-

48. See Wythe, *Industry in Latin America*.

49. See a study undertaken on behalf of the Carnegie Foundation: I. S. Rowe, *Early Effects of the European War upon the Finance, Commerce and Industry of Chile*, Oxford University Press, New York, 1918.

50. See J. H. Williams, 'Latin America's Foreign Exchange and International Balances During the War', *Quarterly Journal of Economics*, 33, 1918/19.

cern the effects of the shipping shortage and perhaps also of the intensified blockade. The Central Powers were almost completely cut off from overseas supplies while the European Allies could not import as much as they wished for lack of shipping. And, as rationing in Europe became more stringent, so the volume of food exports from Latin America declined. Moreover, in 1917 grain exports reflected the poor harvest. President Irigoyen of Argentina imposed a temporary grain embargo but agreed to release wheat to Britain provided an equal quantity was shipped from Australia to the Argentine.[51] Rising prices ensured that, despite diminishing quantities, the value of exports continued to increase. Wheat rose from 10 pesos per 100 kg in July 1914 to 19 pesos in June 1917, wool from 7–12 pesos in July 1914 to 8–18 pesos in March 1917 and 20–32 pesos in January 1918. Speculation lifted the price of nitrate from 7s. per quintal (101·41 lb) in 1914 to 17s. at the end of 1917. Early in the following year consultations between the Chilean, U.S. and British governments resulted in the price coming down to a lower, controlled level. Since imports rose throughout more slowly than exports, the Latin American countries achieved substantial export surpluses.

TABLE 29

LATIN AMERICA: EXPORTS OF STAPLES, 1913–17 (QUANTITIES)

	Argentina and Uruguay		Brazil		Chile	
	Meat (millions of tons)	Grain (millions of tons)	Coffee (millions of sacks)	Rubber (millions of tons)	Nitrate (millions of tons)	Copper (thousands of tons)
1913	—	—	13·3	36·2	2·7	41
1914	8·2	5·8	11·3	33·5	1·8	45
1915	8·0	8·3	17·1	35·2	2·0	54
1916	8·8	6·5	13·0	31·5	3·0	72
1917	7·6	2·2	10·6	34·0	2·8	78

SOURCE: J. H. Williams 'Latin America's Foreign Exchange and International Balances during the War', *Quarterly Journal of Economics*, 33, 1918/19, pp. 436–59.

1 sack of coffee = 132 lb.

The active balance of trade led to an improvement in the rates of exchange: towards the end of the war, the Argentine peso stood at

51. ibid., p. 437.

13 per cent and the Uruguayan peso at 28 per cent above the dollar parity. The Chilean paper peso, hitherto constantly below par, approached parity (18d), while the discount of the Brazilian milreis against the dollar was temporarily reduced from 31 per cent to 12 per cent. The strong currency position of Argentina and Uruguay can also be gauged from the fact that the governments of these countries were able to give credit to the Allies.

TABLE 30

LATIN AMERICA: FOREIGN TRADE, 1914–19. MILLIONS OF PESOS
(ARGENTINA, CHILE, URUGUAY). MILLIONS OF POUNDS STERLING
(BRAZIL)

	Argentina		Brazil		Chile		Uruguay	
	Ex-ports	Im-ports	Ex-ports	Im-ports	Ex-ports	Im-ports	Ex-ports	Im-ports
1914	403	323	47	35	309	270	58	37
1915	582	305	54	30	335	152	73	41
1916	573	366	56	40	523	223	74	53
1917	550	380	63	45	723	339	104	67
1918	801	501	61	53	811	395	116	101
1919	1,031	656	130	78	331	387	147	113

SOURCE: League of Nations, *Memorandum on Balances of Payments and Foreign Trade Balances 1910–1924*, 2 vols, Geneva, 1925. vol. II, pp. 467, 515, 692.

Unit of currency in Argentina, gold peso, in Chile, peso (18d), in Uruguay, peso. Brazil's foreign trade figures were published in her own currency (milreis) and in pounds sterling. At par one pound sterling equalled 8·9 milreis.

Under the Grain Convention of January 1918 Argentina granted Great Britain and France, and later also the United States, government credits of up to 240 million U.S. dollars for the purchase of Argentinian wheat, while Uruguay provided the U.S.A. and Britain with credits of up to 115 million U.S. dollars. By contrast, Brazil's currency position remained relatively weak because her export surpluses lagged behind those of the neighbouring republics and also because, up till 1914, the milreis had been substantially bolstered by capital imports which the war had now interrupted.

The war boom temporarily relieved the Latin American governments of all concern for the diversification of exports since, contrary to expectations, the traditional staples again proved useful earners of foreign exchange. The rubber planters in Brazil and Peru who, in 1914, were fighting a rearguard action against Asian competition, were accorded a respite by the war. There was considerable growth in the exploitation of minerals – mining in Bolivia, Chile, Ecuador, Mexico and Peru, oil production in Peru and Mexico. It was during the Great War that the vast oil resources of Venezuela were first tapped.[52] It must be recognized that the problems arising from overdependance on too narrow a range of exports were at best postponed, not solved, by the war, a case in point being Chile whose export boom based on nitrate for the explosives industry collapsed with the Armistice. The Chilean paper peso, quoted at 7d–8d in the summer of 1914, rose to 17d in September 1918, thus almost attaining parity (18d). Thereafter it fell sharply, and by December had come back to 9d–10d.[53]

TABLE 31
BRAZIL: IMPORTS AND DOMESTIC PRODUCTION OF COTTON CLOTH, 1911–20

	Import	Production		Import	Production
	Thousand kg.	Millions of metres		Thousand kg.	Millions of metres
1911	6,781	378·6	1916	2,004	474·3
1912	4,913	400·0	1917	2,128	548·1
1913	3,631	385·0	1918	2,395	494·4
1914	1,208	314·3	1919	1,616	584·4
1915	1,092	470·8	1920	3,455	587·2

SOURCE: S. J. Stein, 'Brazilian Cotton Textile Industry, 1850–1950', S. Kuznets, W. E. Moore, J. Spengler, eds, *Economic Growth: Brazil, India, Japan*, Duke University Press, Durham, 1955.

In Latin America the export boom was accompanied by a widespread move towards import substitution, itself a consequence of the war. The extent to which domestic products replaced imports may best be seen in Brazil where, towards the end of the war, 75 to

52. On the above, see Wythe, *Industry in Latin America*. On Peru, also I. S. Rowe, *Early Effects of the War upon the Finance, Commerce and Industry of Peru*, Oxford University Press, New York, 1920. In Venezuela in 1921 mineral oil already accounted for 9 per cent of the value of all exports; see International Bank for Reconstruction and Development, *The Economic Development of Venezuela. Report of a Mission Organized by the International Bank for Reconstruction and Development at the Request of the Government of Venezuela*, John Hopkins Press, Baltimore, 1961, p. 482.

53. Williams, 'Latin America's Foreign Exchange', pp. 444, 448.

85 per cent of domestic requirements in cotton goods were supplied from home production. Cheap and medium qualities were also exported, and only the very highest qualities continued to be imported from Britain. The war boom also benefited the smaller textile industries of Argentina, Columbia, Ecuador, Venezuela and Peru; during the war the latter country applied factory methods to woollen spinning and weaving. But Latin America did not stop at the textile industry. Her enforced isolation from European producers led to the *ad hoc* creation in Argentina, Brazil and several other countries, of 'substitute industries' for the manufacture of dyestuffs, soap, beer, shoes, furniture and the like; from 1916 Argentina actually assembled motor vehicles. Often a warehouse would provide the nucleus for the manufacture of the type of imported goods it had previously distributed.[54]

Seen in retrospect, however, the longer-term impact of this surge of industrialization calls for a somewhat cautious assessment. Many of the new factories offered substitutes of inferior quality at higher prices and were unable to meet post-war European competition. Above all, there were no foundations in the shape of heavy industry upon which to build up a new industrial system. The only exception worthy of note was the Brazilian iron industry which, however, produced no more than 4,267 tons of pig iron during the whole of 1916.[55] There was a drastic decline in the import of capital goods: Brazil, for example, imported 13,000 tons of textile machinery in 1913, and only 2,000 tons in 1917. About half of the machinery in Brazil's textile mills in 1945 had been installed and put into operation before 1915; this alone should be enough to warn us against overestimating the impetus given by the war boom to industrialization.[56] Again, in the case of Argentina, it has been suggested that, by interrupting the supply of European capital goods, the Great War tended to retard rather

54. See C. F. Diaz Alejandro, *Essays on the Economic History of the Argentine Republic*, Yale University Press, New Haven, 1970; A. Dorfman, *Evolucion industrial Argentina*, ed., Losada, Buenos Aires, 1942. G. Wythe, *Manufacturing Developments in Argentina*, Government Printing Office, Washington, 1934; Wythe, *Industry in Latin America*.

55. W. Baer, *The Development of the Brazilian Steel Industry*, Vanderbilt University Press, Nashville, 1969, pp. 56ff.

56. See S. J. Stein, *The Brazilian Cotton Manufacture: Textile Enterprise in an Underdeveloped Area, 1850–1950*, Harvard University Press, Cambridge, Mass., 1957, p. 103.

than encourage industrialization.[57] Despite the stimulus of the export boom, and despite certain new departures in the field of import substitution, Latin America failed to achieve any self-sustaining industrial growth during the First World War.

The British Empire

The British Empire may be regarded as a kind of cross-section of the international economic system. The example of countries like India, Canada, Australia, South Africa and New Zealand, which were important components of the world economy, show how diverse could be the effects of the European war upon the foreign trade and the economic development of the non-European countries. One important variable was proximity to the European market. Like the United States, Canada benefited by the concentration of Allied demand on the North Atlantic, itself a consequence of the shortage of shipping space. Canadian grain exports, for instance, increased dramatically at the expense of more distant suppliers such as Australia. A second factor of importance to export economies dependent on a few staple commodities was the extent to which trends in price and demand varied between individual products. Foods of high nutritional value, such as refrigerated meat from New Zealand, were held to justify the long haul, whereas industrial raw materials such as Australian wool and Indian cotton and jute, were subject to comparatively stringent

TABLE 32
BRITISH EMPIRE: SHARES IN WORLD TRADE
(EXPORTS AND IMPORTS) 1913–24

	1913	1924
	%	%
United Kingdom	15·3	16·5
India	3·6	3·7
Canada	2·7	3·6
Australia	2·0	2·5
South Africa	1·4	1·3
New Zealand	0·5	0·9

SOURCE: League of Nations, *Memorandum on Balances of Payments and Foreign Trade Balances, 1910–1924*, 2 vols, Geneva, 1925, vol. 1, p. 90.
　　Merchandize trade. Figures for Australia and South Africa include bullion.

57. Alejandro, *Essays on the Economic History of the Argentine Republic.*

TABLE 33
BRITISH EMPIRE: FOREIGN TRADE, 1913–19

	India (billions of rupees)		Canada (billions of dollars)		Australia (millions of francs)		South Africa (millions of francs)		New Zealand (millions of pounds)	
	Ex-ports	Im-ports	Ex-ports	Im-ports	Ex-ports	Im-ports	Ex-ports	Im-ports	Ex-ports	Im-ports
1913	2,4	1,8	0,4	0,6	77	78	65	41	21	21
1914	2,1	1,6	0,4	0,5	59	71	39	35	25	21
1915	1,8	1,3	0,7	0,5	72	75	33	32	29	20
1916	2,3	1,5	1,2	0,8	95	74	63	39	32	25
1917	2,3	1,5	1,5	1,0	79	60	89	35	30	20
1918	2,4	1,7	1,2	0,9	111	99	67	47	28	24
1919	2,9	1,8	1,2	1,1	145	94	98	49	52	30

SOURCE: League of Nations, *Memorandum on Balances of Payments and Foreign Trade Balances, 1910–1924*, 2 vols, Geneva, 1925, vol. II, pp. 373, 412, 426, 452, 504.

For Australia and South Africa, trade figures include bullion. Fiscal years (April–March) for Canada 1913–19, for Australia–19.

import restrictions. Again, in the case of South Africa and Australia economic life and the balance of payments were both adversely affected by the pegging of the price of gold for reasons of exchange policy: as import prices continued to rise, this entailed a marked deterioration in those countries' terms of trade. Thus the effects of foreign trade on the economies of the various countries were very diverse and equally diverse were the economic responses evoked and the degree of success achieved in adapting to the changes. Three countries, Canada, India and South Africa, will serve to illustrate how differences in economic progress were determined by the economic structure obtaining before the war.

Canada

Prior to 1914, Canada's role in the international economy had been primarily that of a wheat exporter, but at home a phase of rapid industrialization had already diminished the relative importance of agriculture.[58] Shortly before the outbreak of war this

58. See W. T. Easterbrook, H. G. J. Aitken, *Canadian Economic History*, Macmillan, Toronto, 1956. Figures from M. C. Urquart, K. A. H. Buckley, ds, *Historical Statistics of Canada*, Cambridge University Press, 1965.

spate of industrialization had ceased. Moreover, with the temporary interruption of international economic relations that began in August 1914, the Canadian economy seemed to be heading inexorably for a slump. The tide began to turn at the beginning of 1915, when Allied demand and the resulting operation of the foreign trade multiplier acted as a general stimulus to the country's economic development. Like the U.S.A., if on a smaller scale, Canada provided Europe not only with foodstuffs and raw materials (metals) but also with industrial goods. Wheat and meat were the most important export commodities, followed by raw materials and munitions. Rising prices led to an enormous increase in the cultivated area. During the war the average price of 'No. 1 Northern Wheat' rose from 1·07 dollars per bushel (1910–16) to 2·31 dollars (1917–20), while the area under cultivation was increased by more than 4 million acres, i.e. by 80 per cent. Despite poor harvests, high prices meant that farm incomes and the value of exports continued to rise from 1917 onwards. Shortly after the outbreak of war the British government placed orders in Canada for war material, mainly shells, and for a time Canadian industry was supplying between a quarter and a third of the British Army's ammunition requirements.[59] However the progress of industrialization was primarily determined by the flourishing state of home demand. Industrial production, which had increased by 17 per cent between 1910 and 1915, nearly doubled between 1915 and 1919.[60] Before 1914, industrialization had been concentrated primarily on the processing of Canadian natural resources for export – a stage of development which may be regarded as the highest form of primary production. Development during the next four years, however, largely took the form of diversified production for the domestic market.

While there is no doubt that the war gave the Canadian economy a considerable boost, in terms both of growth and of industrializa-

59. F. A. Knox, 'Canadian War Finance and the Balance of Payments, 1914–1918', *Canadian Journal of Economics and Political Science*, 6, 1940, p. 245. On procurements in Canada see also the official British *History of the Ministry of Munitions*, 12 vols. 1921–22, Also D. Carnegie, *The History of Munitions Supply in Canada 1914–1918*, Longman, London, 1925.

60. Index of gross value of industrial production (1935/39 = 100): 1910, 78·5; 1915, 91·8; 1919, 174·7. See G. W. Bertram, 'Economic Growth in Canadian Industry 1870–1915: The Staple Model and the Take-Off Hypothesis', *Canadian Journal of Economics and Political Science*, 29, 1963.

tion, this was to prove not altogether advantageous in the long-term. Before 1914 the central problem of the Canadian economy had been its adjustment to a fall in the rate of growth of world demand for those export commodities, mainly wheat, which had previously been the mainstay of Canada's economic growth. This adverse trend was interrupted, indeed reversed, by the war. In response to wartime demand, a vast amount of labour and capital was diverted to agriculture. Between 1911 and 1921 the population of the prairie provinces increased by 600,000 to 2 million, while farmers acquired a considerable amount of equipment at inflated wartime prices. No one took account of the fact that the agricultural boom, being largely due to the 'concentration on the North Atlantic' of Allied wartime demand, could not be other than short-lived. In the twenties, therefore, the problem of economic structure change again arose, this time in an even acuter form than before the war. Another disadvantage was that the country continued to be heavily dependent on foreign capital. The large surpluses in the balance of merchanize trade were more than offset by interest and dividend payments and by the expenditure of the Canadian forces overseas. On balance, Canada was an importer of capital during the war and, indeed, a substantial one. Private and state credits to the British government must be set against large portfolio and direct investments by the United States in Canada. While the Canadian economy's dependence on Great Britain lessened, its dependence on the U.S.A. increased.

TABLE 34
CANADA: SUMMARY OF THE BALANCE OF PAYMENTS
FROM 1914 TO 1918

	Millions of dollars		Millions of dollars
Interest and dividends	− 849	Balance of trade	+1,141
Armed forces	− 480	Capital receipts	+1,222
Capital payments	− 784		
Currency reserves	− 80	Errors and Omissions	− 170
Total	−2,193	Total	+2,193

SOURCE: F. A. Knox, 'Canadian War Finance and the Balance of Payments, 1914–1928', *Canadian Journal of Economics and Political Science*, 6, 1940, pp. 247ff.

'Errors and Omissions' consist of movement of short-term capital, few of which were recorded, and also include mistakes in other entries.

India

India had a larger share of world trade than Canada, but lagged far behind that country in terms of economic development. The 1918 Report of the Indian Industrial Commission (set up in 1916 to examine the possibilities of industrial development) notes 'how little the march of modern industry has affected the great bulk of the Indian population, which remains engrossed in agriculture, winning a bare subsistence from the soil by antiquated methods of cultivation'.[61] India exported raw materials (cotton, jute, rubber), jute and cotton goods, food grains and tea, in exchange for manufactures, amongst which cotton goods ranked top of the list.[62]

On the eve of the war modern manufacturing industry signified the cotton industry of Bombay and Ahmedabad on the west coast, and the jute industry of Bengal.[63] While both sectors were based on an ample supply of domestic raw materials, their economic contexts were different. The jute industry, controlled by British capital, sold more than 90 per cent of its output abroad, providing bags and balings for a growing world market. The Indian-controlled Bombay cotton industry exported the major part of its yarn output but was less dependent than the jute industry on international trade, since it sold quantities of cotton goods on the domestic market where it competed fairly successfully with local handicrafts and the Lancashire cotton industry. A third modern sector was the iron and steel industry which, for all practical purposes, may be identified with the Tata Iron and Steel Company founded in 1907; the older, but less important, Bengal Iron and Steel Company produced only pig iron.

The war created some additional demand for Indian products; it is estimated that by 1918, besides supplying the wartime requirements of the Indian Army, India had sent 80 million pounds' worth of manufactured jute goods, wolfram, mica, saltpetre, timber

61. Cit. from V. Anstey, *The Economic Development of India*, 4th ed. Longman, London, 1957, p. 218.
62. See G. E. Hubbard, *Eastern Industrialization and its Effect on the West*, Oxford University Press, 1935, p. 251.
63. For a detailed account of India's first bid for industrialization see the penetrating study by A. K. Bagchi, *Private Investment in India 1900–1939*, Cambridge University Press, 1972.

and various other commodities and raw materials to the Allies in Europe.[64] On the other hand the war closed some of India's traditional markets so that total exports declined from a yearly average of 2·3 billion rupees between 1910 and 1913 to 2·2 billion rupees between 1914 and 1918, while the export surplus in the corresponding periods declined from 765 million rupees to 676 million rupees a year.[65] Nevertheless, India improved her trade position vis-à-vis the United Kingdom and this, together with the steep increase in the price of silver, created a number of monetary problems within the Empire. The exchange rate between the pound sterling and the rupee had to be adjusted in favour of India from 1s 4d per rupee before the war to 1s 10d in 1919. The bullion value of the (silver) rupee reached and exceeded the exchange parity of 1s 4d in 1917, with the result that from then on large quantities of rupees were withdrawn from circulation and melted down into bullion.[66] A sectoral analysis of the country's modern manufacturing industries reveals high profits, but in an economy that had not yet reached a phase of self-sustained industrial growth the long-term effects were necessarily limited.[67]

After initial difficulties due to the blockade of its central European markets, the jute industry was soon enjoying a brisk demand for sandbags and other military items, which more than compensated for the fall in civilian demand. Wartime conditions favoured domestic processing: for instance, rather than import raw jute for processing in Dundee, the British authorities had their sandbags made in India, and thus economized on shipping space. A comparison of the five-year averages 1909–13 and 1914–18 shows that annual raw jute exports fell from 222 million rupees to 128 million rupees, while exports of jute manufactures rose from 203 million rupees to 402 million rupees.[68] Thus, the jute mill owners were in the happy position of being able to buy raw material and labour in a buyer's market and sell their products in a seller's market. Though the British authorities eventually tried to gain

64. Anstey, *Economic Development of India*, p. 216.

65. League of Nations, *Memorandum on Balances of Payments and Foreign Trade Balances, 1910–1924*, 2 vols., Geneva, 1925, vol. II, p. 373.

66. See J. L. Laughlin, 'Indian Currency Since the World War', *Journal of Political Economy*, 35, 1927.

67. See Bagchi, *Private Investment in India 1900–1939*.

68. Anstey, *Economic Development of India*, pp. 626ff.

control of the sandbag trade from fibre to finished article,[69] profits remained considerable; according to official estimates, the ratio of profits – excluding interest – to paid-up capital was 10 per cent in 1914, 58 per cent in 1915, 75 per cent in 1916 and 49 per cent in 1917.[70]

The cotton industry not only benefited from wartime conditions, but also gained added protection when in 1917 the import duty on cotton piece goods was raised from 3·5 per cent to 7·5 per cent, while at the same time the excise duty remained unchanged at 3·5 per cent. The Indian cotton mills increased their share of the domestic market for cotton piece goods relative both to imports and to handloom production. Though exports also rose, they were still unimportant by comparison with the home market. The major change took place in the composition of India's wartime cotton imports after the Japanese mills had begun to challenge Britian's monopoly; while the British share of imports of cotton piece goods fell from 97 per cent in 1913 to 77 per cent in 1918, the Japanese share rose from less than 1 per cent in 1913 to 21 per cent in 1918.

TABLE 35

INDIA: PRODUCTION, IMPORTS AND EXPORTS OF COTTON PIECE GOODS, 1913–18

	Domestic production (million yards)	Share of mills in domestic production (per cent)	Imports (million yards)	Exports (million yards)
1913	2,190	54	3,042	130
1914	2,311	51	2,327	110
1915	2,439	61	2,019	161
1916	2,252	71	1,771	309
1917	2,357	60	1,505	234
1918	2,372	63	955	187

SOURCE: A. K. Bagchi, *Private Investment in India 1900–1939*, Cambridge University Press, 1972, p. 226.

Whatever the mill owners might do with their profits, they could not plough them back since there was a dearth of investment goods due to the increasing difficulty of importing machinery. Both the

69. E. V. Morgan, *Studies in British Financial Policy, 1914–1925*, Macmillan, London, 1952, pp. 38ff.

70. Bagchi, *Private Investment in India 1900–1939*, p. 276.

jute and the cotton industry increased their labour force to meet expanding demand but, according to Bagchi's estimates, real investment fell during the war to 26 per cent of its pre-war level in the cotton industry, and to 19 per cent in the jute industry.

To an even greater extent than the textile industry, the Tata Iron and Steel Company faced a wartime demand that was to all intents and purposes unlimited. Indian imports of iron, steel and railway materials declined from 1·3 million tons in 1913–14 to 0·2 million tons in 1918–19. Thus private customers, cut off from their normal supplies, had to compete with the government whose demand for shells and railway materials was constantly increasing.[71] The Tata Company placed most of its output at the disposal of the government at the controlled prices then prevailing in Britain. Though considerably higher prices were obtainable in the private market, the company chose to take a long-term view and to build up a fund of governmental good will upon which to draw in less prosperous times. Tata increased its Indian labour force from 3,685 employees in 1913–14 to 7,570 employees in 1918–19. Extensions to plant presented more of a problem since there was a general shortage both of machinery and shipping-space during the war; moreover, some consignments were actually lost as a result of submarine attacks. After 1918 the company got its reward for keeping on the right side of officialdom when it was helped over the lean post-war years by large government contracts and the protective tariff of 1924.

The profits and progress made in some sectors must not be allowed to obscure the fact that, on balance, the war represented an economic loss for India and brought to an end the country's limited prosperity.[72] As for the mass of the population, the cost was a decline in real wages and standards of consumption.

South Africa

South Africa's economic structure, with its particular emphasis on mining and agriculture, resembled that of many Latin-American countries.[73] In 1917, a year of interest to the economic

71. ibid., p.313.   72. ibid., p. 78.
73. See M. H. De Kock, *The Economic Development of South Africa*, Westminster, 1935. I am indebted to Professor Arnt Spandau of the University of Witwatersrand for his advice on the section that follows.

historian more on account of the industrial census than of the war boom, mining represented 25 per cent of the gross domestic product, agriculture 23 per cent and manufacturing only 8 per cent; the share of the service sector at 45 per cent was surprisingly large.[74] During the war South Africa's foreign trade suffered by reason of the fact that gold, being probably the only metal not immediately essential to the war effort, did not increase in price; despite the worldwide rise in the general level of prices, the average value of South African foreign trade for the war years was less than that in the preceding period. This did not mean that the individual trader was worse off, since the shortage of supplies enabled him to raise his prices and dispose of goods which would have been unsaleable in more normal times. In this connection the report of the Cost of Living Commission cites an observation made by the Durban Chamber of Commerce: 'The war has benefited us to the extent that we can get rid of any bad stock we had and we can sell today anything that comes in, no matter what it is like.'[75]

As in other countries, the shortage of imported goods encouraged attempts at import substitution. The number of registered manufacturing concerns (of all sizes) rose dramatically from 3,638 in 1915/16 to 5,287 in 1918/19, and the gross value of their output from 36 million pounds to 59 million pounds.[76] In the manufacturing sector, as in trade and agriculture, large war profits were made, and the distribution of incomes shifted significantly from labour to capital.[77] However, the contribution to real economic development was less impressive than might at first appear since the 65 per cent increase in production by value must be set against a general price rise of 43 per cent between 1915 and 1918;[78] the greater part of the growth by value, therefore, must be attributed

74. See A. Spandau, *Income Distribution and Economic Growth in South Africa*, D. Com. Thesis, University of South Africa, Pretoria, 1971. vol. II. Table 48.

75. 'Cost of Living Commission, Profits Report', *Cape Times* (government printers), Cape Town, 1919. p. 4.

76. Bureau of Census and Statistics, *Union Statistics for Fifty Years. Jubilee Issue 1910–1960*, Pretoria, 1960. Table L–3.

77. See Spandau, *Income Distribution and Economic Growth*, vol. II, Tables 7 and 9.

78. Bureau of Census and Statistics, *Union Statistics for Fifty Years. Jubilee Issue 1910–1960*, Pretoria, 1960, Table H–15.

10

The Legacy of the Great War

There are turning-points in history whose significance is at once economic, social and political. That the Great War undoubtedly qualified as such was already recognized by contemporary observers, a view which the intervening years have done nothing to change. On the other hand certain structural elements in the international economy were at most only temporarily, and never more than superficially, affected by the Great War. This, the final chapter of the book, picks up the threads of the first in an attempt to demonstrate certain instances of continuity and change in the international economy. The observations are, of course, of a provisional nature, the hypotheses being stated rather than substantiated. Indeed the after effects of the war, no less than the imperialist developments that led up to it, call for painstaking studies in their own right.

Immediately after the conclusion of hostilities, an attempt was made to express in round figures how much the Great War had cost the world. Professor Bogart, whose investigation made at the behest of the Carnegie Institute was the most thorough of its kind, isolated six cost elements: government war expenditure ('direct costs'); loss of life; the destruction of material assets on land and sea; loss of production; war subsidies, in so far as they were not included in the state budget; and finally the costs and/or losses

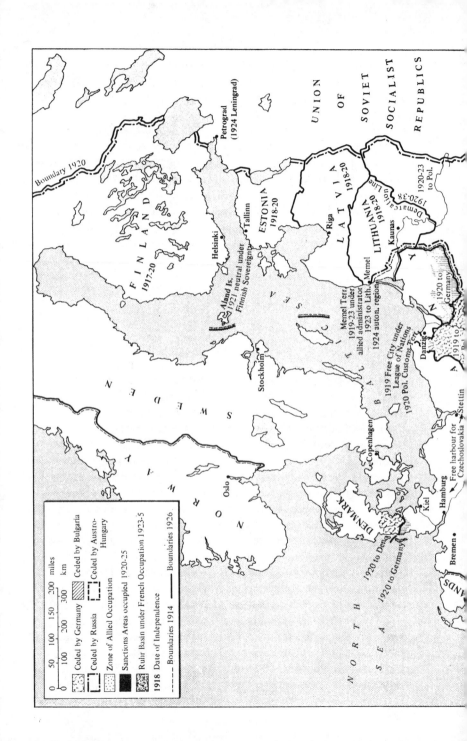

Boundary 1920

Petrograd (1924 Leningrad)

UNION

OF

SOVIET

SOCIALIST

REPUBLICS

F I N L A N D
1917-20

Åland Is. 1921 neutral under
Finnish Sovereignty

Helsinki

Tallinn

ESTONIA
1918-20

L A T V I A
1918-20

Riga

LITHUANIA
1918-20

Kaunas

Demarcation Line
1920-38

1920-23
to Pol.

Memel Terr.
1919-23 under
allied administr.
1923 to Lith.
1924 auton. region

Memel

1920 to
Germany

Stockholm

N

S W E D E N

B A L T I C   S E A

Danzig

1919 Free City under
League of Nations
1920 Pol. Customs Terr.

1919 to

Copenhagen

Stettin

Free harbour for
Czechoslovakia

N O R W A Y

Oslo

DENMARK

1920 to Deutsch

1920 to Germany

Kiel

Hamburg

Bremen

N O R T H

S E A

NDS

miles
0   50   100   150   200
0   100   200   300
km

Ceded by Germany   Ceded by Bulgaria

Ceded by Russia   Ceded for Austro-
                          Hungary

Zone of Allied Occupation

Sanctions Areas occupied 1920-25

Ruhr Basin under French Occupation 1923-5

1918 Date of Independence

————— Boundaries 1914   ———— Boundaries 1926

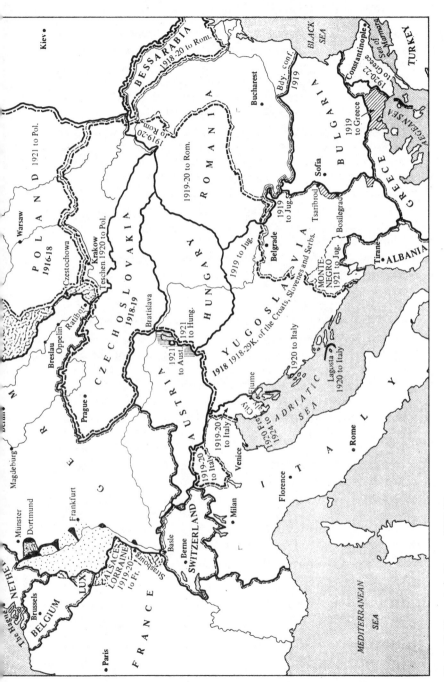

Treaty Settlements in Europe 1919–26.

sustained by the neutrals as a result of the war.[1] Bogart calculated the war expenditure of the states involved as the difference between total war expenditure and a figure representing an extrapolation of the last pre-war budgets, thus arriving at the sum of 186 billion dollars.[2] He estimated the monetary cost of the loss of life by calculating the present productivity that might have been expected of the average worker, having regard to the state of the productive forces in the country concerned. For instance, Bogart placed a cash value of 4,720 dollars on a dead American soldier, while a dead Russian, Serbian or Turk was rated at 2,020 dollars. In accordance with this formula, total loss of life, both military and civilian, worked out at 67 billion dollars. Capital losses occasioned by the war were estimated at 30 billion dollars on land and 7 billion dollars at sea (ships and cargoes). Since the state paid no more than a pittance to the troops in its service, armaments expenditure did not reflect the actual demands made on the factors of production for warlike purposes. Production losses had to be separately calculated as opportunity costs and Bogart estimated them at an all-in figure of 45 billion dollars. War subsidies were put at one billion dollars and losses sustained by the neutrals at two billion dollars. According to this estimate, the total cost of the First World war was 186 billion dollars on 'direct' account and 152 billion dollars on 'indirect' account, making 338 billion dollars in all.

The problems involved in calculating the cost of the war have already been touched on in connection with war finance. Bogart's estimate of government war expenditure is neither better nor worse than subsequent calculations of this kind although, so soon after the war, his material was necessarily incomplete. If the estimates of the 'direct' or 'indirect' cost of the war have not been revised in the light of the latest available material, it is because the whole basis of the calculation has been recognized as inappropriate. In the final analysis, the economic significance of the Great War does not emerge more clearly for being expressed in monetary terms.

1. See E. L. Bogart, *Direct and Indirect Costs of the Great World War*, 2nd (rev.) ed., Oxford University Press, New York, 1920. See also résumé in A. S. Milward, *The Economic Effects of the World Wars on Britain*, Macmillan, London, 1970, pp. 12–16.

2. Bogart has converted the various national currencies into U.S. dollars at the pre-war parity.

A more meaningful equation is that used by W. A. Lewis to assess the extent to which economic development was interrupted by the Great War.[3] The question he poses is this: how much sooner would the 1929 production level have been reached if, after 1913, the international economy had continued to develop at the same average annual growth rate as between 1890 and 1913? According to Lewis's calculations, the delay was 5·2 years in food production, 4·5 years in industrial production and 1·25 years in raw material production; in other words, if we extrapolate on the basis of pre-war growth rates, the 1929 world production level would have been reached in the case of foodstuffs by 1923, of industrial goods by 1924, and of raw materials by 1927. This comparison gives a very clear idea of the 'braking' effect of the Great War, although of course the weaknesses of the method should not be overlooked: firstly, changes in the trend of economic development after 1913 are attributed solely to the war, without any regard for other factors such as demographic growth, technical advances, and changes in consumers' preferences. Secondly, and this is related to the first point, his simple extrapolation does not necessarily indicate a true economic loss. The greatest braking effect is shown in the case of food production, even though during the twenties supplies were ample in relation to effective demand; even before 1913 the growth rate in food production was already so substantial that, while it did not outstrip objective requirements (for everywhere in the world people were still starving to death), it certainly kept ahead of demand backed by purchasing power, as may be seen from the relative decline in food prices.

Today attention is devoted, less to the quantitative evaluation of the economic losses involved, than to the structural changes initiated or accelerated by the Great War. By the time of the Armistice, Europe's importance within the international economy had noticeably declined. Its share of world production had dropped from 43 per cent (1913) to 34 per cent (1923), and of world trade from 59 per cent (1913) to 50 per cent (1924).[4] The

3. See W. A. Lewis, 'World Production, Prices and Trade, 1870–1960', *The Manchester School of Economic and Social Studies*, 20, 1952. For an application of the method to Europe, see I. Svennilson, *Growth and Stagnation in the European Economy*, United Nations Commission for Europe, Geneva, 1954, p. 19.

4. League of Nations, *Memorandum on Production and Trade, 1913 and 1923–1926*, Geneva, 1928, pp. 29 and 51. The estimates of shares in production

decline was due less to the depredations of the war, which by 1924 may be assumed to have been largely made good, than to the growth of overseas competition, particularly from the U.S.A. and Japan. Moreover, Europe's wartime isolation continued to have the effect of stimulating trade between the non-European national economies. Nor should it be forgotten that Russia, up till 1914 an important European trading nation, virtually withdrew from international commerce after the socialist revolution.[5] There can be no doubt that, by and large, this decentralization of world trade was a positive development, and the mood of pessimism prevalent in the literature of the day would scarcely seem to be justified, even in the light of Europe's special situation. A country's imports tend to grow in step with national output. Hence, so far as the industrial nations of Europe were concerned, the long-term implication of industrialization and economic growth overseas was not just intensified competition, but also the possibility of new markets.[6] Nevertheless, if this potential was to be realized, it was essential for the European exporting nations to make an initial, once-and-for-all adjustment to the new situation. This applied more especially to Great Britain, whose export trade still depended to a great extent on the 'industrial staples' of the eighteenth and nineteenth centuries, textiles and ironware. She had side-stepped increasing competition on the Continent by having recourse to overseas markets; instead of looking for new products for her old markets, she had sought new markets for her old products. After the war, this export strategy ran into difficulties, for it was precisely in these easily manufactured basic products that the competition of newly industrialized countries was bound to make itself felt. Brazil, which had previously imported considerable quantities of British cotton goods, now supplied almost all her own requirements from domestic production; in south-east

relate to the production of important staples and are, of course, approximate; the estimates of world trade should be regarded with some reservation. In both cases trends are more revealing than the figures for individual years.

5. Russia's recorded share of world trade fell from 3·9 per cent (1913) to 0·5 per cent (1924); see League of Nations, *Memorandum on Balances of Payments and Foreign Trade Balances, 1910–1924*, 2 vols, Geneva, 1925, vol. I, p. 90.

6. The positive relationship between industrialization and the volume of world trade is stressed in League of Nations, *Industrialization and Foreign Trade*, Geneva, 1945.

Asia the Japanese cotton industry, with the advantage of cheap labour, was able to win a substantial share of the market. After the collapse of the post-war boom, structural adjustment to changed conditions in the world market became a crucial problem for the European economy.

TABLE 36
PRODUCTION AND WORLD TRADE, 1913–24
(REGIONAL DISTRIBUTION IN PERCENTAGES)

| | Share of world production | | Share of world trade | |
	1913	1923	1913	1924
Europe	43	34	59	50
North America	26	32	14	18
Asia	20	21	12	16
Latin America	7	8	8	9
Africa	2	3	4	4
Australia	2	2	3	3

SOURCE: League of Nations, *Memorandum on Production and Trade, 1923 and 1923–1926*, Geneva, 1928, pp. 29, 51.

According to League of Nations estimates, the real levels of world production and world trade in 1913 and in 1923–24 were more or less comparable. According to another estimate, given by Svennilson, world trade did not regain its pre-war level until 1926/27 (cf. I. Svennilson, *Growth and Stagnation in the European Economy*, United Nations Commission for Europe, Geneva, 1954, p. 292),

Of no less importance than the changes in merchandize trade was the change in the structure of international capital movements: Europe, and Britain in particular, were no longer, as before 1914, the world's major creditors.[7] During the war, Great Britain and France had liquidated foreign investments to the order of some 4 million dollars and 700 million dollars respectively. About two-thirds of British sales consisted in U.S. securities, primarily railroad stocks and bonds. Additional losses in the form of direct and portfolio investments, especially in government securities in central and eastern Europe and the Near East, are estimated at 600 million dollars in the case of Britain and 4 billion dollars in the case of France; French losses were exceptionally high because the Soviet government did not honour the debts incurred by the old

7. See United Nations, *International Capital Movements during the Inter-war Period*, Lake Success, 1949.

régime. By this reckoning, Britain and France lost foreign investments amounting in all to somewhere between 4 and 5 billion
dollars, i.e. approximately 25 per cent of British and 50 per cent
of French pre-war foreign investments.[8] During and after the war
Germany lost practically all her foreign investments, amounting
to some 5·8 billion dollars. By contrast, America's foreign indebtedness decreased as a result of the repatriation of securities,
while her foreign investments increased, especially in Canada and
Latin America. Thus, from being a debtor before the war, she had
become a major creditor; gross total of U.S. foreign assets rose
from some 3·5 billion dollars in 1914 to some 7.0 billion dollars
in 1919.[9] Superimposed on these changes in the structure of
international commercial investments there were political debts.
Between 1917 and 1921 the U.S. government made available to
its European allies war and reconstruction credits amounting to
some 10 billion dollars.[10] For their part Britain and France had
granted war credits to the other Allies, more particularly Russia,
Italy and Belgium. Finally, the European Allies were claiming from
the Central Powers, primarily Germany, reparations amounting
to 132 billion marks, or some 33 billion dollars. Thus was created
the well-known triangle of political indebtedness as between Germany, the west European Allies and the U.S.A., which was to
burden the international economy until the Slump.

As might have been foreseen even before 1914, Britain's closest
rival for primacy in the international economy was not Germany
but America. After the war, and largely as its direct consequence,
New York replaced London as the financial capital of the world.
Now, to the extent that America accepted her responsibilities as a
world leader, there was no absolute reason why this shift should
upset the equilibrium of the international economy. But here
certain essential preconditions were lacking. Prior to 1914, the

8. These estimates are, of course, only approximate. According to other
figures Britain lost some 15 per cent and France 55 per cent of her foreign
investments during the war; see W. Ashworth, *A Short History of the International Economy since 1850*, 2nd ed., Longman, London, 1962.

9. C. Lewis, *America's Stake in International Investments*, Brookings Institution, Washington, 1938, p. 606. By comparison with U.S. investment
abroad, foreign investments in the U.S.A. amounted to some 2·7 billion
dollars (1914), or 4 billion dollars (1919), ibid., p. 114.

10. United Nations, *International Capital Movements during the Inter-war
Period*, Lake Success, 1949, p. 5.

international economy had been founded on Britain's free trade policy and the international orientation of London's money and capital market. The United States, on the other hand, had tended towards protectionism. Despite the involvement of individual New York banks, international credit operations as a whole had been relatively unimportant, the inevitable result being lack of interest, experience, and continuity.[11] Indeed, it proved impossible after 1918 to restore either the multilateral equilibrium or the apparently effortless functioning of the gold standard of the pre-war years.[12]

In practice, the decentralization of the world economy meant that its centre of gravity was moving away from Europe, but this is not to say that industrial activity was as yet any more evenly distributed over the world. After the war about two-thirds of the world's production continued to be concentrated in Europe and North America; thus, though their share of world trade had fallen from three-quarters to two-thirds, these areas still retained their dominant position. The continued growth and industrialization taking place in Africa, Asia, Latin America and Australia were as yet of little statistical importance.[13] Significant advances were in any case confined to countries, more notably Japan, which had already been standing on the threshold of industrial power before 1914. In other words, decentralization connoted shifts within the 'imperialist camp'. The polarization of the international economy into dominant industrial powers and dependent primary producers was not greatly altered by the First World War. When the brief war and post-war booms were over, the primary producing countries once again found themselves face to face with the old export problems: namely the low income elasticity of demand for raw materials and food, over-production, and deteriorating terms of trade.[14] Incipient industrialization was held back by the pressure

11. In 1913 foreign investments represented 0·3 per cent, and in 1929, 2 per cent, of the credit transactions of U.S. banks; see R. W. Goldsmith, *Financial Intermediaries in the American Economy since 1900*, Princeton University Press, 1958, p. 143.

12. See H. W. Arndt, *Economic Lessons of the Thirties*, Oxford University Press, 1944; League of Nations, *International Currency Experience. Lessons of the Inter-War Period* (compiled by R. Nurske), 1944.

13. See League of Nations, *Memorandum on Production and Trade, 1913 and 1923–1926*, Geneva, 1928.

14. Using the statistics of the terms of trade between primary and industrial products quoted in Chapter 1, if we take the average of the quinquennium

of competition from Europe, North America and, more latterly, Japan, and by the fact of economic and political dependence. For the political dependence of the primary producers still went hand in hand with economic dependence – this, too, being an element of continuity. The period of territorial expansion had passed its climax, as was plainly evident from the political decentralization of the British Empire, the discussion of the colonial question at the peace negotiations and the espousal of the mandate principle by the League of Nations. But in general these were not so much the concrete results as the harbingers of incipient decolonization. Before its demise, old style colonialism was to enjoy yet one more fling in Japan and Italy.

All in all it is hardly surprising that the peace treaty should have failed to achieve a solution in any of the three areas of conflict mentioned in the first chapter. True, the imperialist race to carve up the world was no longer so keen after the elimination of Germany which, prior to 1914, had been the most aggressive competitor. On the other hand, tension was on the increase in the Far East (Japan), while in Germany there was still an undeniable tendency to seize on every opportunity of channelling internal conflicts into demands for *Lebensraum*.[15] Rivalry between the industrial powers in the field of foreign trade was, if anything, more acute than before the war because many countries were faced with balance of payments problems after the collapse of the multilateral world economic system. Symptomatic of this was Britain's abandonment of free trade. The McKenna Duties of 1915, originally introduced for fiscal reasons and to conserve shipping space, were retained as protective tariffs after the war, while further duties were imposed by the Safeguarding of Industries Act of 1921. Imperial preference, introduced in 1919, showed that tariffs could also be used as an instrument of foreign policy.[16]

1876–80 as 100, then the ratio of primary product to industrial product prices had fallen to an average of 93 for the years 1911–13, and 76 for the quinquennium 1921–25. See United Nations, *Relative Prices of Exports and Imports of Under-developed Countries*, Lake Success, 1949, p. 22.

15. The fact that Germany continued to aspire to world power after 1918 is stressed by F. Fischer, *Der Griff nach der Weltmacht. Die Kriegszielpolitik des kaiserlichen Deutschland 1914/18*, 3rd ed., Droste Düsseldorf, 1964.

16. See W. Ashworth, *An Economic History of England, 1870–1939* Methuen, London, 1960, reprint 1969, pp. 393ff.

The United States, on the other hand, had a long protectionist tradition. Indeed, in imposing the tariffs of 1921 and 1922, the Republicans – in office since 1920 – were pursuing a policy even more restrictive than that of the pre-war period.[17] Least of all did the Great War crystallize the inner social tensions in the industrial capitalist nations. On the contrary, being an imperialist war, it brought the proletariat's class consciousness more nearly into accord with their objective class condition than had previously been the case. Where the ruling classes sought to reduce increasing pressure by means of concessions, there might appear to be a trend towards the harmonization of class relations. This forms the point of departure for the theories evolved by Andrzejewski and others to the effect that a positive correlation exists between the mobilization of large masses for war on the one hand and, on the other, social change tending towards the harmonization and stabilization of social relations, as exemplified in the 'welfare state'.[18]

TABLE 37
1913 RATES OF EXCHANGE (THE VALUE OF THE DOLLAR AND POUND STERLING IN FOREIGN CURRENCIES)

Argentina (peso)	1·04	5·04
Brazil (milreis)	1·83	8·91
Chile (peso)	2·74	13·33
Denmark, Norway, Sweden (crown)	3·73	18·16
Germany (mark)	4·20	20·43
France, Switzerland (franc) Italy (lira)	5·18	25·22
Great Britain (pound)	0·21	—
Japan (yen)	2·01	9·76
Netherlands (guilder)	2·45	12·11
Austria–Hungary (krone)	4·94	24·02
Russia (rouble)	1·94	9·46
Uruguay (peso)	0·97	4·70
U.S.A., Canada (dollar)	—	4·87

SOURCE: League of Nations, *Memorandum on Balances of Payments and Foreign Trade Balances, 1910–1924*, 2 vols, Geneva, 1925, vol. II.

The foregoing is explicitly based on the British experience which

17. See H. U. Faulkner, *Geschichte der amerikanischen Wirtschaft*, Econ, Düsseldorf, 1957, pp. 566–71.

18. See S. Andrzejewski, *Military Organization and Society*, Routledge & Kegan Paul, London, 1954. For a discussion of these theories and further bibliographical information, see A. S. Milward, *The Economic Effects of the World Wars on Britain*, Macmillan, London, 1970, pp. 21–24.

Bibliography

ABBOTT, EDITH, 'English War Statistics of Pauperism', *Journal of Political Economy*, 33, 1925.

ABENDROTH, WOLFGANG, *Sozialgeschichte der europäischen Arbeiterbewegung*, Suhrkamp, Frankfurt, 1965.

AEREBOE, F., *Der Einfluß des Krieges auf die landwirtschaftliche Produktion in Deutschland*, Deutsche Verlags-Anstalt, Stuttgart/Berlin/Leipzig, 1927.

AFTALION, A., *L'industrie textile en France pendant la guerre*, Presses Universitaires de France, Paris, 1924.

ALBERTINI, LUIGI, *The Origins of the War of 1914*, 2nd ed., Oxford University Press, 1952–3.

ALBRECHT-CARRIE, RENÉ, *Italy at the Paris Peace Conference* (The Paris Peace Conference, History and Documents), Columbia University Press, New York, 1938.

ALLEN, G. C. and DONNITHORNE, A. G., *Western Enterprises in Far Eastern Economic Development, China and Japan*, Allen & Unwin, London, 1954.

ANDERSON, B. M., *Effect of the War on Money, Credit and Banking in France and the United States*, Oxford University Press, New York, 1919.

ANDEXEL, RUTH, *Imperialismus – Staatsfinanzen, Rüstung, Krieg*.

Probleme der Rüstungsfinanzierung des deutschen Imperialismus, Akademie-Verlag, Berlin, 1968.

ANDREADES, ANDRÉ, *Les effets économiques et sociaux de la guerre en Grèce*, Presses Universitaires de France, Paris, 1928.

ANDREWS, I. O. and HOBBS, M. A., *Economic Effects of the World War upon Women and Children in Great Britain*, Oxford University Press, New York, 1921.

ANDRZEJEWSKI, S., *Military Organization and Society*, Routledge & Kegan Paul, London, 1954.

ANSTEY, V., *The Economic Development of India*, 4th ed., Longman, London, 1957.

ANWEILER, OSKAR, *Die Rätebewegung in Rußland, 1905–1921*, Brill, Leiden, 1958.

ANTIPA, G., *L'occupation ennemie de la Roumanie et ses conséquences économiques et sociales*, Presses Universitaires de France, Paris, 1929.

ANTSIFEROV, ALEXIS N. and KAYDEN, EUGENE M., *The Cooperative Movement in Russia During the War*, Yale University Press, New Haven, 1929.

APOSTOL, PAUL N., BERNATZKY, MICHAEL W. and MICHELSON, ALEXANDER M., *Russian Public Finance During the War*, Yale University Press, New Haven, 1928.

ARMESON, ROBERT B., *Total Warfare and Compulsory Labour. A Study of the Military–Industrial Complex in Germany during World War I*, Nijhoff, Den Haag, 1964.

ARNDT, H. W., *The Economic Lessons of the Nineteen-Thirties*, Oxford University Press, 1944.

ASHWORTH, WILLIAM, *An Economic History of England, 1870–1939*, Methuen, London, 1960.

ASHWORTH, WILLIAMS, *A Short History of the International Economy Since 1850*, Longman, London, 1962.

ASTROV, NICHOLAS J. and GRONSKY, PAUL P., *The War and the Russian Government*, Yale University Press, New Haven, 1929.

ATALLAH, M. K., *The Long-Term Movement of the Terms of Trade between Agricultural and Industrial Products*, Netherland Economic Institute, Delft, 1958.

AUGÉ – LARIBÉ, MICHEL, *L'agriculture pendant la guerre*, Presses Universitaires de France, Paris, 1925.

BACHI, RICCARDO, *L'alimentazione e la politica annonaria in Italia*, Laterza, Bari, 1926.

BAER, WERNER, *Industrialization and Economic Development in Brazil*, Irwin, Homewood, 1965.

BAER, WERNER, *The Development of the Brazilian Steel Industry*, Vanderbilt University Press, Nashville, 1969.

BAKELESS, JOHN, *The Economic Causes of Modern War, A Study of the Period 1878–1918*. Moffat, New York, 1921.

BAGCHI, A. K., *Private Investment in India, 1900–1939*, Cambridge University Press, 1972.

BANE, S. L. and LUTZ, R. H., *The Blockade of Germany after the Armistice, 1918 to 1919*, Stanford University Press, Palo Alto, 1942.

BARUCH, BERNARD, *The Making of the Reparation and Economic Sections of the Treaty*, Harper, New York, 1920.

BARUÇH, BERNARD, *American Industry in the War. A Report of the War Industries Board*, Government Printing Office, Washington, 1921.

BARUCH, BERNARD, *The Public Years*, Holt/Rinehart/Winston, New York, 1960.

BASLER, WERNER, *Deutschlands Annexionspolitik in Polen und im Baltikum 1914–1918*, Rütten & Loening, Berlin, 1962.

BAUER, M., *Der große Krieg in Feld und Heimat*, Osiander, Tübingen, 1921.

BAUMGART, WINFRIED, *Deutsche Ostpolitik 1918. Von Brest-Litowsk bis zum Ende des Ersten Weltkrieges*, Oldenbourg, Vienna/Munich, 1966.

BAUMGART, WINFRIED, 'Brest-Litowsk und Versailles. Ein Vergleich zweier Friedensschlüsse', *Historische Zeitschrift* 210, 1970.

BELL, A. C., *A History of the Blockade of Germany, Austria-Hungary, Bulgaria, and Turkey 1914–1918*, H.M.S.O., London, 1937.

BENIANS, E. A., 'The Empire in the New Age, 1870–1919', E. A. Benians, J. Butler, E. E. Carrington, *The Empire-Commonwealth 1870–1919 (The Cambridge History of the British Empire*, vol. 3), Cambridge University Press, 1959.

BENTE, HERMAN, 'Die deutsche Währungspolitik von 1914 bis 1924', *Weltwirtschaftliches Archiv* 23, 1926, 1.

BERTRAM, GORDON W., 'Economic Growth in Canadian Industry, 1879–1915: The Staple Model and the Take-Off Hypothesis', *Canadian Journal of Economic and Political Science*, 29, 1963.

reprint, W. T. Easterbrook and M. H. Watkins, *Approaches to Canadian Economic History*, Canadian Publishers, Toronto, 1967.

BEVERIDGE, WILLIAM, *War and Insurance*, Oxford University Press, 1927.

BEVERIDGE, WILLIAM, *British Food Control*, Oxford University Press, 1928.

BIRNBAUM, KARL E., *Peace Moves and U-boat Warfare. A Study of Imperial Germany's Policy toward the United States. April 18, 1916–January 9, 1917*, Almqvist & Wiksell, Stockholm, 1958.

BLANCHARD, R., *Les forces hydro-électriques pendant la guerre*, Presses Universitaires de France, Paris, 1924.

BLANKART, CHARLES, *Die Devisenpolitik während des Weltkrieges (August 1914 bis November 1918)*, Füssli, Zürich, 1919.

BLOOMFIELD, ARTHUR I., *Monetary Policy under the International Gold Standard, 1880–1914*, Federal Reserve Bank, New York, 1964.

Board of Trade and Industries, 'Investigation into Manufacturing Industries in the Union of South Africa (First Interim Report)', *Cape Times*, Cape Town, 1945.

BOELCKE, WILLI A., *Krupp und die Hohenzollern in Dokumenten*, Athenaion, Frankfurt, 1970.

BOGART, ERNEST L., *Direct and Indirect Cost of the Great World War*, Oxford University Press, New York, 1920.

BONNEFOUS, GEORGES, *Histoire politique de la Troisième République*, vol. 2, *La grande guerre 1914–1918*, Presses Universitaires de France, Paris, 1957.

BORCK, FRITZ, 'Die Industrialisierung der Britischen Dominions und die Rückwirkung auf ihre weltwirtschaftliche Stellung', *Weltwirtschaftliches Archiv* 35, 1932.

BOULDING, KENNETH, 'The Role of the War Industry in International Conflict', *The Journal of Social Issues* 23, 1967.

BOWLEY, ARTHUR, *Prices and Wages in the United Kingdom 1914–1920*, Clarendon Press, Oxford, 1921.

BOWLEY, ARTHUR and STAMP, JOSIAH, *The National Income 1924. A Comparative Study of the Income of the United Kingdom in 1911 and 1924*, Clarendon Press, Oxford, 1927.

BOWLEY, A., *Some Economic Consequences of the Great War*, Thornton Butterworth, London, 1930.

BRAND, CARL F., *British Labour's Rise to Power. Eight Studies*, Stanford University Press and Oxford University Press, 1941.

BRAND, CARL F., *The British Labour Party. A Short History*, Stanford University Press, 1964.

BRAND, R. H., *War and National Finance*, Arnold, London, 1921.

BRAUNTHAL, JULIUS, *Geschichte der Internationale*, 3 vols, Dietz, Hanover, 1961–71.

BROWN, WILLIAM A., *The International Gold Standard Reinterpreted, 1914–1934*, 2 vols, Ams Press, New York, 1940.

BRUNEAU, PIERRE, *Le rôle du Haut Commandement au point de vue économic de 1914 à 1921*, Berger-Levrault, Nancy/Paris/Strasbourg, 1924.

BRY, GERHARD, *Wages in Germany 1871–1945*, Princeton University Press, 1960.

BUENGER, SIEGFRIED, *Die sozialistische Antikriegsbewegung in Großbritannien, 1914–1917*, Deutscher Verlag der Wissenschaften, Berlin, 1967.

BURCHARDT, LOTHAR, *Friedenswirtschaft und Kriegsvorsorge. Deutschlands wirtschaftliche Rüstungsbestrebungen vor 1914*, Boldt, Boppard, 1968.

BURCHARDT, LOTHAR, 'Walther Rathenau und die Anfänge der deutschen Rohstoffbewirtschaftung im Ersten Weltkrieg', *Tradition*, 15, 1970.

Bureau International du Travail, *L'accroissement de l'effectiv des syndicats au cours des années 1910–1919*, Geneva, 1921.

Bureau International du Travail, *Fluctuations des salaires dans différents pays de 1914 à 1921*, Geneva, 1922.

Bureau International de Travail, *Fluctuations des salaires dans différents pays de 1914 à 1925*, Geneva, 1926.

Bureau of the Census, *Union Statistics for Fifty Years, Jubilee Issue 1910–1960*, Pretoria, 1960.

BURNETT, PH. M., *Reparation at the Paris Peace Conference. From the Standpoint of the American Delegation* (*The Paris Peace Conference, History and Documents*), 2 vols, Columbia University Press, New York, 1940.

CARMICHAEL, JOEL, *Die Russische Revolution. Von der Volkserhebung zum bolschewistischen Sieg, Februar–Oktober 1917*, Rowohlt, Reinbek, 1967.

CARNEGIE, DAVID, *The History of Munitions Supply in Canada 1914–1918*, Longman, London, 1925.

CARR, E. H., *The Bolshevik Revolution 1917–1923*, 3 vols, Macmillan, London, 1951–3.

CHAMBERLIN, W. H., *Die russische Revolution 1917–1921*, vol. I, Europäische Verlagsanstalt, Frankfurt, 1958.

CHANG, JOHN, 'Industrial Development of Mainland China, 1912–1949', *Journal of Economic History* 27, 1967.

CHANG, JOHN, *Industrial Development in Pre-Communist China. A Quantitative Analysis.* Aldine, Chicago, 1969.

CHARDON, HENRI, *L'organisation de la République pour la paix*, Presses Universitaires de France, Paris, 1926.

CHENG, YU-KWEI, *Foreign Trade and Industrial Development of China*, University Press of Washington, 1956.

CHERNIAVSKY, MICHAEL, *Prologue to Revolution. Notes of A. N. Iakhontov on the Secret Meetings of the Council of Ministers, 1915*, Prentice-Hall, Englewood Cliffs, 1967.

CHESNEAUX, JEAN, 'The Chinese Labour Force in the First Part of the Twentieth Century', C. D. Cowan, ed., *The Economic Development of China and Japan. Studies in Economic History and Political Economy*, Allen & Unwin, London, 1964.

CHOW TSE-TSUNG, *The May Fourth Movement. Intellectual Revolution in Modern China*, 3rd ed., Harvard University Press, Cambridge, Mass., 1967.

CLARK, J. M., HAMILTON, W. H. and MOULTON, H. G., eds, *Readings in the Economics of War*, University of Chicago Press, 1919.

CLARK, JOHN MAURICE, *The Cost of the World War to the American People*, Yale University Press, New Haven, 1931.

CLARKSON, GROSVENOR B., *Industrial America in the World War: The Strategy behind the Line, 1917–1918*, Houghton Mifflin, Boston/New York, 1923.

CLAUS, RUDOLF, *Die Kriegswirtschaft Rußlands bis zur Bolschewistischen Revolution*, Schroeder, Bonn/Leipzig, 1922.

CLEMENTEL, ETIENNE, *La France et la politique économique interalliée*, Presses Universitaires de France, Paris, 1931.

COHN, EINAR, *Danmark under den Store Krig*. Gad, Copenhagen, 1928, rev. English trans. in H. Westergaard ed., *Sweden, Norway, Denmark and Iceland in the World War*, Yale University Press, New Haven, 1930.

COLE, G. D. H., *Labour in the Coal-Mining Industry, 1914–1921*, Clarendon Press, Oxford, 1923.

COLE, G. D. H., *Trade Unionism and Munitions*, Clarendon Press, Oxford, 1923.

COLE, G. D. H., *Workshop Organization*, Clarendon Press, Oxford, 1923.

COLE, G. D. H., *A History of the Labour Party from 1914*, Routledge & Kegan Paul, London, 1948.

COLLINET, PAUL and STAHL, PAUL, *Le ravitaillement de la France occupée*, Presses Universitaires de France, Paris, 1928.

Conférence économique des gouvernement alliés. Programme, procès-verbaux des séances et actes de la conférence, Imprimerie Nationale, Paris, 1916.

CONSETT, MONTAGU W. W. P., *The Triumph of Unarmed Forces (1914–1918)*, Williams & Norgate, London, 1923.

Cost of Living Commission, 'Profits Report', *Cape Times*, Cape Town, 1919.

COURT, W. H. B., 'The Years 1914–1918 in British Economic and Social History', W. H. B. Court, ed., *Scarcity and Choice in History*, Arnold, London, 1970.

CRUTTWELL, C. R. M. F., *A History of the Great War 1914–1918*, 2nd ed., Oxford University Press, 1940.

CROWELL, BENEDICT and WILSON, ROBERT F., *The Giant Hand: Our Mobilization and Control of Industry and Natural Resources, 1917–1918*, vol. I, Yale University Press, New Haven, 1921.

CUFF, ROBERT, D., 'A "Dollar-A-Year Man" in Government: George N. Peek and the War Industries Board', *Business History Review* 41, 1967.

CUFF, ROBERT D., 'Bernard Baruch: Symbol and Myth in Industrial Mobilization', *Business History Review* 43, 1969.

CUNNISON, J. and SCOTT, W. R., *The Industries of the Clyde Valley during the War*, Clarendon Press, Oxford, 1924.

DANAILLOW, GEORGES T., *Les effets de la guerre en Bulgarie*, Presses Universitaires de France, Paris, 1932.

DANIELS, ROBERT V., *Red October. The Bolshevik Revolution of 1917*, Scribner, New York, 1967.

DAVIS, J. S., 'World Currency Expansion during the War and in 1919', *Review of Economic Statistics*, 2 1920.

DAVIS, J. S., 'Recent Developments in World Finance,' *Review of Economic Statistics*, 4 1922.

DEANE, PHYLLIS and COLE, W. A., *British Economic Growth 1688-1959*, 2nd ed., Cambridge University Press, 1967.

DEARLE, N. B., *The Labour Cost of the World War to Great Britain, 1914-1922. A Statistical Analysis*, Yale University Press, New Haven, 1940.

DE KOCK, M. H., *The Economic Development of South Africa*, Westminster, 1935.

DELBRÜCK, CLEMENS VON, *Die wirtschaftliche Mobilmachung in Deutschland 1914*, Verlag für Kulturpolitik, Munich, 1924.

DELEMER, ADOLPHE, *Le bilan de l'étatisme*, Payot, Paris, 1922.

DEMANGEON, A., *Le déclin de l'Europe*. Payot, Paris, 1920.

DIAZ ALEJANDRO, CARLOS HENRICO, *Essays on the Economic History of the Argentine Republic*, Yale University Press, New Haven, 1970.

DOBB, MAURICE, *Soviet Economic Development since 1917*, rev. ed., International Publishers, New York, 1968.

DORFMAN, ADOLFO, *Evolucion industrial Argentina*, ed., Losada, Buenos Aires, 1942.

DULLES, ELEANOR LANSING, *The French Franc, 1914-1918*, Macmillan, New York, 1929.

DUMESNIL, ALEXANDRA, 'Les milieux ouvriers russes et la déclaration de guerre en 1914', *Revue de l'Histoire de la Guerre Mondiale*, 12, 1934.

DRISCOLL, DAVID DANIEL, *Anglo-Swiss Relations 1914-1918. With Special Reference to the Allied Blockade of the Central Powers*, diss, University of London, 1968.

DUNNING, JOHN, H., *Studies in International Investment*, Allen & Unwin, London, 1970.

EASTERBROOK, W. T. and AITKEN, H. G. J., *Canadian Economic History*, Macmillan, Toronto, 1956.

EINAUDI, LUIGI, *La guerra e il sistema tributaria italiana*, Laterza, Bari, 1927.

EINAUDI, LUIGI, *La condotta economica e gli effetti sociali della guerra italiana*, Laterza, Bari, 1933.

EINZIG, PAUL, *World Finance since 1914*, Kegan Paul, London, 1935.

EINZIG, PAUL, *The History of Foreign Exchange*, Macmillan, London, 1962.

EINZIG, PAUL, *Foreign Exchange Crises. An Essay in Economic Pathology*, Macmillan, London, 1968.

ELLSWORTH, P. T., *The International Economy. Its Structure and Operation*, Macmillan, New York, 1950.

EMIN, AHMED, *Turkey in the World War*, Yale University Press, New Haven, 1930.

FAINSOD, MERLE, *International Socialism and the World War*, Harvard University Press, Cambridge, Mass., 1935.

FAIRLIE, JOHN A., *British War Administration*, Oxford University Press, New York, 1919.

FAULKNER, HAROLD U., *Geschichte der amerikanischen Wirtschaft*, Econ, Düsseldorf, 1957.

FAY, SIDNEY, B., *The Origins of the World War*, Macmillan, New York, 1930.

FAY, VICTOR, ed., *La révolution d'octobre et le mouvement ouvrier européen*, Etudes et Documentation Internationales, Paris, 1967.

FAYLE, C. ERNEST, *Seaborne Trade (History of the Great War, by Direction of the Historical Section of the Committee of Imperial Defense)*, 3 vols, Murray, London, 1920–24.

FEARON, PETER, 'The Formative Years of the British Aircraft Industry, 1913–1924', *Business History Review*, 43, 1969.

FEIS, HERBERT, *The Diplomacy of the Dollar, 1919–1932*, Johns Hopkins Press, Baltimore, 1950.

FEIS, HERBERT, *Europe the World's Banker, 1870–1914*, Yale University Press, New Haven, 1930, reprint: Norton, New York, 1965.

FELDMAN, GERALD, *Army, Industry and Labour in Germany 1914–1918*, Princeton University Press, 1966.

FERRO, MARC, *La révolution de 1917. La chute du tsarisme et les origines d'octobre*, Aubier, Paris, 1967.

FEUERWERKER, ALBERT, *China's Early Industrialization. Sheng Hsuan-buai (1844–1916) and Mandarin Enterprise*, Harvard University Press, Cambridge, Mass., 1958.

FEUERWERKER, ALBERT, 'China's Nineteenth Century Industrialization: The Case of the Hanyehping Coal and Iron Company, Limited', C. D. Cowan, ed., *The Economic Development of China and Japan. Studies in Economic History and Political Economy*, Allen & Unwin, London, 1964.

FIELDHOUSE, DAVID K., *Die Kolonialreiche seit dem 18. Jahrhundert*, Fischer, Frankfurt, 1965.

FISCHER, FRITZ, *Der Griff nach der Weltmacht. Die Kriegszielpolitik des kaiserlichen Deutschland 1914/18*, 3rd ed., Droste, Düsseldorf, 1964.

FISCHER, FRITZ, *Weltmacht oder Niedergang. Deutschland im Ersten Weltkrieg*, Europäische Verlags-Anstalt, Frankfurt, 1965.

FISCHER, FRITZ, *Krieg der Illusionen. Die deutsche Politik von 1911 bis 1914*. Droste, Düsseldorf, 1969.

FISK, H. E., *The Inter-Ally Debts. An Analysis of War and Post-War Public Finance, 1914–1923*, Bankers Trust Comp., New York/Paris, 1924.

FLIER, VAN DER M. J., *War Finances in the Netherlands up to 1918*, Clarendon Press, Oxford, 1923.

FLUX, A. W., 'Our Food Supply before and after the War.' *Journal of the Royal Statistical Society* 90, 1930.

FONTAINE, ARTHUR, *L'industrie française pendant la guerre*, Presses Universitaires de France, Paris.

FRANK, A. G., *Capitalism and Underdevelopment in Latin America*, Penguin Books, 1971.

FRIEDMAN, MILTON and SCHWARTZ, ANNA JACOBSON, *A Monetary History of the United States*, Princeton University Press (National Bureau of Economic Research), 1963.

FUCHS, RUDOLF, *Die Kriegsgewinne der verschiedenen Wirtschaftszweige in den einzelnen Staaten an Hand statischer Daten dargestellt*, diss., Zürich, 1918.

FURTADO, CELSO, *The Economic Growth of Brazil. A Survey from Colonial to Modern Times*, University of California Press, Berkeley/Los Angeles, 1963.

FURTADO, CELSO, *Economic Development of Latin America. A Survey from Colonial Times to the Cuban Revolution*, Cambridge University Press, 1970.

GANKIN, OLGA HESS and FISHER, H. H., eds, *The Bolsheviks and the World War. The Origin of the Third International*, Stanford University Press, 1940, reprint 1960.

GARRETT, PAUL W., *Government Control over Prices* (War Industries Board Price Bulletin, No. 3), Government Printing Office Washington, 1920.

GEORGE, OSWALD and MALLET, BERNARD, *British Budgets, 1913/14 to 1920/21*, Macmillan, London, 1929.

GEYER, DIETRICH, *Die Russische Revolution. Historische Probleme und Perspektiven*, Kohlhammer, Stuttgart, 1968.

GIBSON, R. H. and PRENDERGAST, MAURICE, *The German Submarine War 1914–1918*, Constable, London, 1931.

GIDE, CHARLES, 'Des projets d'entente financière après la guerre', *Revue d'Economie Politique*, 32, 1918.

GIDE, CHARLES, 'Des projets d'entente financière après la guerre', *la France*, Presses Universitaires de France, Paris, 1931.

GILBERT, CHARLES, *American Financing of World War I*, Greenwood, Westport, Conn., 1970.

GILBERT, MARTIN, *First World War Atlas*, Weidenfeld & Nicolson, London, 1970.

GOEBEL, OTTO, *Deutschlands Rohstoffwirtschaft im Weltkrieg*, Deutsche Verlags-Anstalt, Stuttgart/Berlin/Leipzig, 1930.

GOLDSMITH, RAYMOND W., *Financial Intermediaries in the American Economy since 1900*, Princeton University Press, 1958.

GOSSWEILER, KURT, *Großbanken, Industriemonopole, Staat. Ökonomie und Politik des staatsmonopolitischen Kapitalismus in Deutschland 1914–1932*, Deutscher Verlag der Wissenschaften, Berlin, 1971.

GOTTLIEB, W. W., *Studies in Secret Diplomacy during the First World War*, Allen & Unwin, London, 1957.

GRATZ, GUSTAV and SCHÜLLER, RICHARD, *Die äußere Wirtschaftspolitik Österreich-Ungarns. Mitteleuropäische Pläne.* Hölder-Pichler-Tempsky, Vienna, 1925.

GRATZ, GUSTAV and SCHÜLLER, RICHARD, *Der Wirtschaftliche Zusammenbruch Österreich-Ungarns*, Hölder-Pichler-Tempsky, Vienna, 1930.

GRAUBARD, STEPHEN, *British Labour and the Russian Revolution, 1917–1924*, Harvard University Press, Cambridge, Mass. 1956.

GREBLER, LEO and WINKLER, WILHELM, *The Cost of the War to Germany and Austria-Hungary*, Yale University Press, New Haven, 1940.

GRINEWITSCH, W., *Die Gewerkschaftsbewegung in Rußland*, Verlagsgesellschaft des Allgemeinen Deutschen Gewerkschaftsbundes, Berlin, 1927.

GROENER, WILHELM, *Lebenserinnerungen. Jugend, Generalstab, Weltkrieg*, Vandenhoeck & Ruprecht, Göttingen, 1957.

GROSS, NACHUM, *Industrialization in Austria in the Nineteenth Century*, diss., University of California, Berkeley, 1966.

GRUBBS, FRANK L., *The Struggle for Labor Loyalty: Gompers, the A. F. of L., and the Pacifists, 1917–1920*, Duke University Press, Durham, 1968.

GÜNTHER, ADOLF, *Die Folgen des Krieges für Einkommen und Lebenshaltung der mittleren Volksschichten Deutschlands*, Deutsche Verlags-Anstalt, Stuttgart/Berlin/Leipzig, 1932.

GUICHARD, LOUIS, *Histoire du Blocus Naval (1914–1918)*, Payot, Paris, 1929.

GUILHON, RAYMOND, *Les consortiums en France pendant la guerre*, Librairie Générale, Paris, 1924.

GUINN, PAUL, *British Strategy and Politics 1914 to 1918*, Oxford University Press, 1965.

GUNZENHÄUSER, MAX, *Die Bibliographien zur Geschichte des Ersten Weltkriegs, Literaturbericht und Bibliographie*, Bernard & Graefe, Frankfurt, 1964.

GUNZENHÄUSER, MAX, *Die Pariser Friedenskonferenz 1919 und die Friedensverträge 1919–1920. Literaturbericht und Bibliographie*, Bernard & Graefe, Frankfurt, 1970.

GUTSCHE, WILLIBALD, 'Erst Europa – und dann die Welt. Probleme der Kriegszielpolitik des deutschen Imperialismus im Ersten Weltkrieg', *Zeitschrift für Geschichtswissenschaft* 12, 1964.

HAIMSON, LEOPOLD, 'The Problem of Social Stability in Urban Russia, 1905–1917', *Slavic Review* 23, 1964 and 24, 1965.

HALL, H. DUNCAN, 'The British Commonwealth and the Founding of the League Mandate System', K. Bourne and D. C. Watt, eds, *Studies in International History*, Longman, London, 1967.

HALLGARTEN, G. W. F., *Imperialismus vor 1914. Die soziologischen Grundlagen der Außenpolitik europäischer Großmächte vor dem Ersten Weltkrieg*, 2nd ed., 2 vols, Beck, Munich, 1963.

HALLGARTEN, G. W. F., *Das Schicksal des Imperialismus im 20, Jahrhundert. Drei Abhandlungen über Kriegsursachen in Vergangenbeit und Gegenwart*, Europäische Verlags-Anstalt, Frankfurt, 1969.

HANCOCK, W. K., *Four Studies of War and Peace in this Century*, Cambridge University Press, 1916.

HARDACH, GERD, 'Französische Rüstungspolitik 1914–1918',

H. A. Winkler, ed., *Organisierter Kapitalismus. Voraussetzungen und Anfänge*, Vandenhoeck & Ruprecht, Göttingen, 1973.

HARMAJA, LEO, *Effects of the War on Economic and Social Life in Finland*, Yale University Press, New Haven, 1933.

HAUPT, GEORGES, *La Deuxième Internationale 1889–1914. Etude critique des sources. Essai bibliographique*. Mouton, Paris/La Haye, 1964.

HAUPT, GEORGES, *Der Kongreß fand nicht statt. Die Sozialistische Internationale 1914*, Europa–Verlag, Wien/Frankfurt/Zürich, 1967.

HECKSCHER, E., ed., *Bidrag till Sveriges ekonomiska och sociala historia under och efter väldskriget*. Norstedt, Stockholm, 1926, rev. Engl. trans. in H. Westergaard, ed., *Sweden, Norway, Denmark and Iceland in the World War*, Yale University Press, New Haven, 1930.

HELFFERICH, KARL, *Der Weltkrieg*, 3 vols, Ullstein, Berlin, 1919.

HELFFERICH, KARL, *Das Geld*, 6th ed., Hirschfeld, Leipzig, 1923.

HENDERSON, HUBERT D., *The Cotton Control Board*, Clarendon Press, Oxford, 1922.

HENDERSON, W. O., 'Walter Rathenau. A Pioneer of the Planned Economy', *Economic History Review* 4, 1951/52.

HENNING, HEINZ, 'Der Aufbau der deutschen Kriegswirtschaft im ersten Weltkrieg', *Wehrwissenschaftliche Rundschau* 6, 1956.

HENRY, ALBERT, *Le ravitaillement de la Belgique pendant l'occupation Allemande*, Presses Universitaires de France, Paris, 1924.

HERZFELD, HANS, *Die deutsche Rüstungspolitik vor dem Weltkrieg*, Schroeder, Bonn/Leipzig, 1923.

HERZFELD, HANS, *Der Erste Weltkrieg*, dtv, Munich, 1968.

HESSE, FRIEDRICH, *Die deutsche Wirtschaftslage von 1914–1923, Krieg, Geldblähe und Wechsellagen*, Fischer, Jena, 1938.

HIBBARD, BENJAMIN, *Effects of the Great War upon Agriculture in the United States and Great Britain*, Oxford University Press, New York, 1919.

HINTON, J., *The First Shop Stewards' Movement*, Allen & Unwin, London, 1973.

HIRST, F. W. and ALLEN, J. E., *British War Budgets*, Oxford University Press, 1926.

HIRST, FRANCIS W., *The Consequence of the War to Great Britain*, Oxford University Press, 1934.

History of the Ministry of Munitions, 12 vols, 1921–22.

HOBSBAWM, ERIC, 'Trends in the British Labour Movement since 1850', *Labouring Men, Studies in the History of Labour*, Basic Books, New York, 1964.

HOBSON, J. A., *Imperialism, A Study*, George Allen & Unwin, London, 1902.

HOFFMANN, LUTZ, *Importsubstitution und wirtschaftliches Wachstum in Entwicklungsländern. Unter besonderer Berücksichtigung von Argentinien, Brasilien, Chile und Columbien*, Mohr, Tübingen, 1970.

HOFFMANN, W., GRUMBACH, F. and HESSE, H., *Das Wachstum der deutschen Wirtschaft seit der Mitte des 19. Jahrhunderts*, Springer, Berlin/Heidelberg/New York, 1965.

HOU, CHI-MING, 'External Trade, Foreign Investment, and Domestic Development: The Chinese Experience, 1840–1937', *Economic Development and Cultural Change* 10, 1961/62.

HOU, CHI-MING, *Foreign Investment and Economic Development in China 1840–1937*, Harvard University Press, Cambridge, 1965.

HUBBARD, G. E., *Eastern Industrialization and its Effect on the West*, Oxford University Press, 1935.

HUMBERT-DROZ, JULES, *Der Krieg und die Internationale. Die Konferenzen von Zimmerwald und Kienthal*, Europa-Verlag, Vienna/Frankfurt/Zürich, 1964.

HURD, ARCHIBALD, *The Merchant Navy (History of the Great War, by Direction of the Historical Section of the Committee of Imperial Defense)*, 3 vols, Murray, London, 1921–29.

HURWITZ, SAMUEL J., *State Intervention in Great Britain. A Study of Economic Control and Social Response, 1914–1919*, Columbia University Press, New York, 1949, reprint, Cass, London, 1968.

HUSTON, J. A., 'The Allied Blockade of Germany 1918–1919', *Journal of Central European Affairs* 10, 1950.

IMLAH, ALBERT H., *Economic Elements in the Pax Britannica. Studies in British Foreign Trade in the Nineteenth Century*, Harvard University Press, Cambridge, Mass., 1958.

Institut für Geschichte an der Deutschen Akademie der Wissenschaften, *Revolutionäre Ereignisse und Probleme in Deutschland während der Periode der Großen Sozialistischen Oktoberrevolution 1917/1918*, Akademie-Verlag, Berlin, 1957.

Institut für Marxismus-Leninismus beim ZK der KPdSU,

Geschichte der Kommunistischen Partei der Sowjetunion, 6 vols, Verlag Progress, Moscow.

Institut für Marxismus-Leninismus beim Zentralkomitee der SED, *Geschichte der deutschen Arbeiterbewegung*, vols II-III, Dietz, Berlin, 1966.

International Commission for the Teaching of History, *The Two World Wars: Selective Bibliography*, Pergamon Press, Oxford, 1964.

IONESCO-SISESTI, G., *L'agriculture de la Roumanie pendant la guerre*, Presses Universitaires de France, Paris, 1929.

Istituto Centrale di Statistica, *Sommario di Statistiche Storiche Italiane*, Istituto Poligrafico dello Stato, Rome, 1958.

JÉZE, GASTON, *Les dépenses de guerre de la France*, Presses Universitaires de France, Paris, 1926.

JINDRA, Z., 'Über die ökonomischen Grundlagen der "Mitteleuropa"-Ideologie des deutschen Imperialismus', K. Obermann, ed., *Probleme der Ökonomie und Politik in den Beziehungen zwischen Ost- und Westeuropa vom 17. Jahrhundert bis zur Gegenwart*, Rütten & Loening, Berlin, 1960.

KATKOV, GEORGE, *Russia 1917. The February Revolution*, Longman, London, 1967.

KAULISCH, BALDUR, 'Die Auseinandersetzung über den uneingeschränkten U-Boot-Krieg innerhalb der herrschenden Klassen im zweiten Halbjahr 1916 und seine Eröffnung im Februar 1917', F. Klein, ed., *Politik im Krieg 1914–1918*, Akademie Verlag, Berlin, 1964.

KEILHAU, WILHELM, *Norge og Verdenskrigen*, Aschehoug, Oslo, 1927, rev. Engl. trans., H. Westergaard, ed., *Sweden, Norway, Denmark and Iceland in the World War*, Yale University Press, New Haven, 1930.

KEITH, ARTHUR BERRIEDALE, *War Government of the British Dominions*, Clarendon Press, Oxford, 1922.

KENDALL, WALTER, *The Revolutionary Movement in Britain 1900–1921, The Origins of British Communism*, Weidenfeld & Nicolson, London, 1969.

KERCHOVE DE DENTERGHEM, CHARLES, *L'industrie belge pendant l'occupation Allemande, 1914–1918*, Presses Universitaires de France, Paris, 1927.

KESTER, RANDALL B., *The War Industries Board, 1917–1918*, 'A Study in Industrial Mobilization', *American Political Science Review* 34, 1940.

KEYNES, JOHN MAYNARD, 'The Economic Consequences of the Peace', *Collected Writings*, vol. 2, Macmillan, London, 1971.

KEYNES, JOHN MAYNARD, 'A Revision of the Treaty', *Collected Writings*, vol. 3, Macmillan, London, 1971.

KEYNES, JOHN MAYNARD, 'A Tract on Monetary Reform', *Collected Writings*, vol. 4, Macmillan, London, 1971.

KEYNES, JOHN MAYNARD, *The General Theory of Employment, Interest and Money*, Macmillan, London, 1951.

KINDLEBERGER, CHARLES P., *Economic Growth in France and Britain, 1851–1950*, Harvard University Press, Cambridge, Mass., 1964.

KLEIN, FRITZ, ed., *Politik im Krieg 1914–1918. Studien zur Politik der deutschen herrschenden Klassen im ersten Weltkrieg*, Akademie-Verlag, Berlin, 1964.

KLEIN, FRITZ, ed., *Deutschland im Ersten Weltkrieg*, 3 vols, Akademie-Verlag, Berlin, 1970.

KLEINE-NATROP, *Devisenpolitik in Deutschland vor dem Kriege und in der Kriegs- und Nachkriegszeit*, Preiss, Berlin, 1922.

KLÖSS, ERHARD, ed., *Von Versailles zum Zweiten Weltkrieg. Verträge zur Zeitgeschichte 1918–1939*, dtv, Munich, 1965.

KNOX, F. A., 'Canadian War Finance and the Balance of Payments, 1914–1918', *Canadian Journal of Economics and Political Science* 6, 1940.

KOBAYASHI, USHISABURO, *Military Industries of Japan*, Oxford University Press, New York, 1922.

KOBAYASHI, USHISABURO, *The Basic Industries and Social History of Japan, 1914–1918*, Yale University Press, New Haven, 1930.

KOCKA, JÜRGEN, *Klassengesellschaft im Krieg. Deutsche Sozialgeschichte 1914–1918*, Vandenhoeck & Ruprecht, Göttingen, 1973.

KÖHLER, LUDWIG VON, *Die Staatsverwaltung der besetzten Gebiete*, Erster Band: *Belgien*, Deutsche Verlags-Anstalt, Stuttgart/Berlin/Leipzig, 1927.

KÖHLER, S., *Die russische Industriearbeiterschaft von 1905–1917*, Teubner, Leipzig/Berlin, 1921.

KÖNIG, HELMUT, *Lenin und der italienische Sozialismus*, Böhlau, Cologne/Graz, 1967.

KOHN, STANISLAS and MEYENDORFF, ALEXANDER F., *The Cost of the War to Russia*, Yale University Press, New Haven, 1932.

KOISTINEN, PAUL A. C., 'The "Industrial-Military Complex" in Historical Perspective: World War I', *Business History Review* 41, 1967.

Kommission der Historiker der DDR und der UdSSR, *Die Oktoberrevolution und Deutschland*, Akademie-Verlag, Berlin, 1958.

KRIEGEL, ANNIE, *Aux origines du communisme Français, 1914– 1920*, 2 vols, Mouton, Paris/La Haye, 1964.

KRUCK, WERNER, *Geschichte des Alldeutschen Verbandes 1890– 1939*, Steiner, Wiesbaden, 1954.

KRÜGER, PETER, *Deutschland und die Reparationen 1918/19*, Deutsche Verlags-Anstalt, Stuttgart, 1972.

KUCZYNSKI, JÜRGEN, *Der Ausbruch des Ersten Weltkrieges und die deutsche Sozialdemokratie*, Akademie-Verlag, Berlin, 1957.

KUCZYNSKI, JÜRGEN, *Zur Frühgeschichte des deutschen Monopolkapitals und des staatsmonopolistischen Kapitalismus. (Die Geschichte der Lage der Arbeiter unter dem Kapitalismus*, vol. XIV), Akademie-Verlag, Berlin, 1962.

KUCZYNSKI, JÜRGEN: *Studien zur Geschichte des staatsmonopolistischen Kapitalismus in Deutschland 1918 bis 1945. (Die Geschichte der Lage der Arbeiter unter dem Kapitalismus*, vol. XVI), Akademie-Verlag, Berlin, 1965.

KUCZYNSKI, JÜRGEN, *Darstellung der Lage der Arbeiter in Deutschland von 1900 bis 1917/18 (Die Geschichte der Lage der Arbeiter unter dem Kapitalismus*, vol. IV), Akademie-Verlag, Berlin, 1967.

LADEMACHER, HORST, ed., *Die Zimmerwalder Bewegung. Protokolle und Korrespondenz*, 2 vols, Mouton, Den Haag/ Paris, 1967.

LANDES, DAVID, *The Unbound Prometheus. Technological Change and Industrial Development in Western Europe from 1750 to the Present*, Cambridge U.P., 1970.

LANK, R., *Der Wirtschaftskrieg und die Neutralen 1914–1918*, Junker & Dünnhaupt, Berlin, 1940.

LAPP, K., *Die Finanzierung der Weltkriege 1914/18 und 1939/45 in*

Deutschland. Ein wirtschafts- und finanzpolitische Untersuchung, diss, Nürnberg, 1957

LAQUEUR, WALTER, *Mythos der Revolution. Deutungen und Fehldeutungen der Sowjetgeschichte,* Fischer, Frankfurt, 1967.

LARIGALDIE, PIERRE, *La politique économique interalliée. Les organismes interalliés de controle économique,* Longin, Paris, 1926.

LARY, HAL B., *The United States in the World Economy,* Government Printing Office, Washington, D.C., 1943.

LAUGHLIN, J. LAURENCE, 'Indian Currency since the World War', *Journal of Political Economy,* 35, 1927.

LAURENS, ADOLPHE: *Le blocus et la guerre sous-marine, 1914–1918,* Colin, Paris, 1924.

LAURENS, ADOLPHE, *Histoire de la guerre sous-marine allemande (1914–1918),* Societé d'Editions Géographiques, Maritimes et Coloniales, Paris, 1930.

LEAGUE OF NATIONS, *Memorandum on Balances of Payments and Foreign Trade Balances, 1910–1924,* 2 vols, Geneva, 1925.

LEAGUE OF NATIONS, *Memorandum on Currency and Central Banks, 1913–1924,* 2 vols, Geneva, 1925.

LEAGUE OF NATIONS, *Memorandum on Production and Trade,* Geneva, 1926.

LEAGUE OF NATIONS, *The Network of World Trade,* Geneva, 1942.

LEAGUE OF NATIONS, *Agricultural Production in Continental Europe during the 1914–18 War and the Reconstruction Period,* Geneva, 1943.

LEAGUE OF NATIONS, *Europe's Overseas Needs 1919–1920 and How They Were Met,* Geneva, 1943.

LEAGUE OF NATIONS, *International Currency Experience. Lessons of the Inter-War Period,* Geneva, 1944.

LEAGUE OF NATIONS, *Industrialization and Foreign Trade,* Geneva, 1945.

LEAGUE OF NATIONS, *Raw Material Problems and Policies,* Geneva, 1946.

LEAGUE OF NATIONS, *The Course and Control of Inflation. A Review of Monetary Experience in Europe after World War I,* Geneva, 1946.

LENIN, V. I., *Ausgewählte Werke in zwei Bänden,* Dietz, Berlin, 1959–60.

LENIN, N. and SINOVIEV, G., *Gegen den Strom. Aufsätze aus den Jahren 1914–1916*, Verlag der Kommunistischen Internationale, 1921.

LEWIS, CLEONA, *America's Stake in International Investments*, Brookings Institution, Washington, D.C., 1938.

LEWIS, W. A., *Economic Survey 1919–1939*, Allen, London, 1949.

LEWIS, W. A., 'World Production, Prices and Trade, 1870–1960', *The Manchester School of Economic and Social History Studies* 20, 1952.

LLOYD, E. M. H., *Experiments in State Control*, Oxford University Press, 1924.

LLOYD GEORGE, DAVID, *War Memoirs*, 6 vols, Nicholson & Watson, London, 1933–6.

LOCKWOOD, WILLIAM W., *The Economic Development of Japan. Growth and Structural Change 1868–1938*, Princeton University Press, 1954.

LOCKWOOD, WILLIAM W. 'The Scale of Economic Growth in Japan, 1868–1938', S. Kuznets, W. E. Moore and J. Spengler, eds, *Economic Growth: Brazil, India, Japan*, Duke University Press, Durham, 1955.

LOEWENFELD-RUSS, HANS, *Die Regelung der Volksernährung im Kriege*, Hölder-Pichler-Tempsky, Vienna, 1926.

LOTZ, WALTHER, *Die deutsche Staatsfinanzwirtschaft im Kriege*, Deutsche Verlags-Anstalt, Stuttgart/Berlin/Leipzig, 1927.

LUCKAU, ALMA, *The German Delegation at the Paris Peace Conference. (The Paris Peace Conference, History and Documents.)* Columbia University Press, New York, 1941.

MANEN, CHARLOTTE A. VAN, *De Nederlandsche Overzee Trustmaatschappij. Middelpunt het Verkeer van Onzijdig Nederland met het Buitenland tijdens den Wereldoorlog, 1914 tot 1919.* Nijhoff, Den Haag, 1935.

MANTOUX, P., ed., *Les Délibérations du Conseil des Quatre*, 2 vols, C.N.R.S., Paris, 1955.

MARCH, LUCIEN, *Mouvement des prix et des salaires la guerre*, Presses Universitaires de France, Paris, 1925.

MARTINI, P. A., *Blockade im Weltkrieg*, Dümmler, Berlin/Bonn, 1932.

MARWICK, A., *The Deluge. British Society and the World War*, London, 1965.

MARX, K. and ENGELS, F., 'Manifest der Kommunistischen Partei', K. Marx, F. Engels, *Werke*, vol. IV, Dietz, Berlin, 1969.

MAUERSBERG, HANS, *Deutsche Industrien im Zeitgeschehen eines Jahrhunderts*, Fischer, Stuttgart, 1966.

MAYER, A. J., *Political Origins of the New Diplomacy, 1917–1918*, Yale University Press, New Haven, 1959.

MENDEL, ARTHUR P., 'Peasant and Worker on the Eve of the First World War', *Slavic Review* 24, 1965.

MENDELSSOHN-BARTHOLDY, ALBRECHT, *The War and German Society. The Testament of a Liberal*, Yale University Press, New Haven, 1937.

MENDERSHAUSEN, HORST, *The Economics of War*, Prentice-Hall, New York, 1941.

MEYER, HENRY CORD, *Mitteleuropa in German Thought and Action 1815–1945*, Nijhoff, The Hague, 1955.

MEYNELL, HILDEMARIE, 'The Stockholm Conference of 1917', *International Review of Social History* 5, 1960.

MIDDLETON, THOMAS HUDSON, *Food Production in War*, Clarendon Press, Oxford, 1923.

MILWARD, A. S., *The Impact of the World Wars on the British Economy*, Macmillan, London, 1970.

MITCHELL, B. R., *Abstract of British Historical Statistics*, Cambridge University Press, 1962.

MITCHELL, WESLEY C., *International Price Comparisons*, Government Printing Office, Washington, D.C., 1919.

MITCHELL, WESLEY C., *Income in the United States. Its Amount and Distribution 1909–1919*, Harcourt Brace, New York, 1921.

MITRANY, DAVID, *The Land and Peasant in Rumania. The War and Agrarian Reform (1917–1921)*, Oxford University Press, 1930.

MITRANY, DAVID, *The Effect of the War in South-Eastern Europe*, Yale University Press, New Haven, 1936.

MOMMSEN, WOLFGANG, *Das Zeitalter des Imperialismus*, Fischer, Frankfurt, 1969.

MORGAN, E. V., *Studies in British Financial Policy, 1914–1925*, Macmillan, London, 1952.

MOULTON, H. G. and MCGUIRE, C. E., *Germany's Capacity to Pay. A Study of the Reparation Problem*, McGraw-Hill, New York, 1923.

MOULTON, HAROLD G. and PASVOLSKY, LEO, *World War Debt Settlements*, Macmillan, New York, 1926.

MOULTON, HAROLD G. and PASVOLSKY, LEO, *War Debts and World Prosperity*, Brookings Institution, Washington, D.C., 1932.

MÜLLER, ALFRED, *Die Kriegsrohstoffbewirtschaftung 1914–1918 im Dienste des deutschen Monopolkapitals*, Akademie-Verlag, Berlin, 1955.

Munitions Industry. Final Report of the Chairman of the United States War Industries Board to the President of the United States, Government Printing Office, Washington, D.C., 1935.

NECK, RUDOLF, ed., *Arbeiterschaft und Staat im Ersten Weltkrieg 1914–1918*, Europa-Verlag, Vienna, 1964.

NELSON, HARALD I., *Land and Power. British and Allied Policy on Germany's Frontiers 1916–1919*, Routledge & Kegan Paul, London, 1963.

NEWBOLT, HENRY, *Naval Operations. (History of the Great War, by Direction of the Historical Section of the Committee of Imperial Defence.)* Vols IV–V, Longman, London, 1928–31.

NOGARO, B. and WEIL, L., *La main-d'œuvre étrangère et coloniale pendant la guerre*, Presses Universitaires de France, Paris, 1926.

NOLDE, E., *Russia in the Economic War*, Yale University Press, New Haven, 1928.

NORTH, DOUGLAS, 'International Capital Movements in Historical Perspective', Raymond F. Mikesell, ed., *U.S. Private and Government Investment Abroad*, University of Oregon Books, Eugene, 1962.

OCHSENBEIN, HEINZ, *Die verlorene Wirtschaftsfreiheit 1914–1918. Methoden ausländischer Wirtschaftskontrollen über die Schweiz*, Stämpfli, Bern, 1971.

OGAWA, GOTARO and YAMASAKI, KAKUJIRO, *The Effect of the World War Upon the Commerce and Industry of Japan*, Yale University Press, New Haven, 1929.

OLSON, MANCUR, *The Economics of the Wartime Shortage. A History of British Food Supply in the Napoleonic War and in World Wars I and II*, Duke University Press, Durham, 1963.

OUALID, WILLIAM and PICQUENARD, CHARLES, *Salaires et tarifs. Conventions collectives et grèves*, Presses Universitaires de France, Paris, 1928.

PARKER, R. A. C., *Das Zwanzigste Jahrhundert I, 1918–1945*, Fischer, Frankfurt, 1967.

PARMELEE, MAURICE, *Blockade and Sea Power. The Blockade, 1914–1919, and its Significance for a World State*, Hutchinson, London, 1924.

PASSELECQ, FERNAND, *Déportation et travail forcé des ouvriers et de la population civile de la Belgique occupée*, Presses Universitaires de France, Paris, 1928.

PICARD, ROGER, *Le mouvement syndical durant la guerre*, Presses Universitaires de France, Paris, 1927.

PIGOU, A. C., *The Political Economy of War*, rev. ed,, Macmillan, London, 1940.

PINOT, PIERRE, *Le contrôle du ravitaillement de la population civile*, Presses Universitaires de France, Paris, 1925.

PINOT, ROBERT, *Le Comité des Forges de France au service de la nation.* (*Août 1914–Novembre 1918*), Colin, Paris, 1919.

PIRENNE, J. and VAUTHIER, M., *La législation et l'administration allemandes en Belgique*, Presses Universitaires de France, Paris, 1925.

PLACHETKA, MANFRED GÜNTHER, *Die Getreide-Autarkiepolitik Bismarcks und seiner Nachfolger im Reichskanzleramt*, diss. Bonn, 1969.

POMMERY, LOUIS, *Aperçu d'histoire économique contemporaire* (*1980–1939*), Médicis, Paris, 1952.

POPOVICS, ALEXANDER, *Das Geldwesen im Kriege*, Hölder-Pichler-Tempsky, Vienna, 1925.

PRIBICEVIC, B., *The Shop Stewards' Movement and Workers' Control, 1910–1922*, Blackwell, Oxford, 1959.

RADKEY, OLIVER H., *The Agrarian Foes of Bolshevism. Promise and Default of the Russian Socialist Revolutionaries, February to October 1917*, Columbia University Press, New York, 1958.

RATHMANN, LOTHAR, *Stoßrichtung Nah-Ost 1914–1918. Zur Expansionspolitik des deutschen Imperialismus im Ersten Weltkrieg*, Rütten & Loening, Berlin, 1963.

RATNER, SIDNEY, *Taxation and Democracy in America*, Science Editions, New York, 1967.

READER, W. J., *Imperial Chemical Industries: A History*, vol. I: *The Forerunners 1870 to 1926*, Oxford University Press, 1970.

REBOUL, C., *Mobilisation industrielle*, vol. I, *Les fabrications de guerre en France de 1914 à 1918*, Berger-Levrault, Nancy/Paris/Strasbourg, 1925.

REDMAYNE, R. A. S., *The British Coal Mining Industry during the War*, Clarendon Press, Oxford, 1923.

Reichsarchiv, Kriegsrüstung und Kriegswirtschaft. Erster Band, *Die militärische wirtschaftliche und finanzielle Rüstung Deutschlands von der Reichsgründung bis zum Ausbruch des Weltkrieges*, with appendices, 2 vols, Mittler, Berlin, 1930.

REISBERG, ARNOLD, *Lenin und die Zimmerwalder Bewegung*, Dietz, Berlin, 1966.

RENOUVIN, PIERRE, *Les formes du gouvernement de guerre*, Presses Universitaires de France, Paris, 1925.

RENOUVIN, PIERRE, *Les Crises du 20e siècle: De 1914 à 1929* (*Histoire des relations internationales*, vol. VII), Hachette, Paris, 1957.

RENOUVIN, PIERRE, *La crise européenne et la première guerre mondiale*, 5th ed., Presses Universitaires de France, Paris, 1969.

RENOUVIN, PIERRE, 'Die Kriegsziele der französischen Regierung 1914–1918', W. Schieder, ed., *Erster Weltkrieg. Ursachen, Entstehung, Kriegsziele*, Kiepenheuer & Witsch, Cologne/Berlin, 1969.

RÉPACI, F. A., *La finanza Italiana nel ventento 1913–1932*, Einaudi, Torino, 1934.

RÉPACI, F. A., 'Il costo finanziaro in Italia della prima guerra mondiale, *Studi in Onore di Gaetano Pietra*, Cappelli, Rocca San Casciano, 1955.

REUBENS, EDWIN P., 'Foreign Capital and Domestic Development in Japan', S. Kuznets, W. E. Moore and J. Spengler, eds, *Economic Growth: Brazil, India, Japan*, Duke University Press, Durham, 1955.

RICHTER, WERNER, *Gewerkschaften, Monopolkapital und Staat im ersten Weltkrieg und in der Novemberrevolution (1914–1919)*, Verlag Tribüne, Berlin, 1959.

RIEDL, RICHARD: *Die Industrie Österreichs während des Krieges*. Hölder-Pichler-Tempsky, Vienna, 1932.

RIST, C. and SCHWOB, PH., *Vingt-cinq ans d'évolution dans la balance des paiements française*, Revue d'Economie Politique, 53, 1939.

RISTO, OLAV, *The Neutral Ally: Norway's Relations with Belliger-*

ent Powers in the First World War, Universitetsforlaget, Oslo, and Allen & Unwin, London, 1965.

RITCHIE, H., *The 'Navicert' System During the World War*, Carnegie Endowment for International Peace, Washington, D.C., 1938.

RITTER, GERHARD, *Staatskunst und Kriegshandwerk. Das Problem des Militarismus in Deutschland*, 4 vols, Oldenbourg, Munich, 1960–68.

ROBBINS, LIONEL, *The Economic Causes of War*, Jonathan Cape, London, 1939.

ROBERTS, B. C., *The Trade Union Congress, 1868–1921*, Allen & Unwin, London, 1958.

ROESLER, KONRAD, *Die Finanzpolitik des Deutschen Reiches im Ersten Weltkrieg*, Duncker & Humblot, Berlin, 1967.

ROSMER, ALFRED, *Le mouvement ouvrier pendant la guerre*, Part 1, *De l'union sacrée à Zimmerwald*, Librairie du Travail, Paris, 1936. Part 2, *De Zimmerwald à la Révolution russe*, Mouton, Paris/La Haye, 1959.

ROTHWELL, V. H., *British War Aims and Peace Diplomacy, 1914–1918*, Clarendon Press, Oxford, 1971.

ROWE, L. S., *Early Effects of the European War upon the Finance, Commerce and Industry of Chile*, Oxford University Press, New York, 1918.

ROWE, L. S., *Early Effects of the War upon the Finance, Commerce and Industry of Peru*, Oxford University Press, New York, 1920.

ROWELL, N. W., 'Canada and the Empire, 1884–1921', E. A. Benians, W. P. M. Kennedy, A. P. Newton and J. H. Rose, eds, *Canada and Newfoundland. (The Cambridge History of the British Empire*, vol. VI.) Cambridge University Press, 1930.

Royal Institute of International Affairs, *The Problem of International Investment*, Oxford University Press, 1937.

SALTER, J. A., *Allied Shipping Control. An Experiment in International Administration*, Clarendon Press, Oxford, 1921.

SARTER, ADOLPH, *Die deutschen Eisenbahnen im Kriege*, Deutsche Verlags-Anstalt, Stuttgart/Berlin/Leipzig, 1930.

SARTORIUS VON WALTERSHAUSEN, A., *Die Umgestaltung der zwischenstaatlichen Wirtschaft*, Fischer, Jena, 1935.

SAUL, S. B., *Studies in British Overseas Trade, 1870–1924*, Liverpool University Press, 1960.

SAUVAIRE-JOURDAN, F., 'Les clauses économiques du traité de paix', *Revue d'Economie Politique* 33, 1919.

SAUVY, ALFRED, 'L'inflation en France jusqu'à la dévaluation de 1928', *Mélanges d'histoire économique et sociale en hommage au professeur Antony Babel*, vol. II, Geneva, 1963.

SCHÄDLICH, KARL-HEINZ, 'Der "Unabhängige Ausschuß für einen Deutschen Frieden" als ein Zentrum der Annexionspropaganda des deutschen Imperialismus im ersten Weltkrieg', F. Klein, ed., *Politik im Krieg 1914–1918*, Akademie-Verlag, Berlin, 1964.

SCHIEDER. WOLFGANG, ed., *Erster Weltkrieg. Ursachen, Entstehung und Kriegsziele*, Kiepenheuer & Witsch, Cologne/Berlin, 1969.

SCHLARP, KARL-HEINZ, *Ursachen und Entstehung des Ersten Weltkrieges im Lichte der sowjetischen Geschichtsschreibung*, Metzner, Frankfurt, 1971.

SCHORSKE, CARL E., *German Social Democracy 1905–1917. The Development of the Great Schism*, Harvard University Press, Cambridge, Mass., 1955.

SCHRÖTER, ALFRED, *Krieg–Staat–Monopol 1914–1918. Die Zusammenhänge von imperialistischer Kriegswirtschaft, Militarisierung der Volkswirtschaft und staatsmonopolistischer Kapitalismus in Deutschland während des ersten Weltkrieges*, Akademie-Verlag, Berlin, 1965.

SCHULTZE, ERNST, *Die Zerrüttung der Weltwirtschaft*, Kohlhammer, Berlin/Stuttgart/Leipzig, 1923.

SCHULZ, GERHARD, *Revolutionen und Friedensschlüsse 1917–1920*, 2nd ed., dtv, Munich, 1969.

SCHUMPETER, J. A., *Business Cycles: A Theoretical, Historical and Statistical Analysis of the Capitalist Process*, New York/London, 1939.

SCOTT, J. B., ed., *The Paris Peace Conference. History and Documents*, 6 vols, Columbia University Press, New York, 1934–42.

SEIDENZAHL, FRITZ, *100 Jahre Deutsche Bank, 1870–1970*, Frankfurt, 1970.

SHARP, M. U., 'Allied Wheat Buying in Relationship to Canadian Marketing Policy 1914 to 1918', *Canadian Journal of Economics and Political Science* 6, 1940.

SHORTT, ADAM, *Early Effects of the European War upon Canada* Oxford University Press, New York, 1918.

SICHLER, RICHARD and TIBURTIUS, JOACHIM, *Die Arbeiter-frage, eine Kernfrage des Weltkrieges. Ein Beitrag zur Erklärung des Kriegsausgangs*, Deutsche Verlags-AG, Berlin.

SILBERNER, E., *Le guerre et la paix dans l'histoire des doctrines économiques*, Sirey, Paris, 1957.

SIMON, MATTHEW, 'The Pattern of New British Portfolio Foreign Investment, 1865–1914', A. R. Hall, ed., *The Export of Capital from Britain 1870–1914*, Methuen, London, 1968.

SINEY, MARION, C., *The Allied Blockade of Germany, 1914–1916*, University of Michigan Press, Ann Arbor, 1957.

SINEY, MARION C., 'British Official Histories of the Blockade of the Central Powers during the First World War,' *American Historical Review* 68, 1963.

SINEY, MARION C., *The Allied Blockade Committee and the Inter-Allied Trade Committees: The Machinery of Economic Warfare, 1917–1918*, K. Bourne and D. C. Watt, eds, *Studies in International History*, Longman, London, 1967.

SKALWEIT, AUGUST, *Die deutsche Kriegsernährungswirtschaft*, Deutsche Verlags-Anstalt, Berlin/Leipzig/Stuttgart, 1927.

SPANDAU, ARNT, *Income Distribution and Economic Growth in South Africa*, 2 vols, D. Com. Thesis, University of South Africa, Pretoria, 1971.

STAMP, JOSIAH, *The Financial Aftermath of War*, Benn, London, 1932.

STAMP, JOSIAH, *Taxation during the War*, Oxford University Press, 1932.

STANSKY, PETER, ed., *The Left and War: The British Labour Party and World War I*, Oxford University Press, 1969.

STEGEMANN, BERND, *Die deutsche Marinepolitik 1916–1918*, Duncker & Humblot, Berlin, 1970.

STEIN, STANLEY J., 'Brazilian Cotton Textile Industry, 1850–1950', S. Kuznets, W. E. Moore and J. Spengler, eds, *Economic Growth: Brazil, India, Japan*, Duke University Press, Durham, 1955.

STEIN, STANLEY J., *The Brazilian Cotton Manufacture: Textile Enterprise in an Underdeveloped Area, 1850–1950*, Harvard University Press, Cambridge, Mass., 1957.

STERN, LEO, *Der Einfluß der Großen Sozialistischen Oktober-revolution auf Deutschland und die deutsche Arbeiterbewegung*, Rütten & Loening, Berlin, 1958.

STOLPER, G., HÄUSER, K. and BORCHARDT, K., *Deutsche Wirtschaft seit 1870*, 2nd ed., Mohr, Tübingen, 1966.

STUDENSKI, PAUL, *The Income of Nations. Theory, Measurements, and Analysis: Past and Present*, New York University Press, 1958.

SVENNILSON, INGVAR, *Growth and Stagnation in the European Economy*, United Nations Commission for Europe, Geneva, 1954.

TAWNEY, R. H., 'The Abolition of Economic Controls, 1918–1921', *Economic History Review* 13, 1943.

TAYLOR, A. J. P., 'The War Aims of the Allies in the First World War', R. Pares and A. J. P. Taylor, eds, *Essays Presented to Sir Lewis Namier*, Macmillan, London, 1956.

TEMPERLEY, H. W. V., ed., *A History of the Peace Conference of Paris*, Published under the Auspices of the Institute of International Affairs, 6 vols, Oxford University Press, 1920–4.

THORSTEINSON, THORSTEINN, *Island under og efter Verdenskrigen*, Gad, Copenhagen, 1928, rev. Engl. trans. in: H. Westergaard, ed., *Sweden, Norway, Denmark and Iceland in the World War*, Yale University Press, New Haven, 1930.

TILLMAN, P., *Anglo-American Relations at the Paris Peace Conference 1919*, Princeton University Press, 1961.

TRASK, D. F., *The United States and the Supreme War Council. American War Aims and Interallied Strategy, 1917–1918*, Wesleyan University Press, Middletown, 1961.

TREUE, WILHELM, *Die Feuer verlöschen nie. August-Thyssen-Hütte 1890–1926*, Econ, Düsseldorf/Vienna, 1966.

TRUCHY, HENRI, *Les finances de guerre de la France*, Presses Universitaires de France, Paris, 1926.

TRUMPENER, V., *Germany and the Ottoman Empire*, Princeton University Press, 1968.

TSUZUKI, CHUSHICHI, *H. M. Hyndman and British Socialism*, Oxford University Press, 1961.

ULAM, ADAM B., *Die Bolschewiki. Vorgeschichte und Verlauf der kommunistischen Revolution in Rußland*, Kiepenheuer & Witsch, Cologne/Berlin, 1967.

UMBREIT, PAUL, *Der Krieg und die Arbeitsverhältnisse. Die*

deutschen Gewerkschaften im Kriege, Deutsche Verlags-Anstalt, Stuttgart/Berlin/Leipzig, 1928.

UNITED NATIONS, *International Capital Movements during the Inter-War-Period*, Lake Success, 1949.

UNITED NATIONS, *Relative Prices of Exports and Imports of Under-developed Countries*, Lake Success, 1949.

U.S. DEPARTMENT OF COMMERCE, BUREAU OF THE CENSUS, *Historical Statistics of the United States. Colonial Times to 1957*, Government Printing Office, Washington, D.C., 1961.

UNITED STATES SENATE, *Special Committee on Investigation of the Munitions Industry. Preliminary Report on Wartime Taxation and Price Control*, Government Printing Office, Washington, D.C., 1935.

URQUHART, M. C. and BUCKLEY, K. A. H., eds, *Historical Statistics of Canada*, Cambridge University Press, 1965.

VINACKE, HAROLD, *Problems of Industrial Development in China*, Princeton University Press, 1926.

VINER, JACOB, 'Who Paid for the War?' *Journal of Political Economy* 28, 1920.

Völkerrecht im Weltkrieg 1914–1918, Dritte Reihe im Werk des Parlamentarischen Untersuchungsausschusses, 4 vols, Deutsche Verlagsgesellschaft für Politik und Geschichte, Berlin, 1927.

WEBER, F. G., *Eagles on the Crescent. Germany, Austria and the Diplomacy of the Turkish Alliance, 1914–1918*, Cornell University Press, Ithaca, 1970.

WEBER, HELLMUTH, *Ludendorff und die Monopole. Deutsche Kriegspolitik 1916–1918*, Akademie-Verlag, Berlin, 1966.

WHEARE, K. C., 'The Empire and the Peace Treaties', E. A. Benians, J. Butler and C. E. Carrington, eds, *The Empire-Commonwealth 1870–1919* (*The Cambridge History of the British Empire*, vol. 3), Cambridge University Press, 1959.

WILLIAMS, J. H., 'Latin America's Foreign Exchange and International Balances during the War', *Quarterly Journal of Economics* 33, 1918–19.

WILLIAMS, J. H., 'The Future of Our Foreign Trade: A Study of our International Balances in 1919', *Review of Economic Statistics* 2, 1920, supplement.

WINKLER, H. A., ed., *Organisierter Kapitalismus. Voraussetzungen und Anfänge*, Vandenhoeck & Ruprecht, Göttingen, 1973.

WOHL, ROBERT, *French Communism in the Making, 1914–1924*, Stanford University Press, 1966.

WOHLGEMUTH, HEINZ, *Burgkrieg, nicht Burgfriede! Der Kampf Karl Liebknechts, Rosa Luxemburgs und ihrer Anhänger um die Rettung der deutschen Nation in den Jahren 1914–1916*, Dietz, Berlin, 1963.

ZUNKEL, F., 'Die ausländischen Arbeiter in der deutschen Kriegswirtschaftspolitik des Ersten Weltkrieges', G. A. Ritter, ed., *Entstehung und Wandel der modernen Gesellschaft*, Gruyter, Berlin, 1970.

ZUNKEL, F., *Industrie und Staatssozialismus. Der Kamf um die Wirtschaftsordnung in Deutschland 1914–1918*, Droste, Düsseldorf, 1974.

Index